Communications in Computer and Information Science   **596**

Commenced Publication in 2007
Founding and Former Series Editors:
Alfredo Cuzzocrea, Dominik Ślęzak, and Xiaokang Yang

More information about this series at http://www.springer.com/series/7899

Cyrille Artho · Peter Csaba Ölveczky (Eds.)

Formal Techniques for Safety-Critical Systems

Fourth International Workshop, FTSCS 2015
Paris, France, November 6–7, 2015
Revised Selected Papers

 Springer

Editors
Cyrille Artho
AIST Ikeda
Ikeda, Osaka
Japan

Peter Csaba Ölveczky
University of Oslo
Oslo
Norway

ISSN 1865-0929   ISSN 1865-0937 (electronic)
Communications in Computer and Information Science
ISBN 978-3-319-29509-1   ISBN 978-3-319-29510-7 (eBook)
DOI 10.1007/978-3-319-29510-7

Library of Congress Control Number: 2015961022

Printed on acid-free paper

This Springer imprint is published by SpringerNature
The registered company is Springer International Publishing AG Switzerland

Preface

This volume contains the proceedings of the *Fourth International Workshop on Formal Techniques for Safety-Critical Systems* (FTSCS 2015), held in Paris on November 6–7, 2015, as a satellite event of the ICFEM conference.

The aim of FTSCS is to bring together researchers and engineers who are interested in the application of formal and semi-formal methods to improve the quality of safety-critical computer systems. FTSCS strives to promote research and development of formal methods and tools for industrial applications, and is particularly interested in industrial applications of formal methods. Specific topics of the workshop include, but are not limited to:

- case studies and experience reports on the use of formal methods for analyzing safety-critical systems, including avionics, automotive, medical, and other kinds of safety-critical and QoS-critical systems;
- methods, techniques, and tools to support automated analysis, certification, debugging, etc., of complex safety/QoS-critical systems;
- analysis methods that address the limitations of formal methods in industry (usability, scalability, etc.);
- formal analysis support for modeling languages used in industry, such as AADL, Ptolemy, SysML, SCADE, Modelica, etc; and
- code generation from validated models.

FTSCS 2015 received 41 regular paper submissions and five work-in-progress paper submissions. Each submission was reviewed by at least three reviewers. Based on the reviews and on extensive discussions, the program committee selected 15 of these regular papers and two work-in-progress papers for presentation at the workshop. This volume contains revised versions of those 15 regular papers, as well as an invited paper by José Meseguer. As was the case for FTSCS 2012–2014, a special issue of the *Science of Computer Programming* journal will be devoted to extended versions of selected papers from FTSCS 2015.

Many colleagues and friends contributed to FTSCS 2015. We thank José Meseguer for accepting our invitation to give an invited talk and the authors who submitted their work to FTSCS 2015 and who made this workshop an interesting event. We are particularly grateful to the members of the program committee, who all provided timely, insightful, and detailed reviews.

We also thank the editors of Springer's *Communications in Computer and Information Science* (CCIS) series for publishing the proceedings of FTSCS 2015, Bas van Vlijmen for accepting our proposal to devote a special issue of *Science of Computer Programming* to extended versions of selected papers from FTSCS 2015, and Fatiha Zaïdi and Étienne André for their help with local arrangements.

December 2015
Cyrille Artho
Peter Csaba Ölveczky

Organization

Program Chairs

Cyrille Artho   AIST, Japan
Peter Csaba Ölveczky   University of Oslo, Norway

Program Committee

Musab AlTurki	King Fahd University of Petroleum & Minerals, Saudi Arabia
Étienne André	University Paris 13, France
Toshiaki Aoki	JAIST, Japan
Cyrille Artho	AIST, Japan
Kyungmin Bae	SRI International, USA
David Broman	KTH, Sweden and UC Berkeley, USA
Bernd Fischer	Stellenbosch University, South Africa
Osman Hasan	National University of Sciences & Technology, Pakistan
Klaus Havelund	NASA JPL, USA
Fuyuki Ishikawa	National Institute of Informatics, Japan
Takashi Kitamura	AIST, Japan
Alexander Knapp	Augsburg University, Germany
Brian Larson	Kansas State University, USA
Wenchao Li	SRI International, USA
Robi Malik	University of Waikato, New Zealand
Frédéric Mallet	Université Nice Sophia-Antipolis, France
Roberto Nardone	University of Napoli Federico II, Italy
Thomas Noll	RWTH Aachen University, Germany
Peter Csaba Ölveczky	University of Oslo, Norway
Charles Pecheur	Université catholique de Louvain, Belgium
Paul Pettersson	Mälardalen University, Sweden
Camilo Rocha	Escuela Colombiana de Ingeniería, Colombia
Markus Roggenbach	Swansea University, UK
Ralf Sasse	ETH Zürich, Switzerland
Oleg Sokolsky	University of Pennsylvania, USA
Sofiène Tahar	Concordia University, Canada
Jean-Pierre Talpin	Inria Rennes, France
Chen-Wei Wang	State University of New York, Korea
Alan Wassyng	McMaster University, Canada
Michael Whalen	University of Minnesota, USA
Huibiao Zhu	East China Normal University, China

Additional Reviewers

Ahmed, Waqar
Asavoae, Irina Mariuca
Bohórquez, Jaime
Cailliau, Antoine
Causevic, Adnan
Elleuch, Maissa
Enoiu, Eduard Paul
Filipovikj, Predrag
Gentile, Ugo

Guo, Jian
Hachani, Ahmed
Inoue, Jun
James, Phillip
Khan, Shahid
Limbrée, Christophe
Marinescu, Raluca
Matheja, Christoph
Nakagawa, Hiroyuki

Seddiki, Ons
Siddique, Umair
Su, Wen
Sun, Youcheng
Wang, Xu
Wu, Xi
Yokogawa, Tomoyuki
Zhang, Min

Contents

Invited Paper

Variant-Based Satisfiability in Initial Algebras

José Meseguer$^{(\boxtimes)}$

Department of Computer Science, University of Illinois at Urbana-Champaign,
Urbana, Illinois, USA
meseguer@illinois.edu

Abstract. Although different satisfiability decision procedures can be combined by algorithms such as those of Nelson-Oppen or Shostak, current tools typically can only support a finite number of theories to use in such combinations. To make SMT solving more widely applicable, *generic* satisfiability algorithms that can allow a potentially infinite number of decidable theories to be *user-definable*, instead of needing to be built in by the implementers, are highly desirable. This work studies how *folding variant narrowing*, a generic unification algorithm that offers good extensibility in unification theory, can be extended to a generic *variant-based satisfiability* algorithm for the initial algebras of its user-specified input theories when such theories satisfy Comon-Delaune's *finite variant property* (FVP) and some extra conditions. Several, increasingly larger infinite classes of theories whose initial algebras enjoy decidable variant-based satisfiability are identified and illustrated with examples.

Keywords: Finite variant property (FVP) · Constructor variant · Constructor unifier · Folding variant narrowing · Satisfiability in initial algebras

1 Introduction

The use of decision procedures for theories axiomatizing data structures and functions commonly occurring in software and hardware systems is currently one of the most effective methods at the heart of state-of-the art theorem provers and model checkers. It offers the promise, and often even the reality, of scaling up such verification efforts to handle large systems used in industrial practice. In the area of decision procedures two important phases stand out. The first is the discovery in the late 70's and early 80's of *combination methods* by Nelson and Oppen [73] and Shostak [78] to achieve satisfiability in combinations of decidable theories. The second is the marriage of SAT-solving technology with decision procedures for certain theories, an approach pioneered independently by a number of different groups [5,7,14,45,46,72] and distilled in the influential DPLL(T) architecture [75]. This approach has been key to the success of SMT, as witnessed by a vast literature on the subject.

However, one important challenge is the lack of *extensibility* of current SMT tools. This may seem somewhat paradoxical to say, since obviously the

© Springer International Publishing Switzerland 2016
C. Artho and P.C. Ölveczky (Eds.): FTSCS 2015, CCIS 596, pp. 3–34, 2016.
DOI: 10.1007/978-3-319-29510-7_1

Nelson-Oppen (NO) combination method [73,76] offers unlimited extensibility by theory combinations under some conditions on the combined theories. This is true enough, but:

1. One needs to have algorithms and implementations for each of the theories supported by the SMT solver, which requires a non-trivial effort and in any case limits at any given time each SMT solver to support a *finite* (and in practice not very large) library of theories that it can handle.
2. What we need are *generic* —i.e., not for a single theory, but for a possibly infinite class of theories— and easily *user-definable* satisfiability decision procedures that are supported by an SMT solver tool, so that the tool's repertory of individual decidable theories becomes potentially *infinite* and easily specifiable by the tool's *users*, as opposed to its implementers.

Achieving extensibility in this, more ambitious sense can have large payoffs for SMT solving technology, because it can widely extend both its *scope* and its *effectiveness*. In formal verification practice this would allow automating larger fragments of the verification effort, both in theorem proving and in model checking, and therefore scaling up to effectively handle larger problems.

This paper is all about making SMT solving extensible in the just-mentioned sense by what I call *variant-based satisfiability* methods. The best way for me to explain the key ideas is to place them in the context of a recent sea change in *unification theory* that has been quietly taking place thanks to *variant-based unification* [41,42], inspired by the Comon-Delaune notion of variant [31].

Note that unification theory is not just a *neighboring area* of SMT solving, but actually a *subfield*: specifically, the subfield obtained by: (i) considering theories of the form $th(T_{\Sigma/E}(X))$, associated to equational theories (Σ, E), where $th(T_{\Sigma/E}(X))$ denotes the theory of the free (Σ, E)-algebra $T_{\Sigma/E}(X)$ on countably many variables X, and (ii) restricting ourselves to *positive* quantifier-free (QF) formulas of the form $\varphi = \bigvee_i \bigwedge G_i$, with each $\bigwedge G_i$ a conjunction of equations. A finitary E-unification algorithm then gives us a *decision procedure* for satisfiability of such formulas φ not only in the *free* (Σ, E)-algebra $T_{\Sigma/E}(X)$, but also in the *initial* (Σ, E)-algebra $T_{\Sigma/E}$ when all sorts of $T_{\Sigma/E}$ are non-empty.

Unification theory is not only a subfield of SMT solving but what might be called a *microcosm*, where many problems and challenges of SMT solving already show up, including the extensibility problem. For example, the Nelson-Oppen (NO) combination algorithm [73,76] is mirrored by algorithms for combining unification procedures, such as those of Baader and Schulz [8] and Boudet [19] (see [10] for a unified treatment of both NO and the Baader-Schulz algorithms). Also, as for SMT solving, extensibility *is* a problem for the exact same reasons: although combination methods exist, E-unification algorithms require substantial implementation efforts and a tool can only support so many of them.

One important advantage of unification theory is that it has had for a long time *generic* E-unification semi-algorithms, namely, *narrowing-based* [44, 57,58,79] and *transformation-based* [47,80] ones. But one important drawback of these semi-algorithms is that, since E-unification for arbitrary E is undecidable, in general they only provide a *semi-decision* procedure, which is useless for *deciding* unifiability, i.e., satisfiability of formulas $\varphi = \bigvee_i \bigwedge G_i$ in the initial algebra $T_{\Sigma/E}$, *unless* they can be proved *terminating* for a given equational theory E. For theories E whose equations can be oriented as convergent rewrite rules R, some termination results for narrowing-based unification, mostly based on the *basic narrowing* strategy [57], do exist for some quite restrictive classes of rules R (see [1,2], and references there, for a comprehensive and up-to-date treatment). Instead, the more general case of termination for narrowing-based unification for equational theories $E \uplus B$ for which the equations E can be oriented as convergent rules R *modulo* axioms B having a finitary B-unification algorithm, has been a real *terra incognita* until very recently, because *negative* results, like the impossibility of using basic narrowing when B is a set of associative-commutative (AC) axioms [31], seemed to dash any hopes not just of termination, but even of efficient implementation. Many of these limitations have now disappeared thanks to the *folding variant narrowing* algorithm [41,42]. Let me summarize the current state of the matter after [42]:

1. When B has a finitary unification algorithm, folding variant narrowing with convergent oriented equations E modulo B will terminate on any input term (including unification problems expressed in an extended signature) iff $E \uplus B$ has the *finite variant property*[1] (FVP) in the Comon-Delaune sense [31].
2. No other complete narrowing strategy can terminate more often than folding variant narrowing; in particular, basic narrowing (when applicable, e.g., $B = \varnothing$) terminates strictly less often.
3. FVP is a semi-decidable property and, when it actually holds, can be easily checked by existing tools, assuming convergence [23].
4. Both folding variant narrowing and variant-based unification for theories $E \uplus B$, where B can be any combination of associativity, commutativity and identity axioms, except associativity without commutativity, are already supported by tools such as Maude [25] in its latest 2.7 version.

There are by now papers, e.g., [31,39,40], many cryptographic protocol specifications, e.g., [22,40,53,77,84], and several verification tools, e.g., [22,40,77], demonstrating that FVP equational theories are omni-present in cryptographic protocol verification and that variant-based unification and narrowing are very general and effective formal reasoning methods to verify such protocols. In this paper I give many examples showing that, in a similar way, QF satisfiability in initial algebras of FVP theories is decidable under reasonable conditions.

The key question addressed in this paper should now be obvious: can the good properties of variant-based unification as a *theory-generic*, finitary $E \uplus B$-unification algorithm for FVP theories be extended to a, likewise generic, variant-based $E \uplus B$-satisfiability algorithm for the initial algebras $T_{\Sigma/E \uplus B}$ of an infinite

---

[1] Roughly, u is an E,B-*variant* of a term t if u is the E,B-canonical form of a substitution instance, $t\theta$, of t (for a more careful definition see Definition 5). Therefore, the variants of t are intuitively the "irreducible patterns" to which t can be symbolically evaluated by the rules E modulo B. $E \uplus B$ has the *finite variant property* if there is a *finite* set of *most general* variants, which are computed by *folding variant narrowing*.

number of such FVP theories $E \uplus B$ under suitable conditions? If this were possible, the advances in increasing the *extensibility* of unification theory could then be leveraged to make SMT solving substantially more extensible than it is at present. Answering this question is non-trivial, because unification only deals with positive, i.e., negation-free, formulas, whereas satisfiability must deal with *all* QF formulas. This is precisely what is done in this work, which answers this main question in the affirmative as follows:

1. After some preliminaries in Sect. 2, Sect. 3 discusses an incorrect first attempt, in [31], to relate satisfiability and initial FVP algebras. Section 4 then proposes new notions of *constructor variant* and *constructor unifier* as key concepts towards a solution.
2. Section 5 gives a general "descent theorem" reducing satisfiability in an initial algebra to satisfiability in a simpler initial algebra on a subsignature Ω of constructors, and outlines a general satisfiability algorithm when the initial algebra of constructors has decidable satisfiability for QF formulas.
3. General conditions under which the initial algebra of constructors associated to an initial algebra $T_{\Sigma/E \uplus B}$ has decidable satisfiability and makes, in turn, satisfiability in $T_{\Sigma/E \uplus B}$ decidable are investigated. A key notion is that of an *OS-compact theory*, which generalizes in several ways that of a compact theory in [29]. In particular, it is shown that $T_{\Omega/B}$ has decidable QF satisfiability for B any combination of associativity, commutativity and identity axioms, except associativity without commutativity; furthermore, various relevant examples of decidable initial algebras whose initial algebra of constructors are of the form $T_{\Omega/B}$ are given.
4. Section 7 shows that various parameterized data types, such as lists, compact lists [33,34], multisets, and hereditarily finite (HF) sets, are *satisfiability-preserving* under very general conditions; that is, they map a target initial algebra with decidable QF satisfiability, like integers with addition, to the initial algebra of the corresponding instance of the parameterized module, like sets of integers, also with decidable QF satisfiability.
5. Related work is discussed in Sect. 8; and a fuller discussion of the entire work is given in Sect. 9.

Proofs are omitted; they can be found in [69].

2 Order-Sorted Algebra, Rewriting, and Variants

I summarize the order-sorted algebra, order-sorted rewriting, and FVP notions needed in the paper. The material, adapted from [42,66], extends ideas in [31,51]. It assumes the notions of many-sorted signature and many-sorted algebra, e.g., [37], which include unsorted signatures and algebras as a special case.

Definition 1. *An* order-sorted (OS) signature *is a triple* $\Sigma = ((S, \leqslant), \Sigma)$ *with* $(S, \leqslant)$ *a poset and* (S, Σ) *a many-sorted signature.* $\widehat{S} = S/\equiv_{\leqslant}$, *the quotient of* S *under the equivalence relation* $\equiv_{\leqslant} = (\leqslant \cup \geqslant)^{+}$, *is called the set of* connected components *of* $(S, \leqslant)$. *The order* $\leqslant$ *and equivalence* $\equiv_{\leqslant}$ *are extended to sequences of same length in the usual way, e.g.,* $s'_1 \ldots s'_n \leqslant s_1 \ldots s_n$ *iff* $s'_i \leqslant s_i$, $1 \leqslant i \leqslant n$. Σ *is called* sensible *if for any two* $f : w \to s, f : w' \to s' \in \Sigma$, *with* w *and* w' *of same length, we have* $w \equiv_{\leqslant} w' \Rightarrow s \equiv_{\leqslant} s'$. *A many-sorted signature* Σ *is the special case where the poset* $(S, \leqslant)$ *is discrete, i.e.,* $s \leqslant s'$ *iff* $s = s'$. $\Sigma = ((S, \leqslant), \Sigma)$ *is a* subsignature *of* $\Sigma' = ((S', \leqslant'), \Sigma')$, *denoted* $\Sigma \subseteq \Sigma'$, *iff* $S \subseteq S'$, $\leqslant \subseteq \leqslant'$, *and* $\Sigma \subseteq \Sigma'$.

For connected components $[s_1], \ldots, [s_n], [s] \in \widehat{S}$

$$f^{[s_1] \ldots [s_n]}_{[s]} = \{ f : s'_1 \ldots s'_n \to s' \in \Sigma \mid s'_i \in [s_i], \ 1 \leqslant i \leqslant n, \ s' \in [s] \}$$

denotes the family of "subsort polymorphic" operators f. $\square$

I will always assume that Σ's poset of sorts $(S, \leqslant)$ is *locally finite*, that is, that for any $s \in S$ its connected component $[s]$ is a finite set.

Definition 2. *For* $\Sigma = (S, \leqslant, \Sigma)$ *an OS signature, an* order-sorted Σ-algebra *A is a many-sorted (S, Σ)-algebra A such that:*

- *whenever* $s \leqslant s'$, *then we have* $A_s \subseteq A_{s'}$, *and*
- *whenever* $f : w \to s, f : w' \to s' \in f^{[s_1] \ldots [s_n]}_{[s]}$ *and* $\overline{a} \in A^w \cap A^{w'}$, *then we have* $A_{f:w \to s}(\overline{a}) = A_{f:w' \to s'}(\overline{a})$, *where* $A^{\epsilon} = 1$ *(ϵ denotes the empty string and* $1 = \{0\}$ *is a singleton set), and* $A^{s_1 \ldots s_n} = A_{s_1} \times \ldots \times A_{s_n}$.

An order-sorted Σ-homomorphism *$h : A \to B$ is a many-sorted (S, Σ)-homomorphism such that whenever $[s] = [s']$ and $a \in A_s \cap A_{s'}$, then we have $h_s(a) = h_{s'}(a)$. We call h* injective, *resp.* surjective, *resp.* bijective, *iff for each $s \in S$ h_s is injective, resp. surjective, resp. bijective. We call h an* isomorphism *if there is another order-sorted Σ-homomorphism $g : B \to A$ such that for each $s \in S$, $h_s; g_s = 1_{A_s}$, and $g_s; h_s = 1_{B_s}$, with $1_{A_s}, 1_{B_s}$ the identity functions on A_s, B_s. This defines a category* **OSAlg**$_{\Sigma}$. $\square$

Theorem 1 *[66]. The category* **OSAlg**$_{\Sigma}$ *has an initial algebra. Furthermore, if Σ is sensible, then the term algebra T_{Σ} with:*

- *if* $a : \epsilon \to s$ *then* $a \in T_{\Sigma,s}$,
- *if* $t \in T_{\Sigma,s}$ *and* $s \leqslant s'$ *then* $t \in T_{\Sigma,s'}$,
- *if* $f : s_1 \ldots s_n \to s$ *and* $t_i \in T_{\Sigma,s_i}$ $1 \leqslant i \leqslant n$, *then* $f(t_1, \ldots, t_n) \in T_{\Sigma,s}$,

is initial, i.e., there is a unique Σ-homomorphism from T_{Σ} to each Σ-algebra.

T_{Σ} will (ambiguously) denote both the above-defined S-sorted set and the set $T_{\Sigma} = \bigcup_{s \in S} T_{\Sigma,s}$. For $[s] \in \widehat{S}$, $T_{\Sigma,[s]} = \bigcup_{s' \in [s]} T_{\Sigma,s'}$. An OS signature Σ is said to *have non-empty sorts* iff for each $s \in S$, $T_{\Sigma,s} \neq \varnothing$. Unless explicitly stated otherwise, I will assume throughout that Σ has non-empty sorts. An OS signature Σ is called *preregular* [51] iff for each $t \in T_{\Sigma}$ the set $\{s \in S \mid t \in T_{\Sigma,s}\}$ has a least element, denoted $ls(t)$. I will assume throughout that Σ is preregular.

An S-sorted set $X = \{X_s\}_{s \in S}$ of *variables*, satisfies $s \neq s' \Rightarrow X_s \cap X_{s'} = \varnothing$, and the variables in X are always assumed disjoint from all constants in Σ.

The Σ-*term algebra* on variables X, $T_\Sigma(X)$, is the *initial algebra* for the signature $\Sigma(X)$ obtained by adding to Σ the variables X *as extra constants*. Since a $\Sigma(X)$-algebra is just a pair (A, α), with A a Σ-algebra, and α an *interpretation of the constants* in X, i.e., an S-sorted function $\alpha \in [X \to A]$, the $\Sigma(X)$-initiality of $T_\Sigma(X)$ can be expressed as the following corollary of Theorem 1:

Theorem 2. *(Freeness Theorem). If Σ is sensible, for each $A \in \mathbf{OSAlg}_\Sigma$ and $\alpha \in [X \to A]$, there exists a unique Σ-homomorphism, $\_\alpha : T_\Sigma(X) \to A$ extending α, i.e., such that for each $s \in S$ and $x \in X_s$ we have $x\alpha_s = \alpha_s(x)$.*

In particular, when $A = T_\Sigma(X)$, an interpretation of the constants in X, i.e., an S-sorted function $\sigma \in [X \to T_\Sigma(X)]$ is called a *substitution*, and its unique homomorphic extension $\_\sigma : T_\Sigma(X) \to T_\Sigma(X)$ is also called a *substitution*. Define $dom(\sigma) = \{x \in X \mid x \neq x\sigma\}$, and $ran(\sigma) = \bigcup_{x \in dom(\sigma)} vars(x\sigma)$. A *variable specialization* is a substitution ρ that just renames a few variables and may lower their sort. More precisely, $dom(\rho)$ is a finite set of variables $\{x_1, \ldots, x_n\}$, with respective sorts $s_1, \ldots, s_n$, and ρ injectively maps the $x_1, \ldots, x_n$ to variables $x'_1, \ldots, x'_n$ with respective sorts $s'_1, \ldots, s'_n$ such that $s'_i \leqslant s_i$, $1 \leqslant i \leqslant n$.

The first-order language of *equational Σ-formulas* is defined in the usual way: its atoms are Σ-*equations* $t = t'$, where $t, t' \in T_\Sigma(X)_{[s]}$ for some $[s] \in \widehat{S}$ and each X_s is assumed countably infinite. The set $Form(\Sigma)$ of *equational Σ-formulas* is then inductively built from atoms by: conjunction ($\wedge$), disjunction ($\vee$), negation ($\neg$), and universal ($\forall x{:}s$) and existential ($\exists x{:}s$) quantification with sorted variables $x{:}s \in X_s$ for some $s \in S$. The literal $\neg(t = t')$ is denoted $t \neq t'$.

Given a Σ-algebra A, a formula $\varphi \in Form(\Sigma)$, and an assignment $\alpha \in [Y \to A]$, with $Y = fvars(\varphi)$ the free variables of φ, the *satisfaction relation* $A, \alpha \models \varphi$ is defined inductively as usual: for atoms, $A, \alpha \models t = t'$ iff $t\alpha = t'\alpha$; for Boolean connectives it is the corresponding Boolean combination of the satisfaction relations for subformulas; and for quantifiers: $A, \alpha \models (\forall x{:}s)\ \varphi$ (resp. $A, \alpha \models (\exists x{:}s)\ \varphi$) holds iff for all $a \in A_s$ (resp. some $a \in A_s$) we have $A, \alpha \uplus \{(x{:}s, a)\} \models \varphi$, where the assignment $\alpha \uplus \{(x{:}s, a)\}$ extends α by mapping $x{:}s$ to a. Finally, $A \models \varphi$ holds iff $A, \alpha \models \varphi$ holds for each $\alpha \in [Y \to A]$, where $Y = fvars(\varphi)$. We say that φ is *valid* (or *true*) in A iff $A \models \varphi$. We say that φ is *satisfiable* in A iff $\exists \alpha \in [Y \to A]$ such that $A, \alpha \models \varphi$, where $Y = fvars(\varphi)$. For a subsignature $\Omega \subseteq \Sigma$ and $A \in \mathbf{OSAlg}_\Sigma$, the *reduct* $A|_\Omega \in \mathbf{OSAlg}_\Omega$ agrees with A in the interpretation of all sorts and operations in Ω and discards everything in $\Sigma - \Omega$. If $\varphi \in Form(\Omega)$ we have the equivalence $A \models \varphi \Leftrightarrow A|_\Omega \models \varphi$.

An OS *equational theory* is a pair $T = (\Sigma, E)$, with E a set of Σ-equations. $\mathbf{OSAlg}_{(\Sigma, E)}$ denotes the full subcategory of $\mathbf{OSAlg}_\Sigma$ with objects those $A \in \mathbf{OSAlg}_\Sigma$ such that $A \models E$, called the (Σ, E)-*algebras*. $\mathbf{OSAlg}_{(\Sigma, E)}$ has an *initial algebra* $T_{\Sigma/E}$ [66]. Given $T = (\Sigma, E)$ and $\varphi \in Form(\Sigma)$, we call φ T-*valid*, written $E \models \varphi$, iff $A \models \varphi$ for each $A \in \mathbf{OSAlg}_{(\Sigma, E)}$. We call φ T-*satisfiable* iff there exists $A \in \mathbf{OSAlg}_{(\Sigma, E)}$ with φ satisfiable in A. Note that φ is T-*valid* iff $\neg\varphi$ is T-*unsatisfiable*.

The inference system in [66] is *sound and complete* for OS equational deduction, i.e., for any OS equational theory (Σ, E), and Σ-equation $u = v$ we have an equivalence $E \vdash u = v \Leftrightarrow E \models u = v$. Deducibility $E \vdash u = v$ is often abbreviated as $u =_E v$ and called *E-equality*. A preregular signature Σ is called *E-preregular* iff for each $u = v \in E$ and variable specialization ρ, $ls(u\rho) = ls(v\rho)$.

In the above logical notions there is only an *apparent* lack of predicate symbols: full order-sorted first-order logic can be *reduced* to order-sorted algebra and the above language of equational formulas. The essential idea is to view a predicate $p(x_1:s_1, \ldots, x_n:s_n)$ as a function symbol $p : s_1 \ldots s_n \to Pred$, with $Pred$, a new sort having a constant tt. An atomic formula $p(t_1, \ldots, t_n)$ is then expressed as the equation $p(t_1, \ldots, t_n) = tt$. Let me just give a few technical details. An *order-sorted first-order logic signature*, or just an OS-FO signature, is a pair (Σ, Π) with Σ an OS signature with set of sorts S, and Π an S^*-indexed set $\Pi = \{\Pi_w\}_{w \in S^*}$ of *predicate symbols*. An OS (Σ, Π)-*model* M is an OS Σ-algebra M together with an S^*-indexed mapping $M_\_ : \Pi \to \{\mathcal{P}(M^w)\}_{w \in S^*}$ interpreting each $p \in \Pi_w$ as a subset $M_p \subseteq M^w$. Since p can be overloaded, we sometimes write $M_{p_w} \subseteq M^w$. M must also satisfy the additional condition that *overloaded predicates agree on common data*. That is, if $w \equiv_{\leqslant} w'$, $p \in \Pi_w$ and $p \in \Pi_{w'}$, then for any $\bar{a} \in M^w \cap M^{w'}$ we have $\bar{a} \in M_{p_w} \Leftrightarrow \bar{a} \in M_{p_{w'}}$. The language of *first-order (Σ, Π)-formulas* extends that of equational Σ-formulas by adding as atomic formulas predicate expressions of the form $p(t_1, \ldots, t_n)$, with $p \in \Pi_w$ and $(t_1, \ldots, t_n) \in T_\Sigma(X)^w$. The satisfaction relation is likewise extended by defining $M, \alpha \models p(t_1, \ldots, t_n)$ iff $(t_1\alpha, \ldots, t_n\alpha) \in M_p$.

The reduction to OS algebra is achieved as follows. We associate to an OS-FO signature (Σ, Π) an OS signature $(\Sigma \cup \Pi)$ by the above-mentioned method of adding to Σ a new sort $Pred$ with a constant tt in its own separate connected component $\{Pred\}$, and viewing each $p \in \Pi_w$ as a function symbol $p : s_1 \ldots s_n \to Pred$. The reduction at the model level is now very simple: each OS $(\Sigma \cup \Pi)$-algebra A defines a (Σ, Π)-model A° with Σ-algebra structure $A|_\Sigma$ and having for each $p \in \Pi_w$ the predicate interpretation $A_p^\circ = A_{p:w \to Pred}^{-1}(tt)$. The reduction at the formula level is also quite simple: we map a (Σ, Π)-formula φ to an equational formula $\widetilde{\varphi}$, called its *equational version*, by just replacing each atom $p(t_1, \ldots, t_n)$ by the equational atom $p(t_1, \ldots, t_n) = tt$. The *correctness* of this reduction is just the easy to check equivalence:

$$A^\circ \models \varphi \Leftrightarrow A \models \widetilde{\varphi}.$$

An OS-FO *theory* is just a pair $((\Sigma, \Pi), \Gamma)$, with (Σ, Π) an OS-FO signature and Γ a set of (Σ, Π)-formulas. Call $((\Sigma, \Pi), \Gamma)$ *equational* iff $(\Sigma \cup \Pi, \widetilde{\Gamma})$ is an OS equational theory. By the above equivalence and the completeness of OS equational logic such theories allow a sound and complete use of equational deduction also with predicate atoms. Note that if $((\Sigma, \Pi), \Gamma)$ is equational, it is a very simple type of theory in OS Horn Logic with Equality and therefore has an initial model $T_{\Sigma, \Pi, \Gamma}$ [52]. A useful, easy to check fact is that we have an identity: $T_{\Sigma \cup \Pi / \widetilde{\Gamma}}^\circ = T_{\Sigma, \Pi, \Gamma}$. I will give natural examples of OS-FO equational theories later in the paper.

Recall the notation for term positions, subterms, and term replacement from [32]: (i) positions in a term viewed as a tree are marked by strings $p \in \mathbb{N}^*$

specifying a path from the root, (ii) $t|_p$ denotes the subterm of term t at position p, and (iii) $t[u]_p$ denotes the result of *replacing* subterm $t|_p$ at position p by u.

Definition 3. *A* rewrite theory *is a triple* $\mathcal{R} = (\Sigma, B, R)$ *with* (Σ, B) *an order-sorted equational theory and* R *a set of* Σ-*rewrite rules, i.e., sequents* $l \to r$, *with* $l, r \in T_\Sigma(X)_{[s]}$ *for some* $[s] \in \widehat{S}$. *In what follows it is always assumed that:*

1. *For each* $l \to r \in R$, $l \notin X$ *and* $vars(r) \subseteq vars(l)$.
2. *Each rule* $l \to r \in R$ *is sort-decreasing, i.e., for each variable specialization* ρ, $ls(l\rho) \geqslant ls(r\rho)$.
3. Σ *is* B-*preregular.*
4. *Each equation* $u = v \in B$ *is regular, i.e.,* $vars(u) = vars(v)$, *and linear, i.e., there are no repeated variables in* u, *and no repeated variables in* v.

The one-step R, B-*rewrite relation* $t \to_{R,B} t'$, *holds between* $t, t' \in T_\Sigma(X)_{[s]}$, $[s] \in \widehat{S}$, *iff there is a rewrite rule* $l \to r \in R$, *a substitution* $\sigma \in [X \to T_\Sigma(X)]$, *and a term position* p *in* t *such that* $t|_p =_B l\sigma$, *and* $t' = t[r\sigma]_p$. *Note that, by assumptions (2)–(3) above,* $t[r\sigma]_p$ *is always a well-formed* Σ-*term.*

$\mathcal{R}$ *is called: (i)* terminating *iff the relation* $\to_{R,B}$ *is well-founded; (ii)* strictly B-coherent *[68] iff whenever* $u \to_{R,B} v$ *and* $u =_B u'$ *there is a* v' *such that* $u' \to_{R,B} v'$ *and* $v =_B v'$:

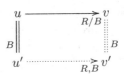

(iii) confluent *iff* $u \to^*_{R,B} v_1$ *and* $u \to^*_{R,B} v_2$ *imply that there are* w_1, w_2 *such that* $v_1 \to^*_{R,B} w_1$, $v_2 \to^*_{R,B} w_2$, *and* $w_1 =_B w_2$ *(where* $\to^*_{R,B}$ *denotes the reflexive-transitive closure of* $\to_{R,B}$*); and (iv)* convergent *if (i)–(iii) hold. If* $\mathcal{R}$ *is convergent, for each* Σ-*term* t *there is a term* u *such that* $t \to^*_{R,B} u$ *and* $(\nexists v) u \to_{R,B} v$. *We then write* $u = t!_{R,B}$ *and* $t \to!_{R,B} t!_{R,B}$, *and call* $t!_{R,B}$ *the* R, B-*normal form of* t, *which, by confluence, is unique up to* B-*equality.*

Given a set E of Σ-equations, let $R(E) = \{u \to v \mid u = v \in E\}$. A *decomposition* of an order-sorted equational theory (Σ, E) is a convergent rewrite theory $\mathcal{R} = (\Sigma, B, R)$ such that $E = E_0 \uplus B$ and $R = R(E_0)$. The key property of a decomposition is the following:

Theorem 3. *(Church-Rosser Theorem) [59, 68] Let* $\mathcal{R} = (\Sigma, B, R)$ *be a decomposition of* (Σ, E). *Then we have an equivalence:*

$$E \vdash u = v \iff u!_{R,B} =_B v!_{R,B}.$$

If $\mathcal{R} = (\Sigma, B, R)$ is a decomposition of (Σ, E), and X an S-sorted set of variables, the *canonical term algebra* $C_\mathcal{R}(X)$ has $C_\mathcal{R}(X)_s = \{[t!_{R,B}]_B \mid t \in T_\Sigma(X)_s\}$, and interprets each $f : s_1 \ldots s_n \to s$ as the function $C_\mathcal{R}(X)_f :$

$([u_1]_B, \ldots, [u_n]_B) \mapsto [f(u_1, \ldots, u_n)!_{R,B}]_B$. By the Church-Rosser Theorem we then have an isomorphism $h : T_{\Sigma/E}(X) \cong C_{\mathcal{R}}(X)$, where $h : [t]_E \mapsto [t!_{R,B}]_B$. In particular, when X is the empty family of variables, the canonical term algebra $C_{\mathcal{R}}$ is an initial algebra, and is the most intuitive possible model for $T_{\Sigma/E}$ as an algebra of *values* computed by R, B-simplification.

Quite often, the signature Σ on which $T_{\Sigma/E}$ is defined has a natural decomposition as a disjoint union $\Sigma = \Omega \uplus \Delta$, where the elements of $C_{\mathcal{R}}$, that is, the *values* computed by R, B-simplification, are Ω-terms, whereas the function symbols $f \in \Delta$ are viewed as *defined functions* which are *evaluated away* by R, B-simplification. Ω (with same poset of sorts as Σ) is then called a *constructor subsignature* of Σ. Call a decomposition $\mathcal{R} = (\Sigma, B, R)$ of (Σ, E) *sufficiently complete* with respect to the *constructor subsignature* Ω iff for each $t \in T_\Sigma$ we have: (i) $t!_{R,B} \in T_\Omega$, and (ii) if $u \in T_\Omega$ and $u =_B v$, then $v \in T_\Omega$. This ensures that for each $[u]_B \in C_{\mathcal{R}}$ we have $[u]_B \subseteq T_\Omega$. Of course, we want Ω as *small as possible* with these properties. I give in what follows many examples of such decompositions $\Sigma = \Omega \uplus \Delta$ into constructors and defined functions. In Example 1 below, $\Omega = \{\top, \bot\}$ and $\Delta = \{\_ \wedge \_, \_ \vee \_\}$. Tools based on tree automata [27], equational tree automata [56], or narrowing [55], can be used to automatically check sufficient completeness of a decomposition $\mathcal{R}$ with respect to constructors Ω under some assumptions.

As the following definition shows, sufficient completeness is closely related to the notion of a *protecting* theory inclusion, which is itself a special case of an *extending* theory inclusion.

Definition 4. *An equational theory* (Σ, E) *protects (resp. extends) another theory* (Ω, E_Ω) *iff* $(\Omega, E_\Omega) \subseteq (\Sigma, E)$ *and the unique* Ω-*homomorphism* $h : T_{\Omega/E_\Omega} \to T_{\Sigma/E}|_\Omega$ *is an isomorphism* $h : T_{\Omega/E_\Omega} \cong T_{\Sigma/E}|_\Omega$ *(resp. is injective). A decomposition* $\mathcal{R} = (\Sigma, B, R)$ *protects (resp. is a conservative extension of) another decomposition* $\mathcal{R}_0 = (\Sigma_0, B_0, R_0)$ *iff* $\mathcal{R}_0 \subseteq \mathcal{R}$, *i.e.,* $\Sigma_0 \subseteq \Sigma$, $B_0 \subseteq B$, *and* $R_0 \subseteq R$, *and for all* $t, t' \in T_{\Sigma_0}(X)$ *we have: (i)* $t =_{B_0} t' \Leftrightarrow t =_B t'$, *(ii)* $t = t!_{R_0,B_0} \Leftrightarrow t = t!_{R,B}$, *and (iii)* $C_{\mathcal{R}_0} = C_{\mathcal{R}}|_{\Sigma_0}$ *(resp.* $C_{\mathcal{R}_0} \subseteq C_{\mathcal{R}}|_{\Sigma_0}$). $\mathcal{R}_\Omega = (\Omega, B_\Omega, R_\Omega)$ *is a constructor decomposition of* $\mathcal{R} = (\Sigma, B, R)$ *iff* $\mathcal{R}$ *protects* $\mathcal{R}_\Omega$ *and* Σ *and* Ω *have the same poset of sorts, so that by (iii) above* $\mathcal{R}$ *is sufficiently complete with respect to* Ω. *Furthermore,* Ω *is called a subsignature of* free constructors modulo B_Ω *iff* $R_\Omega = \varnothing$, *so that* $C_{\mathcal{R}_0} = T_{\Omega/B_\Omega}$.

The case where all constructor terms are in R, B-normal form is captured by Ω being a subsignature of free constructors modulo B_Ω. Note also that conditions (i) and (ii) are, so called, "no confusion" conditions, and for protecting extensions (iii) is a "no junk" condition, that is, $\mathcal{R}$ does not add new data to $C_{\mathcal{R}_0}$, whereas for conservative extensions (iii) is relaxed to the "no confusion" condition $C_{\mathcal{R}_0} \subseteq C_{\mathcal{R}}|_{\Sigma_0}$, which is already implicit in (i) and (ii). Therefore, protecting extensions are a stronger kind of conservative extensions.

Given an OS equational theory (Σ, E) and a system of Σ-equations, that is, a conjunction $\phi = u_1 = v_1 \wedge \ldots \wedge u_n = v_n$ of Σ-equations, an E-*unifier* of it is a substitution σ such that $u_i\sigma =_E v_i\sigma$, $1 \leqslant i \leqslant n$. An E-*unification algorithm* for (Σ, E) is an algorithm generating a *complete set* of E-unifiers $Unif_E(\phi)$ for any system of Σ equations ϕ, where "complete" means that for any E-unifier σ of ϕ there is a $\tau \in Unif_E(\phi)$ and a substitution ρ such that $\sigma =_E \tau\rho$, where $=_E$ here means that for any variable x we have $x\sigma =_E x\tau\rho$. Such an algorithm is called *finitary* if it always terminates with a *finite set* $Unif_E(\phi)$ for any such ϕ.

The notion of *variant* answers, in a sense, two questions: (i) how can we best describe symbolically the elements of $C_{\mathcal{R}}(X)$ that are *reduced substitution instances* of a *pattern term* t? and (ii) given an original pattern t, how many other patterns do we need to describe the reduced instances of t in $C_{\mathcal{R}}(X)$?

Definition 5. *Given a decomposition* $\mathcal{R} = (\Sigma, B, R)$ *of an OS equational theory* (Σ, E) *and a* Σ-*term* t, *a variant*[2] *[31,42] of* t *is a pair* (u, θ) *such that: (i)* $u =_B (t\theta)!_{R,B}$, *(ii) if* $x \notin vars(t)$, *then* $x\theta = x$, *and (iii)* $\theta = \theta!_{R,B}$, *that is,* $x\theta = (x\theta)!_{R,B}$ *for all variables* x. (u, θ) *is called a* ground variant *iff, furthermore,* $u \in T_\Sigma$. *Note that if* (u, θ) *is a ground variant of some* t, *then* $[u]_B \in C_{\mathcal{R}}$. *Given variants* (u, θ) *and* (v, γ) *of* t, (u, θ) *is called* more general *than* (v, γ), *denoted* $(u, \theta) \sqsupseteq_{R,B} (v, \gamma)$, *iff there is a substitution* ρ *such that: (i)* $\theta\rho =_B \gamma$, *and (ii)* $u\rho =_B v$. *Let* $[\![t]\!]_{R,B} = \{(u_i, \theta_i) \mid i \in I\}$ *denote a* most general complete set of variants *of* t, *that is, a set of variants such that: (i) for any variant* (v, γ) *of* t *there is an* $i \in I$, *such that* $(u_i, \theta_i) \sqsupseteq_{R,B} (v, \gamma)$; *and (ii) for* $i, j \in I$, $i \neq j \Rightarrow ((u_i, \theta_i) \not\sqsupseteq_{R,B} (u_j, \theta_j) \wedge (u_j, \theta_j) \not\sqsupseteq_{R,B} (u_i, \theta_i))$. *A decomposition* $\mathcal{R} = (\Sigma, B, R)$ *of* (Σ, E) *has the* finite variant property *[31] (FVP) iff for each* Σ-*term* t *there is a* finite most general complete set of variants $[\![t]\!]_{R,B} = \{(u_1, \theta_1), \ldots, (u_n, \theta_n)\}$.

If B has a finitary unification algorithm, the *folding variant narrowing* strategy described in [42] provides an effective method to generate $[\![t]\!]_{R,B}$. Furthermore, $[\![t]\!]_{R,B}$ is finite for each t, so that the strategy *terminates*, iff $\mathcal{R}$ is FVP.

Example 1. Let $\mathcal{B} = (\Sigma, B, R)$ with Σ having a single sort, say *Bool*, constants $\top, \bot$, and binary opertors $\_ \wedge \_$ and $\_ \vee \_$, B the associativity and commutativity (AC) axioms for both $\_ \wedge \_$ and $\_ \vee \_$, and R the rules: $x \wedge \top \rightarrow x$, $x \wedge \bot \rightarrow \bot$, $x \vee \bot \rightarrow x$, and $x \wedge \top \rightarrow \top$. Then $\mathcal{B}$ is FVP. For example, $[\![x \wedge y]\!]_{R,B} = \{(x \wedge y, id), (y, \{x \mapsto \top\}), (x, \{y \mapsto \top\}), (\bot, \{x \mapsto \bot\}), (\bot, \{y \mapsto \bot\})\}$.

FVP is a *semi-decidable* property [23], which can be easily verified (when it holds) by checking, using folding variant narrowing, that for each function symbol f the term $f(x_1, \ldots, x_n)$, with the sorts of the $x_1, \ldots, x_n$ those of f, has a finite number of most general variants. Given an FVP decomposition $\mathcal{R}$ its *variant complexity* is the total number n of variants for all such $f(x_1, \ldots, x_n)$, provided f has some associated rules of the form $f(t_1, \ldots, t_n) \rightarrow t'$. This gives a rough measure of how costly it is to perform variant computations *relative to* the cost of performing B-unification. For example, the variant complexity of $\mathcal{B}$ above is 10.

---

[2] For a discussion of similar but not exactly equivalent versions of the variant notion see [23]. Here I follow the formulation in [42].

Folding variant narrowing provides also a method for generating a *complete set of E-unifiers*. I give below a method for generating such a set that is different from the one given in [42], because in Sect. 4 this will allow me to express the notion of constructor E-unifier in a straightforward way. Let (Σ, E) have a decomposition $\mathcal{R} = (\Sigma, B, R)$ with B having a finitary B-unification algorithm.

To be able to express systems of equations, say, $u_1 = v_1 \wedge \ldots \wedge u_n = v_n$, as *terms*, we can extend Σ to a signature $\Sigma^{\wedge}$ by adding:

1. for each connected component $[s]$ that does not already have a top element, a fresh new sort $\top_{[s]}$ with $\top_{[s]} > s'$ for each $s \in [s]$. In this way we obtain a (possibly extended) poset of sorts $(S_\top, \geqslant)$;
2. fresh new sorts *Lit* and *Conj* with a subsort inclusion *Lit* < *Conj*, with a binary conjunction operator $\_ \wedge \_ : Lit\ Conj \rightarrow Conj$, and
3. for each connected component $[s] \in \widehat{S_\top}$ with top sort $\top_{[s]}$, binary operators $\_ = \_ : \top_{[s]}\ \top_{[s]} \rightarrow Lit$ and $\_ \neq \_ : \top_{[s]}\ \top_{[s]} \rightarrow Lit$.

Theorem 4. *Under the above assumptions on $\mathcal{R}$, let $\phi = u_1 = v_1 \wedge \ldots \wedge u_n = v_n$ be a system of Σ-equations viewed as a $\Sigma^{\wedge}$-term of sort Conj. Then*

$$\{\theta\gamma \mid (\phi', \theta) \in [\![\phi]\!]_{R,B} \wedge \gamma \in Unif_B(\phi') \wedge (\phi'\gamma, \theta\gamma) \text{ is a variant of } \phi\}$$

is a complete set of E-unifiers for ϕ, where $Unif_B(\phi')$ denotes a complete set of most general B-unifiers for each variant $\phi' = u'_1 = v'_1 \wedge \ldots \wedge u'_n = v'_n$.

Since if $\mathcal{R} = (\Sigma, B, R)$ is FVP, then $\mathcal{R}^{\wedge} = (\Sigma^{\wedge}, B, R)$ is also FVP, Theorem 4 shows that if a finitary B-unification algorithm exists and $\mathcal{R}$ is an FVP decomposition of (Σ, E), then E has a finitary E-unification algorithm.

3   A Satisfiability Puzzle

In Sect. 8 of their paper about the finite variant property [31], Comon-Lundh and Delaune give a theorem (Theorem 3) stating that if (Σ, E) has an FVP decomposition, say $\mathcal{R} = (\Sigma, E', R)$, and satisfiability of quantifier-free (QF) equational Σ-formulas in the initial algebra $T_{\Sigma/E'}$ is decidable,[3] then satisfiability of QF equational Σ-formulas in the initial algebra $T_{\Sigma/E}$ is also decidable. They give the following proof sketch for this theorem:

> *To prove this, simply compute the variants $\phi_1, \ldots, \phi_n$ of the formula ϕ. (In such a computation, logical connectives are seen as free symbols). For every substitution σ, there is an index i and a substitution θ such that $\phi\sigma!_{R,E'} =_{E'} \phi_i\theta$. In particular, ϕ is solvable modulo E iff one of the ϕ_i is solvable modulo E'.*

---

[3] Such decidable QF satisfiability is of course equivalent to the decidability of whether a sentence in the existential closure of such QF formulas belongs to the theory of $T_{\Sigma/E'}$, which is how the decidability property is actually stated in [31].

The actual text in [31] only differs from the one above by the use of a different notation for the normal form $\phi\sigma!_{R,E'}$. Their theorem, however, is incorrect, as shown below. Since it is well-known that, putting a QF formula in DNF we can reduce satisfiability of a QF formula to satisfiability of a conjunction of literals, we can further simplify the above proof sketch by focusing on such conjunctions.

What the proof sketch then means is that, since $(\Sigma^\wedge, E)$ has an FVP decomposition $\mathcal{R}^\wedge = (\Sigma^\wedge, E', R)$, and each conjunction of literals, say, $\phi = B_1 \wedge \ldots \wedge B_k$, with each B_i either a Σ-equation or a Σ-disequation, is a $\Sigma^\wedge$-term, the proof sketch is a claim that ϕ is satisfiable in $T_{\Sigma/E}$ iff for some R, E'-variant (ϕ_i, θ_i) of ϕ the conjunction ϕ_i is satisfiable in $T_{\Sigma/E'}$.

Example 2. The following counterexample shows that Theorem 3 in [31] is incorrect as stated. Let Σ have sorts *Nat* and *Bool*, with constants 0 of sort *Nat* and $\top, \bot$ of sort *Bool*, a unary successor operator s of sort *Nat*, and a unary *zero?* : *Nat* $\rightarrow$ *Bool*. Let n be a variable of sort *Nat*, and E the equations $zero?(s(n)) = \bot$ and $zero?(0) = \top$. Then $(\Sigma, \varnothing, R(E))$ is an FVP decomposition of (Σ, E) of variant complexity 3 (i.e., in the above notation $E' = \varnothing$). Let ϕ be the formula $x = zero?(n) \wedge x \neq \top \wedge x \neq \bot$. It has a complete set of three most general $R(E), \varnothing$-variants, namely: (ϕ, id), $(\phi', \{n \mapsto s(n')\})$, and $(\phi'', \{n \mapsto 0\})$, with n' of sort *Nat*, id the identity substitution, the other substitutions specified by how they map the variable n in ϕ, and where ϕ' is the formula $x = \bot \wedge x \neq \top \wedge x \neq \bot$, and ϕ'' is the formula $x = \top \wedge x \neq \top \wedge x \neq \bot$. The formula ϕ is clearly unsatisfiable in $T_{\Sigma/E}$. However, for the variant (ϕ, id) the formula ϕ *is* satisfiable in T_Σ for *any* substitution $\sigma = \{n \mapsto t, x \mapsto zero?(t)\}$ with t a ground term of sort *Nat*; for example for $\sigma = \{n \mapsto 0, x \mapsto zero?(0)\}$.

A question still remains: whether, under suitable conditions, some analogue of the (incorrect) Theorem 3 in [31] could somehow be obtained. That is, can we find some results relating satisfiability in the *initial* algebras $T_{\Sigma/E}$ and in $T_{\Sigma/B}$ (or some initial algebra related to $T_{\Sigma/B}$) when $\mathcal{R} = (\Sigma, B, R)$ is an FVP decomposition of (Σ, E)? I address this question in Sects. 5, 6 and 7. The key to answer the question is the new notion of constructor variant that I present next.

4   Constructor Variants and Constructor Unifiers

Intuitively, an R, B-variant of a term t is another term v which is the normal form of an instance $t\theta$ of t; i.e., such variants v are *patterns* covering the normal forms of instances of t. But we can ask: what variants cover the normal forms of the *ground* instances of t? I call them the *constructor variants* of t. Likewise, a *constructor unifier* of ϕ is a special type of constructor variant of ϕ in the extended decomposition $\mathcal{R}^\wedge = (\Sigma^\wedge, B, R)$, and every R, B-normalized *ground* unifier of ϕ is "covered" by a constructor unifier.

Definition 6. *Let* $\mathcal{R} = (\Sigma, B, R)$ *be a decomposition of* (Σ, E), *and let* $\mathcal{R}_\Omega = (\Omega, B_\Omega, R_\Omega)$ *be a constructor decomposition of* $\mathcal{R}$. *Then an* R, B-*variant* (u, θ) *of a* Σ-*term* t *is called a* constructor R, B-variant *of* t *iff* $u \in T_\Omega(X)$.

Suppose, furthermore, that B has a finitary B-unification algorithm, so that, given a unification problem $\phi = u_1 = v_1 \wedge \ldots \wedge u_n = v_n$, Theorem 4 allows us to generate the complete set of E-unifiers

$$\{\theta\gamma \mid (\phi', \theta) \in [\![\phi]\!]_{R,B} \wedge \gamma \in \mathit{Unif}_B(\phi') \wedge (\phi'\gamma, \theta\gamma) \text{ is a variant of } \phi\}$$

Then a constructor E-unifier of ϕ is either: (1) a unifier $\theta\gamma$ in the above set such that $\phi'\gamma \in T_{\Omega^\wedge}(X)$; or otherwise, (2) a unifier $\theta\gamma\rho$ such that: (i) $\theta\gamma$ belongs the above set, (ii) ρ is a variable specialization[4] of the variables in $\mathit{ran}(\theta\gamma)$ such that $\phi'\gamma\rho \in T_{\Omega^\wedge}(X)$, (iii) $(\phi'\gamma\rho, \theta\gamma\rho)$ is a variant of ϕ, and (iv) the specialization ρ is maximal[5] satisfying conditions (ii) and (iii) in the order $\rho \geqslant \tau$ between variable specializations with same domain that holds iff for each $x:s$ in the domain, if $x:s\rho = x':s'$ and $x:s\tau = x'':s''$, then $s' \geqslant s''$.

Recall that if (v, δ) is a ground variant of t, then $[v]_B \in C_{\mathcal{R}}$, so that v is an Ω-term. Therefore, any ground variant (v, δ) of t is "covered" by some constructor variant (u, θ) of t, i.e., $(u, \theta) \sqsupseteq_{R,B} (v, \delta)$. Likewise, suppose that δ is an R, B-normalized *ground* unifier of ϕ. Then, (i) $(\bigwedge_i (u_i\delta)!_{R,B} = (v_i\delta)!_{R,B}) \in T_{\Omega^\wedge}(X)$; (ii) $((\bigwedge_i(u_i\delta)!_{R,B} = (v_i\delta)!_{R,B}), \delta)$ is a variant of ϕ, and (iii) $(u_i\delta)!_{R,B} =_B (v_i\delta)!_{R,B}, 1 \leqslant i \leqslant n$. Therefore, there is a constructor unifier $\theta\gamma\rho$ and a substitution α such that $\delta =_B \theta\gamma\rho\alpha$.

If (Σ, E) has a decomposition $\mathcal{R} = (\Sigma, B, R)$, B has a finitary B-unification algorithm and we are only interested in characterizing the *ground solutions* of an equation in the initial algebra $T_{\Sigma/E}$, only constructor E-unifiers are needed, since they completely cover all such solutions. Likewise, if we are only interested in *unifiability* of a system of equations only constructor E-unifiers are needed.

---

[4] By the assumption that Σ's poset of sorts $(S, \leqslant)$ is locally finite, up to variable renaming the specializations of a finite set of variables form always a *finite* set. When $\phi'\gamma \notin T_{\Omega^\wedge}(X)$ we may still have $\phi'\gamma\rho \in T_{\Omega^\wedge}(X)$ for some variable specialization ρ because a constructor symbol $f : w \to s$ may have a subsort-overloaded typing $f : w' \to s'$ that is *not* a constructor but a *defined* symbol (see Footnote 5 below for an example).

[5] The following example illustrates all the issues involved. In the FVP decomposition $\mathcal{Z}_+$ of the integers with addition of Example 10 in Sect. 6.2, the signature Ω of constructors contains two typings for $+$, namely, $\_+\_ : Nat\ Nat \to Nat$ and $\_+\_ : NzNat\ NzNat \to NzNat$, with $NzNat$ the subsort of non-zero naturals, and both operations associative-commutative, and having 0 as unit element (ACU). Instead, the typing $\_+\_ : Int\ Int \to Int$ (also ACU) is *not* a constructor, but a function defined by equations. Let ϕ be the equation $x + y = x' + y'$, where all variables have sort Int. It has the variant $(x + y = x' + y', id)$, and $\gamma = \{x \mapsto x', y \mapsto y'\}$ is one of the ACU-unifiers of $x + y = x' + y'$. Case (1) fails because $x' + y'$ is *not* an Ω-term. However, the variable specialization $\rho = \{x' \mapsto x'' : Nat, y' \mapsto y'' : Nat\}$ yields the constructor unifier $id\gamma\rho = \{x \mapsto x'' : Nat, y \mapsto y'' : Nat, x' \mapsto x'' : Nat, y' \mapsto y'' : Nat\}$ because now $x'' : Nat + y'' : Nat$ is an Ω-term (property (ii) holds) and property (iii) also holds. Furthermore, ρ is maximal with properties (ii) and (iii). For example, $\rho > \tau$ for $\tau = \{x' \mapsto x''' : NzNat, y' \mapsto y''' : NzNat\}$, so that the less general unifier $id\gamma\tau$ is unnecessary.

Theorem 5. *Let (Σ, E) have a decomposition $\mathcal{R} = (\Sigma, B, R)$ with B having a finitary B-unification algorithm. Then, for each system of Σ-equations $\phi = u_1 = v_1 \wedge \ldots \wedge u_n = v_n$, where $Y = vars(\phi)$, we have:*

1. *(Completeness for Ground Unifiers). If $\delta \in [Y \rightarrow T_\Sigma]$ is a ground E-unifier of ϕ, then there is a constructor E-unifier $\theta\gamma\rho$ and a substitution α such that $\delta =_E \theta\gamma\rho\alpha$, i.e., $x\delta =_E x\theta\gamma\rho\alpha$ for each variable x.*
2. *(Unifiability). $T_{\Sigma/E} \models (\exists Y) \phi$ iff ϕ has a constructor E-unifier. Furthermore, we have equivalences:*

$$E \models (\exists Y) \phi \; \Leftrightarrow \; T_{\Sigma/E}(X) \models (\exists Y) \phi \; \Leftrightarrow \; T_{\Sigma/E} \models (\exists Y) \phi.$$

Example 3. Let (Σ, E) be the OS equational theory of Example 2 and $\mathcal{R} = (\Sigma, \varnothing, R(E))$ its associated FVP decomposition. The term $zero?(n)$ has three variants: $(zero?(n), id)$, $(\bot, \{n \mapsto s(n')\})$, and $(\top, \{n \mapsto 0\})$. Since all ground instances of $zero?(n)$ are $R(E)$-reducible, only the last two are constructor variants.

The E-unification problem $zero?(n) = zero?(m)$ has three unifiers: $\{n \mapsto m\}$, obtained from the variant $(zero?(n) = zero?(m), id)$, $\{n \mapsto s(n'), m \mapsto s(m')\}$, obtained from the variant $(\bot = \bot, \{n \mapsto s(n'), m \mapsto s(m')\})$, and $\{n \mapsto 0, m \mapsto 0\}$, obtained from the variant $(\top = \top, \{n \mapsto 0, m \mapsto 0\})$. Only the last two are constructor unifiers.

Example 4. Consider the unsorted theory (Σ, E) where Σ has a constant 0, a unary s and a binary $\_+\_$, and E has the equations $n+0 = n$, $n+s(m) = s(n+m)$. (Σ, E) is not FVP, but it has an obvious decomposition $\mathcal{R} = (\Sigma, \varnothing, R(E))$. The variants of the term $x + y$ are of the following types: (i) $(x+y, id)$, (ii) $(x, \{y \mapsto 0\})$, (iii) $(s^n(x+y'), \{y \mapsto s^n(y')\})$, $n \geqslant 1$, and (iv) $(s^n(x), \{y \mapsto s^n(0)\})$, $n \geqslant 1$. Only variants of types (ii) and (iv) are constructor variants.

The E-unification problem $x + y = z + 0$ has the following types of E-unifiers: (i) $\{z \mapsto x + y\}$, associated to the variant $(x + y = z, id)$, (ii) $\{z \mapsto x, y \mapsto 0\}$, associated to the variant $(x = z, \{y \mapsto 0\})$, (iii) $\{z \mapsto s^n(x + y'), y \mapsto s^n(y')\}$, associated to the variants $(s^n(x + y') = z, \{y \mapsto s^n(y')\})$, $n \geqslant 1$, and (iv) $\{z \mapsto s^n(x), y \mapsto s^n(0)\}$, associated to the variants $(s^n(x) = z, \{y \mapsto s^n(0)\})$, $n \geqslant 1$. Only unifiers of types (ii) and (iv) are constructor unifiers.

As the above examples show, there can be considerably fewer constructor E-unifiers than general E-unifiers, so using constructor unifiers can be considerably more efficient for various purposes.

5   Satisfiability in Initial Algebras: Descent Results

Using the constructor variant notion from Sect. 4 we can associate the failure of Theorem 3 of [31] in Example 2 to the fact that for ϕ the formula $x = zero?(n) \wedge x \neq \top \wedge x \neq \bot$, the variant (ϕ, id) is *not* a constructor variant. One might conjecture that if $\mathcal{R} = (\Sigma, B, R)$ is an FVP decomposition of (Σ, E), a QF equational formula ϕ is satisfiable in $T_{\Sigma/E}$ iff for some *constructor variant* (ϕ', θ) ϕ' is satisfiable in $T_{\Sigma/B}$. But this conjecture fails in general:

Example 5. Let Σ be the unsorted signature with a constant 0 and a unary s, and E consist of the single equation $s(s(0)) = 0$. Then, $\mathcal{N}_2 = (\Sigma, \varnothing, R(E))$ is an FVP decomposition of (Σ, E). Let ϕ be the formula $x \neq 0 \wedge x \neq s(0)$. Its only $R(E), \varnothing$-variant is (ϕ, id), which is a constructor variant, since it has, for example, the ground variant $(0 \neq 0 \wedge 0 \neq s(0), \{x \mapsto 0\})$ as an instance. Obviously, ϕ is unsatisfiable in $T_{\Sigma/E}$, but it is clearly satisfiable in $T_{\Sigma/\varnothing} = T_\Sigma$, for example with the ground substitution $\{x \mapsto s(s(0))\}$. Of course, since $T_{\Sigma/E}$ is a *finite* algebra, satisfiability in $T_{\Sigma/E}$ is decidable anyway, but *not as conjectured.*

A key reason for the failure of the above conjecture in Example 5 is that the rules in $R(E)$ *rewrite constructor terms*, so that not all constructor terms are in normal form. Therefore, the conjecture's mistake was to focus on $T_{\Sigma/B}$, when we should focus on the *canonical algebra of constructors* $C_{\mathcal{R}_\Omega}$ associated to a constructor decomposition $\mathcal{R}_\Omega = (\Omega, B_\Omega, R_\Omega)$ of the given FVP decomposition $\mathcal{R} = (\Sigma, B, R)$. Note that the canonical term algebra $C_{\mathcal{R}}$ and the canonical constructor algebra $C_{\mathcal{R}_\Omega}$ are related by the equality $C_{\mathcal{R}}|_\Omega = C_{\mathcal{R}_\Omega}$. This allows us to *reduce* satisfiability in $C_{\mathcal{R}}$ to satisfiability in $C_{\mathcal{R}_\Omega}$ as follows:

Theorem 6. *(Descent Theorem).* Let a decomposition $\mathcal{R} = (\Sigma, B, R)$ of an OS equational theory (Σ, E) protect a constructor decomposition $\mathcal{R}_\Omega$ with equational theory (Ω, E_Ω). Then, a QF Σ-conjunction of literals ϕ is satisfiable in $T_{\Sigma/E}$ iff there is a constructor variant (ϕ', θ) of ϕ such that ϕ' is satisfiable in T_{Ω/E_Ω}.

This theorem has a useful corollary for equational OS-FO theories:

Corollary 1. *Let an FVP decomposition $\mathcal{R} = (\Sigma \cup \Pi, B, R)$ of an OS-FO equational theory $((\Sigma, \Pi), \Gamma)$, with B having a finitary unification algorithm, protect a constructor decomposition $\mathcal{R}_{(\Omega, \Delta)} = (\Omega \cup \Delta, B_\Omega, R_{(\Omega, \Delta)})$ of a theory $((\Omega, \Delta), \Gamma_0)$, with $=_{B_\Omega}$ decidable and such that satisfiability of QF (Ω, Δ)-formulas in $T_{\Omega, \Delta, \Gamma_0}$ is decidable. Then, satisfiability of any QF (Σ, Π)-formula ϕ in $T_{\Sigma, \Pi, \Gamma}$ is decidable.*

Given an OS equational theory (Σ, E), call a Σ-equality $u = v$ *E-trivial* iff $u =_E v$, and a Σ-disequality $u \neq v$ *E-consistent* iff $u \neq_E v$. Likewise, call a conjunction $\bigwedge D$ of Σ-disequalities *E-consistent* iff each $u \neq v$ in D is so.

Corollary 1 can be "unpacked" into an actual *generic algorithm* to decide the satisfiability in $T_{\Sigma, \Pi, \Gamma}$ of any QF (Σ, Π)-formula ϕ. We can first of all shift the problem to the equivalent one of satisfiability of the equational version $\widetilde{\phi}$ in $T_{\Sigma \cup \Pi / \widetilde{\Gamma}}$ and, by assuming $\widetilde{\phi}$ in DNF,[6] we can reduce to deciding whether some conjunction of literals $\bigwedge G \wedge \bigwedge D$, with G equations and D disequations in such a DNF is satisfiable. The algorithm is as follows:

1. Thanks to Theorem 5 we need only compute the variant-based *constructor* $\widetilde{\Gamma}$-unifiers of $\bigwedge G$, and reduce to the case of deciding the satisfiability of

---

[6] Using a lazy *DPLL(T)* solver (see, e.g., [13]) we do *not* have to assume that φ is in DNF: the *DPLL(T)* solver will efficiently extract from φ the appropriate conjunctions of *T*-literals to check for satisfiability.

some conjunction of disequalities $(\bigwedge D\alpha)!_{R,B}$, for some constructor unifier α, discarding any $(\bigwedge D\alpha)!_{R,B}$ containing a B-inconsistent disequality.

2. For each remaining $(\bigwedge D\alpha)!_{R,B}$ we can then compute a finite, complete set of most general R, B-variants $[\![(\bigwedge D\alpha)!_{R,B}]\!]_{R,B}$ by folding variant narrowing, and obtain from them[7] the B_Ω-consistent constructor variants $\bigwedge D'$.

3. We can then decide the satisfiability in $T_{\Omega,\Delta,\Gamma_0}$ of each such $\bigwedge D'$, so that $\bigwedge G \wedge \bigwedge D$ will be satisfiable in $T_{\Sigma,\Pi,\Gamma}$ iff some $\bigwedge D'$ is so in $T_{\Omega,\Delta,\Gamma_0}$.

In a sequential implementation of such an algorithm, steps (1) and (2) should be computed *incrementally*: one unifier, resp. variant, at a time. Maude 2.7 supports incremental computation of variants and variant-based unifiers with caching to reduce the cost of computing the next variant, resp. unifier.

The simplest case in which the above algorithm can be exploited is for $\mathcal{R} = (\Sigma, B, R)$ FVP with a finitary B-unification algorithm, Ω a signature of free constructors modulo B_Ω, and satisfiability of QF formulas in T_{Ω/B_Ω} decidable. In Sect. 6 I study such decidability for the commonly occurring case when B_Ω is any (possibly empty) combination of commutativity, associativity-commutativity, and identity axioms for some binary function symbols in Σ. Exploiting the descent theorem when $R_\Omega \neq \varnothing$ is postponed until Sect. 7.

6   OS-Compact Theories and Satisfiability in $T_{\Omega/ACCU}$

The simplest application of Theorem 6 is when $\mathcal{R} = (\Sigma, B, R)$ is FVP with a finitary B-unification algorithm, Ω is a signature of free constructors modulo B_Ω, and satisfiability of QF formulas in T_{Ω/B_Ω} is decidable. Generalizing a similar result in [29] for the unsorted and AC case, I show below that, when $B_\Omega = ACCU$ —where $ACCU$ stands for any combination of associativity-commutativity (AC), commutativity (C), and/or left- or right-identity (U) axioms for some binary function symbols— satisfiability of QF formulas in $T_{\Omega/ACCU}$ is decidable. But, generalizing again another result in [29], we can view such a satisfiability result as part of a broader one, namely, decidable satisfiability in $T_{\Sigma,\Pi,\Gamma}$ or, equivalently, in $T_{\Sigma\cup\Pi/\widetilde{\Gamma}}$ when $((\Sigma,\Pi),\Gamma)$ is an OS-*compact* equational OS-FO theory.

Call a sort $s \in S$ *finite* in both (Σ, E) and $T_{\Sigma/E}$ iff $T_{\Sigma/E,s}$ is a finite set, and *infinite* otherwise. Here is the key notion:

Definition 7. *An equational OS-FO theory $((\Sigma,\Pi),\Gamma)$ is called* OS-compact *iff: (i) for each sort s in Σ we can effectively determine whether s is finite or infinite in $T_{\Sigma\cup\Pi/\widetilde{\Gamma}}$, and, if finite, can effectively compute a representative ground term $rep([u]) \in [u]$ for each $[u] \in T_{\Sigma\cup\Pi/\widetilde{\Gamma},s}$; (ii) $=_{\widetilde{\Gamma}}$ is decidable and $\widetilde{\Gamma}$ has a finitary unification algorithm; and (iii) any finite conjunction $\bigwedge D$ of*

---

[7] A complete set of constructor variants for a term t is obtained by inspecting each $(u,\theta) \in [\![t]\!]_{R,B}$ and either: (1) choosing (u,θ) when $u \in T_\Omega(X)$, or otherwise (2) choosing those $(u\rho,\theta\rho)$ such that ρ is a variable specialization and: (i) $u\rho \in T_\Omega(X)$, (ii) $(u\rho,\theta\rho)$ is a variant of t, and (iii) ρ is maximal with properties (i)–(ii).

negated (Σ, Π)-*atoms whose variables have all infinite sorts and such that* $\bigwedge \widetilde{D}$ *is* $\widetilde{\Gamma}$-*consistent is satisfiable in* $T_{\Sigma, \Pi, \Gamma}$.

We call an OS equational theory (Σ, E) OS-*compact* iff the OS-FO theory $((\Sigma, \varnothing), E)$ is so.

Note that this generalizes the notion of *compact theory* in [29] in four ways: (i) from unsorted to OS theories; (ii) by dealing with the phenomenon of possibly having some sorts finite and some infinite; (iii) by extending the notion from equational theories to OS-FO equational theories; and (iv) by including the case of computable *finite initial models*, because an OS-FO theory $((\Sigma, \varnothing), E)$ whose sorts are all finite and for which we can effectively compute representatives has decidable equality and finitary unification, and is OS-compact in a vacuous sort of way; e.g., the Boolean theory $\mathcal{B}$ of Example 1, and the theory $\mathcal{N}_2$ in Example 5 are both OS-compact. I will illustrate with examples that extensions (i)–(iii) are needed in many useful applications.

The key theorem about OS-compact theories is again a generalization of a similar one in [29].

Theorem 7. *Let* $((\Sigma, \Pi), \Gamma)$ *be an* OS-compact *theory. The satisfiability of QF* (Σ, Π)-*formulas in* $T_{\Sigma, \Pi, \Gamma}$ *is decidable.*

This now gives us the following, quite useful corollary of Corollary 1:

Corollary 2. *Let an FVP decomposition* $\mathcal{R} = (\Sigma \cup \Pi, B, R)$ *of an OS-FO equational theory* $((\Sigma, \Pi), \Gamma)$, *with* B *having a finitary unification algorithm, protect a constructor decomposition* $\mathcal{R}_{(\Omega, \Delta)} = (\Omega \cup \Delta, B_{\Omega}, R_{(\Omega, \Delta)})$ *of an OS-compact theory* $((\Omega, \Delta), \Gamma_0)$, *with* $=_{B_{\Omega}}$ *decidable. Then, satisfiability of any QF* (Σ, Π)-*formula* ϕ *in* $T_{\Sigma, \Pi, \Gamma}$ *is decidable.*

This corollary further "unpacks" how the satisfiability in $T_{\Omega, \Delta, \Gamma_0}$ of an $\Omega \cup \Delta$-disjunction of disequalities $\bigwedge D'$ obtained in step (2) of the satisfiability decision procedure "unpacking" Corollary 1 can be checked in step (3) when $((\Omega, \Delta), \Gamma_0)$ is OS-compact, namely, we then replace $\bigwedge D'$ by the disjunction of all the representative ground instantiations $\bigwedge D' rep(\beta)$ of its finite sort variables, and then check whether at least one such $\bigwedge D' rep(\beta)$ is satisfiable by checking the B_{Ω}-consistency of $(\bigwedge D' rep(\beta))!_{R_{(\Omega, \Delta)}, B_{\Omega}}$.

6.1 Theories $(\Omega, ACCU)$ are OS-Compact

Consider now an OS signature Ω where some (possibly empty) subsignature $\Omega_{ACCU} \subseteq \Omega$ of binary operators of the form $f : s\,s \rightarrow s$, for some $s \in S$, satisfy any combination of: (i) the associativity-commutativity (AC) axioms $f(f(x, y), z) = f(x, f(y, z))$ and $f(x, y) = f(y, x)$; (ii) just the commutativity (C) axiom $f(x, y) = f(y, x)$; (iii) the left-unit (LU) axiom $f(e_f, x) = x$ for a unit constant e_f; or (iv) the right-unit (RU) axiom $f(x, e_f) = x$ (note that the standard unit axioms (U) are just the combination of LU and RU). Furthermore, if $f : s\,s \rightarrow s \in \Omega_{ACCU}$ belongs to a subsort polymorphic family $f^{[s]\,[s]}_{[s]}$, then all other members of the family are of the form $f : s' s' \to s'$, $f_{[s]}^{[s]\,[s]} \subseteq \Omega_{ACCU}$, and all operators in such a family satisfy exactly the same axioms. $ACCU$ abbreviates: *any combination of associativity-commutativity and/or commutativity and/or unit axioms*. Since all the above axiom combinations are possible and Ω_{ACCU} can be empty, the acronym $ACCU$, covers in fact *eight* possibilities for each subsort polymorphic family $f_{[s]}^{[s]\,[s]}$ of binary function symbols: (i) the "free" case where f satisfies no axioms; (ii) the case where f is only LU; (iii) the case where f is only RU; (iv) the case where f is only U; (v) the case where f is C; (vi) the case where f is CU; (vii) the case where f is AC; and (viii) the case where f is ACU. Furthermore, I will always assume that Ω is $ACCU$-preregular.

The main goal of this section is to prove that, under the above assumptions, satisfiability of QF Ω-formulas in $T_{\Omega/ACCU}$ is decidable. This result generalizes from the unsorted to the order-sorted case, and from AC to $ACCU$ axioms, a previous result by H. Comon-Lundh [29]. This is done in Theorem 8 below. But we need before the following auxiliary proposition, generalizing to the order-sorted and $ACCU$ case a similar result in [29] for the unsorted and AC case:

Proposition 1. *Under the above assumptions, let $u = v$ be an $ACCU$-nontrivial Ω-equation whose only variable is $x : s$. Then the set of most general $ACCU$-unifiers $Unif_{ACCU}(u = v)$ is finite, and all unifiers in it are ground unifiers, i.e., ground substitution $\{x : s \mapsto w\}$, with $w \in T_{\Omega,s}$. Since ground unifiers cannot be further instantiated, for any $ACCU$-unifier α there is a $\beta \in Unif_{ACCU}(u = v)$ with $\alpha =_{ACCU} \beta$.*

Note that for arbitrary combinations of associativity A, commutativity C, and left LU, and right RU unit axioms, the above proposition is *as general as possible*: any combination of axioms involving associativity without commutativity will violate the requirement that $Unif_{ACCU}(u = v)$ is finite. Not only is it well-known that A and AU unification are in general infinitary: this also remains true when $u = v$ has a single variable x. For example, if $\_\cdot\_$ is an A operator, and a a constant, the equation $a \cdot x = x \cdot a$ has an infinite number of ground A unifiers: $\{x \mapsto a\}$, $\{x \mapsto a \cdot a\}$, $\{x \mapsto a \cdot a \cdot a\}$, and so on.

The following theorem generalizes an analogous one in [29] for the unsorted and AC case.

Theorem 8. *Under the above assumptions, satisfiability of QF Ω-formulas in $T_{\Omega/ACCU}$ is decidable.*

The above theorem yields as a direct consequence the decidable satisfiability of any QF equational formula in the *natural numbers with addition*.

Example 6. (Natural Numbers with $+$). This is an unsorted[8] theory $\mathcal{N}_+^u$ with sort *Nat* The operations in the signature Ω are: $0 :\to Nat$, $1 :\to Nat$, and

---

[8] An order-sorted version $\mathcal{N}_+$ of $\mathcal{N}_+^u$ is obtained by adding a subsort inclusion $NzNat <$ Nat, where $NzNat$ denotes the non-zero naturals, typing 1 with sort $NzNat$, and adding the typing $\_+\_ : NzNat\ NzNat \to NzNat$. $\mathcal{N}_+$ is also OS-compact for the exact same reasons. A reduction of satisfiability in the initial agebra of $\mathcal{N}_+$ to satisfiability in the initial algebra of $\mathcal{N}_+^u$ is discussed in [69]. $\mathcal{N}_+$ makes the language more expressive: instead of stating $x \neq 0$ we can just type x as having sort $NzNat$.

$\_ + \_ : Nat\ Nat \to Nat$, which satisfies the ACU axioms, with 0 as unit. Since the conditions in Theorem 8 are met, satisfiability (and therefore validity) in the initial algebra of $\mathcal{N}_+^u$ is decidable.

Note that, by Theorem 7, deciding satisfiability of a conjunction $\bigwedge G \wedge \bigwedge D$ in the initial algebra of $\mathcal{N}_+^u$ boils down to computing the most general unsorted ACU-unifiers α of $\bigwedge G$, and then checking the ACU-consistency of each $\bigwedge D\alpha$, which amounts to checking for each $u\alpha \neq v\alpha$ in $D\alpha$ that $u\alpha \neq_{ACU} v\alpha$. Note also that unsorted ACU-unification is NP-complete [60].

For example, $n = 0 \vee n + n \neq n$ is a theorem in the initial algebra of $\mathcal{N}_+^u$ because its negation $n \neq 0 \wedge n + n = n$ is such that $n + n = n$ has $\{n \mapsto 0\}$ as its only ACU-unifier, yielding the unsatisfiable disequality $0 \neq 0$.

6.2 The Descent Theorem with Free Constructors Modulo $ACCU$

Thanks to Theorem 8 we can apply Corollary 2 to the case of an FVP decomposition $\mathcal{R} = (\Sigma, B, R)$ of an equational theory (Σ, E), with B having a finitary unification algorithm, and protecting the constructor decomposition $\mathcal{R}_\Omega = (\Omega, ACCU, \varnothing)$ of $(\Omega, ACCU)$ to obtain a method to decide the satisfiability of any QF Σ-formula in $T_{\Sigma/E}$. Let us see some examples.

Example 7. Recall Example 2. Since $\Omega = \Sigma - \{zero?\}$ is a signature of free constructors, the conditions of Corollary 2 are met. Let now ϕ be the formula $x = zero?(n) \wedge x \neq \top \wedge x \neq \bot$. Recall that its two constructor variants are $x = \bot \wedge x \neq \top \wedge x \neq \bot$, and $x = \top \wedge x \neq \top \wedge x \neq \bot$. Solving the equation in each case we get formulas $\bot \neq \top \wedge \bot \neq \bot$, and $\top \neq \top \wedge \top \neq \bot$, which have both $\varnothing$-inconsistent disequalities, so ϕ is unsatisfiable.

Example 8. (Natural Presburger Arithmetic). An FVP decomposition $\mathcal{N}_{+,>^b}^u$ having the natural numbers with $+$ and $>$ as a Boolean-valued predicate[9] as its initial model is obtained as an extension of $\mathcal{N}_+^u$ in Example 6: we just add a new sort *Truth* with constants $\bot$ and $\top$, and a defined function $\_ > \_ : Nat\ Nat \to Truth$ with rules $1 + m + n > n \to \top$ and $m > m + n \to \bot$. This specification is sufficiently complete with $\mathcal{N}_+^u$ extended with $\top, \bot$ as its constructor subspecification, and yields an FVP decomposition with variant complexity 3.

The predicate $\geq$ can either: (i) be explicitly defined by similar rules, or (ii) be defined by the equivalence $x \geq y \Leftrightarrow (x > y \vee x = y)$.

Since $\mathcal{N}_+^u$ extended with $\top, \bot$ is OS-compact, by Corollary 2 satisfiability in the initial algebra of $\mathcal{N}_{+,>^b}^u$ is decidable. For example, the transitivity law $(n > m = \top \wedge m > n' = \top) \Rightarrow n > n' = \top$ of natural Presburger arithmetic is a theorem because its negation is the conjunction $n > m = \top \wedge m > n' = \top \wedge n > n' = \bot$, which has no variant-based unifiers.

Example 9. (Integers Offsets). This is perhaps the simplest possible theory $\mathcal{Z}_{s,p}$ of integers. Decisions procedures for it have been given in [4,17,21]. This example

---

[9] See [69] for a version $\mathcal{N}_{+,>}$ of natural Pressburger arithmetic in which $>$ is only explictly defined in the positive case.

is also interesting because it is usually specified in an unsorted way, for which no signature of free constructors is possible. Instead, an order-sorted presentation makes a signature of free constructors possible and allows Corollary 2 to be applied. The sorts are: *Int*, *Nat*, *Neg*, and *Zero*, with subsort inclusions *Zero* < *Nat Neg* < *Int*. The subsignature Ω of free constructors is $0 :\to Zero$, $s : Nat \to Nat$, and $p : Neg \to Neg$, and the defined symbols[10] $s, p : Int \to Int$. The rules R are just $p(s(m)) \to m$ and $s(p(n)) \to n$, with m of sort *Nat* and n of sort *Neg*.

Since $\mathcal{Z}_{s,p}$ is FVP with variant complexity 4 and is sufficiently complete with signature of free constructors Ω, the conditions of Corollary 2 are met and satisfiability, and therefore validity, in $C_{\mathcal{Z}_{s,p}}$ is decidable. Let us, for example, decide the validity of the inductive theorem $s(x) = s(y) \Rightarrow x = y$, with x, y of sort *Int*. This is equivalent to checking that $s(x) = s(y) \wedge x \neq y$ is unsatisfiable. The only variant-based E-unifier of $s(x) = s(y)$, $\{x \mapsto y\}$, yields the inconsistent disequality $y \neq y$. Thus, $s(x) = s(y) \Rightarrow x = y$ holds in $C_{\mathcal{Z}_{s,p}}$.

Example 10. (Integers with Addition). The decomposition $\mathcal{Z}_+$ for integers with addition imports in a protecting mode the theory $\mathcal{N}_+$ of natural numbers with addition in Footnote 8, and extends its constructor signature by adding two new sorts, *NzNeg*, and *Int*, with subsort inclusions *Nat NzNeg* < *Int*, and a constructor $- : NzNat \to NzNeg$, to get an extended constructor signature Ω. The only defined function symbol is: $\_ + \_ : Int\ Int \to Int$, also *ACU*. The rewrite rules R defining $+$ and making $(\Omega, ACU, \varnothing)$ an *ACU*-free constructor decomposition of $\mathcal{Z}_+$ are the following (with i a variable of sort *Int*, and n, m variables of sort *NzNat*): $i + n + -(n) \to i$, $i + -(n) + -(m) \to i + -(n + m)$, $i + n + -(n + m) \to i + -(m)$, and $i + n + m + -(n) \to i + m$. Note that, by the *ACU* axioms, the initial algebra $C_{\mathcal{Z}_+}$ is automatically a *commutative monoid*. Furthermore, by sufficient completeness $C_{\mathcal{Z}_+}|_\Omega = T_{\Omega/ACU}$, so that the first rule (specialized to $i = 0$) plus the U axioms (specialized to $x = 0$) make $C_{\mathcal{Z}_+}$ into an *abelian group*, since it satisfies the axiom $(\forall x)(\exists y)\, x + y = 0$.

Subsorts make, again, the language of $\mathcal{Z}_+$ considerably more expressive than an untyped language: we do not have to say $x > 0$ (resp. $x < 0$) by additionally defining an order predicate $>$: we just type x with sort *NzNat* (resp. *NzNeg*).

$\mathcal{Z}_+$ is FVP with variant complexity 12. Since the conditions of Corollary 2 are met, satisfiability, and therefore validity, in $C_{\mathcal{Z}_+}$ is decidable. Let us, for example, decide the validity of the inductive theorem $i + j = i + l \Rightarrow j = l$, with i, j, l variables of sort *Int*. This is equivalent to checking that $i + j = i + l \wedge j \neq l$ is unsatisfiable. The only variant unifier of $i + j = i + l$ is $\{j \mapsto l\}$, giving us $l \neq l$, which is *AC*-inconsistent.

Example 11. (Integer Presburger Arithmetic). The FVP theory $\mathcal{Z}_{+,>^b}$ of integer Presburger arithmetic with Boolean-valued[11] $>$ protects $\mathcal{Z}_+$ by adding a new

---

[10] Note the interesting phenomenon, impossible in a many-sorted setting, that a subsort-polymorphic symbol like s or p can be a constructor for some typings and a defined symbol for other typings.

[11] See [69] for an even simpler version $\mathcal{Z}_{+,>}$ of integer Presburger arithmetic in which $>$ is only explicitly defined in the positive case.

sort *Truth* with constants $\bot$ and $\top$, and a defined function $\_ > \_ : Int\ Int \to$ *Truth* with rules $p + n > n \to \top$, $n > -(q) \to \top$, $-(p) > -(p+q) \to \top$, and $i > i + n \to \bot$, were p, q have sort *NzNat*, n has sort *Nat*, and i has sort *Int*. $\mathcal{Z}_{+,>^b}$ is sufficiently complete with constructor subspecification that of $\mathcal{Z}_+$ extended with $\top, \bot$, and FVP with variant complexity 17.

Again, $\geqslant$ can either be explicitly defined, or be defined by an equivalence.

Since the constructor subspecification of $\mathcal{Z}_+$ extended with $\top, \bot$ is OS-compact, by Corollary 2 satisfiability in the initial algebra of $\mathcal{Z}_{+,>^b}$ is decidable. For example, the transitivity law $(i > j = \top \wedge j > k = \top) \Rightarrow j > k = \top$ of integer Presburger arithmetic is a theorem because its negation is the conjunction $i > j = \top \wedge j > k = \top \wedge i > k = \bot$, which has no variant-based unifiers.

See [69] for the example $\mathcal{N}_{+,\dot{-}}$ of the natural numbers with $+$ and a "monus" operator $\dot{-}$. Since we have the constructor decomposition $\mathcal{N}_{+,\dot{-}} \supset \mathcal{N}_+$ with $\mathcal{N}_+$ OS-compact, Corollary 2 applies, and satisfiability in $C_{\mathcal{N}_{+,\dot{-}}}$ is decidable.

7   Satisfiability in Parameterized FVP Data Types

What Corollary 2 achieves is a large increase in the infinite class of decidable OS-FO equational theories for which satisfiability of QF formulas in their initial models is decidable, namely, it grows from the class of OS-compact theories (including those of the form $(\Omega, ACCU)$) to that of all those OS-FO equational theories having an FVP theory decompositions with axioms B having a finitary unification algorithm and protecting an OS-compact constructor subtheory.

But how can we further enlarge the class of OS-FO equational theories for which satisfiability of QF formulas in their initial model is decidable? Here is one idea: since parameterized data types are *theory transformations* applicable to a typically infinite class of input theories and yielding an equally infinite class of instantiations, an appealing idea is to search for *satisfiability-preserving* parameterized data types. That is, parameterized data types that, under suitable conditions, transform an input theory with decidable satisfiability of QF formulas in its initial model into a corresponding instance of the parameterized data type with the same property for *its* initial model.

I will give a full treatment of parameterized FVP data types elsewhere. Here, I illustrate with several examples a general method for substantially enlarging, by means of parameterization, the class of equational OS-FO theories with initial models having decidable QF satisfiability. For my present purposes it will be enough to summarize the basic general facts and assumptions for the case of FVP parameterized data types with a *single parameter* X. That is, I will restrict myself to parameterized FVP theories of the form $\mathcal{R}[X] = (\mathcal{R}, X)$, where $\mathcal{R} = (\Sigma \cup \Pi, B, R)$ is an FVP decomposition of a finitary equational OS-FO theory $((\Sigma, \Pi), \Gamma)$; and X is a sort in Σ (called the *parameter sort*) such that: (i) is empty,[12] i.e., $T_{\Sigma \cup \Pi / \tilde{r}, X} = \varnothing$; and (ii) X is a minimal element in the sort order, i.e., there is no other sort s' with $s' < X$.

---

[12] This violates the general assumption that sorts are non-empty; however, parameter sorts instantiated to target theories with non-empty sorts become non-empty.

Consider now an FVP decomposition $\mathcal{G} = (\Sigma' \cup \Pi', B', R')$ of another finitary OS-FO equational theory $((\Sigma', \Pi'), \Gamma')$, which we can assume without loss of generality[13] disjoint from $((\Sigma, \Pi), \Gamma)$, and let s be a sort in Σ'. The *instantiation* $\mathcal{R}[\mathcal{G}, X \mapsto s] = (\Sigma[\Sigma', X \mapsto s], B \cup B', R \cup R')$ is the decomposition of a theory $(\Sigma[\Sigma', X \mapsto s], E \cup E')$, extending (Σ', E'), where the signature $\Sigma[\Sigma', X \mapsto s]$ is defined as the union $\Sigma[X \mapsto s] \cup \Sigma'$, with $\Sigma[X \mapsto s]$ just like Σ, except for X renamed to s. The set of sorts is $(S - \{X\}) \uplus S'$, and the poset ordering is obtained by combining those of $\Sigma[X \mapsto s]$ and Σ'.

$\mathcal{R}[\mathcal{G}, X \mapsto s]$ is also FVP under fairly mild assumptions. The only problematic issue is termination, because the disjoint union of terminating rewrite theories need not be terminating [83]. However, many useful p-termination properties p ensuring the p-termination of a disjoint union have been found (see, e.g., [54]). Therefore I will assume that either: (i) $\mathcal{R}[X]$ and $\mathcal{G}$ are both p-terminating for a modular termination property p, or (ii) $\mathcal{R}[\mathcal{G}, X \mapsto s]$ has been proved terminating. Convergence of $\mathcal{R}[\mathcal{G}, X \mapsto s]$ then follows easily from termination, because there are no new critical pairs. So does the FVP property, which is a modular property (see, e.g., [18]). In fact one can say more: the variant complexity of $\mathcal{R}[\mathcal{G}, X \mapsto s]$ is the *sum* of those of $\mathcal{R}[X]$ and $\mathcal{G}$. We furthermore require the *parameter protection* property that the unique Σ' homomorphism $h : T_{\Sigma'/E'} \to T_{\Sigma[\Sigma', X \mapsto s]/E \cup E'}|_{\Sigma'}$ is an isomorphism. Typically, parameter protection can be easily proved using a protected constructor subtheory $\mathcal{R}_{(\Omega, \Delta)}[X]$.

Suppose now that B, B' and $B \cup B'$ have finitary unification algorithms and that both $\mathcal{R}[X] = (\mathcal{R}, X)$ and $\mathcal{G}$ protect, respectively, constructor theories,[14] say $\mathcal{R}_{(\Omega, \Delta)}[X] = (\Omega \cup \Delta, B_{(\Omega, \Delta)}, R_{(\Omega, \Delta)})$ and $\mathcal{G}_{(\Omega', \Delta')} = (\Omega' \cup \Delta', B_{(\Omega', \Delta')}, R_{(\Omega', \Delta')})$. Then $\mathcal{R}[\mathcal{G}, X \mapsto s]$ will protect $\mathcal{R}_{(\Omega, \Delta)}[\mathcal{G}_{(\Omega', \Delta')}, X \mapsto s]$. Suppose, further, that $B_{(\Omega, \Delta)}$, $B_{(\Omega', \Delta')}$, and $B_{(\Omega, \Delta)} \cup B_{(\Omega', \Delta')}$ have decidable equality.

The general kind of satisfiability-preserving result we are seeking follows the following pattern: (i) assuming that $\mathcal{G}_{(\Omega', \Delta')}$ is the decomposition of an OS-compact theory, then (ii) under some assumptions about the cardinality of the sort s, prove the OS-compactness of $\mathcal{R}_{(\Omega, \Delta)}[\mathcal{G}_{(\Omega', \Delta')}, X \mapsto s]$. By Corollary 2 this then proves that satisfiability of QF formulas in the initial model of the instantiation $\mathcal{R}[\mathcal{G}, X \mapsto s]$ is decidable.

In [69] the following parameterized data types have been proved satisfiability-preserving following the just-described pattern of proof: (i) $\mathcal{L}[X]$, *parameterized lists*, which is just an example illustrating the general case of any constructor-selector-based [70] parameterized data type; (ii) $\mathcal{L}^c[X]$, *parameterized compact lists*, where any two identical contiguous list elements are identified [33,34]; (iii) $\mathcal{M}[X]$, *parameterized multisets*; (iv) $\mathcal{S}[X]$, *parameterized sets*; and (v) $\mathcal{H}[X]$, *parameterized hereditarily finite sets*. Since $\mathcal{H}[X]$ is the most complex data type, I discuss it in more detail below.

---

[13] There is no real loss of generality because we can make it so by renaming its sorts and operations. In fact, disjointness must in any case be enforced by the "pushout construction" for parameter instantiation, implicitly described in what follows for this simple class of uni-parametric parameterized theories.

[14] For more details about sufficient completeness of parameterized OS theories and methods for checking it see [67].

Example 12. (Hereditarily Finite (HF) Sets). HF sets are a model of set theory without the axiom of infinity. All effective constructions of finitary mathematics —including in particular all effective arithmetic constructions— can be represented within it (see [26], Chap. I). I specify below a data type of HF sets with set union $\cup$ and a set inclusion predicate $\subseteq$ (the predicates $\subset$ and $\in$ are obtained as definitional extensions). As is well-known, all HF sets can be built "ex nihilo" out of the empty set $\varnothing$. However, it is very convenient to also allow "urelements," like $a, b, c, 7, 2/9, \sqrt{2}, \pi$, and so on, as set elements. This can be achieved by making HF sets parametric on a parameter sort X for such "urelements." That is, HF sets is an FVP parameterized data type $\mathcal{H}[X]$ protecting an FVP constructor subtheory $\mathcal{H}_{(\Omega,\Pi)}[X]$ which has the following signature Ω of constructors: there are five sorts: X, *Elt*, *Set*, *Magma*, and *Pred*, and subsort inclusions X *Set* $<$ *Elt* $<$ *Magma*, where *Magma* represents multisets of sets and has an *AC* multiset union constructor $\_,\_ :$ *Magma Magma* $\rightarrow$ *Magma*. There is also the empty set constructor constant $\varnothing :\rightarrow$ *Set*, and a constructor $\{\_\} :$ *Magma* $\rightarrow$ *Set* that builds a set out of a magma. The signature Π of constructor predicates has the usual constructor constant $tt :\rightarrow$ *Pred*, plus the constructor set inclusion predicate $\_ \subseteq \_ :$ *Set Set* $\rightarrow$ *Pred*. Using M, M' as variables of sort *Magma* and U, V as variables of sort *Set*, the rules $R_{(\Omega,\Pi)}$ rewriting constructor terms and constructor predicates are: (i) the "magma idempotency" rules, $M, M \rightarrow M$ and $M, M, M' \rightarrow M, M'$; and (ii) the rules defining the $\subseteq$ predicate, $\varnothing \subseteq U \rightarrow tt$, $\{M\} \subseteq \{M\} \rightarrow tt$, and $\{M\} \subseteq \{M, M'\} \rightarrow tt$.

This constructor decomposition $\mathcal{H}_{(\Omega,\Pi)}[X]$ is extended in a sufficiently complete and *protecting* way by the specification of the union operator $\_ \cup \_ :$ *Set Set* $\rightarrow$ *Set* as a function defined by means of the following rules: $U \cup \varnothing \rightarrow U$, $\varnothing \cup U \rightarrow U$, and $\{M\} \cup \{M'\} \rightarrow \{M, M'\}$. The variant complexity of this decomposition of HF sets is 17.

The predicates $\in$ and $\subset$ need not be explicitly defined, since they can be expressed by the definitional equivalences $x \in V = tt \Leftrightarrow \{x\} \cup V = V$, with x of sort *Elt*, and $U \subset V = tt \Leftrightarrow (U \subseteq V = tt \wedge U \neq V)$.

Let us consider instantiations of HF sets whose actual the parameter is specified by an *infinity-closed* decomposition $\mathcal{G}$, defined as a theory where, if a term t has at least one variable having an infinite sort, then the least sort of t is itself infinite. For example, offset integers (Example 9) have the *Zero* finite sort, but are infinity-closed. The main theorem preservation of OS-compactness for HF sets can be stated as follows:

Theorem 9. *For* $\mathcal{H}[X]$ *the above parameterized HF set module, protecting the constructor decomposition* $\mathcal{H}_{(\Omega,\Pi)}[X]$, $\mathcal{G} = (\Sigma' \cup \Pi', B', R')$ *an infinity-closed FVP decomposition of a finitary OS-FO equational theory* $((\Sigma', \Pi'), \Gamma')$, *where* $\mathcal{G}$ *protects a constructor decomposition* $\mathcal{G}_{(\Omega',\Delta')} = (\Omega' \cup \Delta', B_{(\Omega',\Delta')}, R_{(\Omega',\Delta')})$ *of an equational OS-FO-compact theory* $((\Omega', \Delta'), \Gamma)$, *and* s *a sort of* $\mathcal{G}$ *in* Ω', *if: (i)* $\mathcal{H}[X]$ *and* $\mathcal{G}$ *are both p-terminating for a modular termination property p or* $\mathcal{H}[\mathcal{G}, X \mapsto s]$ *is terminating, (ii)* B' *and* $B' \cup AC$ *have finitary unification algorithms and (iii)* $B_{(\Omega',\Delta')} \cup AC$*-equality is decidable, then* $\mathcal{H}_{\Omega,\Pi}[\mathcal{G}_{(\Omega',\Delta')}, X \mapsto s]$ *is the* *decomposition of an OS-compact theory and therefore satisfiability of QF formulas in the initial model of the instantiation $\mathcal{H}[\mathcal{G}, X \mapsto s]$ is decidable.*

By the above theorem, validity of all QF inductive theorems in an instance of the HF sets module satisfying the requirements in the theorem is decidable. Therefore, we can decide, for example, that $C_{\mathcal{H}[\mathcal{G}, X \mapsto s]}$ satisfies theorems such as: the *extensionality* axiom $(U \subseteq V \land V \subseteq U) \Rightarrow U = V$, the *pairing axiom*, $x \in \{S, S'\} \Leftrightarrow (x \in S \lor x \in S')$, the *extensionality of ordered pairs lemma*, $\{x, \{x, y\}\} = \{x', \{x', y'\}\} \Rightarrow (x = x' \land y = y')$, the *finite union axiom*, $x \in (S \cup S') \Leftrightarrow (x \in S \lor x \in S')$, the equivalence $x \in S = tt \Leftrightarrow S = (S \cup \{x\})$, the *associativity-commutativity and idempotency* of $\cup$, and so on.

The extensionality of ordered pairs lemma holds of course for all instances, including the instance $\mathcal{H}[\mathcal{N}_+^u, X \mapsto Nat]$. Proving this is equivalent to checking the unsatisfiability in $C_{\mathcal{H}[\mathcal{N}_+^u, X \mapsto Nat]}$ of the two conjunctions: $\{x, \{x, y\}\} = \{x', \{x', y'\}\} \land x \neq x'$, and $\{x, \{x, y\}\} = \{x', \{x', y'\}\} \land y \neq y'$. The equation $\{x, \{x, y\}\} = \{x', \{x', y'\}\}$ has the single, variant-based, unifier: $\{x \mapsto x', y \mapsto y'\}$, yielding the unsatisfiable formulas $x' \neq x'$, and $y' \neq y'$, as desired.

8 Related Work

The original paper proposing the concepts of variant and FVP is [31]. These ideas have been further advanced in [18,23,24,42]. In particular, I have used the ideas on folding variant narrowing and variant-based unification from [42], and have provided a different, detailed description of variant-based unifiers in Theorem 4 needed to better clarify the notion of constructor unifier in Sect. 4. To the best of my knowledge the notions of constructor variant and constructor unifier and the results on satisfiability in FVP initial algebras are new.

There is a vast literature on satisfiability in data types, including parameterized ones such as, e.g., [12,20,33,34,62,74,81]. In relation to that large body of work, what the results in this paper provide is both the characterization of a wide class of data types for which satisfiability is decidable, and a new *generic algorithm* to check satisfiability for data types in such a class. In particular, there are interesting parallels between the work on unification and satisfiability for lists, compact lists, sets, and HF sets in [33,34] and that in Sect. 7. Again, an important difference is that in [33,34] specific, inference-rule-based, unification and satisfiability algorithms are developed for each such data type, whereas in Sect. 7 both unification and satisfiability are obtainable as part of generic, variant-based unification and satisfiability procedures. A detailed comparison between the two approaches should be a topic for further research.

There are also various results about decidability of QF or sometimes general first-order formulas in some initial unsorted, many-sorted, and order-sorted algebras modulo some equations, e.g., [9,28–30,65,71], that can be very useful, because, as shown in Sect. 6, they can be used in the reduction from satisfiability in an FVP initial algebra $T_{\Sigma/E}$ to satisfiability in T_{Ω/B_Ω} by ensuring that satisfiability in T_{Ω/B_Ω} is decidable. For example, as already mentioned, Theorem 8 generalizes to the OS and *ACCU* case a similar result in [29] for the unsorted and *AC* case for theories of constructors modulo axioms.

A line of work that is quite close in aims to the present one is the so-called *rewriting-based approach* to satisfiability [4,6,17,36,61,63,64]. Since the present work is also "rewriting-based" in an obvious sense, but quite different from the work just cited, to help the reader appreciate the differences I would rather call that work *superposition-based* satisfiability. That, is, the relevant first-order theory is axiomatized, and then it is proved that a superposition theorem proving inference system terminates for that theory together with any given set of ground clauses representing a satisfiability problem. Common features between the superposition-based and variant-based (both rewriting based!) approaches involve good modularity properties (see [4]), and no need for an explicit NO combination between procedures developed in either approach (although *both* approaches can of course be combined with other satisfiability procedures in the classical NO way[15]). The aims in both approaches are quite similar, but the methods are very different. I view both approaches as complementary and think that exploring potential synergies between them can further increase the extensibility of SMT solving.

Another approach to making SMT solving more extensible is presented in [35]. The goal is to allow a user to define a new theory with decidable QF satisfiability by axiomatizing it according to some requirements, and then making an SMT solver extensible by such a user-defined theory. This is done as follows:

1. A new theory T', extending a given *background theory* T already supported by the SMT solver, is axiomatized by the user in a first-order logic enhanced with the notion of using a literal l as a *trigger* (or dually as a *witness*) in a formula φ, denoted $[l]\varphi$ (resp. $\langle l \rangle \varphi$).
2. If the user proves that T' is *complete* and *terminating* in the precise sense of [35], he/she automatically obtains a QF satisfiability procedure for T'.
3. The DPLL(T) procedure is extended to support theories axiomatized by formulas with triggers. Thus, the satisfiability of a complete and terminating user-defined theory T' can be decided. This extension of DPLL(T) has been implemented in the Alt-Ergo SMT solver [16], and a non-trivial case study on the decidable satisfiability of a theory of doubly-linked lists axiomatized with triggers using this implementation is presented in [35].

The approach in [35] is very different, yet complementary, to the one presented here. Ways of using both approaches together are worth investigating.

Last, but not least, there is also an important connection between the present work and a body of work in *inductive theorem proving* aimed at characterizing classes of algebraic specifications and associated kinds of formulas for which validity in an initial algebra can be decided automatically, e.g., [3,43,48,49]. The obvious relation to that work is that decidable validity and decidable satisfiability in an initial algebra are two sides of the same coin, so this paper might

---

[15] For combining variant-based decision procedures with other decision procedures, the *order-sorted* NO combination method in [82] will be particulary useful.

as well have been entitled "variant-based validity in initial algebras." What this work contributes to inductive theorem proving are new methods and results, complementing those in [3,43,48,49], for bringing large classes of initial algebras within the fold of decidable validity. In particular, to the best of my knowledge, the methods for decidable inductive validity for *parameterized* data types presented in Sect. 7 seem to be new.

9   Conclusions and Future Work

This work has made two main contributions:

1. **To Unification Theory**: The new notion of *constructor unifier* can make the use of the generic variant-based unification algorithm considerably more efficient by generating fewer unifiers than up to now. This can have a substantial impact in reducing the search space of variant-unification-based model checking methods such as those used in, e.g., [11,40].
2. **To Extensible Satisfiability Methods**: The new *generic algorithm for variant-based satisfiability* presented in this paper brings an infinite class of theories for which satisfiability in their initial algebras is decidable within the fold of SMT solving, thus making SMT solving considerably more extensible. Such theories are in fact *user-definable*, their required properties easy to check (by existing methods and tools for checking confluence, termination, sufficient completeness, and FVP), and quite modular. Also, combining satisfiability procedures for such theories is very simple (just theory union), without any need for a NO infrastructure. Specifically, the classes of theories to which these methods can be applied to make satisfiability in their initial algebras decidable has been extended in four concentric circles: (i) theories $(\Omega, ACCU)$, which are all OS-compact; (ii) FVP theories having a constructor decomposition of type (i); (iii) parameterized data types (several examples have been given to illustrate the general method) that transform input theories with an OS-compact core into corresponding instantiations of the parameterized data type, also having an OS-compact core, including input theories such as those in (ii), and *nested* instantiations of different parameterized data types; and (iv) a still broader class of theories that can be reduced to cases (i)–(iii) by means of the *descent maps* discussed in [69].

Much work remains ahead. I have already pointed out that variant-based satisfiability *complements*, and can be synergistic with, other methods, such as superposition-based satisfiability, decidable theories defined by means of formulas with triggers, or the NO combination method. Indeed, NO combinations remain essential, since one obviously wants to combine generic procedures based on variant-based, superpositon-based, or trigger-based algorithms with efficiently implemented ones for well-known theories and with each other. In this regard, my focus in this work on satisfiability in *initial algebras* could be misunderstood as exclusive, when actually it is not. The general picture emerging from such NO combinations is that of combinations of theories which may have some "initiality constraints" (more generally understood as *freeness* constraints, as in the case of formulas valid in *uninstantiated* parameterized data types, which I have mentioned *en passant* in the HF sets example) as well as some other unconstrained theories with a "loose semantics," in the sense of Goguen and Burstall [50].

What all this suggests as a longer-term goal is the development of an *extensible framework and tools* for the definition, prototyping and combination of satisfiability procedures. Within such a framework one would already have available a library of dedicated and generic procedures that would make quite easy for *users* to *prototype* a first version of a new satisfiability procedure by *combining* existing procedures with a newly specified one. There are of course tensions and tradeoffs between the efficiency of a generic algorithm and that of an optimized, domain-specific one; but the whole point of an extensible framework is precisely to make it easy to migrate in a *correct*, tool-supported, and seamless way prototypes into efficient algorithms. In this regard, the notion of *descent map* in [69] can be an important tool in such a framework, and can be applied very broadly to both generic and dedicated algorithms, and to quantified and unquantified formulas. Also, the computational cost of deciding satisfiability is seldom that of a single procedure but is instead the *overall* cost. Here interesting situations may arise. For example, we may have a combination of four procedures obtained by generic methods and two by dedicated algorithms. Although the dedicated ones may be more efficient, since the three generic ones may be combined as their *union*, NO will only have to deal with the interactions between *three* procedures, as opposed to six, thus reducing the computational cost of the combination.

On a shorter time frame, all the algorithms presented here, and suitable extensions or optimizations of them, should be implemented; and new descent maps should be developed. A first implementation should then be used to evaluate the practical effectiveness of variant-based satisfiability, and to compare it with that of other existing methods and tools such as those for superposition-based and trigger-based satisfiability [4,6,17,35,36,61,63,64], constraint logic programming methods such as those in [33,34] and others, and state of the art SMT solvers. The implementation task will be made easier by the fact that Maude 2.7 already supports the computation of variants and of variant-based unifiers. It will also be made easier by Maude's reflective capabilities, which allow easy transformation and manipulation of theories by built-in and user-definable meta-level functions.

Last, but not least, besides experimental performance comparisons, *computational complexity bounds* should be developed for different satisfiability algorithms. This of course is impossible for a generic algorithm such as variant-based narrowing, superposition theorem proving, or trigger-based satisfiability algorithms, whose complexity depends on the input theory; but it may become possible when the input theory T is fixed. For example, in superposition theorem proving results along the lines of [4,6,15,63] do exactly this. For variant-based satisfiability this will be a non-trivial task, because —besides the fact that complexity issues for variant-based computations have not yet been investigated— all R, B-variant-based computations first of all invoke order-sorted B-unification algorithms which themselves do not have just the complexity of their unsorted version, but the added complexity of their sort computations (which itself depends on the given subsort hierarchy) (see [38] for a detailed complexity analysis when only free function symbols are involved).

Acknowledgements. I thank the organizers of FTSCS 2015 for inviting me to present these ideas in Paris, and the FTSCS participants for their interest and very helpful comments. I thank Andrew Cholewa, Steven Eker, Santiago Escobar, Ralf Sasse, and Carolyn Talcott for their contributions to the development of the theory and Maude implementation of folding variant narrowing. I have learned much about satisfiability from Maria-Paola Bonacina, Vijay Ganesh and Cesare Tinelli along many conversations; I am most grateful to them for their kind enlightenment. I also thank the following persons for their very helpful comments on earlier drafts: Maria-Paola Bonacina, Santiago Escobar, Dorel Lucau, Peter Ölveczky, Vlad Rusu, Ralf Sasse, Natarajan Shankar, and Cesare Tinelli. The pioneering work of Hubert Comon-Lundh about compact theories [29], and that of him with Stephanie Delaune about the finite variant property [31], have both been important sources of inspiration for the ideas presented here. This work has been partially supported by NSF Grant CNS 13-19109.

References

1. Alpuente, M., Escobar, S., Iborra, J.: Termination of narrowing revisited. Theor. Comput. Sci. **410**(46), 4608–4625 (2009)
2. Alpuente, M., Escobar, S., Iborra, J.: Modular termination of basic narrowing and equational unification. Log. J. IGPL **19**(6), 731–762 (2011)
3. Aoto, T., Stratulat, S.: Decision procedures for proving inductive theorems without induction. In: Proceedings of PPDP2014, pp. 237–248. ACM (2014)
4. Armando, A., Bonacina, M.P., Ranise, S., Schulz, S.: New results on rewrite-based satisfiability procedures. ACM Trans. Comput. Log. 10(1) (2009)
5. Armando, A., Castellini, C., Giunchiglia, E.: SAT-based procedures for temporal reasoning. In: Biundo, S., Fox, M. (eds.) ECP 1999. LNCS, vol. 1809, pp. 97–108. Springer, Heidelberg (2000)
6. Armando, A., Ranise, S., Rusinowitch, M.: A rewriting approach to satisfiability procedures. Inf. Comput. **183**(2), 140–164 (2003)
7. Audemard, G., Bertoli, P.G., Cimatti, A., Kornilowicz, A., Sebastiani, R.: A SAT based approach for solving formulas over boolean and linear mathematical propositions. In: Voronkov, A. (ed.) CADE 2002. LNCS (LNAI), vol. 2392, pp. 195–210. Springer, Heidelberg (2002)
8. Baader, F., Schulz, K.: Unification in the union of disjoint equational theories: combining decision procedures. J. Symbolic Comput. **21**, 211–243 (1996)
9. Baader, F., Schulz, K.U.: Combination techniques and decision problems for disunification. Theor. Comput. Sci. **142**(2), 229–255 (1995)
10. Baader, F., Schulz, K.U.: Combining constraint solving. In: Comon, H., Marché, C., Treinen, R. (eds.) CCL 1999. LNCS, vol. 2002, pp. 104–158. Springer, Heidelberg (2001)
11. Bae, K., Meseguer, J.: Infinite-state model checking of LTLR formulas using narrowing. In: Escobar, S. (ed.) WRLA 2014. LNCS, vol. 8663, pp. 113–129. Springer, Heidelberg (2014)

12. Barrett, C., Shikanian, I., Tinelli, C.: An abstract decision procedure for satisfiability in the theory of inductive data types. J. Satisfiability Boolean Model. Comput. **3**, 21–46 (2007)
13. Barrett, C., Tinelli, C.: Satisfiability modulo theories. In: Clarke, E., Henzinger, T., Veith, H. (eds.) Handbook of Model Checking. Springer (2017, to appear)
14. Barrett, C.W., Dill, D.L., Stump, A.: Checking satisfiability of first-order formulas by incremental translation to SAT. In: Brinksma, E., Larsen, K.G. (eds.) CAV 2002. LNCS, vol. 2404, pp. 236–249. Springer, Heidelberg (2002)
15. Basin, D.A., Ganzinger, H.: Automated complexity analysis based on ordered resolution. J. ACM **48**(1), 70–109 (2001)
16. Bobot, F., Conchon, S., Contejean, E., Lescuyer, S.: Implementing polymorphism in SMT solvers. In: Proceedings of 6th International Workshop on Satisfiability Modulo Theories and 1st International Workshop on Bit-Precise Reasoning. SMT 2008/BPR 2008, pp. 1–5. ACM (2008)
17. Bonacina, M.P., Echenim, M.: On variable-inactivity and polynomial $\mathcal{T}$-satisfiability procedures. J. Log. Comput. **18**(1), 77–96 (2008)
18. Lynch, C., Gero, K.A., Narendran, P., Bouchard, C.: On forward closure and the finite variant property. In: Fontaine, P., Ringeissen, C., Schmidt, R.A. (eds.) FroCoS 2013. LNCS, vol. 8152, pp. 327–342. Springer, Heidelberg (2013)
19. Boudet, A.: Combining unification algorithms. J. Symb. Comput. **16**(6), 597–626 (1993)
20. Bradley, A.R., Manna, Z.: The Calculus of Computation - Decision Procedures with Applications to Verification. Springer, Heidelberg (2007)
21. Bryant, R.E., Lahiri, S.K., Seshia, S.A.: Modeling and verifying systems using a logic of counter arithmetic with lambda expressions and uninterpreted functions. In: Brinksma, E., Larsen, K.G. (eds.) CAV 2002. LNCS, vol. 2404, pp. 78–92. Springer, Heidelberg (2002)
22. Chadha, R., Kremer, S., Ciobâcă, Ş.: Automated verification of equivalence properties of cryptographic protocols. In: Seidl, H. (ed.) Programming Languages and Systems. LNCS, vol. 7211, pp. 108–127. Springer, Heidelberg (2012)
23. Cholewa, A., Meseguer, J., Escobar, S.: Variants of variants and the finite variant property. Technical report, CS Department University of Illinois at Urbana-Champaign, February 2014. http://hdl.handle.net/2142/47117
24. Ciobaca, S.: Verification of composition of security protocols with applications to electronic voting. Ph.D. thesis, ENS Cachan (2011)
25. Clavel, M., Durán, F., Eker, S., Lincoln, P., Martí-Oliet, N., Meseguer, J., Talcott, C. (eds.): All About Maude. LNCS, vol. 4350. Springer, Heidelberg (2007)
26. Cohen, P.: Set Theory and the Continuum Hypothesis. W.A. Benjamin, New York (1966)
27. Comon, H., Dauchet, M., Gilleron, R., Löding, C., Jacquemard, F., Lugiez, D., Tison, S., Tommasi, M.: Tree automata techniques and applications (2007). http://www.grappa.univ-lille3.fr/tata. 12th October 2007
28. Comon, H., Lescanne, P.: Equational problems and disunification. J. Symbolic Comput. **7**, 371–425 (1989)
29. Comon, H.: Complete axiomatizations of some quotient term algebras. Theor. Comput. Sci. **118**(2), 167–191 (1993)
30. Comon, H., Delor, C.: Equational formulae with membership constraints. Inf. Comput. **112**(2), 167–216 (1994)
31. Delaune, S., Comon-Lundh, H.: The finite variant property: how to get rid of some algebraic properties. In: Giesl, J. (ed.) RTA 2005. LNCS, vol. 3467, pp. 294–307. Springer, Heidelberg (2005)

32. Dershowitz, N., Jouannaud, J.P.: Rewrite systems. In: van Leeuwen, J. (ed.) Handbook of Theoretical Computer Science, vol. B, pp. 243–320. North-Holland, Amsterdam (1990)
33. Dovier, A., Piazza, C., Rossi, G.: A uniform approach to constraint-solving for lists, multisets, compact lists, and sets. ACM Trans. Comput. Log. **9**(3) (2008)
34. Dovier, A., Policriti, A., Rossi, G.: A uniform axiomatic view of lists, multisets, and sets, and the relevant unification algorithms. Fundam. Inf. **36**(2–3), 201–234 (1998)
35. Dross, C., Conchon, S., Kanig, J., Paskevich, A.: Adding Decision Procedures to SMT Solvers using Axioms with Triggers. Journal of Automated Reasoning (2016) (accepted for publication). https://hal.archives-ouvertes.fr/hal-01221066
36. Echenim, M., Peltier, N.: An instantiation scheme for satisfiability modulo theories. J. Autom. Reasoning **48**(3), 293–362 (2012)
37. Ehrig, H., Mahr, B.: Fundamentals of Algebraic Specification 1. Springer, Heidelberg (1985)
38. Eker, S.: Fast sort computations for order-sorted matching and unification. In: Agha, G., Danvy, O., Meseguer, J. (eds.) Formal Modeling: Actors, Open Systems, Biological Systems. LNCS, vol. 7000, pp. 299–314. Springer, Heidelberg (2011)
39. Lynch, C.A., Narendran, P., Escobar, S., Meseguer, J., Liu, Z., Santiago, S., Kapur, D., Sasse, R., Meadows, C., Erbatur, S.: Asymmetric unification: a new unification paradigm for cryptographic protocol analysis. In: Bonacina, M.P. (ed.) CADE 2013. LNCS, vol. 7898, pp. 231–248. Springer, Heidelberg (2013)
40. Escobar, S., Meadows, C., Meseguer, J.: Maude-NPA: cryptographic protocol analysis modulo equational properties. In: Aldini, A., Barthe, G., Gorrieri, R. (eds.) FOSAD 2007/2008/2009 Tutorial Lectures. LNCS, vol. 5705, pp. 1–50. Springer, Heidelberg (2009)
41. Escobar, S., Sasse, R., Meseguer, J.: Folding variant narrowing and optimal variant termination. In: Ölveczky, P.C. (ed.) WRLA 2010. LNCS, vol. 6381, pp. 52–68. Springer, Heidelberg (2010)
42. Escobar, S., Sasse, R., Meseguer, J.: Folding variant narrowing and optimal variant termination. J. Algebraic Log. Program. **81**, 898–928 (2012)
43. Falke, S., Kapur, D.: Rewriting induction + Linear arithmetic = Decision procedure. In: Gramlich, B., Miller, D., Sattler, U. (eds.) IJCAR 2012. LNCS, vol. 7364, pp. 241–255. Springer, Heidelberg (2012)
44. Fay, M.: First-order unification in an equational theory. In: Proceedings of the 4th Workshop on Automated Deduction, pp. 161–167 (1979)
45. Filliâtre, J.-C., Owre, S., Rueß, H., Shankar, N.: ICS: Integrated Canonizer and Solver. In: Berry, G., Comon, H., Finkel, A. (eds.) CAV 2001. LNCS, vol. 2102, pp. 246–249. Springer, Heidelberg (2001)
46. Flanagan, C., Joshi, R., Ou, X., Saxe, J.B.: Theorem proving using lazy proof explication. In: Hunt Jr., W.A., Somenzi, F. (eds.) CAV 2003. LNCS, vol. 2725, pp. 355–367. Springer, Heidelberg (2003)
47. Gallier, J.H., Snyder, W.: Complete sets of transformations for general E-unification. Theor. Comput. Sci. **67**(2–3), 203–260 (1989). http://dx.doi.org/10.1016/0304-3975(89)90004--2
48. Giesl, J., Kapur, D.: Decidable classes of inductive theorems. In: Goré, R.P., Leitsch, A., Nipkow, T. (eds.) IJCAR 2001. LNCS (LNAI), vol. 2083, pp. 469–484. Springer, Heidelberg (2001)
49. Giesl, J., Kapur, D.: Deciding inductive validity of equations. In: Baader, F. (ed.) CADE 2003. LNCS (LNAI), vol. 2741, pp. 17–31. Springer, Heidelberg (2003)

50. Goguen, J., Burstall, R.: Institutions: abstract model theory for specification and programming. J. ACM **39**(1), 95–146 (1992)
51. Goguen, J., Meseguer, J.: Order-sorted algebra I. Theor. Comput. Sci. **105**, 217–273 (1992)
52. Goguen, J., Meseguer, J.: Models and equality for logical programming. In: Ehrig, H., Kowalski, R., Levi, G., Montanari, U. (eds.) TAPSOFT'87. LNCS, vol. 250, pp. 1–22. Springer, Heidelberg (1987)
53. Escobar, S., Meseguer, J., Santiago, S., Meadows, C., González-Burgueño, A.: Analysis of the IBM CCA security API protocols in Maude-NPA. In: Chen, L., Mitchell, C. (eds.) SSR 2014. LNCS, vol. 8893, pp. 111–130. Springer, Heidelberg (2014)
54. Gramlich, B.: Modularity in term rewriting revisited. Theor. Comput. Sci. **464**, 3–19 (2012)
55. Hendrix, J., Meseguer, J., Clavel, M.: A sufficient completeness reasoning tool for partial specifications. In: Giesl, J. (ed.) RTA 2005. LNCS, vol. 3467, pp. 165–174. Springer, Heidelberg (2005)
56. Meseguer, J., Ohsaki, H., Hendrix, J.: A sufficient completeness checker for linear order-sorted specifications modulo axioms. In: Furbach, U., Shankar, N. (eds.) IJCAR 2006. LNCS (LNAI), vol. 4130, pp. 151–155. Springer, Heidelberg (2006)
57. Hullot, J.M.: Canonical forms and unification. In: Bibel, W., Kowalski, R. (eds.) 5th Conference on Automated Deduction. LNCS, vol. 87, pp. 318–334. Springer, Heidelberg (1980)
58. Jouannaud, J.P., Kirchner, C., Kirchner, H.: Incremental construction of unification algorithms in equational theories. In: Diaz, J. (ed.) Automata, Languages and Programming. LNCS, vol. 154, pp. 361–373. Springer, Heidelberg (1983)
59. Jouannaud, J.P., Kirchner, H.: Completion of a set of rules modulo a set of equations. SIAM J. Comput. **15**, 1155–1194 (1986)
60. Kapur, D., Narendran, P.: Complexity of unification problems with associative-commutative operators. J. Autom. Reasoning **9**(2), 261–288 (1992)
61. Ringeissen, C., Tran, D.-K., Ranise, S., Kirchner, H.: On superposition-based satisfiability procedures and their combination. In: Van Hung, D., Wirsing, M. (eds.) ICTAC 2005. LNCS, vol. 3722, pp. 594–608. Springer, Heidelberg (2005)
62. Krstić, S., Goel, A., Tinelli, C., Grundy, J.: Combined satisfiability modulo parametric theories. In: Grumberg, O., Huth, M. (eds.) TACAS 2007. LNCS, vol. 4424, pp. 602–617. Springer, Heidelberg (2007)
63. Lynch, C., Morawska, B.: Automatic decidability. In: Proceedings of LICS 2002, p. 7. IEEE Computer Society (2002)
64. Tran, D.-K., Lynch, C.: Automatic decidability and combinability revisited. In: Pfenning, F. (ed.) CADE 2007. LNCS (LNAI), vol. 4603, pp. 328–344. Springer, Heidelberg (2007)
65. Maher, M.J.: Complete axiomatizations of the algebras of finite, rational and infinite trees. In: Proceedings of LICS 1988, pp. 348–357. IEEE Computer Society (1988)
66. Meseguer, J.: Membership algebra as a logical framework for equational specification. In: Parisi-Presicce, F. (ed.) WADT 1997. LNCS, vol. 1376, pp. 18–61. Springer, Heidelberg (1998)
67. Meseguer, J.: Order-sorted parameterization and induction. In: Palsberg, J. (ed.) Semantics and Algebraic Specification. LNCS, vol. 5700, pp. 43–80. Springer, Heidelberg (2009)

68. Meseguer, J.: Strict coherence of conditional rewriting modulo axioms. Technical report, C.S. Department, University of Illinois at Urbana-Champaign, August 2014. http://hdl.handle.net/2142/50288
69. Meseguer, J.: Variant-based satisfiability in initial algebras. Technical report, University of Illinois at Urbana-Champaign, November 2015. http://hdl.handle.net/2142/88408
70. Meseguer, J., Goguen, J.: Order-sorted algebra solves the constructor-selector, multiple representation and coercion problems. Inf. Comput. **103**(1), 114–158 (1993)
71. Meseguer, J., Skeirik, S.: Equational formulas and pattern operations in initial order-sorted algebras. In: Falaschi, M., et al. (eds.) LOPSTR 2015. LNCS, vol. 9527, pp. 36–53. Springer, Heidelberg (2015). doi:10.1007/978-3-319-27436-2_3
72. de Moura, L., Rueß, H.: Lemmas on demand for satisfiability solvers. In: Proceedings of the Fifth International Symposium on the Theory and Applications of Satisfiability Testing (SAT 2002), May 2002
73. Nelson, G., Oppen, D.C.: Simplification by cooperating decision procedures. ACM Trans. Program. Lang. Syst. **1**(2), 245–257 (1979)
74. Nelson, G., Oppen, D.C.: Fast decision procedures based on congruence closure. J. ACM **27**(2), 356–364 (1980)
75. Nieuwenhuis, R., Oliveras, A., Tinelli, C.: Solving SAT and SAT modulo theories: from an abstract Davis-Putnam-Logemann-Loveland Procedure to DPLL(T). J. ACM **53**(6), 937–977 (2006)
76. Oppen, D.C.: Complexity, convexity and combinations of theories. Theor. Comput. Sci. **12**, 291–302 (1980)
77. Schmidt, B., Meier, S., Cremers, C.J.F., Basin, D.A.: Automated analysis of Diffie-Hellman protocols and advanced security properties. In: Proceedings of CSF 2012, pp. 78–94. IEEE (2012)
78. Shostak, R.E.: Deciding combinations of theories. J. ACM **31**(1), 1–12 (1984)
79. Slagle, J.R.: Automated theorem-proving for theories with simplifiers commutativity, and associativity. J. ACM **21**(4), 622–642 (1974)
80. Snyder, W.: A Proof Theory for General Unification. Birkhäuser, Basel (1991)
81. Stump, A., Barrett, C.W., Dill, D.L., Levitt, J.R.: A decision procedure for an extensional theory of arrays. In: Proceedings of LICS 2001, pp. 29–37. IEEE Computer Society (2001)
82. Tinelli, C., Zarba, C.G.: Combining decision procedures for sorted theories. In: Alferes, J.J., Leite, J. (eds.) JELIA 2004. LNCS (LNAI), vol. 3229, pp. 641–653. Springer, Heidelberg (2004)
83. Toyama, Y.: Counterexamples to termination for the direct sum of term rewriting systems. Inf. Process. Lett. **25**(3), 141–143 (1987)
84. Yang, F., Escobar, S., Meadows, C., Meseguer, J., Narendran, P.: Theories of homomorphic encryption, unification, and the finite variant property. In: Proceedings of PPDP 2014, pp. 123–133. ACM (2014)

Timed Systems

An Executable Semantics of Clock Constraint Specification Language and Its Applications

Min Zhang[1]([✉]) and Frédéric Mallet[1,2,3]

[1] Shanghai Key Laboratory of Trustworthy Computing,
East China Normal University, Shanghai, China
zhangmin@sei.ecnu.edu.cn
[2] University of Nice Sophia Antipolis, I3S, UMR 7271 CNRS, Nice, France
Frederic.Mallet@unice.fr
[3] INRIA Sophia Antipolis Méditerranée, Valbonne, France

Abstract. The Clock Constraint Specification Language (CCSL) is a language to specify logical and timed constraints between logical clocks. Given a set of clock constraints specified in CCSL, formal analysis is preferred to check if there exists a schedule that satisfies all the constraints, if the constraints are valid or not, and if the constraints satisfy expected properties. In this paper, we present a formal executable semantics of CCSL in rewriting logic and demonstrate some applications of the formal semantics to its formal analysis: (1) to automatically find bounded or periodic schedules that satisfy all the given constraints; (2) to simulate the execution of schedules with customized simulation policies; and (3) to verify LTL properties of CCSL constraints by bounded model checking. Compared with other existing modeling approaches, advantages with the rewriting-based semantics of CCSL are that we do not need to assume a bounded number of steps for the formalization, and we can exhaustively explore all the solutions within a given bound for the analysis.

1 Introduction

Logical time such as defined by Lamport [9] gives a flexible abstraction to compare and order occurrences of events when appealing to more traditional physical measures is either not possible or not desirable. This is the case in a great variety of application domains, from widely distributed systems, for which maintaining a global clock can be costly, to deeply embedded software or in latency-insensitive designs [3], for which the complexity of the control mechanisms (like frequency scaling) makes it neither desirable nor efficient. In the latter case, synchronous languages [2,14] have shown that logical clocks can give a very adequate tool to represent any recurrent event uniformly, whether occurring in a periodic fashion or not.

The Clock Constraint Specification Language (CCSL) [11] is a language that handles logical clocks as first-class citizens. While synchronous languages mainly focus on signals and values and use logical clocks as a controlling mechanism, CCSL discards the values and only focuses on clock-related issues. The formal

C. Artho and P.C. Ölveczky (Eds.): FTSCS 2015, CCIS 596, pp. 37–51, 2016.
DOI: 10.1007/978-3-319-29510-7_2

operational semantics of CCSL was initially defined in a research report [1] in a bid to provide a reference semantics for building simulation tools, like TimeSquare [6]. We are interested here in studying the properties of a CCSL specification and we give another formal executable semantics in rewriting logic and demonstrate the benefits of this new semantics. The first benefit is that rewriting logic gives a direct implementation of the operational semantics while TimeSquare provides a Java-based implementation, which is prone to introduce accidental complexity.

The second and most important benefit is that we can directly use rewriting logic tooling to model-check a CCSL specification. Previous works on studying CCSL properties [13], rely on several intermediate transformations to automata and other specific formats so that model-checking becomes possible when a CCSL specification is finite (or safe) [12]. It either meant, reducing to a safe subset of CCSL [8] or detecting that the specification was finite even though relying on unsafe operators. In this contribution, we rely on Maude environment [4] to provide a direct analysis support from the operational semantics and we can explore unsafe specifications by using bounded-model checking and do not restrict to the safe subset. While before, successive intermediate transformations could each introduce variations in the semantics, if not careful enough, we rely here on the strong, widely used, generic tooling provided by Maude, rather than on an ad-hoc manual implementation.

More precisely, in this paper, we introduce the notions of bounded and periodic schedules for a CCSL specification. Periodic schedules are useful to reason on specifications that rely on unsafe operators. With periodic schedules, we can use bounded model-checking to verify temporal logic properties on CCSL models. The tooling and automatic verification directly comes with the newly introduced semantics and the Maude environment.

The rest of the paper is organized as follows. Sections 2 and 3 give a brief introduction to CCSL and Maude. In Sect. 4 we present the formal definition of semantics of CCSL in Maude, and in Sect. 5 we demonstrate four applications of the formal semantics to the analysis of CCSL. Section 6 mentions some related work and Sect. 7 concludes the paper.

2 CCSL

2.1 Syntax and Semantics of CCSL

In CCSL, there are four primitive constraint operators which are binary relations between clocks, and five kinds of clock definitions [11]. The four constraint operators are called *precedence, causality, subclock* and *exclusion*; and the five clock definitions are called *union, intersection, infimum, supremum,* and *delay.*

The meaning of the nine primitive operators (see Fig. 1) is given using the notions of *schedule* and *history.* Given a set C of clocks, a schedule of C is used to decide which clocks can tick at a given step, and a history is used to calculate the number of ticks of each clock at a given step.

1. $\delta \vDash c_1 \prec c_2$	$\Longleftrightarrow \forall n \in \mathbb{N}^+.\chi(c_1,n) = \chi(c_2,n) \Rightarrow c_2 \notin \delta(n+1)$	(Precedence)
2. $\delta \vDash c_1 \preceq c_2$	$\Longleftrightarrow \forall n \in \mathbb{N}^+.\chi(c_1,n) \geq \chi(c_2,n)$	(Causality)
3. $\delta \vDash c_1 \subseteq c_2$	$\Longleftrightarrow \forall n \in \mathbb{N}^+.c_1 \in \delta(n) \Rightarrow c_2 \in \delta(n)$	(Subclock)
4. $\delta \vDash c_1 \# c_2$	$\Longleftrightarrow \forall n \in \mathbb{N}^+.c_1 \notin \delta(n) \vee c_2 \notin \delta(n)$	(Exclusion)
5. $\delta \vDash c_1 \triangleq c_2 + c_3$	$\Longleftrightarrow \forall n \in \mathbb{N}^+.(c_1 \in \delta(n) \Longleftrightarrow c_2 \in \delta(n) \vee c_3 \in \delta(n))$	(Union)
6. $\delta \vDash c_1 \triangleq c_2 \times c_3$	$\Longleftrightarrow \forall n \in \mathbb{N}^+.(c_1 \in \delta(n) \Longleftrightarrow c_2 \in \delta(n) \wedge c_3 \in \delta(n))$	(Intersection)
7. $\delta \vDash c_1 \triangleq c_2 \wedge c_3$	$\Longleftrightarrow \forall n \in \mathbb{N}^+.\chi(c_1,n) = max(\chi(c_2,n),\chi(c_3,n))$	(Infimum)
8. $\delta \vDash c_1 \triangleq c_2 \vee c_3$	$\Longleftrightarrow \forall n \in \mathbb{N}^+.\chi(c_1,n) = min(\chi(c_2,n),\chi(c_3,n))$	(Supremum)
9. $\delta \vDash c_1 \triangleq c_2 \,\$\, d$	$\Longleftrightarrow \forall n \in \mathbb{N}^+.\chi(c_1,n) = max(\chi(c_2,n) - d, 0)$	(Delay)

Fig. 1. Definition of 9 primitive CCSL operators

Definition 1 (Schedule). *Given a set C of clocks, a schedule of C is a total function $\delta : \mathbb{N}^+ \to 2^C$ such that for any n in $\mathbb{N}^+$, $\delta(n) \neq \varnothing$.*

Note that a schedule must be non-trivial such that there is at least one clock ticking at any execution step. This condition excludes from schedules those steps where no clocks tick. Such steps are called *empty steps* and are trivial in that adding them to a schedule does not affect the logical relations among clocks.

Definition 2 (History). *A history of a schedule $\delta : \mathbb{N}^+ \to 2^C$ over a set C of clocks is a function $\chi : C \times \mathbb{N} \to \mathbb{N}$ such that for any clock $c \in C$ and $n \in \mathbb{N}$:*

$$\chi(c,n) = \begin{cases} 0 & \text{if } n = 0 \\ \chi(c,n-1) & \text{if } n \neq 0 \wedge c \notin \delta(n) \\ \chi(c,n-1) + 1 & \text{if } n \neq 0 \wedge c \in \delta(n) \end{cases}$$

We use $\delta \vDash \phi$ to denote that schedule δ satisfies constraint ϕ. Figure 1 shows the definition of the satisfiability of a constraint ϕ with regards to a schedule δ. We take the definition of precedence for example. $\delta \vDash c_1 \prec c_2$ holds if and only if for any n in $\mathbb{N}$, c_2 must not tick at step $n + 1$ if the number of ticks of c_1 is equal to the one of c_2 at step n. Precedence and causality are asynchronous constraints and they forbid clocks to tick depending on what has happened on other clocks in the earlier steps. Subclock and exclusion are synchronous constraints and they force clocks to tick or not depending on whether another clock ticks or not in the same step. Union defines a clock c_1 which ticks whenever c_2 or c_3 ticks; intersection defines a clock c_1 which ticks whenever both c_2 and c_3 tick; supremum defines the slowest clock c_1 which is faster than both c_2 and c_3; infimum defines the fastest clock c_1 which is slower than both c_2 and c_3; and delay defines the clock c_1 which is delayed by c_2 with d steps. More details can be found in a recent study on CCSL [13].

Given a set Φ of clock constraints and a schedule δ, δ satisfies Φ (denoted by $\delta \vDash \Phi$) if for any ϕ in Φ there is $\delta \vDash \phi$. In particular, we use $\delta; k \vDash \phi$ to denote that δ satisfies ϕ at step $k(k \in \mathbb{N}^+)$. We use $\delta; k \vDash \Phi$ to denote that δ satisfies all the constraints in Φ at step k, i.e., $\forall \phi \in \Phi$, $\delta; k \vDash \phi$.

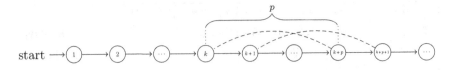

Fig. 2. Periodic schedule

2.2   Satisfiability Problem of CCSL

Given a set Φ of CCSL constraints, one of the most important problems is to decide if there exist some schedules that satisfy Φ. However, it is still an open problem whether the satisfiability of a given arbitrary set of CCSL constraints is decidable or not. We consider two kinds of schedules called *bounded schedule* and *periodic schedule* from the pragmatic point of view and show the satisfiability problem of an arbitrary given set of CCSL constraints with regards to bounded schedule and periodic schedule is decidable.

Definition 3 (Bounded schedule). *Given a set Φ of clock constraints on clocks in C, and a function $\delta : \mathbb{N}_{\leq n} \to 2^C$, δ is called an n-bounded schedule if for any $i \leq n$, $\delta; i \vDash \Phi$.*

We denote the bounded satisfiability relation by $\delta \vDash_n \Phi$, which means that δ is an n-bounded schedule of Φ. It is obvious that given a bound n it is decidable to check if there exists an n-bounded schedule for a set of CCSL constraints because the number of candidate schedules is finite, i.e., $(2^{|C|} - 1)^n$, where $|C|$ denotes the number of clocks in C. If there does not exist an n-bounded schedule for a set Φ of clock constraints, there must not be a schedule that satisfies Φ, although not vice versa.

Bounded schedule is sometimes too restrictive in practice because we usually do not assign a bound to clocks in real-time embedded systems, but assume that reactive systems run forever and only terminate when shutdown. Thus, clocks should tick infinitely often from the theoretical point of view. There is another class of schedules which are unbounded and force all the clocks to occur periodically. We call them *periodic schedules*.

Definition 4 (Periodic schedule). *A schedule δ is periodic if there exist k, p in $\mathbb{N}$ such that for any $k' \geq k$, $\delta(k' + p) = \delta(k')$.*

Figure 2 depicts a periodic schedule whose period is p. Each node denotes a time point, and each arrow denotes the elapse of a time unit. The dashed line indicates that, for any clock, it ticks at one point if and only if it ticks at the other point. From step k, the schedule starts to repeat every p steps infinitely. To decide whether there exists a periodic schedule for a given set of clock constraints is also an open problem. In the rest of this section, we propose an approach to constructing a periodic schedule from a bounded one when the bounded one satisfies certain conditions which are to be introduced below.

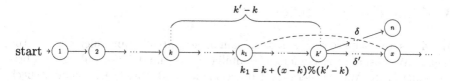

Fig. 3. Construction of periodic schedule δ' from an n-bounded schedule δ

Lemma 1. *Given a schedule $\delta : \mathbb{N}^+ \to 2^C$ and two natural numbers k, k', if there exists $m \in \mathbb{N}$ such that for any c in C $\chi(c, k) + m = \chi(c, k')$ and $\chi(c, k+1) + m = \chi(c, k'+1)$ then $\delta(k+1) = \delta(k'+1)$.*

Proof. It is equal to prove that for any $c \in C$, $c \in \delta(k+1) \iff c \in \delta(k'+1)$.

($\Rightarrow$): $c \in \delta(k+1)$ implies that $\chi(c, k+1) = \chi(c, k) + 1$. Thus, $\chi(c, k+1) + m = \chi(c, k'+1) = \chi(c, k) + 1 + m = \chi(c, k') + 1$. Thus, $c \in \delta(k'+1)$.

($\Leftarrow$): $c \in \delta(k'+1)$ implies that $\chi(c, k'+1) = \chi(c, k') + 1$. Namely, $\chi(c, k+1) + m = \chi(c, k) + m + 1$. Thus, $\chi(c, k+1) = \chi(c, k) + 1$, and hence we have $c \in \delta(k+1)$. $\square$

Theorem 1. *Given a schedule $\delta : \mathbb{N}^+ \to 2^C$, a clock constraint ϕ, and two natural numbers k, k', $\delta; k \models \phi \Rightarrow \sigma; k' \models \phi$ if all the following three conditions are true:*

1. *$\delta(k) = \delta(k')$;*
2. *There exists m in $\mathbb{N}$ such that $m > 0$ and for any c in C, $\chi(c, k) + m = \chi(c, k')$ and $\chi(c, k+1) + m = \chi(c, k'+1)$;*
3. *If $\phi \equiv (c_1 \triangleq c_2 \$ d)$, $\chi(c_2, k) \geq d$.*

Theorem 1 can be proved with Lemma 1. We omit the proof due to the limit of space. From Theorem 1 we can directly derive the following corollary.

Corollary 1. *Given a schedule $\delta : \mathbb{N}^+ \to 2^C$, a set Φ of clock constraints, and two natural numbers n, k', $\delta; k \models \Phi \Rightarrow \sigma; k' \models \Phi$ if the three conditions in Theorem 1 are satisfied.*

Given an n-bounded schedule δ of a set Φ of clock constraints, if there exist two natural numbers $k, k' \leq n$, which satisfy the three conditions in Theorem 1, we can define a periodic schedule δ' based on δ such that δ' satisfies Φ.

$$\delta'(x) = \begin{cases} \delta(x) & \text{if } x \leq k' \\ \delta(k + (x - k)\%(k' - k)) & \text{if } x > k' \end{cases}$$

Figure 3 shows the construction of δ' based on δ. From k', the schedule δ' repeats infinitely the steps from k to $k' - 1$. By Corollary 1, it is obvious that for any k'' such that $k'' > k'$, we have $\delta'; k'' \models \Phi$ because we can find a natural number $k_1 = k + (k'' - k)\%(k' - k)$ such that $\delta; k_1 \models \Phi$, $\delta(k_1) = \delta'(k_1)$ and k'', k_1, δ' satisfy the three conditions in Theorem 1. Thus, we have $\delta' \models \Phi$.

3 Maude in a Nutshell

Maude is rewriting-based algebraic language and also an efficient rewriting engine. We assume the readers are familiar with Maude, and only give a brief introduction to Maude meta-level functionality and Maude LTL model checking, which is used in this paper. More details about Maude can be found in the Maude book [4].

The underlying logic of Maude is rewriting logic, which is reflective in the sense that it can be faithfully interpreted in itself [4]. The reflectivity allows us to reason with a specified rewrite theory in customized strategies by Maude. Intuitively, we define a rewrite theory $\mathcal{R}$ and then define a metatheory $\mathcal{U}$ where $\mathcal{R}$ is treated as data. A rewrite theory $\mathcal{R}$ is a tripe $\langle \Sigma, E, R \rangle$, where Σ is called the signature specifying the type structure, E is a set of equations and R is a set of rewrite rules. Maude provides efficient function by command search to find if there exist some paths from a given term t to a target term t' by repeatedly applying the rewrite rules in R. It also provides a corresponding meta-level searching function metaSearch which takes $\mathcal{R}$, t and t' as arguments and returns the searching result. An LTL model checker has been implemented based on Maude to verify LTL properties of a rewrite theory when the set of states that are reachable from an initial state in the rewrite theory is finite [7].

4 Formal Semantics of CCSL in Maude

We formalize a clock as a triple (c, ℓ, n), consisting of the clock identifier c, a list ℓ of records, with each value being *tick* or *idle* (abbreviated by t or i respectively), representing that the clock ticks or not at the corresponding step, and a natural number n to indicate the numbers of ticks in ℓ. ℓ represents a bounded schedule of c whose bound is equal to the length of ℓ. Initially, ℓ is empty and n is 0. Let $\mathcal{C}$ be the set of such clock triples of a set C of clocks. We call $\mathcal{C}$ a *configuration*. We suppose that the length of the lists in each clock triple in $\mathcal{C}$ are equal, e.g. n. $\mathcal{C}$ essentially represents an n-bounded schedule for all the clocks in C.

We declare a predicate satisfy which takes three arguments: a configuration $\mathcal{C}$, a non-zero natural number k, and a set Φ of constraints, and returns true if $\mathcal{C}$ satisfies Φ at step k, and otherwise false. We consider each possible constraint form in Φ when defining satisfy. For instance, the following two equations are defined to specify a configuration $\mathcal{C}$ satisfies precedence and infimum at step k:

```
1 ceq satisfy(C, k, c1 < c2) = (num(ℓ1,k) >= num(ℓ2, k)) and
2   (if num(ℓ1,k-1) == num(ℓ2, k-1) then t-val(ℓ2,k) =/= t else true fi)
3 if (c1, ℓ1, n1) := getConf(C, c1) /\ (c2, ℓ2, n2) := getConf(C, c2).
4 ceq satisfy(C, k, c1 ≜ c2 ∧ c3) = (if n2 > n3 then n1 == n2 else n1 == n3 fi)
5 if (c1, ℓ1, n1) := getConf(C, c1) /\ (c2, ℓ2, n2) := getConf(C, c2)
6   /\ (c3, ℓ3, n3) := getConf(C, c2) .
```

The first equation says that satisfy returns true with $\mathcal{C}$, k and $c_1 < c_2$ when the number of ticks of c_1 up to step k is greater than or equal to the one of c_2 and further if the number of ticks of c_1 up to step $k-1$ is the same as the one of c_2 then c_2 must not tick at step k (as represented by $\texttt{t-val}(\ell_2, k)$ $\texttt{=/=}$ t, where $\texttt{t-val}$ is a function returning the kth value in the list ℓ_2). The equation has a condition which is a conjunction of two matching equations [4]. The two conjuncts are used to retrieve the tick list and the number of ticks of c_1 (and c_2) by function $\texttt{getConf}$ and assign them to ℓ_1 and n_1 (and ℓ_2 and n_2). The second equation defines the semantics of infimum relation, namely, at any step k the number of ticks of c_1 must be the minimum of those of c_2 and c_3. The correspondence between the formalization of the constraints and their formal semantics defined in Fig. 1 should be clear. Other constraints can be formalized in Maude likewise, and we omit them from the paper.

Next we formalize one-step ticking from k to $k + 1$ of all clocks by a set of rewrite rules. The basic idea is as follows. From step k to $k+1$ each clock decides to tick or not (be idle). After all the clocks make a decision, we check if the bounded schedule satisfies all the constraints at step $k + 1$. The first rewrite rule at Line 1 specifies the behavior that clock c ticks at step $k + 1$. The list ℓ is changed into $\ell\ t$. The rule is conditional because we need the condition that c is not the last clock which makes a decision. If c is the last one, we need to check if all the constraints in Φ are satisfied at step $k + 1$. The step k can be represented by the length of the list ℓ of an arbitrary clock triple in $\mathcal{C}$, i.e., $k = \texttt{size}(\ell)$, where $\texttt{size}(\ell)$ returns the length of ℓ. Thus, $k + 1$ is equal to $\texttt{size}(\ell) + 1$, and hence we use the latter one in the condition of the fourth equation on Line 6.

Similarly, if c decides to remain idle next step and c is not the last clock, its corresponding tick list is changed from ℓ to $\ell\ i$, which is specified by the rule on Line 2. If c is the last clock in this case, we also need to guarantee that from step k to $k + 1$ there must be at least one clock ticking (represented by the formula $\texttt{not allIdle}(\mathcal{C}')$) and all the clocks satisfy the constraints in Φ at step $k + 1$.

```
1 crl ((c,ℓ,n) C ; C' ; Φ) => (C ; C' (c,ℓ t,n+1) ; Φ) if C =/= nil .
2 crl ((c,ℓ,n) C ; C' ; Φ) => (C ; C' (c,ℓ i,n) ; Φ)    if C =/= nil .
3 crl ((c,ℓ,n) ; C' ; Φ)    => (nil ; C' (c,ℓ t,n+1) ; Φ )
4        if satisfy(C' (c,ℓ t,n+1), size(ℓ) + 1, Φ) .
5 crl ((c,ℓ,n) ; C' ; Φ)    => (nil ; C' (c,ℓ i,n) ; Φ)
6        if not allIdle(C') /\ satisfy(C' (c,ℓ i,n), size(ℓ) + 1, Φ) .
```

We assume that $\mathcal{C}$ is a k-bounded schedule of a set Φ of CCSL constraints. If there is a rewriting sequence from $(\mathcal{C};\ \texttt{nil};\ \Phi)$ to a new one $(\texttt{nil};\ \mathcal{C}';\ \Phi)$ with the above four rules, $\mathcal{C}'$ must be a $k + 1$-bounded schedule of Φ because $\mathcal{C}'$ satisfies Φ up to $k + 1$ steps. We can define the following rule to specify the one-step ticking of all the clocks from step k to $k + 1$.

```
1 crl < C ; k ; Φ > => < C' ; k+1 ; Φ > if (C ; nil ; Φ) => (nil ; C' ; Φ) .
```

The condition of the rule is a *rewrite condition* [4], which is true if and only if there exists a rewriting sequence from the term at the left-hand side of => to the one at the right-hand side when the condition is true. In the above rule, $\mathcal{C}'$ represents an arbitrary immediate successor of $\mathcal{C}$ such that $\mathcal{C}'$ satisfies Φ up to $k + 1$ steps.

5   Applications of the Formal Semantics

In this section, we show four applications of the executable formal semantics of CCSL in Maude.

5.1   Bounded Scheduling

Given a bound n and a set of clock constraints Φ, we can use Maude's **search** function to find automatically if there exists an n-bounded schedule of Φ. If Maude cannot find a schedule within a given bound n, it means that there must not exist such an n-bounded schedule, and further we can conclude that there must not exist a schedule that satisfies Φ. However, if a schedule is found up to bound n, we can only conclude that the returned schedule is n-bounded, but cannot guarantee the existence of a schedule for Φ.

We show an example of finding bounded schedules for a given set of clock constraints using Maude's **search** command.

Example 1. Given a set of constraints $\Phi_1 = \{c_1 < c_2, c_3 \triangleq c_1 \$ 1, c_2 < c_3$, we can use Maude's **search** command to find a 100-bounded schedule.

```
1 search [2,100] init(Φ₁) =>* < C ; 100 ; (Φ₁) > .
2 states: 101  rewrites: 629424
3 C -->
4  (c₁,t i t i t i t i t i t i t i t i t i t i t i t i t i t i t i t i t i t i t
5       i t i t i t i t i t i t i t i t i t i t i t i t i t i t i t i t i t i t i
6       t i t i t i t i t i t i t i t i t i t i t i t i t i t i t i t i t i i,50)
7  (c₂,i t i t i t i t i t i t i t i t i t i t i t i t i t i t i t i t i t i t i
8       t i t i t i t i t i t i t i t i t i t i t i t i t i t i t i t i t i t i t
9       i t i t i t i t i t i t i t i t i t i t i t i t i t i t i t i t i t,50)
10 (c₃,i i t i t i t i t i t i t i t i t i t i t i t i t i t i t i t i t i t i t i t
11      i t i t i t i t i t i t i t i t i t i t i t i t i t i t i t i t i t i t i t i
12      t i t i t i t i t i t i t i t i t i t i t i t i t i t i t i t i t i t i i,49)
```

Maude's **search** command takes two optional arguments in the square brackets. The first one is used to specify the number of expected solutions, and the second one is used to specify the maximal depth of searching. Function **init** takes a set Φ of constraints and generates an initial configuration $< C_0 ; 0 ; \Phi >$, where C_0 is a set of clock triples, each of which is of the form $(c, \text{nil}, 0)$. The operator =>* indicates there are zero or more rewritings from the given initial term to the expected term that can be matched by the target term.

In this example, the target term represents those configurations where the current step is 200. C is a configuration which is assigned by Maude. The result is obtained by repeatedly applying the rewrite rule. Maude only returns one result with the command. It means that there is only one possible 100-bounded schedule for the constraints. The schedule shows that c_1 and c_3 only tick at all odd steps except that c_3 does not tick at the first step, because of the constraint $c_3 \triangleq c_1 \$ 1$. c_2 only ticks at all even steps. The returned bounded schedule coincides with the result in an earlier work of the second author [13].

5.2   Customized Simulation

Given a set Φ of clock constraints, it is also desirable to have a customized schedule which satisfies not only Φ but also some customized requirements, e.g., at each step if a clock can tick it must tick, or if a clock does not have to tick, it must not tick. We only consider three basic scheduling policies, called *randomness*, *maximum* and *minimum* respectively.

– *Randomness*: If a clock can tick and not tick at next step, we randomly choose whether it ticks or not.
– *Maximum*: If a clock can tick at next step, it must tick.
– *Minimum*: If a clock may not to tick at next step, it must not tick.

Based on the four rewrite rules defined in Sect. 4, we can achieve customized scheduling for a given set of clock constraints using Maude's meta-level facility. We first find all the possible immediate successors of a set C of clock triples using Maude's metaSearch function, and then choose the successor that satisfies the customized policy given by users. The following rewrite rule is defined for customized scheduling.

```
1 --- the rewrite rule is defined for customized scheduling
2 crl < C ; k ; Φ ; ρ > => < C' ; k+1 ; Φ ; ρ > if C' := conf(sucs(C, Φ), ρ)

3 --- the equation needs the meta-level function metaSearch to compute all successors
4 ceq sucsAux(C, Φ, j) = downTerm(T, nil), sucsAux(C, Φ, j+1)
5 if RT := metaSearch(upModule('ONE-STEP-TICKING, false),
6         ''(_;_;_')[upTerm(C), 'nil.Conf, upTerm(Φ)],
7         ''(_;_;_')['nil.Conf, C', upTerm(Φ)],nil,'*,unbounded,i) /\
8     (C' <- T) := getSubstitution(RT) .
```

In the rule, ρ is a variable, denoting the customized policy given by users, e.g. rand for randomness, max for maximum or min for minimum. The function sucs used in the condition returns the set of all the successors of C that satisfy Φ, and conf returns one among them according to the customized policy ρ. The equation above is used to define a recursive function sucsAux, which is the main auxiliary function to define sucs. Function sucsAux takes three arguments, C, Φ and a natural number j, which indicate that we want metaSearch to find the $j^{th}(j \geq 0)$ successor of C. The metaSearch function takes a meta-module of the module ONE-STEP-TICKING where the four rewrite rules in Sect. 4 are defined, a term from which searching begins, a target term that the result term can match, and other three arguments, and returns a searching result. The searching result contains a meta-level term which substitutes for C'. We change it to the object level by the built-in function downTerm. The object-level term represents the ith successor of C. We omit the detailed explanation about the usage of metaSearch. Interested readers can refer to the work [4] for the details.

Example 2. Let Φ_2 be the set of the following constraints:

$$in_1 \preccurlyeq step_1 \qquad step_1 \prec step_3 \qquad in_2 \preccurlyeq step_2$$
$$step_2 \prec step_3 \qquad step_3 \preccurlyeq out$$

We show the simulations of the bounded schedules that satisfy Φ_2 with maximum and minimum policy. We use Maude's `rew` command to rewrite the initial configuration $< \mathcal{C}_0 \; ; \; 0 \; ; \; \Phi \; ; \; \rho >$ by applying the rewrite rule defined in this section 10 times with `max` and `min` respectively. The initial configuration is generated by function `init1`, which takes a set Φ of CCSL constraints and a simulation policy ρ as its arguments. The commands and returned results are shown as follows.

```
1 rew [10] init1(Φ₂, max) .
2 result CCC: ('in1,   t t t t t t t t t t,10)('in2,   t t t t t t t t t t,10)
3             ('out,   i t t t t t t t t t,9) ('step1,t t t t t t t t t t,10)
4             ('step2,t t t t t t t t t t,10)('step3,i t t t t t t t t t,9)
                    ...
5 rew [10] init1(Φ₂, min) .
6 result CCC: ('in1,   i i i i i i i i i i,0) ('in2,   t i t i t i t i t i,5)
7             ('out,   i i i i i i i i i i,0) ('step1,i i i i i i i i i i,0)
8             ('step2,i t i t i t i t i t,5) ('step3,i i i i i i i i i i,0)
                    ...
```

For the first schedule, the number of ticking clocks is always maximal, while for the second one the number of ticking clocks is always minimal.

5.3 Periodic Scheduling

We also can find automatically periodic schedules of a given set of CCSL constraints by Maude's `search` command with the rewriting-based semantics of CCSL in Maude. The basic idea is to compute all possible immediate successors of the current k-bounded schedule at every step $k (k \geq 1)$ and check if there exists a successor that satisfies all the three conditions in Theorem 1. If such a successor exists, a periodic schedule is found, and the step $k + 1$ is the first step of the second iteration. We also can compute the period of the schedule. The following rewrite rule is defined for periodic scheduling.

```
1 --- the rewrite rule is defined to represent periodic schedules
2 crl < C ; k ; Φ ; 0 > =>
3     if C" == nil then < C' ; k+1 ; Φ ; 0 > else < C" ; k+1 ;  Φ ; p > fi
4 if (CS₁,C',CS₂) := sucs(CF,CTS) /\ <C"; p> := checkOcc((CS₁, C',CS₂),k+1)
```

The term on the left-hand side of the rule is a 4-tuple, where the last argument, i.e., 0 indicates that the k-bounded schedule does not satisfy the three conditions in Theorem 1. Function `checkOcc` is used to check if there exists a $k + 1$-bounded schedule that satisfies all the constraints in Φ and also the three conditions in Theorem 1. If that is the case, `checkOcc` returns the schedule C'' and the period $p (p > 0)$, and otherwise nil and 0. Once a periodic schedule is found, the rewrite rule cannot be applied and Maude returns the result. Note that the rule may cause non-termination if no periodic schedule is found and no bound to the times of rewriting is set.

As an example, we use Maude's `search` command to find periodic schedules of the precedence constraint $c_1 < c_2$. The command is as follows:

```
1 search [4] init2(c₁ < c₂) =>* < C; k ; c₁ < c₂ ; p > such that p =/= 0 .
```

Table 1. Four periodic schedules that satisfy $c_1 \prec c_2$

schedule	clock/step	1	2	3	4	5	6	...	period p
1	c_1	t	t	t	t	t	t	...	1
	c_2	i	t	t	t	t	t	...	
2	c_1	t	i	t	i	t	i	...	2
	c_2	i	t	i	t	i	t	...	
3	c_1	t	t	t	t	t	t	...	1
	c_2	i	i	t	t	t	t	...	
4	c_1	t	t	t	i	t	i	...	2
	c_2	i	i	i	t	i	t	...	

Function `init2` takes a set Φ of CCSL constraints and returns an initial configuration $< \mathcal{C}_0 ; 0 ; \Phi ; 0 >$, where the last natural number is used to record the period of the current bounded schedule. We provide an upper bound (e.g. 4) to the expected periodic schedules. In the command, $\mathcal{C}$ is a set of two clock triples of c_1 and c_2 returned by Maude when a periodic schedule is found. k indicates the step where the first period of the schedule ends, and p indicates the period of the schedule. The condition $p =/= 0$ means that $\mathcal{C}$ represents a periodic schedule. Table 1 shows four periodic schedules found by Maude for $c_1 \prec c_2$ when the bound is set to 4. The red steps for each schedule are the beginning of the first and second iterations of the period. We also can give p a concrete value and use Maude to search those periodic schedules with a fixed period.

5.4 Bounded Model Checking

Given a set of clock constraints, it is desired to know if the constraints satisfy some properties, e.g. if all the clocks can tick infinitely often, or a clock must tick immediately after another clock ticks. Based on the formal semantics of CCSL in Maude, we can model check LTL properties of a given set of CCSL constraints by Maude LTL model checker. Maude model checker requires the reachable state space being verified must be finite, while the reachable state space specified by the rewrite theory of a set of clock constraints may be infinite if there exist some non-periodic schedules. For periodic schedules, we force the schedule to repeat from step n to n' where n and n' are the beginning and ending steps of the first period. As depicted by Fig. 4, by setting a bound we can compute all periodic schedules up to the bound. The periodic schedules compose a finite state space which can be used for model checking. Figure 4 (left) shows an example of an unbounded state space. Each path represents a schedule. The path with a loop represents a periodic schedule. There are three periodic schedules in the figure when the bound is set to 3. The three periodic schedules constitute a finite state space which can be model checked, as shown in Fig. 4 (right).

Next, we show some basic properties that clock constraints are expected to satisfy and their representations in LTL formula. Let *tick* be a parameterized predicate on states, which takes a clock c as argument and returns true if c ticks in a state and otherwise false.

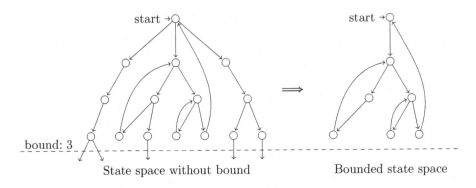

State space without bound   Bounded state space

Fig. 4. Bounded state-space of periodic schedulers

- *Repeated ticking*: all clocks must tick infinitely often, which can be formalized as: $\bigwedge_{c \in C} \Box \Diamond\, tick(c)$.
- *Simultaneous ticking*: two clocks c_1 and c_2 must tick simultaneously, which can be formalized as: $\Box(tick(c_1) \iff tick(c_2))$.
- *Leading-to ticking*: if a clock c_1 ticks, it must cause another clock c_2 to tick eventually, which can be formalized as: $\Box(tick(c_1) \to \Diamond tick(c_2))$.
- *Alternating ticking*: two clocks c_1 and c_2 must always tick immediately after each other, which can be formalized as: $\Box(tick(c_1) \to \bigcirc tick(c_2) \wedge tick(c_2) \to \bigcirc tick(c_1))$.

As an example, we model check if the constraints Φ_1 in Example 1 satisfy the alternating ticking property.

```
1 --- definition of the state predicate tick in Maude
2 ceq <(C; k; Φ; p> |= tick(c) = (tval(ℓ,k) == t) if (c,ℓ,n) := getConf(C, c)

3 --- the following command is used for model checking in Maude
4 red modelCheck(init2((c₁ < c₂)(c₃ ≜ c₁ $ 1 )(c₂ < c₃)),
5     [](tick(c₁) -> O tick(c₂) /\ tick(c₂) -> O tick(c₁))) .
6 Result: true
```

The first equation is used to define the state predicate `tick`, and `modelCheck` is a built-in function to do model checking in Maude. It takes an initial state (configuration) and an LTL formula. Maude returns true with the above command, which means that the constraints Φ_1 indeed satisfies the alternating ticking property. This result coincides with the one obtained by encoding CCSL into finite-state transition systems [13].

By bounded model checking in Maude we also can find invalid schedules of a given set of clock constraints. A schedule is called invalid if it prevents some clocks from ticking after some step, namely, it does not satisfy the repeated ticking property. A set Φ of CCSL constraints are called invalid if there exist invalid schedules that satisfy Φ. Once Maude finds such a periodic schedule that violates the repeated ticking property, we can conclude that the constraints are not valid. However, it cannot guarantee the constraints are valid if no invalid schedules are found because not all schedules are model checked.

Table 2. Eight deadlock schedules found by Maude for CCSL constraints Φ_2'

No.	in_1	in_2	$step_1$	$step_2$	$step_3$	out	tmp_1	tmp_2
1	t	i	t	i	i	i	t	i
2	i	t	i	t	i	i	t	i
3	t i	i i	i t	i i	i i	i i	t i	i i
4	i i	t i	i i	i t	i i	i i	t i	i i
5	t i t	t i i	t i t	t i i	i t i	i t i	t i t	i i t
6	t i i	t i t	t i i	t i t	i t i	i t i	t i t	i i t
7	t i t	t i i	t i t	i t i	i t i	i t i	t i t	i i t
8	t i i	t i t	t i i	i t t	i t i	i t i	t i t	i i t

A special invalid case of CCSL constraints is that some schedules may prevent all clocks from ticking after some step. We call them *deadlock schedules*. We can use Maude to find if there exist deadlock schedules within a given bound. Let us consider a case of Example 2. Assume that we introduce the following four new constraints to Φ_2 and denote the new set as Φ_2':

$$tmp_1 \triangleq in_1 + in_2 \qquad tmp_1 < out \qquad tmp_2 \triangleq tmp_1 \,\$\, 1 \qquad out < tmp_2$$

The four constraints mean that clocks tmp_1 and out must alternatively tick. We can find a number of schedules satisfying all the constraints in Φ_2'. However, some of them may cause deadlock. We find 8 deadlock schedules by searching within 3 steps in Maude with the command:

```
1 search [10,3] init(Φ₂')=>! CF .
```

In the command $\mathcal{CF}$ is a variable to which a 4-tuple is going to be assigned by Maude, and =>! means that the value assigned to $\mathcal{CF}$ must be rewritten by any rewrite rules. Namely, the value assigned to $\mathcal{CF}$ is a deadlock schedule. Table 2 shows the eight deadlock schedules. We take the first one as an example. According to the first schedule, only three clocks, i.e. in_1, $step_1$ and tmp_1 tick at the first step. In next step, no clocks can tick because of the newly introduced four constraints. For instance, in_2 cannot tick in next step. If in_2 ticked, so did tmp_1 (by constraint $tmp_1 \triangleq in_1 + in_2$) and tmp_2 (by constraint $tmp_2 \triangleq tmp_1 \,\$\, 1$), which violates the constraint $out < tmp_2$. Because in_2 cannot tick, $step_2$ cannot tick either by constraint $in_2 < step_2$. Other clocks also cannot tick because of the corresponding constraints, leading to a deadlock.

6 Related Works and Discussion

CCSL mainly deals with logical clocks, i.e., unbounded increasing sequences of integers. The semantics of clock constraints may depend on boolean parameters, in which case, we remain in a finite world and can rely on traditional verification and analysis results and tools. The constraints may also depend on unbounded integer values, for instance, the number of times a given clock has ticked. In this latter case, the constraint is called unsafe [12]. A specification is safe if it does not use any unsafe constraint.

The reference semantics of CCSL was given in a research report [1] mainly to be able to define a simulation tool called TimeSquare [6]. TimeSquare encodes the operational semantics of CCSL in Java and captures boolean constraints symbolically using Binary Decision Diagrams (BDD). TimeSquare works step by step and at each step, finding a solution reduces to a satisfiability problem. After deciding if and how many valid solutions can be found at a step, TimeSquare clock engine picks one solution according to its simulation policy, updates the state space and moves forward. TimeSquare does not consider the unbounded specification as a whole and only produce one finite possible trace that satisfies all the constraints up to a given number of steps. In this work, we use bounded model-checking, we can then explore all the solutions reached in a given number of steps, instead of only one.

Other works have tried to make an exhaustive exploration of the entire state space (not up to a pre-defined number of steps). A comprehensive list of such works has been summarized in a recent survey [13]. However, one aspect is to be able to decide whether the state space can be represented with a finite abstraction even though the specification is unsafe. Another way is to force a finite space by restricting to safe constraints [8,15,16]. In this work, we do not make any assumptions on whether the specification is safe or not.

The most important achievement in this paper is that, thanks to Maude environment, all the analyses performed result directly from the operational semantics without intermediate transformations, so without the need to prove that the semantics is preserved. Yu et al. proposed to encode CCSL in Signal before transforming it to the internal format of Sigali [16]. We hope that the encoding in Maude will allow to conduct automated verification for all the transformational approaches that use CCSL as a step. Maude also gives a framework to define the simulation policies formally. Some undocumented simulation policies are available in TimeSquare [6]. In Sect. 4, we give a simple formal interpretation for three of these simulation policies.

Finally, abstract interpretation [5] or infinite model-checking [10] would allow reasoning on the global CCSL specification without restrictions. However, the encoding is likely to introduce semantic variations and we do not know at the moment how to encode CCSL constraints in a compositional way.

7   Conclusion and Future Work

We have proposed a new semantic model for CCSL constraints. We have also introduced the notion of bounded and periodic schedules. The satisfiability problem for CCSL specifications, which is still an open problem in the general case, is proved to be decidable with regards to bounded and periodic schedules even when using unsafe constraints. This is the first main result. The second result is to use the Maude encoding to perform bounded scheduling, customized simulation with different policies, periodic scheduling, and bounded model-checking.

The notion of periodic schedule seems promising but a bit constraining. In the future, we shall try to provide a more general definition where the behavior might slightly vary between successive periods while still maintaining decidability.

References

1. André, C.: Syntax and semantics of the Clock Constraint Specification Language (CCSL). Research Report 6925, INRIA (2009)
2. Benveniste, A., Caspi, P., Edwards, S.A., Halbwachs, N., Le Guernic, P., de Simone, R.: The synchronous languages 12 years later. Proc. IEEE **91**(1), 64–83 (2003)
3. Carloni, L.P., McMillan, K.L., Sangiovanni-Vincentelli, A.L.: Theory of latency-insensitive design. IEEE Trans. CAD Integr. Circ. Syst. **20**(9), 1059–1076 (2001)
4. Clavel, M., Durán, F., Eker, S., Lincoln, P., Martí-Oliet, N., Meseguer, J., Talcott, C. (eds.): All About Maude. LNCS, vol. 4350. Springer, Heidelberg (2007)
5. Cousot, P.: Abstract interpretation. ACM Comput. Surv. **28**(2), 324–328 (1996)
6. Mallet, F., DeAntoni, J.: TimeSquare: treat your models with logical time. In: Furia, C.A., Nanz, S. (eds.) TOOLS 2012. LNCS, vol. 7304, pp. 34–41. Springer, Heidelberg (2012)
7. Eker, S., Meseguer, J., Sridharanarayanan, A.: The maude LTL model checker. In: 4th WRLA. ENTCS, vol. 71, pp. 162–187. Elsevier (2002)
8. Gascon, R., Mallet, F., DeAntoni, J.: Logical time and temporal logics: comparing UML MARTE/CCSL and PSL. In: Combi, C., Leucker, M., Wolter, F. (eds.) TIME, pp. 141–148. IEEE (2011)
9. Lamport, L.: Time, clocks, and the ordering of events in a distributed system. Commun. ACM **21**(7), 558–565 (1978)
10. Sutre, G., Leroux, J.: Flat counter automata almost everywhere!. In: Peled, D.A., Tsay, Y.-K. (eds.) ATVA 2005. LNCS, vol. 3707, pp. 489–503. Springer, Heidelberg (2005)
11. Mallet, F., André, C., de Simone, R.: CCSL: specifying clock constraints with UML/Marte. Innovations Syst. Softw. Eng. **4**(3), 309–314 (2008)
12. Mallet, F., Millo, J.V., de Simone, R.: Safe CCSL specifications and marked graphs. In: 11th ACM/IEEE International Conference on Formal Methods and Models for Codesign, pp. 157–166. IEEE (2013)
13. Mallet, F., de Simone, R.: Correctness issues on MARTE/CCSL constraints. Sci. Comput. Program. **106**, 78–92 (2015)
14. Potop-Butucaru, D., de Simone, R., Talpin, J.: The Synchronous Hypothesis and Polychronous Languages, chap. 6. CRC Press (2009)
15. Yin, L., Mallet, F., Liu, J.: Verification of MARTE/CCSL time requirements in Promela/SPIN. In: Perseil, I., Breitman, K., Sterritt, R. (eds.) ICECCS, pp. 65–74. IEEE Computer Society (2011)
16. Yu, H., Talpin, J., Besnard, L., Gautier, T., Marchand, H., Guernic, P.L.: Polychronous controller synthesis from MARTE/CCSL timing specifications. In: 9th IEEE/ACM International Conference on Formal Methods and Models for Codesign, MEMOCODE, pp. 21–30. IEEE (2011)

What's Decidable About Parametric Timed Automata?

Étienne André[1,2(✉)]

[1] Université Paris 13, Sorbonne Paris Cité, LIPN, CNRS, UMR 7030,
93430 Villetaneuse, France
etienne.andre@lipn.univ-paris13.fr
[2] École Centrale de Nantes, IRCCyN, CNRS, UMR 6597, Nantes, France

Abstract. Parametric timed automata (PTA) are a powerful formalism to reason, simulate and formally verify critical real-time systems. After two decades of research on PTA, it is now well-understood that any non-trivial problem studied is undecidable for general PTA. We provide here a survey of decision and computation problems for PTA. On the one hand, bounding time, bounding the number of parameters or the domain of the parameters does not (in general) lead to any decidability. On the other hand, restricting the number of clocks, the use of clocks (compared or not with the parameters), and the use of parameters (e.g., used only as upper or lower bounds) leads to decidability of some problems.

1 Introduction

The absence of undesired behaviors in real-time critical systems is of utmost importance in order to ensure the system safety. Model checking aims at formally verifying a model of the system against a correctness property. Timed automata (TA) are a popular formalism to model and verify safety critical systems with timing constraints. TA extend finite state automata with clocks, i.e., real-valued variables increasing linearly [1]. These clocks can be compared with integer constants in guards (sets of linear inequalities that must be satisfied to take a transition) and invariants (sets of linear inequalities that must be satisfied to remain in a location). TA have been widely studied, and several state-of-the-art model checkers (such as UPPAAL [28] or PAT [33]) support TA as an input language.

TA benefit from many interesting decidable properties, such as the emptiness of the accepted language, the reachability of a control state, etc. However, TA also suffer from some limitations. First, they cannot be used to specify and verify systems incompletely specified (i.e., whose timing constants are not known yet), and hence cannot be used in early design phases. Second, verifying a system for a *set* of timing constants usually requires to enumerate all of them one by one if they are supposed to be integer-valued; in addition, TA cannot be used anymore

This work is partially supported by the ANR national research program PACS (ANR-14-CE28-0002).

C. Artho and P.C. Ölveczky (Eds.): FTSCS 2015, CCIS 596, pp. 52–68, 2016.
DOI: 10.1007/978-3-319-29510-7_3

if these constants are rational- or real-valued, and can be taken from a dense interval. Third, robustness in TA often assumes that all guards can be enlarged or shrinked by the same small variation; considering independent variations or considering both enlarging and shrinking was not addressed, and it is actually unclear whether this can be even considered for TA.

Parametric timed automata (PTA) overcome these limitations by allowing the use of parameters (i.e., unknown constants) in guards and invariants [3]. This increased expressive power comes at the price of the undecidability of most interesting problems – at least in the general case.

Tools such as an extension of UPPAAL [24], ROMÉO [29] or IMITATOR [5] take PTA as input formalism. Beyond the usual academic examples (such as variants of train controllers [3,24]), PTA were also used to successfully specify and verify numerous interesting case studies such as the root contention protocol [24], Philip's bounded retransmission protocol [24], a 4-phase handshake protocol [27], the alternating bit protocol [25], an asynchronous circuit commercialized by ST-Microelectronics [17], (non-preemptive) schedulability problems [25], a distributed prospective architecture for the flight control system of the next generation of spacecrafts designed at ASTRIUM Space Transportation [20], an unmanned aerial video system by Thales, and even analysis of music scores [19].

In this paper, we survey decision problems for PTA proposed in the past two decades. On the one hand, bounding time, bounding the number of parameters or the domain of the parameters does not (in general) lead to any decidability. On the other hand, restricting the number of clocks, the use of clocks (compared or not with the parameters), and the use of parameters (e.g., used only as upper or lower bounds) can lead to the decidability of some problems.

Related Surveys. To the best of our knowledge, no survey was dedicated specifically to decision problems for PTA. In addition, recent results in the field in the past two years (e.g., [8,10,16,25,32]) justify the need for a clear picture of these updated (un)decidability results.

Related works include a work by Henzinger *et al.* [21], that is not a survey, but exhibits decidable subclasses of hybrid automata, an extension of timed automata where variables can have (in general) arbitrary rates. Then, Asarin *et al.* proposed a work [9] acting both as a survey and as a contribution paper that studies hybrid automata with "low dimensions", i.e., with few variables. Our survey is also concerned (in Sect. 4) with decidability results for PTA with few variables (i.e., clocks and parameters). Various problems related to the robustness in TA were also surveyed [12].

Outline. In Sect. 2, we propose a unified syntax for PTA, and we define the decision problems that we will consider throughout this manuscript. In Sect. 3, we recall general undecidability for PTA. We then study in Sect. 4 the decidability when restricting the syntax of PTA (number of variables, syntax of the constraints, etc.). We consider specifically in Sect. 5 the subclass of L/U-PTA. We conclude by emphasizing open problems in Sect. 6.

Table 1. Syntax of operators in guards

Operator	Definition
$\sim$	$\{<, \leq, =, \geq, >\}$
$\lessgtr$	$\{\leq, \geq\}$
$<>$	$\{<, >\}$
$\preceq$	$\{<, \leq\}$

2 Parametric Timed Automata and Problems

2.1 Clocks, Parameters and Constraints

Let $\mathbb{Z}$, $\mathbb{N}$, $\mathbb{Q}^+$ and $\mathbb{R}^+$ denote the sets of (possibly negative) integer numbers, (non-negative) natural numbers, non-negative rational numbers, and non-negative real numbers, respectively. In the following, $\mathbb{T}$ denotes the domain of time, and $\mathbb{P}$ the domain of the parameters; these domains will be instantiated with $\mathbb{N}$, $\mathbb{Q}^+$ or $\mathbb{R}^+$ later on. Throughout this survey, let d denote an integer constant in $\mathbb{Z}$, and d^+ denote a non-negative constant in $\mathbb{N}$.

Let us assume a set $X = \{x_1, \ldots, x_H\}$ of *clocks*, that are $\mathbb{T}$-valued variables that evolve at the same rate. Let us assume a set $P = \{p_1, \ldots, p_M\}$ of *parameters*, i.e., unknown constants. A parameter *valuation* v is a function $v : P \to \mathbb{P}$. Throughout this survey, symbols x, x_i denote clocks whereas p, p_i denote parameters.

A parametric linear term is $\sum_{1 \leq i \leq M} \alpha_i p_i + d$, with $\alpha_i \in \mathbb{Z}$; in the following *plt* will denote a parametric linear term.

A (linear) inequality is $x \sim plt$, where x is a clock, *plt* a parametric linear term, and $\sim \in \{<, \leq, =, \geq, >\}$. We give in Table 1 the conventions used throughout this survey concerning comparison operators. A (linear) constraint is a set of linear inequalities.

A simple inequality is either $x \sim p$ or $x \sim d^+$. A simple constraint is a set of simple inequalities.

2.2 A Unified Syntax for Parametric Timed Automata

The syntax of PTA varies a lot in the literature; we give below a definition that includes any definition in the literature. That is, any definition of PTA can be obtained from the following one by adding restrictions such as removing the set of accepting locations, forbidding invariants, restricting the domain of clocks or parameters, simplifying the syntax of the guards and invariants, etc.

Definition 1. *A PTA is a tuple* $\mathsf{A} = (\Sigma, L, l_0, F, X, P, I, E)$, *where:*

- Σ *is a finite set of actions,*
- L *is a finite set of locations,*
- $l_0 \in L$ *is the initial location,*

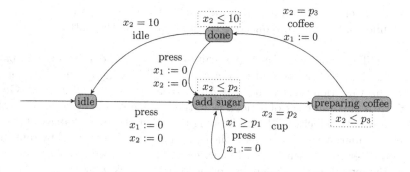

Fig. 1. A coffee machine modeled using a PTA

- $F \subseteq L$ is a set of accepting (or final) locations,
- X is a set of clocks with domain $\mathbb{T} = \mathbb{R}^+$,
- P is a set of parameters with domain $\mathbb{P} = \mathbb{R}^+$,
- I is the invariant, assigning to every $l \in L$ a constraint $I(l)$, and
- E is a set of edges (l, g, a, R, l') where $l, l' \in L$ are the source and destination locations, g is a constraint which is the transition guard, $a \in \Sigma$, and $R \subseteq X$ is a set of clocks to be reset.

Given a PTA A and a parameter valuation v, the *valuation* of A with v, denoted by $v(A)$, is the (non-parametric) TA where each occurrence of p is replaced with $v(p)$.

We say that a PTA is *deterministic* if, for any $l \in L$, for any $a \in \Sigma$, there exists at most one edge $(l, g, a, R, l') \in E$, for some g, R, l'. (Note that it differs from a rather common definition of determinism for TA, that allows two or more outgoing transitions with the same action label provided that the corresponding guards are pairwise disjoint.)

A clock is said to be a *parametric clock* if it is compared with at least one parameter in at least one guard or invariant; otherwise, it is a *non-parametric clock*. This notion is central when studying the decidability of problems for PTA with few clocks and parameters.

Example 1. Consider the coffee machine in Fig. 1, modeled using a PTA with 4 locations, 2 clocks (x_1 and x_2) and 3 parameters (p_1, p_2, p_3). This PTA is deterministic; both clocks x_1 and x_2 are parametric clocks. The machine can initially idle for an arbitrarily long time. Then, whenever the user presses the (unique) button (action press), the PTA enters location "add sugar", resetting both clocks. The machine can remain in this location as long as the invariant ($x_2 \leq p_2$) is satisfied; there, the user can add a dose of sugar by pressing the button (action press), provided the guard ($x_1 \geq p_1$) is satisfied, which resets x_1. That is, the user cannot press twice the button (and hence add two doses of sugar) in a time less than p_1. Then, p_2 time units after the machine left the idle mode, a cup is delivered (action cup), and the coffee is being prepared; eventually, p_2 time units after the machine left the idle mode, the coffee (action coffee) is delivered. Then, after 10 time units, the machine returns to the idle mode – unless a user again requests a coffee by pressing the button.

Semantics. The semantics of a PTA A can be defined as the union over all parameter valuations v of the semantics of $v(A)$. In the following, given $\delta \in \mathbb{R}^+$, $w+\delta$ denotes the valuation such that $(w + \delta)(x) = w(x) + \delta$, for all $x \in X$. Given $R \subseteq X$, we define the *reset* of a clock valuation w, denoted by $[w]_R$, as the valuation resetting the clocks in R, and keeping the other clocks unchanged. Given a parameter valuation v, $v(C)$ denotes the constraint over X obtained by replacing each parameter p in C with $v(p)$. Likewise, given a clock valuation w, $w(v(C))$ denotes the expression obtained by replacing each clock x in $v(C)$ with $w(x)$. We use the notation $w|v \models C$ to indicate that $w(v(C))$ evaluates to true.

Definition 2 (Semantics of a TA). *Given a PTA* $A = (\Sigma, L, l_0, X, P, I, E)$, *and a parameter valuation* v, *the semantics of* $v(A)$ *is given by the timed transition system* $(Q, q_0, \Rightarrow)$, *with*

- $Q = \{(l, w) \in L \times \mathbb{R}^{+H} \mid v|w \models I(l)\}$,
- $q_0 = (l_0, X = 0)$,
- $((l, w), e, (l', w')) \in \Rightarrow$ *if* $\exists w'' : (l, w) \overset{e}{\to} (l', w'') \overset{\delta}{\to} (l', w')$, *with:*
  - *discrete transitions:* $(l, w) \overset{e}{\to} (l', w')$, *if* $(l, w), (l', w') \in Q$, *there exists* $e = (l, g, a, R, l') \in E$, $w' = [w]_R$, *and* $v|w \models g$;
  - *delay transitions:* $(l, w) \overset{\delta}{\to} (l, w+\delta)$, *with* $\delta \in \mathbb{R}^+$, *if* $\forall \delta' \in [0, \delta], (l, w+\delta') \in Q$.

A run of a TA is an alternating sequence of states of Q and edges of the form $(l_0, w_0) \overset{e_0}{\Rightarrow} (l_1, w_1) \overset{e_1}{\Rightarrow} \cdots \overset{e_{m-1}}{\Rightarrow} (l_m, w_m)$, such that for all $i = 0, \ldots, m - 1$, $e_i \in E$, and $((l_i, w_i), e_i, (l_{i+1}, w_{i+1})) \in \Rightarrow$.

Note that time elapsing can still be a 0-duration ($d \in \mathbb{R}^+$ allows $d = 0$); in other words, TA allow to model Zeno behaviors, i.e., an infinite number of actions within a 0-time or, more generally, a finite time (see e.g., [34]). The accepted timed language is the set of timed words (alternating sequences of actions and time elapsing) associated with an accepting run, i.e., a run ending in a location of F (or, in some works, passing infinitely often by a location in F). Note that some works make a difference between finite and infinite runs. The untimed language of a TA is the timed language projected onto the actions. The set of traces (or trace set) is the set of accepting runs projected onto the locations and actions, i.e., a set of alternating locations and actions.

A *symbolic semantics* is also defined for PTA as a parametric zone graph [4, 24, 25], where a symbolic state is made of a discrete part (the current location) and a symbolic, continuous part (a set of diagonal constraints, i.e., $x_i - x_j \sim plt$, sometimes allowing disjunctions).

Simple PTA. We defined *simple PTA* as the subclass of PTA where guards and invariants are simple constraints. We define this class to show that, even in this restricted situation, all non-trivial problems are undecidable (Sect. 3).

Variants of the PTA Syntax. PTA were first defined in the seminal paper [3] using a set of accepting locations. This is similar to timed automata [1]. *Timed Safety Automata* (TSA) were introduced later by removing the final states, but adding invariants to locations [23]; many subsequent papers then refer to timed safety automata as simply "timed automata". In contrast, timed automata with accepting locations are often referred to as timed Büchi automata (TBA). The timed expressive power of TSA is strictly less than that of TBA [22].

The syntax of PTA differs in most of the papers in the literature. Concerning guards and invariants, in work [3] (resp. [30]), guards (resp. guards and invariants) are conjunctions of inequalities of the form $x \sim p$. In works [13,24], guards are conjunctions of inequalities of the form $x_i - x_j \preceq plt \cup \{\infty\}$; in work [24] invariants have the same form as guards (invariants are not considered in work [13]). In work [18], guards and invariants are all open, i.e., of the form $x <> p$ or $x <> d^+$. In work [25], guards and invariants are conjunctions of inequalities of the form $x \sim plt$, and invariants can only bound clocks from above (i.e., $x \preceq plt$). In work [10], guards are conjunctions of inequalities of the form $x \sim p$ and invariants can only bound clocks from above (i.e., $x \preceq p$). In work [8], guards and invariants are conjunctions of inequalities of the form $x \sim p + d$, $x \sim d^+$ or $p \sim d$ (although the proofs of undecidability only need inequalities of the form $x \sim p$ or $x \sim d^+$).

A set of accepting locations is considered in several previous works [3,10,13], but only one [13] is interested in infinite accepting runs, i.e., runs that pass infinitely often by an accepting location; hence this latter work considers what could be referred to as parametric timed Büchi automata. In contrast, other previous approaches [4,8,18,24,25] consider parametric timed safety automata (i.e., without accepting locations).

Expressiveness. A comparison of the expressiveness of these different syntactic models remains to be done. Whereas it is likely that allowing constraints of the form $x \sim plt$ may be simulated using constraints of the form $x \sim p$ (perhaps adding additional locations, clocks and parameters), the expressiveness may differ when adding a set of accepting locations (just as the timed expressive power of TSA is strictly less than that of TBA [22]). In fact, the expressiveness of a PTA was not even defined; we believe that shall be studied in the future.

2.3 Decision and Computation Problems

We follow here the presentation of a previous approach [25]. Given a class of decision problems $\mathcal{P}$ (reachability, unavoidability, etc.), let us define the $\mathcal{P}$-emptiness, the $\mathcal{P}$-universality and the $\mathcal{P}$-finiteness. Given a PTA A and an instance ϕ of $\mathcal{P}$, the $\mathcal{P}$-emptiness, $\mathcal{P}$-universality and $\mathcal{P}$-finiteness ask whether the set of parameter valuations v such that $v(A)$ satisfies ϕ is empty, is equal to $\mathbb{P}^{|P|}$ and is finite, respectively.

In this survey, we mainly focus on reachability and unavoidability properties, and call them EF and AF respectively.[1] We will also mention the EG property,

---

[1] The names EF, AF, EG, AG were first used for PTA by Jovanović *et al.* [25], and come from the CTL syntax.

that checks whether there exists a maximal run along which the locations remain in a subset G of the locations, and the AG property that checks whether the locations remain in G for all runs.[2]

Additionally, we will survey the language (resp. trace) preservation (emptiness) problem [8]: given a PTA A and a parameter valuation v, does there exist another valuation $v' \neq v$ such that the untimed languages (resp. sets of traces) of $v(A)$ and $v'(A)$ are the same?

We finally define the $\mathcal{P}$-synthesis problem: Given a PTA A and an instance ϕ of $\mathcal{P}$, compute the parameter valuations such that $v(A)$ satisfies ϕ.

Example 2. Let us exemplify some decision and computation problems for the PTA in Fig. 1. Assume the unique target location is "done", i.e., $G = \{done\}$. EF-emptiness asks whether at least one parameter valuation can reach location "done" for some run; this is true (e.g., $p_1 = 1$, $p_2 = 2$, $p_3 = 3$). EF-universality asks whether all parameter valuations can reach location "done" for some run; this is false (no parameter valuation such that $p_2 > p_3$ can reach "done"). AF-emptiness asks whether at least one parameter valuation can reach location "done" for all runs; this is true (e.g., $p_1 = 1$, $p_2 = 2$, $p_3 = 3$). EF-synthesis consists in synthesizing all valuations for which a run reaches location "done"; the resulting set of valuations is $0 \leq p_2 \leq p_3 \leq 10 \wedge p_1 \geq 0$.

3   Almost Everything is Undecidable for Simple PTA

In this entire section, we consider simple PTA without restriction on the number of clocks and parameters. In that situation, all non-trivial problems studied in the literature are undecidable, with the exception of the membership problem (that asks whether the language of a valuated PTA is empty) – which is rather a problem for TA. By non-trivial, we mean requiring a semantic analysis, and not, e.g., a sole analysis of the syntax of the PTA (e.g., "is the number of clocks even", or any problem defined in Sect. 2.3 by setting $G = L$).

We also survey that bounding time (Sect. 3.3) or the parameter domain for rational-valued parameters (Sect. 3.4) preserves the undecidability. However, we will show in Sect. 4 that bounding the number of clocks and/or parameters brings decidability.

All proofs of undecidability reduce from either the halting problem, or the boundedness problem, of a 2-counter machine, known to be undecidable [31].

3.1   Decidability of the Membership

In the seminal PTA paper [3], the membership problem for PTA is defined as follows: given a PTA A and a parameter valuation v, is the language of $v(A)$ empty? The membership problem is not strictly speaking a problem for PTA, but rather for TA, since it considers a valuated PTA. As a consequence,

---

[2] Note that EF-, AF-, EG-, and AG-emptiness are equivalent to AG-, EG-, AF-, EF-universality, respectively.

the decidability of this problem only relies on known results for TA [1]: the membership problem is decidable (and PSPACE-complete) for PTA over discrete time ($\mathbb{T} = \mathbb{N}$ and $\mathbb{P} = \mathbb{N}$), over dense time with integer-valued parameters ($\mathbb{T} = \mathbb{R}^+$ and $\mathbb{P} = \mathbb{N}$), and over dense time with rational-valued parameters ($\mathbb{T} = \mathbb{R}^+$ and $\mathbb{P} = \mathbb{Q}$). However, it becomes undecidable with real-valued (in fact irrational) parameters [30].

3.2 General Undecidable Problems

EF-, AF, EG, AG-emptiness. The seminal paper on PTA [3] showed that the EF-emptiness problem is undecidable for PTA, both for discrete time, and for dense-time (real-valued clocks and real-valued parameters). Although not explicitly stated in that paper, the proof of undecidability, that consists in reducing from the halting problem of a 2-counter machine, also works for real-valued clocks with integer-valued parameters.

It was then proved that the AF-emptiness is undecidable for L/U-PTA (a subclass of PTA, see Sect. 5), and hence for PTA as well [25]. Again, the proof of undecidability consists in reducing from the halting problem of a 2-counter machine.

AG- and EG-emptiness are also undecidable [7].

Language and trace preservation problems. Both language preservation and trace preservation problems are undecidable for simple PTA [8]. The *continuous* (or robust) versions of those problems additionally require that the language (resp. set of traces) is preserved under any intermediary valuation of the form $\lambda \cdot v + (1 - \lambda) \cdot v'$, for $\lambda \in [0, 1]$ (with the classical definition of addition and scalar multiplication). These problems are also undecidable for simple PTA.

The language preservation problems and its continuous version are undecidable for a PTA with at least 4 parametric clocks. The trace preservation and its continuous version require either an *unbounded* number of non-parametric clocks and diagonal constraints (that go beyond the usual syntax of PTA), or an *unbounded* number of parametric clocks. This is due to the fact that the proof encodes the 2-counter machine with a fixed number of locations, which thus requires to encode each location with a different clock. It remains open whether this problem is undecidable for a bounded number of clocks.

3.3 Bounding Time

Bounded-time model checking consists in checking a property *within a bounded time domain*. Undecidable problems might become decidable in this situation, or be of a lower complexity. For example, time-bounded reachability becomes decidable for a special subclass of hybrid automata with monotonic rates [14].

In contrast, the EF-emptiness problem remains undecidable for (general) PTA over bounded, dense time [26, Theorem 3.4].

This said, we emphasize that (quite trivially) model checking *discrete-time* PTA over bounded-time would become decidable. (This remains to be shown formally though.)

3.4 Bounding the Parameter Domain

Bounding the parameter domain consists in setting a minimal and a maximal bound on the possible parameter valuations of a PTA.

For integer parameters, any problem for a PTA over a bounded parameter domain is decidable iff the corresponding problem is decidable for a TA. In fact, the $\mathcal{P}$-emptiness problem for PTA with bounded integer is PSPACE-complete for any class of problems $\mathcal{P}$ that is PSPACE-complete for TA [25]. Indeed, it suffices to enumerate all parameter valuations, of which there is a finite number. As a consequence, EF-, AF-, EG-, AG-emptiness are all decidable; and so are language and trace preservation. A symbolic method was proposed to compute EF- and AF-synthesis [25]; experiments showed that this symbolic computation is faster than an exhaustive enumeration (using UPPAAL).

For rational-valued parameters, the EF-emptiness problems is undecidable for a single parameter in $[1, 2]$ [30]. EG- and AG-emptiness [7], and language and trace preservation [8] are also undecidable for a single parameter in $[0, 1]$.

4   Bounding the Numbers of Clocks and Parameters

4.1 EF-Emptiness

Since the seminal paper on PTA [3], the decidability of the EF-emptiness problem was studied in various settings, by bounding the number of parametric clocks, of non-parametric clocks, and of parameters. The syntax was also restrained. We summarize these results in Table 2 (partially inspired by a similar table in a previous work [18], improved by adding more dimensions, and more recent results). The open question of the syntax expressiveness requires to consider a multi-dimensional table: we need to consider not only the number of clocks and parameters, but also the syntax allowed in guards and invariants. For example, a recent paper [16] improves the complexity of the seminal PTA papers [3] (NEXPTIME-complete instead of non-elementary) over $\mathbb{N}$ for 1 clock, but requires non-strict inequalities, and uses invariants; it is hence unclear whether the result of the seminal paper [3] is really subsumed by that more recent paper [16].

Let us extract the most important results out of Table 2. The decidability is clearly impacted by the number of parametric clocks. First, let us consider PTA with a single parametric clock: the EF-emptiness problem is decidable over discrete time with arbitrarily many non-parametric clocks (NEXPTIME-complete when only large inequalities are used [16], and non-elementary otherwise [3]). It is NP-complete over dense time with no non-parametric clock [30]. It is open over dense time with two non-parametric clocks, and undecidable with three non-parametric clocks [30]; note that this problem is decidable over discrete time [3,16], which exhibits a difference between dense and discrete time [30].

Second, let us consider PTA with two parametric clocks: the EF-emptiness problem is decidable over discrete time with a single parameter [16]; this result is claimed in the same paper to extend to dense time with integer-valued parameters. Any other case with two parametric clocks remains open. Third, the EF-emptiness problem is undecidable in all settings with three (or more) parametric

Table 2. Decidability of the EF-emptiness problem for general PTA

T	P	Guards	Invariants	P-clocks	NP-clocks	Params	Decidability	Main ref.
N	N	$x \lessgtr p|d^+$		1	any	any	NEXPTIME-compl.	[16]
N	N	$x \in I$	None	1	any	any	non-elementary	[3]
N	N	$x \lessgtr p|d^+$		2	any	1	PSPACE^{NEXP}-hard	[16]
N	N	any		2	any	>1	open	
N	N	$x \sim p|d$	None	3	0	1	undecidable	[10]
N	N	$x <> p$		any	any	any	open	
N	N bounded	$x \sim plt$	$x \preceq plt$	any	any	any	decidable	[25] (conseq.)
R$^+$	N	$x \in I$	None	1	0	any	non-elementary	[3] (conseq.)
R$^+$	N	$x \sim p|d$	$x \preceq p$	1	any	any	NEXPTIME	[10]
R$^+$	N	$x \lessgtr p|d^+$		2	any	1	PSPACE^{NEXP}-hard	[16]
R$^+$	N	any		2	any	>1	open	
R$^+$	N	$x \sim p|d$	None	3	0	1	undecidable	[10]
R$^+$	N	$x \sim plt$	$x \preceq plt$	3	0	2	undecidable	[25]
Q$^+$/R$^+$	N	$x <> p$		any	any	any	open	
R$^+$	N bounded	$x \sim plt$	$x \preceq plt$	any	any	any	PSPACE-complete	[25]
R$^+$	R$^+$	$x \in I$	None	1	0	any	non-elementary	[3]
R$^+$	Q$^+$	$x \sim p|d$		1	0	any	NP-complete	[30]
R$^+$	Q$^+$	$x \sim p|d$		1	0	bounded	PTIME	[30]
R$^+$	R$^+$	any		1	1 or 2	1	open	
R$^+$	Q$^+$	$x \sim p|d$		1	3	1	undecidable	[30]
R$^+$	R$^+$	any		2	any	any	open	
R$^+$	R$^+$	$x \in I$	None	3	0	6	undecidable	[3]
R$^+$	Q$^+$	$x \sim p|d$		3	0	1	undecidable	[30]
R$^+$	R$^+_{[1;2]}$	$x \sim p|d$		1	3	1	undecidable	[30]
R$^+$	R$^+_{[1;2]}$	$x \sim p|d$		3	0	1	undecidable	[30]
Q$^+$/R$^+$	Q$^+$/R$^+$	$x <> p$		<2	<3	<2	open	
Q$^+$/R$^+$	Q$^+$/R$^+$	$x <> p$		2	3	2	undecidable	[18]

clocks. Finally, using only strict inequalities, the EF-emptiness is undecidable over dense time for two parametric clocks, three non-parametric clocks and two parameters [18]; this situation was not considered over discrete time.

4.2 Language and Trace Preservation

The language- and trace-preservation problems are decidable for deterministic PTA with a single clock, and with linear parameter constraints allowed in guards and invariants, i.e., of the form $x \sim plt$ or $plt \sim 0$ [8]. A procedure to compute parameter valuations with the same trace set as a given valuation is proposed (close to the "inverse method" [4]), that is complete for deterministic PTA, and terminates in the case of a single clock [8].

4.3 Parametric Model Checking

Parametric model checking was addressed in different settings: verifying a non-parametric model against a parametric formula, or a parametric model against a non-parametric formula, or a parametric model against a parametric formula.

Non-parametric Model/Parametric Formula. An extension of LTL with parameters in the formula ("PLTL") was studied [2]. When only parametric "always" modalities are allowed of the form "$\leq p$", checking emptiness of the valuation set is PSPACE-complete. The solution to the synthesis problem is doubly exponential in the number of parameters. However, when allowing equality in PLTL, the emptiness problem becomes undecidable [2].

Parametric Model/Non-parametric Formula. It is shown that model checking PTA with the (non-parametric) logic MTL is undecidable, even with a single clock and a single parameter, and even when the PTA is deterministic [32]. This negative result comes in contrast to the decidability of the EF-emptiness problem for one-clock PTA. Note that the proof of undecidability requires the parameters to be rational-valued (integer-valued parameters are not sufficient – and this latter case can hence be considered as open).

Parametric Model/Parametric Formula. Model checking a PTA over discrete-time with a single parametric clock against a PTCTL formula (a parametric version of TCTL) is decidable, provided the formula does not use equality constraints; otherwise the problem becomes undecidable [15].

5   The Disappointing Class of L/U-PTA

Lower-bound/upper-bound parametric timed automata (L/U-PTA) restrict the use of parameters in the model [24]. A parameter is said to be an *upper-bound parameter* if, whenever it is compared with a clock, it is compared as an upper bound, i.e., it only appears in inequalities of the form $x \preceq p$. Conversely, a parameter is a *lower-bound parameter* if it is only compared with clocks as a lower bound, i.e., of the form $p \preceq x$.

An L/U-PTA is a PTA where the set of parameters is partitioned into upper-bound parameters and lower-bound parameters. Two additional subclasses were introduced later [13]: L-PTA (resp. U-PTA) are PTA with only lower-bound (resp. upper-bound) parameters.

Example 3. Consider again the coffee machine in Fig. 1, modeled using a PTA A. This PTA is not an L/U-PTA; indeed, the guard $x_2 = p_2$ (resp. $x_2 = p_3$) makes p_2 (resp. p_3) be compared with clocks both as a lower-bound and as an upper-bound. (Recall that = stands for $\leq$ and $\geq$.)

However, if one replaces $x_2 = p_2$ with $x_2 \leq p_2$ and one replaces $x_2 = p_3$ with $x_2 \leq p_3$, then A becomes an L/U-PTA with lower-bound parameter p_1 and upper-bound parameters $\{p_2, p_3\}$. Note that equalities are not forbidden in L/U-PTA (e.g., $x_1 = 10$), but only equalities involving parameters.

Several case studies fit into the class of L/U-PTA: the root contention protocol, the bounded retransmission protocol and the Fischer mutual exclusion protocol are all modeled with L/U-PTA in the paper introducing L/U-PTA [24]; in two works [24,27], both the Fischer mutual exclusion protocol and a producer-consumer are verified using L/U-PTA. Interestingly, the two case studies of the seminal paper on PTA [3] (viz., a toy railroad crossing model and a model of

Fischer mutual exclusion protocol) are also L/U-PTA. In addition, most models of asynchronous circuits with bi-bounded delays (i.e., where each delay between the change of an input signal and the change of the corresponding output is a parametric interval) can be modeled using L/U-PTA.

5.1 Decidability Results

The first (and main) positive result for L/U-PTA is the decidability of the EF-emptiness problem [24]. L/U-PTA benefit from the following interesting property: increasing the value of an upper-bound parameter or decreasing the value of a lower-bound parameter necessarily relaxes the guards and invariants, and hence can only add behaviors. Hence, checking the EF-emptiness of an L/U-PTA can be achieved by replacing all lower-bound parameters with 0, and all upper-bound parameters with ∞; this yields a non-parametric TA, for which emptiness is PSPACE [1]. This procedure is not only sound but also complete.

Further decidability results are exhibited [13], for infinite runs acceptance properties, i.e., where a location is met infinitely often (to which we refer hereafter as BüEF). Note that, in contrast to the first paper on L/U-PTA [24] where the parameters are valued with non-negative reals, the results this later work [13] consider integer-valued parameters (though time is dense, i.e., clocks are real-valued). It is shown in this later work [13] that emptiness, universality, finiteness of the valuation set are PSPACE-complete for infinite runs acceptance properties. Remark that the decidability of the BüEF-finiteness is due to the integerness of the parameters; in short, a sufficient bound is computed on the parameters, and then valuations smaller or equal to this bound are enumerated, which would not be feasible for real-valued parameters.

A parametric extension of the dense-time linear temporal logic $MITL_{0,\infty}$ (denoted "$PMITL_{0,\infty}$") is proposed [13]; when parameters are used only as lower or upper bound in the formula (to which we refer as $L/U\text{-}PMITL_{0,\infty}$), satisfiability and model checking are PSPACE-complete; this is obtained by translating the formula into an L/U-automaton and checking an infinite acceptance property.

5.2 Undecidability Results

The first undecidability results for L/U-PTA are shown in works by Bozelli *et al.* [13]: the *constrained* EF-emptiness problem and constrained EF-universality problem (for infinite runs acceptance properties) are undecidable for L/U-PTA. By constrained it is meant that some parameters of the L/U-PTA can be constrained by an initial linear constraint, e.g., $p_1 \leq 2 \times p_2 + p_3$. Indeed, using linear constraints, one can constrain an upper-bound parameter to be equal to a lower-bound parameter, and hence build a 2-counter machine using an L/U-PTA. However, when no upper-bound parameter is compared to a lower-bound parameter (i.e., when no initial linear inequality contains both an upper-bound and a lower-bound parameter), these two problems retrieve decidability [13].

A second negative result is shown by Jovanović *et al.* [25]: the AF-emptiness problem is undecidable for L/U-PTA. This is achieved by a reduction from a

Table 3. Decision problems for L/U-PTA

Problem	$\mathbb{P}$	Complexity	Main ref.
EF-emptiness	$\mathbb{R}^+$	PSPACE	[24]
AG-emptiness	$\mathbb{R}^+$	PSPACE	[24]
AF-emptiness	$\mathbb{R}^+$	undecidable	[25]
EG-emptiness	$\mathbb{R}^+$	open	
BüEF-emptiness	$\mathbb{N}$	PSPACE-complete	[13]
BüEF-universality	$\mathbb{N}$	PSPACE-complete	[13]
BüEF-finiteness	$\mathbb{N}$	PSPACE-complete	[13]
constrained BüEF-emptiness	$\mathbb{N}$	undecidable	[13]
constrained BüEF-universality	$\mathbb{N}$	undecidable	[13]
L/U-constrained BüEF-emptiness	$\mathbb{N}$	PSPACE-complete	[13]
L/U-constrained BüEF-universality	$\mathbb{N}$	PSPACE-complete	[13]
Language preservation	$\mathbb{N}$	undecidable	[8]
Language preservation	$\mathbb{R}^+$	undecidable	[8]
L/U-PMITL$_{0,\infty}$-emptiness	$\mathbb{N}$	PSPACE-complete	[13]
L/U-PMITL$_{0,\infty}$-universality	$\mathbb{N}$	PSPACE-complete	[13]

2-counter machine where a lower-bound parameter is equal to an upper-bound parameter iff AF holds. This restricts again the use of L/U-PTA, as AF is essential to show that all possible runs of a system eventually reach a (good) state.

Then, it is shown that the language preservation problem is undecidable for L/U-PTA [8]. Again, this is achieved by a reduction from a 2-counter machine where a lower-bound parameter is equal to an upper-bound parameter iff the language is preserved.

We summarize in Table 3 decision problems for L/U-PTA.

5.3   Intractability of the Synthesis

The most disappointing result concerning L/U-PTA is shown by Jovanović *et al.* [25]: if it can be computed, the solution to the EF-synthesis problem for L/U-PTA cannot be represented using a formalism for which the emptiness of the intersection with equality constraints is decidable. The proof relies on the undecidability of the constrained emptiness problem of Bozelli *et al.* [13]. A very annoying consequence is that such a solution cannot be represented as a finite union of polyhedra (since the emptiness of the intersection with equality constraints is decidable).

5.4   Two Open Classes: L-PTA and U-PTA

L-PTA and U-PTA (introduced by Bozelli *et al.* [13]) are very open classes, in the sense that to the best of our knowledge, no result known to be decidable for L-PTA (or U-PTA) was shown undecidable for L/U-PTA (and is hence either decidable or open). Conversely, and even stronger, no result known to be undecidable for L/U-PTA was shown decidable for L-PTA (or U-PTA) – and is always open.

To summarize, the AF-emptiness, the language- and trace-preservation problems, are all undecidable for L/U-PTA, but remain open for L-PTA and U-PTA.

In fact, the only result that could be described as a difference between L/U-PTA and U-PTA (resp. L-PTA) is as follows [8]: the language-preservation problem is decidable for deterministic U-PTA (resp. deterministic L-PTA) with a single integer-valued parameter, whereas this problem is proved undecidable for L/U-PTA. However, one could argue that an L/U-PTA with a single parameter is necessarily either an L-PTA (if the unique parameter is a lower-bound parameter) or a U-PTA (otherwise).

Synthesis. The synthesis for L-PTA and U-PTA was not much addressed, with the exception of integer-valued parameters: in that case, it is possible to synthesize the solution to the BüEF-synthesis problem in the form of a union of linear constraints doubly exponential in the number of parameters [13]. The authors note that it remains open whether one can construct a linear constraint with a single exponential blow-up. This result does not extend in a straightforward manner to rational-valued parameters, as the technique of Bozelli *et al.* [13] (for U-PTA) requires the computation of a sufficient upper bound, and then an exhaustive enumeration of parameters below this bound.

6   Open Questions

Syntax and Expressiveness. A first perspective is to compare the expressiveness of the various syntaxes of PTA defined in the literature. This implies to first agree on a definition of the expressiveness of a PTA. We propose as a perspective two possible definitions: either the union over all parameter valuations of the timed language, or the union over all parameter valuations of the untimed language. Comparing the expressiveness of the syntaxes in the literature would reduce the number of dimensions for the various decidability results of the EF-emptiness problem studied in Table 2.

Decidability Problems. A main open problem is the decidability of PTA with two clocks, that was only studied with a single parameter and over discrete time [16]. Studying further the EG-, AF- and AG-emptiness problems for few clocks and parameters (as it was quite extensively done for EF-emptiness) remains to be done too, although the theoretical or practical interest may be somehow debatable. More interesting (and promising) are the two open classes of L-PTA and U-PTA. These classes are non-trivial, and relate to the robust analysis of TA: most robustness problems (see [12]) consider an enlargement of all guards by (usually) the same constant factor, whereas U-PTA allow to enlarge or decrease *some* of the upper-bound guards by a possibly different parameter, which gives an orthogonal definition of robustness. The language preservation problem remains open for U-PTA [8], and the question of the synthesis is also challenging.

Also note that formalisms close to PTA (not surveyed here for lack of space) include subclasses of hybrid automata [14] and parametric interrupt timed automata [11], that benefit from promising decidability results.

Synthesis. Whereas decision problems (surveyed in this document) were much studied, little interest has been dedicated to the synthesis of parameters, which should however be a main practical challenge. Despite undecidability (in general [3]) or intractability (for L/U-PTA [25]), semi-algorithms or approximated procedures could be devised; SMT-based techniques [27], or the integer hull approximation [6,25] can serve as a basis for future works.

Are PTA a Useless Formalism? Despite many undecidability problems, PTA were often used to model and verify various case studies (see Sect. 1). This can be seen as a paradox considering the numerous undecidability results PTA suffer from. In fact, as all of the aforementioned analyses terminate, it is challenging to understand why, and perhaps to exhibit further classes for which the problems considered in this survey become decidable.

Acknowledgements. This manuscript benefited from discussions with Didier Lime, Nicolas Markey, and Olivier H. Roux.

References

1. Alur, R., Dill, D.L.: A theory of timed automata. Theoret. Comput. Sci. **126**(2), 183–235 (1994)
2. Alur, R., Etessami, K., La Torre, S., Peled, D.: Parametric temporal logic for "model measuring". ACM Trans. Comput. Logic **2**(3), 388–407 (2001)
3. Alur, R., Henzinger, T.A., Vardi, M.Y.: Parametric real-time reasoning. In: STOC, pp. 592–601. ACM (1993)
4. André, É., Chatain, Th., Encrenaz, E., Fribourg, L.: An inverse method for parametric timed automata. IJFCS **20**(5), 819–836 (2009)
5. André, É., Fribourg, L., Kühne, U., Soulat, R.: IMITATOR 2.5: a tool for analyzing robustness in scheduling problems. In: Giannakopoulou, D., Méry, D. (eds.) FM 2012. LNCS, vol. 7436, pp. 33–36. Springer, Heidelberg (2012)
6. André, É., Lime, D., Roux, O.H.: Integer-complete synthesis for bounded parametric timed automata. In: Bojanczyk, M., Lasota, S., Potapov, I. (eds.) RP 2015. LNCS, vol. 9328, pp. 7–19. Springer, Heidelberg (2015). doi:10.1007/978-3-319-24537-9_2
7. André, É., Lime, D., Roux, O.H.: Decision problems for parametric timed automata (submitted, 2016)
8. André, É., Markey, N.: Language preservation problems in parametric timed automata. In: Sankaranarayanan, S., Vicario, E. (eds.) FORMATS 2015. LNCS, vol. 9268, pp. 27–43. Springer, Heidelberg (2015)
9. Asarin, E., Mysore, V., Pnueli, A., Schneider, G.: Low dimensional hybrid systems – decidable, undecidable, don't know. Inf. Comput. **211**, 138–159 (2012)

10. Beneš, N., Bezděk, P., Larsen, K.G., Srba, J.: Language emptiness of continuous-time parametric timed automata. In: Halldórsson, M.M., Iwama, K., Kobayashi, N., Speckmann, B. (eds.) ICALP 2015, Part II. LNCS, vol. 9135, pp. 69–81. Springer, Heidelberg (2015)
11. Bérard, B., Haddad, S., Jovanović, A., Lime, D.: Parametric interrupt timed automata. In: Abdulla, P.A., Potapov, I. (eds.) RP 2013. LNCS, vol. 8169, pp. 59–69. Springer, Heidelberg (2013)
12. Bouyer, P., Markey, N., Sankur, O.: Robustness in timed automata. In: Abdulla, P.A., Potapov, I. (eds.) RP 2013. LNCS, vol. 8169, pp. 1–18. Springer, Heidelberg (2013)
13. Bozzelli, L., La Torre, S.: Decision problems for lower/upper bound parametric timed automata. Formal Meth. Syst. Des. **35**(2), 121–151 (2009)
14. Brihaye, T., Doyen, L., Geeraerts, G., Ouaknine, J., Raskin, J.-F., Worrell, J.: Time-bounded reachability for monotonic hybrid automata: complexity and fixed points. In: Van Hung, D., Ogawa, M. (eds.) ATVA 2013. LNCS, vol. 8172, pp. 55–70. Springer, Heidelberg (2013)
15. Bruyère, V., Raskin, J.F.: Real-time model-checking: parameters everywhere. Logical Meth. Comput. Sci. **3**(1: 7), 1–30 (2007)
16. Bundala, D., Ouaknine, J.: Advances in parametric real-time reasoning. In: Csuhaj-Varjú, E., Dietzfelbinger, M., Ésik, Z. (eds.) MFCS 2014, Part I. LNCS, vol. 8634, pp. 123–134. Springer, Heidelberg (2014)
17. Chevallier, R., Encrenaz-Tiphène, E., Fribourg, L., Xu, W.: Timed verification of the generic architecture of a memory circuit using parametric timed automata. Formal Meth. Syst. Des. **34**(1), 59–81 (2009)
18. Doyen, L.: Robust parametric reachability for timed automata. Inf. Process. Lett. **102**(5), 208–213 (2007)
19. Fanchon, L., Jacquemard, F.: Formal timing analysis of mixed music scores. In: International Computer Music Conference (2013)
20. Fribourg, L., Lesens, D., Moro, P., Soulat, R.: Robustness analysis for scheduling problems using the inverse method. In: TIME, pp. 73–80. IEEE Computer Society Press (2012)
21. Henzinger, T.A., Kopke, P.W., Puri, A., Varaiya, P.: What's decidable about hybrid automata? J. Comput. Syst. Sci. **57**(1), 94–124 (1998)
22. Henzinger, T.A., Kopke, P.W., Wong-Toi, H.: The expressive power of clocks. In: Fülöp, Z. (ed.) ICALP 1995. LNCS, vol. 944, pp. 417–428. Springer, Heidelberg (1995)
23. Henzinger, T.A., Nicollin, X., Sifakis, J., Yovine, S.: Symbolic model checking for real-time systems. Inf. Comput. **111**(2), 193–244 (1994)
24. Hune, T., Romijn, J., Stoelinga, M., Vaandrager, F.W.: Linear parametric model checking of timed automata. JLAP **52–53**, 183–220 (2002)
25. Jovanović, A., Lime, D., Roux, O.H.: Integer parameter synthesis for timed automata. IEEE Trans. Softw. Eng. **41**(5), 445–461 (2015)
26. Jovanović, A.: Parametric verification of timed systems. Ph.D. thesis , École Centrale Nantes, France (2013)
27. Knapik, M., Penczek, W.: Bounded model checking for parametric timed automata. In: Jensen, K., Donatelli, S., Kleijn, J. (eds.) ToPNoC V. LNCS, vol. 6900, pp. 141–159. Springer, Heidelberg (2012)
28. Larsen, K.G., Pettersson, P., Yi, W.: UPPAAL in a nutshell. Int. J. Softw. Tools Technol. Transfer **1**(1–2), 134–152 (1997)

29. Lime, D., Roux, O.H., Seidner, C., Traonouez, L.-M.: Romeo: a parametric model-checker for petri nets with stopwatches. In: Kowalewski, S., Philippou, A. (eds.) TACAS 2009. LNCS, vol. 5505, pp. 54–57. Springer, Heidelberg (2009)

30. Miller, J.S.: Decidability and complexity results for timed automata and semi-linear hybrid automata. In: Lynch, N.A., Krogh, B.H. (eds.) HSCC 2000. LNCS, vol. 1790, p. 296. Springer, Heidelberg (2000)

31. Minsky, M.L.: Computation: Finite and Infinite Machines. Prentice-Hall Inc., Englewood Cliffs (1967)

32. Quaas, K.: MTL-model checking of one-clock parametric timed automata is undecidable. SynCoP. EPTCS **145**, 5–17 (2014)

33. Sun, J., Liu, Y., Dong, J.S., Pang, J.: PAT: towards flexible verification under fairness. In: Bouajjani, A., Maler, O. (eds.) CAV 2009. LNCS, vol. 5643, pp. 709–714. Springer, Heidelberg (2009)

34. Wang, T., Sun, J., Wang, X., Liu, Y., Si, Y., Dong, J.S., Yang, X., Li, X.: A systematic study on explicit-state non-zenoness checking for timed automata. IEEE Trans. Softw. Eng. **41**(1), 3–18 (2015)

Compositional Predictability Analysis of Mixed Critical Real Time Systems

Abdeldjalil Boudjadar[1]([✉]), Juergen Dingel[2],
Boris Madzar[2], and Jin Hyun Kim[3]

[1] Linköping University, Linköping, Sweden
abdeldjalil.boudjadar@liu.se
[2] Queen's University, Kingston, Canada
[3] INRIA, Rennes, France

Abstract. This paper introduces a compositional framework for analyzing the predictability of component-based embedded real-time systems. The framework utilizes automated analysis of tasks and communication archittdepicts the structureectures to provide insight on the schedulability and data flow. The communicating tasks are gathered within components, making the system architecture hierarchical. The system model is given by a set of Parameterized Stopwatch Automata modeling the behavior and dependency of tasks, while we use Uppaal to analyze the predictability. Thanks to the Uppaal language, our model-based framework allows expressive modeling of the behavior. Moreover, our reconfigurable framework is customizable and scalable due to the compositional analysis. The analysis time and cost benefits of our framework are discussed through an avionic case study.

1 Introduction

Since the Apollo Guidance Computer has been recognized as one of the first successful embedded systems designed early in the 60's, embedded software functions have been increasing in number, complexity and scale in the design of automotive and avionic systems. In some application areas, for example avionics, human life might be dependent on the reliability of such embedded systems which makes these systems highly critical. To demonstrate the reliability of safety critical systems, an intensive effort has been jointly undertaken by researchers and practitioners. Such a pursuit includes the definition of appropriate software engineering principles [23] (modularity, abstraction, separation of concerns, etc.) and the development of powerful analysis tools [3,17,27].

A common execution requirement to be guaranteed when designing an embedded system is the response time [19], which is the end-to-end delay of the system execution. To be able to guarantee response times, (1) the execution times of actions must be bounded; (2) an analysis must demonstrate that the system produces its results under all relevant circumstances and all ways to resolve internal non-determinism (due to, e.g., concurrency and communication delays) and external non-determinism (due to, e.g., changes in input values/arrival times).

© Springer International Publishing Switzerland 2016
C. Artho and P.C. Ölveczky (Eds.): FTSCS 2015, CCIS 596, pp. 69–84, 2016.
DOI: 10.1007/978-3-319-29510-7_4

Predictability [16] has been identified as an input related requirement. It ascertains that the externally observable behavior of a process or a system remains the same despite internal non-determinism while removing external non-determinism (i.e., keeping the inputs and their timing unchanged).

Proving the predictability [25] means that the system analysis is successfully passed regarding both data flow and time-constrained behavior under any execution assumption, for example concerning failure and workload. An example of the predictability property is the Emergency Brake System [26] mounted in Volvo FH truck series since 2013 to avoid rear end collisions. Such a feature is a component of the Adaptive Cruise Control (ACC) system. Once the radar of a moving truck discovers an obstacle on the route of the truck, it communicates the distance information to a computation process that calculates the braking pressure to be applied based on the obstacle distance and the truck speed and delivers the braking pressure value to the braking system. The radar component is a composition of sensors and cameras. A danger state is determined by the presence of a stationary or a moving vehicle just in the front of the truck with a very slower speed than the truck's. The computation must output the correct brake pressure at the expected time, which is a couple of micro seconds after the detection of the obstacle. An unpredictable computation process might deliver different outputs in response to the same inputs, which could result in bugs that are hard to detect.

Different techniques have been introduced to analyze the predictability of real-time systems [12,14,15,28], where the analysis does not leverage the system structure and systems are analyzed monolithically. This may lead to a state space explosion, making large systems non-analyzable. To the best of our knowledge, compositional analysis techniques for predictability have not received a lot of attention in the literature (discussed in Sect. 3).

By compositional analysis [5], we mean that the analysis of a system relies on the individual analysis of its components separately, since they are independent. In such a design architecture, when a component violates its requirements it does not affect the execution of other components because the faulty component cannot request more than the resource budgeted by its interface (Sect. 5.2).

The system architecture we consider in this paper is structured in terms of components having different criticality levels. During execution, criticality levels will be used as static priorities to sort components. Each component is the composition of either other components (hierarchical) or basic processes (periodic tasks) having deterministic behavior. Each component will be analyzed individually and independently from the other system components thanks to its abstraction through an interface. We use parameterized stopwatch automata (PSA) to model the system while we use Uppaal toolsuite for simulation and formal analysis. The contributions of this paper include:

- How to support the predictability of hierarchical real-time systems through certain design restrictions.
- A scalable predictability analysis framework due to the component-based design and compositional analysis.

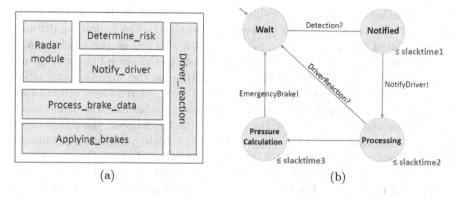

Fig. 1. Volvo's emergency brake system.

- Flexible and customizable framework due to the parametrization and instantiation mechanism of Uppaal.

The rest of the paper is organized as follows: Sect. 2 motivates the predictability analysis through an industrial example. Section 3 cites relevant related work. Section 4 introduces the predictability notion we adopt as well as schedulability as a sufficient condition for the predictability. In Sect. 5, we introduce a compositional analysis technique. Section 6 shows our model-based analysis for the predictability of component-based real-time systems using the Uppaal. Section 7 presents a case study. Section 8 concludes the paper.

2   Motivating Example

Figure 1 depicts the structure (Fig. 1(a)) and abstract behavior (Fig. 1(b)) of Volvo's emergency brake system mentioned above. The system consists of 6 concurrent components, each of which is given a set of timing attributes as well as a priority level. Once an input is generated by component **Radar module**, the component **Determine_risk** determines whether a potential obstacle is present or not. The component **Notify_driver** is responsible for notifying the driver in case a risk occurs. Based on the driver reaction, received and analyzed by component **Driver_reaction**, the system decides which action to take next. If the driver reaction is continuously missing for a certain duration, component **Process_brake_data** calculates the necessary brake pressure according to certain input data such as distance, truck speed and obstacle speed. Once the pressure value is handed over to component **Applying_brakes**, it brakes the truck.

Figure 1(b) depicts an abstract behavior of the overall emergency brake system. The system execution is initially in state **Wait** waiting to be triggered by the radar (external sensor) via a signal through channel *detection*. Once such a notification occurs, the system moves to state **Notified** waiting for the emergency data acquisition before notifying the truck driver. The data communication could be done via shared memory, bus, etc. The maximum waiting time for data acquisition must not exceed **slacktime1** time units. If the data is communicated late during the allowed interval [0, slacktime1], the remaining distance to the collision will not be the same, i.e., much shorter, as the truck is moving. After notifying the driver, the system moves to the state **Processing** and keeps calculating the remaining distance and time to the collision until either the driver reacts, and thus moves to the initial state, or reaches a critical time **slacktime2** by which it moves to state **PressureCalculation**. The slack time is calculated on the fly according to the distance, the truck speed, the elapsed time since detection and the obstacle speed. Once the brake pressure is calculated, the system activates the hardware through a signal on channel *EmegencyBrake* and moves to the initial state. The pressure calculation must be done within **slacktime3** time units. A safety property expected from this system is that it must deliver the right brake pressure at the expected time (bounded by the slack times). The later the notification arrives, the stronger the brake pressure has to be. In fact, the brake pressure delivered at time x, is different of that delivered at time $x + 1$, and strongly dependent to the input values and the acquisition time of such inputs. Moreover, such a brake pressure must be predictable in a way that it is the same whenever the system is in the same configuration (data arrival time, elapsed time since the collision detection, the initial distance, the truck speed, etc.). If the brake pressure is wrongly calculated (not sufficient) or delivered late, the truck will probably collide with the obstacle.

3   Related Work

In the literature, several model-based frameworks for the predictability analysis of real-time systems have been proposed [12,14,15,28]. However, only few proposals consider the behavior of system processes (tasks) when analyzing predictability. Moreover, to the best of our knowledge it is very rare that the system predictability is analyzed in a compositional way.

The authors of [12] presented a model-based architectural approach for improving predictability of performance in embedded real-time systems. This approach is component-based and utilizes automated analysis of task and communication architectures. The authors generate a runtime executive that can be analyzed using the MetaH language and the underlying toolset. However the tasks considered are abstract units given via a set of timing requirements. Without considering the concrete behavior of system tasks, the analysis could be pessimistic and may lead to over-approximated results.

The authors of [22] defined a predictable execution model PREM for COTS (commercial-off-the-shelf) based embedded sysestimated the resource utilizationtems. The purpose of such a model is to control the use of each resource in the way that it does not exceed its saturation limit. Accordingly, each resource must be assigned at the expected time thus avoiding any delay at the operation points. This work focuses on resource utilization rather than data flow in case of communicating architectures. Moreover, analyzing the whole system at once might not be possible.

Garousi *et al.* introduced a predictability analysis approach [15], for real-time systems, relying on the control flow analysis of the UML 2.0 sequence diagrams as well as the consideration of the timing and distribution information. The analysis includes resource usage, load forecasting/balancing and dynamic dependencies. However, analyzing the whole system at once makes the identification of faulty processes/components not trivial.

The authors of [4] introduced a compositional analysis technique enabling predictable deployment of component-based real time systems running on heterogeneous multi-processor platforms. The system is a composition of software and hardware models according to a specific operational semantics. Such a framework is a simulation-based analysis, thus it cannot be used as a rigorous analysis means for critical systems.

Our paper introduces a compositional model-based framework for the predictability analysis of component-based real time systems, so that faulty components can easily be identified. The framework uses the expressive real-time formalism of parameterized stopwatch automata to describe the system/components behavior. We rely on the advances made in the area of model-checking by analyzing each component formally using the Uppaal model checker. The compositionality and parametrization lead our framework to be scalable and flexible.

4 Predictable Real Time Systems

Concurrent real-time systems [18] are usually specified by a set of communicating processes called tasks. Each task performs a specific job such as data acquisition, computation and data actuation. Moreover, tasks are constrained by a set of features, such as roundness and execution time, as well as a dependency relation capturing the data flow between processes.

- *Roundness* includes the activation rhythm (periodic, aperiodic, sporadic) and the necessary time interval for each activation.
- *Execution time* specifies the amount of processing time required to achieve the execution of one task activation on a given platform.
- *Dependency* [10] describes the communication and synchronization order between tasks, meaning that a dependent task cannot progress if the task on which it depends has not reached a certain execution step or delivered a specific message.

Another property to be considered in case of dependency is the manipulation of correct data. So that when a task T_1 interacts with (or preempts) another task T_2, task T_1 must reload the data possibly modified by the execution of T_2 in order to avoid using out of date or inconsistent data. Powerful synchronization mechanisms enable to capture the interaction, and thus determine the time point at which the data produced by a task must be delivered to the consumer task.

In the literature, recent work [2,22] enhances the predictability of real-time systems by restraining the observability of data in such a way that a consumer task can only access the data produced by a run-until-completion execution of

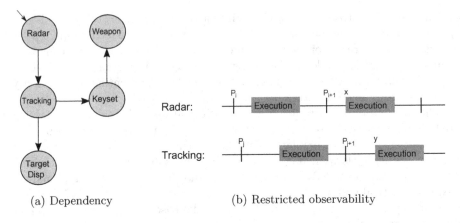

(a) Dependency   (b) Restricted observability

Fig. 2. Example of dependency and restricted observability.

the corresponding producer task. Moreover, such data must be produced before the consumer starts it current execution. For data consistency, tasks read and write data only on the beginning and the end of their period execution respectively. This implies that any data update made after the release of a given task will be ignored by that task for the current execution. This notion of run-to-completion data consistency is called *restricted observability* [2].

For example, if a consumer task synchronizes with a producer task, the legal data values to be used by the consumer after the synchronization must be the data issued before the consumer started its current job. This means that if the producer does not complete its execution before a synchronization point, the data value to be considered by the consumer for its current execution (potentially released at the synchronization time point) is not the value computed until the synchronization time but rather it is the data delivered at the termination of the previous execution period of the producer.

Figure 2(a) illustrates a dependency relation between different tasks of a mission control computer system. An arrow from one task T_1 to another task T_2 means that T_2 depends on T_1. Once the radar component captures the presence of a potential enemy engine it outputs data concerning the enemy position to the tracking task which in turn identifies the enemy status, speed, etc. Meanwhile, the tracking task unlocks the display task with the updated data for the target display on the screen. Once the enemy is positioned in a reachable distance, the keyset task will be unlocked to enable the aircraft pilot activating the weapon task to destroy the enemy engine.

Figure 2(b) depicts a data flow example following the restricted observability. For the period P_{j+1}, Tracking is released at time y while Radar is still running under its period P_{i+1}, the data to be considered by Tracking must be that issued by Radar before time x which means before the beginning of period P_{i+1}. Thus, the data considered by task Tracking during the period P_{j+1} is the update made by task Radar at the end of its execution for period P_i.

Technically, the predictability property we consider consists of 2 requirements: (1) data consistency; (2) execution order.

- *Data consistency* ensures that all tasks have the same observability of the data regardless of their dependencies. The non-preemption of tasks ensures that tasks access the shared data only at the scheduling time points, i.e. a dependent task execution considers the data update made by the tasks on which it depends before its current release (scheduling) for the whole current period. Any other data update made externally during the task execution is ignored and can only be considered in the next scheduling of the task. A scheduling time point is the time instant when the execution of a running tasks is done and the scheduler releases another ready task. This approach to data observability is known as *predictable intervals* [22].
- *Execution order* between tasks follows the scheduling mechanism adopted by the real-time system, and must not be in contradiction with the dependency relation so that a dependent task cannot first execute before the tasks on which it depends.

Therefore, for real-time systems specified using non-preemptive tasks if the execution order, reflecting both scheduling mechanism and data consistency, is guaranteed then the schedulability is a sufficient condition for predictability [2]. Accordingly, predictability will simply be analyzed through schedulability.

Apart from the temporal partitioning [24] of the system workload to tasks, the separation of concerns [21] allows gathering collaborative and dependent tasks within components. Thus making the system architecture modular.

5   Compositional Framework for Predictability Analysis

In this section, we consider real-time systems structured as a set of independent components while we analyze system predictability, relying on the schedulability as a sufficient condition, in compositional way so that each component will be analyzed individually.

5.1   Hierarchical Real-Time Systems

Hierarchical scheduling systems [11,13] have been introduced as a component-based representation of real-time systems, allowing temporal partitioning and separation of concerns. A major motivation of the separation of concerns [21] is that it allows isolation and modular design to accommodate changes in the system such that the impact of a change is isolated to the smallest component. An example of the increasing use of hierarchical scheduling systems is the standard ARINC-653 [1] for avionics real-time operating systems.

An example of a hierarchical scheduling system running on a single core platform is depicted in Fig. 3. It consists of 2 independent components, Component1 and Component2, scheduled by the system level according to FPS (Fixed Priority

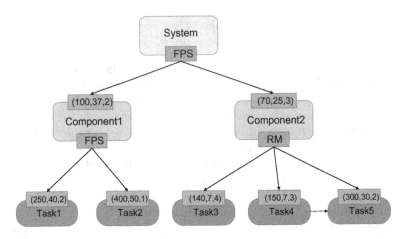

Fig. 3. Example of a hierarchical scheduling system.

Scheduling). For compositionality purposes, each component is given an interface (*period, budget, criticality*) e.g. (100,37,2) for Component1, where *budget* is the CPU time required by component for a time interval *period*. In our context, *criticality*[1] is handled as static priority to sort components at their parent level, so that in Fig. 3 Component2 has priority over Component1 $(2 < 3)$. Each component in turn is a composition of tasks scheduled according to a local scheduler, FPS for Component1 and RM (Rate Monotonic) for Component2. Each task is also assigned an interface *(period, exectime, prio)*, where *exectime* and *prio* are respectively the execution time and priority. Of course, the priority will be considered if a static priority scheduling scheduler is adopted. We also consider dependencies between tasks (the dashed arrow from Task4 to Task5), so that the execution of a dependent task (Task5) cannot start until the task on which it depends (Task4) finishes it execution. In this work, we only consider periodic non-preemptive tasks.

At the system level, each component will be abstracted as a task given by the interface *(period, budget, criticality)* regardless of its child tasks. The interface of a component is a contract that the system level supplies such a component with *budget* CPU time every time interval of size *period*. Once a component is scheduled by the system level, it schedules one of its local tasks according to its scheduler, i.e. a component can trigger its child tasks only when it is allocated the CPU resource.

5.2   Compositional Analysis

By compositional analysis [5] we mean that the analysis process of a system relies on the individual analysis of each component separately, since components

---

[1] We do not consider the criticality related features like fault tolerance for soft critical components.

are independent. In such a design architecture, when a component violates its requirements it does not affect the execution of other components. The misbehavior cannot propagate because the faulty component, even though it is not satisfied with the resource budget it has been granted, cannot request more than the resource budgeted by its interface. Thus, the other concurrent components will not be deprived and remain supplied with the same budgeted resource amounts as in case of the successful behavior.

The analysis of each component consists in checking the feasibility of its tasks against its interface (*period, budget*), which is a guarantee that the component always supplies its tasks with the budgeted resource amount every period. To check that the tasks are feasible whatever the budget supply time, we consider all possible scenarios. We model the resource supply by a periodic process (*supplier*) having a non-deterministic behavior. For each period, the supplier provides the resource amount specified in the component interface (*budget*). Thereafter, we use a model checker to explore the state space, by considering all potential supply times, and verify whether all tasks are satisfied for all supply scenarios. For further description and illustration of our compositional analysis technique, we refer readers to [7, 8].

Depending on the interpretation of the deadline miss, the faulty component can either be suspended for the current period execution, discarded from the system (blocked) or just be kept running. The deadline miss interpretation strongly depends on the criticality and the application area of the failed component/system. Since we are considering criticality, in our framework the occurrence of a deadline miss implies a suspension of the execution, thus tasks termination (by deadline) is not guaranteed (the system is not schedulable). This implies that tasks cannot output data at the expected time (deadline), thus violate the predictability property.

5.3   Conceptual Design

Basically, the dependency relation can be viewed as order on the tasks execution in the way that a dependent task cannot run while the task on which it depends does hand out the event or data expected by the dependent task (in our context it is just a run-to-termination of the task execution for the current period). Tasks are usually given with a period *period*, an offset *offset*, an execution time *execTime*, a priority *prio* and a deadline *deadline*. Moreover, in our framework we consider a dependency relation *Dependency* between tasks. Throughout this paper we assume that the task period is greater or equal to the deadline. Moreover, the deadline must be greater than the execution time.

Figure 4 depicts a conceptual model of tasks with dependency. The task is initially in state Wait Offset expiry waiting for the expiration of its offset. In state Wait dependency, the task waits execution termination of the immediate tasks on which it depends while its deadline is not missed yet. Once a task obtains the requested inputs it becomes ready to be scheduled and thus waiting for the CPU. A ready task moves to state Running when it is scheduled. Since the task behavior we consider is not preemptive, a scheduled task keeps running until

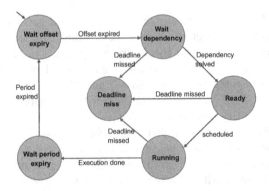

Fig. 4. Conceptual model of tasks.

satisfying the execution requirement or missing its deadline by which it joins the state Deadline miss. After having satisfied the execution requirement the task enters state Wait period expiry waiting for the expiry of its current period.

Namely, the dependency relation is a direct acyclic graph where nodes represent tasks execution and transitions are the dependency order. A transition from a node to another means once the execution of the source node task is done the target node task is unlocked. Of course this does mean that the execution of such a task will start immediately but only becomes ready to be scheduled. A task must not depend to its dependent tasks nor to the tasks depending to one of its dependent tasks so far. The dependency of task must be applied for each period. Accordingly, a dependent task waits for its dependency to be satisfied whenever a new period starts. In turn, such a task unlocks its dependent tasks just for the execution of their current periods.

6   Uppaal System Model

UPPAAL [3] is a tool environment for modeling, simulation and formal verification of real-time systems modeled as composition of inter-communicating processes. Each process is an instance of a template model. Our system model consists of a set of independent components, each of which is modeled separately and will be analyzed individually. Each template is a Parameterized Stopwatch Automata (PSA), offering the ability to use stopwatch clocks [9] and instantiation with different parameters.

Components Modeling. Each component is given by an interface (*period, budget, criticality*), a local scheduler and a workload. The workload of a component is either a set of tasks (i.e., basic component) or other components (i.e., hierarchical component). Components are independent and viewed by their parents as single periodic tasks having deadlines the same as periods. Such components are scheduled by their parent level's scheduler according to their *criticality*.

Each component consists of a task model, a scheduler model, a CPU resource model, a supplier model [5] and a dependency relation.

Task Model. Tasks are instances of the task template with the corresponding attributes (*tid, period, offset, exectime, deadline, prio*) as parameters. The task identifier *tid* is used to distinguish between tasks. Figure 5 shows the PSA template we designed to model tasks. We use two stopwatch variables exeTime[tid] and curTime[tid] to keep track of the execution time and the current time respectively of a given task *tid*. Such variables are continuous but do not progress when their derivatives are set to 0.

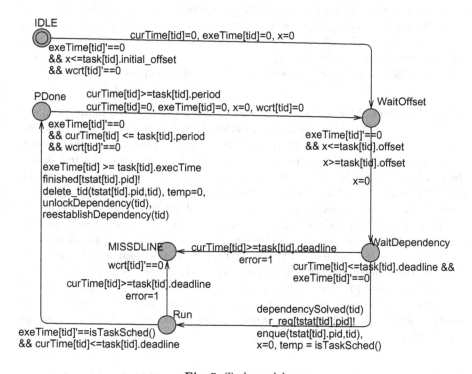

Fig. 5. Task model.

Once started, the task model waits for the expiry of the initial offset at location IDLE. At location WaitOffset, the task waits until its periodic offset expires then moves to location WaitDependency. At both locations IDLE and WaitOffset the stopwatch exeTime[tid] does not progress because the task is not running yet. At location WaitDependency, the task is waiting until either its deadline is missed (curTime[tid]≥ task[tid].deadline) or its dependency gets unlocked (dependencySolved(tid)). The stay at such a location is constrained by the invariant curTime[tid]≤ task[tid].deadline, during which the stopwatch exeTime[tid] does not progress. Once the deadline is missed, the task moves to location MISSDLINE. Otherwise, the task is ready and it requests the CPU resource through an event r_req[tstat[tid].pid]! on channel r_req and moves to location Run. Through such an edge, the task enqueues its identifier tid into the queue of the resource model identified by *pid*. In fact, location Run corresponds to both ready and running status thanks to the stopwatch. Once the task gets scheduled through function isTaskSched() it keeps running while it is scheduled and its execution requirement is not fully satisfied. Thus, the stopwatch exeTime[tid] measuring the execution time increases continuously while isTaskSched() holds, i.e., exeTime[tid]'==isTaskSched().

For analysis performance, whenever a deadline is missed the faulty task updates the global variable error to one. Thus, the schedulability will be checked upon the content of this variable. When the execution requirement $execTime$ is satisfied, exeTime[tid]$\geq$task[tid].execTime, the task moves to location PDone waiting for the expiry of the current period. Through such an edge, the task releases the CPU, unlocks the dependent tasks waiting for such a termination and reestablishes its original dependency for the next period.

CPU Resource Model. Figure 6 depicts the CPU resource model. Once it starts, the CPU resource moves to location Idle, because the initial location (with double circles) is committed, and waits for a request from tasks through channel r_req[rid]. Through a resource request, the CPU model moves to location ReqSched and immediately calls the underlying scheduler. At location WaitSched, the CPU model is waiting for a notification from the scheduler through which the CPU will be assigned to a particular task at location Assign. Such a task will immediately be removed from the resource queue by the edge leading to the location InUse. As we consider non-preemptive execution only, if a task requests the CPU while it is assigned to another task such a request will be declined. However the requesting task will immediately be enqueued. Whenever the CPU resource is released by the current scheduled task, the resource model calls the scheduler to determine to which task it will be assigned if the queue is not empty (location ReqSched). Otherwise, the resource model moves to location Idle waiting for task requests.

Dependency Relation Modeling. Given n tasks, we model their dependencies by a matrix of 2 dimensions each of which has n elements. A row i represents the dependencies of all tasks to the task having identifier $tid = i$, whereas a column j states the identifiers of tasks on which the task $tid = j$ depends. The content of each cell is Boolean, so that $cell[i, j]$ states whether task $tid = j$ depends on the task having identifier $tid = i$. Accordingly, the dependencies of a task x are satisfied if the cells of column x are all *False*. Table. 1 shows the matrix representation of the dependency relation given in Fig. 2(a).

To manipulate the dependencies of tasks during components execution, we introduce the following functions:

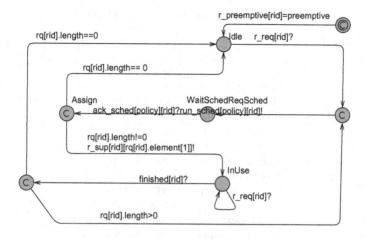

Fig. 6. CPU resource model.

Table 1. Implementation of the dependency relation of Fig. 2(a).

Dependency	Radar	Tracking	Target	Keyset	Weapon
Radar	*False*	**True**	*False*	*False*	*False*
Tracking	*False*	*False*	**True**	**True**	*False*
Target	*False*	*False*	*False*	*False*	*False*
Keyset	*False*	*False*	*False*	*False*	**True**
Weapon	*False*	*False*	*False*	*False*	*False*

- dependencySatisfied(tid) checks whether all tasks on which a given task *tid* depends have already updated their status to *Done* (execution finished for one period). This is done by verifying that all cells of the tid^{th} column of the dependency matrix are *False*.
- unlockDependent(tid) unlocks all tasks dependent on a given task *tid* when the execution of such a task is finished. This is done by updating the cells of row *tid* to *False*.
- reestablishDependency(tid) establishes the original dependency relation of a given task *tid* when its execution is done. This is done by updating the cells of column *tid*, corresponding to the tasks on which task *tid* originally depends, to *True*. Such a reestablishment is because, as stated earlier, the dependency relation is applicable every task period.

7   Case Study

To show the applicability and scalability of our analysis framework, we modeled and analyzed an avionics system [20]. Table 2 lists the system components, tasks and their underlying timing attributes. Columns two and three list the

Table 2. Avionics mission control system

Component	Criticality	Tasks	p_i	e_i	d_i	$prio_i$	Task dependency
Display	1	Status update (T_1)	200	3	200	12	T_2, T_3, T_5
		Keyset (T_2)	200	1	200	16	—
		Hook update (T_3)	80	2	80	36	—
		Graph display (T_4)	80	9	80	40	T_1, T_3
		Store updates (T_5)	200	1	200	20	T_2
RWR	3	Contact mgmt (T_6)	25	5	25	72	—
Radar	3	Target update (T_7)	50	5	50	60	T_8
		Tracking filter (T_8)	25	2	25	84	—
NAV	2	Nav update (T_9)	59	8	59	56	T_{10}
		Steering cmds (T_{10})	200	3	200	24	—
		Nav status (T_{11})	1000	1	1000	4	T_9
Tracking	1	Target update (T_{12})	100	5	100	32	—
Weapon	4	Weapon protocol (T_{13})	200	1	200	28	T_{15}
		Weapon release (T_{14})	200	3	200	98	T_{13}
		Weapon aim (T_{15})	50	3	50	64	—
BIT	0	Equ stat update (T_{16})	1000	1	1000	8	—
Data bus	2	Poll bus (T_{17})	40	1	40	68	—

Table 3. Analysis results of the case study.

Component	Period	Budget	CPU utilization	Analysis time (s)	Memory space (KB)
Display	80	13	13/80	0.016	8852
Radar	10	2	2/10	0.016	7656
NAV	20	3	3/20	0.016	7784
Weapon	50	4	4/50	0.015	7748

criticality level and tasks of each component. Columns four to seven list the timing attributes of tasks, whereas the last column describes the tasks on which each task depends. Due to space limitation, we do not consider inter-component dependencies however it can simply be applied since our analysis is recursive where components are viewed by their parent levels as single tasks.

We consider that components having criticality levels less than 2 are not hard critical. Moreover, for the components having one task only, the component period, respectively budget, is the same as the child task period, respectively execution time. Since tasks are non preemptible and satisfy the restricted observability, we check predictability through schedulability. Table 3 summarizes the analysis results. First, we calculate the minimum budget of each composite component using a binary checking while varying the component budget [6].

The analysis time (15 and 16 ms) is very low compared to the system size, while the used memory space is relatively acceptable. In a previous work [20], Locke *et al.* estimated the resource utilization of the whole system to 85 % without considering data flow time. In our paper, while considering data flow between certain tasks we estimated the resource utilization to 86.25 %. Such a utilization is very high and leads the avionic system to be non-schedulable, in particular if the overhead time is also considered. Accordingly, the individual tasks cannot guarantee to output data before their deadlines, thus making the system unpredictable.

8   Conclusion

In this paper we have introduced a compositional model-based framework for the predictability analysis of real-time systems. The architecture we considered is hierarchical where components running on a single core platform may have different criticality levels. The system tasks are periodic and may depend on each other. We analyze each component individually by providing insight on the schedulability and data flow.

Our framework is set using Uppaal while the real-time formalism we used to model tasks and data flow is the stopwatch automata. We believe that our framework is scalable as long as the system is designed in terms of independent (average size) components.

A future work is the introduction of a new task model to capture data flow and analyze the predictability without considering the schedulability as a sufficient condition.

References

1. ARINC 653. Website. https://www.arinc.com/cf/store/documentlist.cfm
2. Aussagues, C., Chabrol, D., David, V., Roux, D., Willey, N., Tournadre, A., Graniou, M.: PharOS, a multicore OS ready for safety-related automotive systems:results and future prospects. In: ERTS2 2010, May 2010
3. Behrmann, G., David, A., Larsen, K.G.: A tutorial on UPPAAL. In: Bernardo, M., Corradini, F. (eds.) SFM-RT 2004. LNCS, vol. 3185, pp. 200–236. Springer, Heidelberg (2004)
4. Bondarev, E., Chaudron, M., de With, P.: Compositional performance analysis of component-based systems on heterogeneous multiprocessor platforms. In: SEAA 2006, pp. 81–91, August 2006
5. Boudjadar, A., Nyman, U., Kim, J.H., Larsen, K.G., Mikučionis, M., Skou, A., David, A.: Hierarchical scheduling framework based on compositional analysis using uppaal. In: Fiadeiro, J.L., Liu, Z., Xue, J. (eds.) FACS 2013. LNCS, vol. 8348, pp. 61–78. Springer, Heidelberg (2014)
6. Skou, A., Boudjadar, A., David, A., Larsen, K.G., Mikučionis, M., Nyman, U., Kim, J.H.: Widening the schedulability of hierarchical scheduling systems. In: Lanese, I., Madelaine, E. (eds.) FACS 2014. LNCS, vol. 8997, pp. 209–227. Springer, Heidelberg (2015)
7. Boudjadar, A., David, A., Kim, J.H., Larsen, K.G., Mikucionis, M., Nyman, U., Skou, A.: A reconfigurable framework for compositional schedulability and power analysis of hierarchical scheduling systems with frequency scaling. Sci. Comput. Program. J. **113**, 236–260 (2015)
8. Boudjadar, A., Kim, J.H., Larsen, K.G., Nyman, U.: Compositional schedulability analysis of an avionics system using Uppaal. In: Proceedings of the International Conference on Advanced Aspects of Software Engineering ICAASE, pp. 140–147 (2014)

9. Cassez, F., Larsen, K.G.: The impressive power of stopwatches. In: Palamidessi, C. (ed.) CONCUR 2000. LNCS, vol. 1877, pp. 138–152. Springer, Heidelberg (2000)

10. Larsen, K.G., Mikučionis, M., David, A., Legay, A.: Schedulability of herschel-planck revisited using statistical model checking. In: Margaria, T., Steffen, B. (eds.) ISoLA 2012, Part II. LNCS, vol. 7610, pp. 293–307. Springer, Heidelberg (2012)

11. Deng, Z., Liu, J.W.S.: Scheduling real-time applications in an open environment. In: RTSS, pp. 308–319 (1997)

12. Feiler, P., Lewis, B., Vestal, S.: Improving predictability in embedded real-timesystems. Technical Report CMU/SEI-2000-SR-011, Carnegie Mellon University, December 2000

13. Feng, X.A., Mok, A.K.: A model of hierarchical real-time virtual resources. In: RTSS 2002, pp. 26–35. IEEE Computer Society (2002)

14. Fredriksson, J.: Improving predictability and resource utilization in component-based embedded real-time systems. Ph.D. thesis, Mälardalen University (2008)

15. Garousi, V., Briand, L.C., Labiche, Y.: A unified approach for predictability analysis of real-time systems using UML-based control flow information (2005)

16. Henzinger, T.A.: Two challenges in embedded systems design: predictability and robustness. Philos. Trans. R. Soc. London Math. Phy. Eng. Sci. **366**(1881), 3727–3736 (2008)

17. Holzmann, G.: The model checker spin. IEEE Trans. Softw. Eng. **23**(5), 279–295 (1997)

18. Hooman, J.: Specification and Compositional Verification of Real-Time Systems. LNCS. Springer, Heidelberg (1991)

19. Joseph, M., Pandya, P.: Finding response times in a real-time system. Comput. J. **29**(5), 390–395 (1986)

20. Locke, C., Vogel, D., Mesler, T.: Building a predictable avionics platform in ADA: a case study. In: Proceedings of RTSS, pp. 181–189 (1991)

21. Panunzio, M., Vardanega, T.: A component-based process with separation of concerns for the development of embedded real-time software systems. J. Syst. Softw. **96**, 105–121 (2014)

22. Pellizzoni, R., Betti, E., Bak, S., Yao, G., Criswell, J., Caccamo, M., Kegley, R.: A predictable execution model for COTS-based embedded systems. In: RTAS 2011, pp. 269–279, April 2011

23. Pfleeger, S.L., Atlee, J.M.: Software Engineering - Theory and Practice, 4th edn. Pearson Education, Upper Saddle River (2009)

24. Purna, K., Bhatia, D.: Temporal partitioning and scheduling data flow graphs for reconfigurable computers. IEEE Trans. Comput. **48**(6), 579–590 (1999)

25. Stankovic, J., Ramamritham, K.: What is predictability for real-time systems? Real-Time Syst. **2**(4), 247–254 (1990)

26. Volvo Trucks Great Britain and Ireland. Driver support systems: Keeping anextra eye on the road. http://www.volvotrucks.com/trucks/uk-market/en-gb/trucks/volvo-fh-series/key-features/Pages/driver-support-systems.aspx

27. Wang, F.: Efficient verification of timed automata with BDD-like data-structures. In: Zuck, L.D., Attie, P.C., Cortesi, A., Mukhopadhyay, S. (eds.) VMCAI 2003. LNCS, vol. 2575, pp. 189–205. Springer, Heidelberg (2002)

28. Yau, S., Zhou, X.: Schedulability in model-based software development for distributed real-time systems. In: Proceedings of WORDS 2002, pp. 45–52 (2002)

Railway Systems

Towards a Body of Knowledge in Formal Methods for the Railway Domain: Identification of Settled Knowledge

Stefan Gruner[1]($\boxtimes$), Apurva Kumar[2], and Tom Maibaum[3]

[1] Department of Computer Science, University of Pretoria, Pretoria, South Africa
sgruner@cs.up.ac.za
[2] Department of Computing and Software, McMaster University, Hamilton, Canada
kumara39@mcmaster.ca
[3] Department of Computing and Software, McMaster University, Hamilton, Canada
tom@maibaum.org

Abstract. Bodies of Knowledge (BoK) are available only in mature technical fields, in which professional practices and technical rules have been well established (i.e.: 'settled'), and are compiled for any prospective or current practitioner to refer to. By their factual establishment they also become professionally normative to a considerable extent. As a precursor to establishing a BoK it is important to determine whether or not a target domain already contains sufficient 'settled' knowledge, and, if yes, how such knowledge can be identified for its reproduction. In the undisputed safety-critical railway domain, formal methods have been applied for several decades in the solution of various modelling and verification problems. The application of many of those formal methods in the railway domain has also reached sufficient levels of maturity or 'stability' — yet no BoK for this domain has ever been compiled so far. Thus the time is ripe now to start such a project. In this paper, with regard to the necessary identification of settled knowledge, we apply the lattice-theoretical methods of Formal Concept Analysis (FCA) in order to structure and organise large amounts of relevant bibliometric data from the railway domain's corpus of literature. In other words, we construct a formal concept lattice, the semantics of which is suitable for revealing the 'settled' parts of this domain. As a result of our formalised domain analysis, we provide a clear and theoretically well-grounded indication of the 'settled' themes and topics which any future BoK on Formal Methods in the Railway Domain ought to contain.

Keywords: Formal methods · Railway domain · Body of knowledge · Settled knowledge · Formal concept analysis · Semantic lattices

1 Introduction: Motivation and Related Work

Engineering disciplines, as well as other science-based disciplines such as medicine, are characterised by high levels of *standardisation* and the subsequent availability of readily applicable *handbook* knowledge, also known as the discipline's

© Springer International Publishing Switzerland 2016
C. Artho and P.C. Ölveczky (Eds.): FTSCS 2015, CCIS 596, pp. 87–102, 2016.
DOI: 10.1007/978-3-319-29510-7_5

Body of Knowledge (BoK). In those disciplines of engineering or applied science, a BoK handbook compiling the key concepts, terms and activities that constitute a professional domain can be found in the office of every serious practitioner [14]. One example is the *Civil Engineering Body of Knowledge for the 21st Century* (2008) released by the American Society of Civil Engineers.

Michael Jackson, in discussing his understanding of engineering practice based on a reading of Vincenti [19], has clarified this notion further. According to Jackson [10], an engineering handbook is not a compendium of scientific laws or fundamental principles; rather it contains a corpus of rules and procedures by which it has been found that those principles can be most easily and effectively applied to the particular design tasks established in the field. The outline design is already given, determined by the established needs and products. In Chap. 11 of his standard textbook on the philosophy of science, the philosopher *Mario Bunge* called those rules *'technological rules'* and clarified their relation to the 'nomological' and 'nomopragmatic statements' on which technological rules are grounded [4]: Nomological statements describe scientific *facts*, nomopragmatic statements describe science-based technical *possibilities*, and technological rules outline the adequate *implementation* of those possibilities. Moreover —now according to Jackson again— the methods of value for engineers are based on so-called *'micro theories'* which describe only small and well understandable parts of an entire domain, and which are closely fitted to the tasks of developing particular well understood components of particular well-understood products within the development phases of so-called *'normal engineering'* [10].

Formal Methods in software science and software engineering have existed at least as long as the term 'software engineering' itself. In many engineering-based and software-supported application areas, particularly in the *railway domain* [3], formal methods —as defined in further details by *Formal Methods Europe* (FME),[1] or similar professional associations— have already reached a level of *maturity* amenable to the compilation a BoK. Its various methods and techniques include algebraic specification, process-algebraic modelling and verification, Petri nets, fuzzy logics, etc. The B-method, for example, has been used successfully to verify the most relevant parts of a model of the Metro underground railway system of the city of Paris (in which this FTSCS workshop is held this year). Also software tool support is already available for a variety of those formal methods, for example in the form of various model checker or SAT solver programs, such that *'formal'* can become *'normal'* to a large extent.

The use of formal methods has also shifted from only *proof*-based applications to also including formal *modelling* of systems and their behaviour. This is an observable trend within the railway domain [6].

When we bring those above-mentioned trains of thought together, then it 'naturally' appears as a fundamental task of applied formal methods research to build a catalogue of such micro-methods in support of the everyday work of formal method engineers, particularly those ones who are working in the safety-critical railway domain. We also call this the *'BoK-ification'* of the domain.

---

[1] http://www.fmeurope.org/.

Alas, one important question has remained unanswered so far, namely: *Which, exactly*, is the domain knowledge that already 'matured' to such an extent that its BoK-ification is *reasonably justified* —in contrast to other knowledge which is still too immature, too recent or 'in the flow'— and *by what rationally grounded method* can such mature knowledge be *recognised* and subsequently 'filtered' out of a topically vast and epistemically diverse domain (such as the Formal-Methods-in-the-Railway domain)? This question is the topic of this paper, and a plausible *answer to this question is our main contribution* to FTSCS'15. Thereby we do not merely indicate which particular parts of the particular Formal-Methods-in-the-Railway domain ought to be selected for its future BoK-ification [8] — we also provide, more importantly, a *general method* by means of which *any* other domain can be analysed for its future BoK-ification, too. As the remainder of this paper will show, this meta-method is *Formal Concept Analysis* (FCA) as it was first introduced by *Ganter* and *Wille* on the basis of mathematical lattice theory [7]. In other words: in this paper, which is based on the recent Master's-dissertation by one of our co-authors [11], we use and apply a formal method, namely FCA, in support of the future BoK-ification of other formal methods, namely the ones in the safety-critical railway domain. To our best awareness this is a *new* solution which had never been presented for the railway domain so far.

2   Method

In order to answer the question: *which knowledge in the railway domain has matured*, it is most important to look at the possible *sources* of domain knowledge within the domain, and what the *definition* of 'settled knowledge' is. It is also necessary to investigate *how* this knowledge is structured within an engineering domain, so that it is easier to identify.

The answers to these questions will decide which formal attributes are included in the concept lattice that will contain the collected knowledge. After constructing the lattice and pruning it with the use of stability indices, the resulting lattice shows the most stable, and therefore, settled knowledge (including its structure) within the railway domain in the context of the dataset used.

2.1   Settled Knowledge

Poser [15], Vincenti [19], Arageorgis and Baltas [1] describe engineering as a multi-level activity. In order to design a device or a system, we need to first understand its operational principle, that is, what it does. That overall goal drives the smaller aspects of design, as the goal is broken up into smaller design tasks that have their own requirements constrained by scientific and practical expertise.

Without a particular goal in mind, engineering activity loses its meaning. This goal is determined by people that need to solve a problem — here: the engineers. Their *purposes* bring a variety of social aspects into the engineering disciplines. These social aspects of engineering are built into its knowledge, and provide the body of knowledge with context information about the form various classes of problems being (or to be) solved. Hence there are *categories of knowledge* which are almost always relevant in any engineering activity [19]. The categories include *explicit* forms of knowledge such as *fundamental design concepts, criteria*, as well as *theoretical tools* (such as formal methods). They also include *tacit* knowledge which is much harder to identify and isolate, i.e.: general 'guidelines' (rather than precisely stipulated rules).

In this context, *settled knowledge* is the knowledge which *can* become 'officially codified' in a BoK. Its structure would be consistent with Vincenti's above-mentioned epistemological categories [19], influenced by relevant external social purposes. This knowledge must be stable and coherent throughout the BoK's domain over a reasonably long period of time, and should appear in similar form for all similar problems to be solved in that domain. *Forms* of engineering knowlege could include mathematical formulae, semi-formal descriptions, or even pictures and diagrams. Such settled knowledge stems from the typical *knowledge-generating activities* which Vincenti has comprehensively described [19].

The aim of the future BoK should be to discover these operational theories —i.e.: theories about methods rather than theories about natural objects [4]— of software engineering for the railway domain, and a starting point would be to find any consistencies of the use of formal methods, by surveying a large amount of sources of railway domain knowledge spread out over a reasonably long period of time.

Applications of formal methods are almost always 'straight-forward' —i.e.: under not too complicated circumstances— with refinements or variations depending on the overall aim of a project. Formal methods are also used widely throughout the railway domain [6]. Identification of the actually applied formal methods is our first step towards creating the afore-mentioned BoK, because they can be easily identified and ectracted from the large amount of knowledge which the railway domain has already accumulated. Other aspects of settled knowledge may not be so easily identified.

Sources of Knowledge. In order to extract settled domain knowledge from the railway domain we need to find sources of domain knowledge within this domain. These sources could consist of

- industry standards and guidelines laid out by governing bodies,
- papers and articles written as a result of research done in the domain (both academic and industrial),
- requirements specifications or other documents produced by domain experts and specialists,

and many more. Papers and articles, written as a result of research done in the domain, are the main source of domain knowledge used for this paper, although a mixture of the above-mentioned source-types would be ideal for a 'holistic' view of the domain. This source is selected because its papers cover a reasonable duration of time (as long as formal methods in railway software engineering have been used) and are relevant with regard to our epistemic purposes. They were also suggested by experts in the domain, (see Acknowledgements). The chosen papers are from the following venues:

- Proceedings IFAC Symposiums on Control in Transportation Systems: 1975–2012 [9],
- Proceedings FORMS-FORMAT: 2010–2014 [9],
- Proceedings SAFECOMP: 2005–2014.

Those conferences provided more than three hundred papers related to the railway domain. Many papers did not relate to the use of formal methods in railways or were discussions or predictions of the current status of the domain. Due to this, only one hundred and fifty were used in our analysis. It is just the beginning of a long list papers that have been published within the railway domain [11].

Classification of Knowledge. The use of formal concept analysis (FCA) in this project provides an attribute-based classification system of knowledge. In the case of formal methods, the simplest classification is the name of the formal method used in each source. Each formal method used in the railway domain is an attribute of the source, though it is also important to look at further pertinent characteristics of the knowledge to the railway domain. Simply including only the names of formal methods is not enough, as different methods are used in different contexts and when solving different problems or classes of problems. Therefore, additional techniques and keywords (context of the knowledge of the domain) is used as attributes for the resulting lattice. A summary of the reasons for each choice is given below and a full explanation can be found in the Master's dissertation of a similar name [11].

It is also necessary to know *where* in the railway domain these formal methods are used. This gives us more context around the use of each formal method. In future, the analysis could even be extended to problems or problem-types being solved within the domain. To this end we record the subdomain of the railway domain each source of knowledge (paper) deals with. This also gives us the added advantage of visualising generic uses of formal methods as opposed to methods only used in specific areas of the domain. For the purposes of this paper, the railway domain is divided into the following subdomains: The Net, Timetables, Scheduling and Allocation, Traffic Monitoring and Control, Rolling Stock, Passenger Handling, Freight Handling. This list was a culmination of the opinion of a number of domain experts (see Acknowledgements), as well as Bjørner's work on the subdomain division of the railway domain [3].

Next, it also seems useful to include the year that each paper was published within our collected domain knowledge. As it was mentioned earlier, knowledge existing over a length of time has a greater chance of being 'settled' than knowledge that is much more recent. Methods that have been studied over time show refinement in their use and therefore, like in the case with most engineering knowledge, are honed until they become standard practice. It is possible that the inclusion of year-attributes may cause extra 'noise' in the lattice which will require the use of noise-removing techniques on the lattice to take out.

Lastly, other keywords and attributes might also be included that add to the structure and context of the knowledge that each paper holds. Some of these keywords measured the *'settled-ness'* of knowledge included in a paper, similar to the scientific maturity scheme outlined by Mary Shaw in [18]. This also includes the *type* of modeling that occurs in each source, such as mathematical, descriptive or analytical modeling as well as commonly used techniques or languages that provide extra context to the general use of formal methods.

2.2   Formal Concept Analysis

A formal *context*, which is a set of objects supplied with their descriptions as sets of attributes, gives rise to a family of formal *concepts*. A formal concept has an intent and an extent. The *extent* of a concept consists of all formal objects which belong to the concept, and the *intent* of a concept consists of all formal attributes that apply to all formal objects of the concept.

In our case, the objects will be the sources of knowledge, i.e.: published papers within the railway domain from relevant journals, conference proceedings or other books. The attributes are a collection of characteristics of these papers: for example, when they were published, which sub-domain the papers deal with, what formal methods are used, etc.

Thus the mathematical model of a formal context includes formal objects, formal attributes, and a relation between the object and attribute sets. The following mathematical descriptions are taken from the book by Ganter and Wille on Formal Concept Analysis [7].

Formal Context. A context $\mathbb{K}$ has a structure $\mathbb{K} := (G, M, I)$ where G and M are sets representing objects and attributes respectively. I is a binary relation between sets G and M where $I \subseteq G \times M$ and gIm indicates that the object g has the attribute m. We define two operators for arbitrary $X \subseteq G$ and $Y \subseteq M$ such that:[2]

$$X \mapsto X^I := m \in M | \forall g \in X gIm$$

$$Y \mapsto Y^I := g \in G | \forall m \in Y gIm$$

Within this context $\mathbb{K}$, we can define a concept as a pair (A, B) with $A \subseteq G$, $B \subseteq M$, $A = B^I$ and $B = A^I$. A and B are called the *extent* and the *intent* of the formal concept (A, B) respectively. The mathematical meaning of the relationship between the subconcept and superconcept is as follows:

$$(A_1, B_1) \leq (A_2, B_2) \iff A_1 \subseteq A_2 (\iff B_1 \supseteq B_2)$$

The set of all formal concepts of context $\mathbb{K}$ together with their defined order relation is denoted by $\mathfrak{B}(\mathbb{K})$. The visual representation of this is referred to as a concept *lattice*. For an object $g \in G$, its object concept $\gamma g := (g^{II}, g^I)$ is the smallest concept in $\mathfrak{B}(\mathbb{K})$ whose extent contains g. Additionally, for an attribute

	needs water	lives in water	lives on land	is mobile
Bream	X	X		X
Frog	X	X	X	X
Dog	X		X	X
Reed	X	X	X	
Corn	X		X	

Fig. 1. Structure of a cross table in FCA: example adapted from [16]

$m \in M$, its attribute concept $\mu m := (m^I, m^{II})$ is the greatest concept in $\mathfrak{B}(\mathbb{K})$ whose intent contains m.

The formal context can be represented as a *cross table*, like the one shown for example in Fig. 1). Each row represents an object and each column represents an attribute. A cross at the intersection of a row and column indicates that the object possesses the particular attribute. In our application of FCA this means that a studied paper describes the use of a specific formal method, or was published in a particular year. Such a cross table can then be translated automatically into a concept lattice to visualise the relationships within the context.

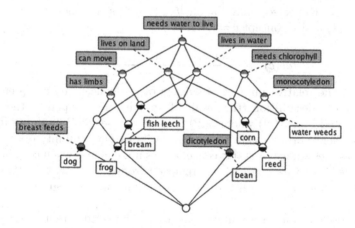

Fig. 2. Concept lattice: example taken from [16]

An example of such a concept lattice can be seen in Fig. 2. Concepts closer to the top are on a *'higher level'* than those below them. Concepts on lower levels are more specific than concepts on a higher level, appearing near the bottom of the lattice. Concepts on higher levels are more general than concepts on lower levels and appear near the top of the lattice. A concept at the top of an edge in the graph is called a *parent* concept, in relation to the concept at the bottom of

---

[2] $\mapsto$ defines a relation pair, and $:=$ precedes a definition statement.

that edge which is called a *child* concept. If a child concept has more than one parent, the parent concepts all share a subset of attributes of the child.

Each node (ball) in a concept lattice, such as depicted, represents a single concept. The radius of the nodes represents the relative number of objects that exist within the concept. If the drawing of a node shows a blue-filled upper semi-circle, there is a so-called own-attribute attached to this concept. This means: not only is the attribute in the concept's intent, it belongs solely to this concept and its children. If a node contains a black-filled lower semicircle, there is an object attached to this concept. This means that the intent of this concept exactly matches the attributes of the object.

The concept lattice at this stage represents all the domain knowledge contained within the sources, but we still need to determine which information within it has matured and which has not. There might be *noise* within the lattice (representing un-settled knowledge) which needs to be filtered out for the sake of accurate analysis results, for example: some formal techniques that were attempted in a few papers but were not successfully adopted as the norm within the domain.

2.3   Stability Index

The definition of stability and the stability index can be found in the papers by Buzmakov, Kuznetsov and Napoli [5,12] and is as follows: For a context $K = (G, M, I)$ and a concept $c = (A, B)$,

$$Stab(c) := \frac{|\{s \in \wp(Ext(c)) \mid s^I = Int(c)\}|}{2^{|Ext(c)|}}$$

That is, the relative number of subsets of the concept extent (denoted by $Ext(c)$), whose description (the result of applying I) is equal to the concept intent (denoted by $Int(c)$) where $\wp(P)$ is the power set of P. Stability indicates the independence of a concept's intent from its extent. Stability does not only provide noise-resistance. A stable concept does not collapse when certain objects (in our case: literature sources) are removed from the context — that is, the concept does not merge with a different concept nor disintegrate into smaller concepts.

In our domain analysis study, noise in the knowledge-representing lattice should be expected. There are, for example, avenues of research that have been unsuccessfully attempted; they are sources of noise in our lattice. Redundancy is an issue to be taken into consideration, too: If a context and its concepts are stable, then the same lattice and the same relations could be seen on the basis of a rather different data set.

As we presume settled knowledge to be integral to the body of knowledge in our domain, we expect settled knowledge to be incorporated in stable concepts rather than unstable ones. So we need to distillate the stable concepts in the lattice and 'prune' the unstable ones away. Thus, we extract the most relevant domain-specific knowledge by selecting concepts with the highest stability indices.

Stability Threshold. Selecting a threshold stability index will decide which concepts are 'stable enough' to be preserved in the final lattice. Previous work in knowledge ontologies allows for a systematic post-processing of the raw data to influence this crucial decision [5,12,13,17]. Picking a stability threshold has the advantage of getting rid of noise but the disadvantage of removing even some potentially relevant data. Therefore, we need to find a balance between both for the best fit lattice. We plot the percentage of data included in the lattice versus the stability threshold indices. The resulting graph will allow us to decide what is an acceptable stability threshold based on the amount of data left out.

After selecting this threshold, we prune the concepts that fall below it and arrive at a clean and stable lattice with concepts that better represent the structure of data within the railway domain. Note that a pruned lattice does not necessarily form a single lattice [17]. If there are formal methods represented in this final lattice, we can conclude that those formal methods are indeed present in the settled knowledge of the railway domain.

Using the stability threshold as a pruning technique has an important advantage. It provides a mathematical measure of the stability of the structure of the lattice. Concepts with low stability rely on too varied a dataset that makes their case as a reliable data point come into question. This allows us to include data that has a number of varied characteristics, and be assured that only those that provide a stable structure remain after the pruning with regard to a chosen stability threshold value.

3   Results

Concept Lattice. A large cross table for the railway domain was constructed with the knowledge collected. From this table, we use the tool ConExp [20] to automatically construct a concept lattice. The resulting lattice is too large and complicated for any meaningful visualisation. Therefore, it is broken up into smaller, easier-to-understand lattices that contain objects and their attributes for specific subdomains of the railway domain. An example subdomain can be seen in Fig. 3; it represents the lattice for the *Rolling Stock* subdomain. There is a similar lattice for each subdomain of the railway domain [11]. Model-Driven Engineering (MDE) can be found as a very prominent technique, as shown in Fig. 3. Tool chains, domain-specific specification as well as further languages are other familiar techniques in this subdomain. We can also see that the sources of that knowledge are from 2000, 2010, 2012 and 2014, and have thus a reasonably long historic duration in this field.

These smaller sub-domain-specific lattices permit the visualisation of a particular set of data, such that relevant relations are easily observable. Important formal techniques within the subdomain can be seen as well as specific and general methods. These smaller lattices also allow a closer look at smaller areas of the wider railway domain, so that more detailed structures can be gleaned from them.

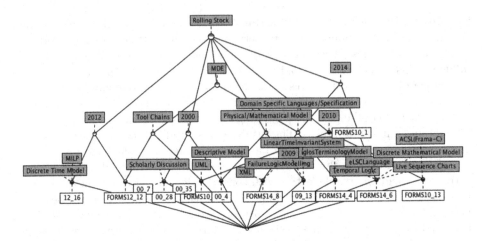

Fig. 3. Lattice representing knowledge in the Rolling stock subdomain in ConExp

Pruning of the Lattice. By manually examining the data, there are a large number of concepts with only one object in their extent. There is no way of knowing whether the corresponding papers are actually pertinent to the overall structure, or if they are merely noise. We would need more data to support either theory, therefore the one-object concepts do not give us any useful information about the structure of the domain or the settled knowledge we seek. Thus, these concepts are pruned from the final lattice.

After examining this lattice, the additional attributes such as the years and non-formal-method papers were also removed from the context, in order to produce a more streamlined visual representation of the final results. We need to not only to distill settled knowledge but also to discover some structure, so removal of deliberate noise was important.

To get a stability threshold value, we plot a graph of the percentage of data included in the lattice versus the stability threshold indices (expressed as percentages). The graph, which can be seen in Fig. 4, shows us the percentage of data left in the lattice if a particular stability index was used as a threshold. Here it is easy to see that there are two significantly large drops in data inclusion: one drop at 25 % and one drop at 50 %. This is due to the mathematics of the formula that is used to calculate stability, and also because of a number of concepts with 3 or more objects in their extent.

Since stability index values below 0.5 do not make sense and keeping 100 % of the data is not needed as per the definition of stability, the data inclusion drop at 25 % is not so meaningful. However, the drop at 50 % is much more reasonable and would highlight the most important concepts within the context while removing noise from the structure. This also coincides with the mathematical prediction that at least 0.5 stability can be considered as 'good enough' to be taken as a stable lattice structure.

Selecting this threshold and removing the noise in the original lattice leads to the final complete lattice as shown in Fig. 5. Acronym definitions for this figure can be found in the dissertation of a similar name [11].

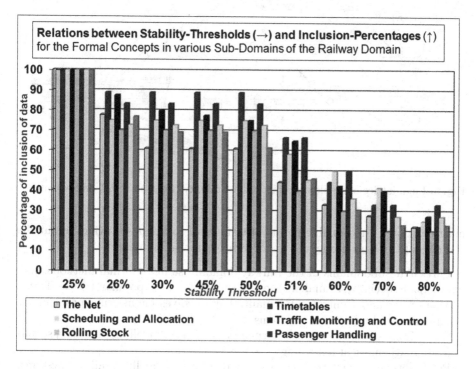

Fig. 4. Changes in percentage data inclusion as a function of the stability threshold indices (expressed as a percentage)

The formal methods included in the final lattice (Fig. 5) are given below. Note that these are considered 'formal' methods within the context of their use in the railway domain and also can be found stated as such in much of the literature [6,8].

– Petri Nets
– Mathematical Models
– Markov Models
– Discrete Mathematical Models
– Discrete Event Systems
– Fuzzy Logic

The final lattice has a non-empty subset of formal methods used both in general problems within the domain and specific problems to a particular subdomain. This directly fulfills one aspect of settled knowledge. The data spans a period of over twenty years and therefore fulfills the main requirement that the knowledge

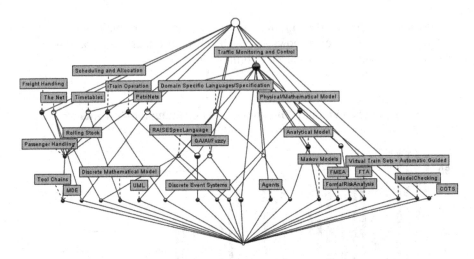

Fig. 5. Final lattice of stable concepts with a stability threshold ≥ 0.5 and extent > 1

must exist over a reasonable period of time. Some other observations about the contents of this knowledge and its structure can also be made:

- Particular subdomains of the railway domain use more formal methods than others. Especially, formal methods seem to be very popular in the Traffic Monitoring and Control subdomain. This involves engineering problems in signalling and interlocking systems.
- The railway domain often uses formal methods for modelling purposes, specifically mathematical modelling.
- Petri Nets are a generic formal method used in modelling railway systems, whereas Markov Models are specifically used for analysing the Traffic Monitoring and Control subdomain. Other techniques like Model Checking are specific to the same domain while Model Driven Engineering (MDE) with Tool Chains is used for the subdomains of Passenger Handling and Rolling Stock.
- UML and the RAISE Specification Language are frequently used in railways, specifically for modelling the subdomain Traffic Monitoring and Control.
- There are some unknown concepts that also exist within the lattice, connecting several concepts which might provide extra context within the domain. For example, there is a connection between Domain Specific Languages, RAISE Language, Analytical Models and the subdomain Traffic Monitoring and Control. It could be noted that the specification language RAISE is used in the domain Traffic Monitoring and Control to create analytical models.

Ultimately, there are at least six formal methods that can be seen as 'settled' in this subset of data. According to our original criteria, as previously mentioned, and in relation to this collected subset of domain knowledge, there is definitely settled knowledge to be found in the railway domain and it can be isolated by interpreting a stable lattice constructed from domain knowledge sources.

4   Discussion: Possible Threats to Validity

The results of our domain analysis were obtained on the basis of several preconditions and rational assumptions. Though these can well be defended —see above— as 'reasonable', we must nevertheless make those preconditions and assumptions *explicit* such as to enable both scholarly critique and future improvements. The following points shall be particularly mentioned:

Notion of 'Settled-ness': In asking which knowledge is sufficiently 'settled' for its BOK-ification, we assumed a notion of 'settled-ness' which is essentially *temporal*. Such knowledge must occur and re-occur sufficiently often over a sufficiently long historic period of time.

- Other epistemologists might thus argue whether or not our notion of 'settled-ness' is appropriate.

Choice of Database: We have sought settled knowledge in the *public domain*, particularly in the *community-relevant* conference proceedings indicated in [9] and [11].

- Other experts might thus argue against us that the chosen conferences are not 'community-relevant' at all, that the set of chosen conferences is insufficiently small such that relevant settled knowledge has been omitted, or that the settled knowledge of the engineering industry exists only in form of corporate secrets rather than being publicly available. We also have to admit that the number of conferences, which we scanned for domain-specific literature, was rather small; only a part of the entire railway domain could be captured so far.

Choice of Attributes for FCA: We have used the attribute-based method of FCA to automatically identify those concepts which we have strongly associated with 'settled' knowledge. Our definition of the relevant attributes, to be used in the lattice matrices such as the one shown in Fig. 1, was done *rationally* upon a thorough hermeneutical reading and interpretation of relevant engineering-philosophical literature.

- Other experts might thus argue against us that our attributes were not defined appropriately, or that we have wrongly omitted important attributes altogether: consequently the automatically generated lattice graphs, such as the one shown in Fig. 3, would not represent an accurate 'image' of the chosen domain or subdomain.

Choice of Stability Threshold: After a first 'raw' lattice with too many 'unstable' concepts had been obtained in the first phase of our FCA, we have selected and included into our recommendable results only those concepts with a stability *above* a particular percentage threshold $(0 < s < 1)$. Though the value v for $s := v$ was chosen carefully on the basis of reasonable considerations (see Fig. 4), it was nevertheless still our *choice*.

– Other experts might thus argue against us that our choice of v was not appropriate, and that an alternative threshold $s := v'$ (with $v' \neq v$) should have been chosen instead of v.

5   Conclusion and Outlook to Future Work

From the preceding sections of this paper, supported by many further details in [11], *two* kinds of conclusions can now be drawn, namely about:

– *how* to proceed methodically, in a rationally well-grounded, mathematically formalised and scientifically repeatable manner, for the identification of *settled knowledge* in any engineering domain which possesses a sufficiently large corpus of scholarly literature;
– *which* topics to include into the future BoK book on the topic of *Formal Methods in the Railway Domain*.

As far as the first point is concerned: We have shown how to 'dissect' a large domain into its most relevant sub-domains (a.k.a. 'divide and conquer'), how to lay out for each sub-domain a many-dimensional 'attribute space' which accommodates all the epistemically relevant entities of that sub-domain, how to use Formal Concept Analysis (FCA) to well-order the entities which 'live' in that space, and how to apply well-defined 'stability' calculations on formal concept lattices in support of a final decision about which concepts are to be regarded as most important (or which ones are merely spurious and may be ignored). From an engineering-philosophical point of view, the thus-identified epistemic entities could possibly belong to any of the six categories of engineering-knowledge in Vincenti's epistemology [19].

As far as the second point is concerned: Our analyses of very large volumes of scholarly literature on the application of Formal Methods in the railway domain, over a long period of more than twenty years, have indicated clearly that at least the following epistemic concepts must now be regarded as well-established or 'settled' in this domain: *Petri Nets* (and similar types of mathematical modelling) in almost all of the domain's subdomains, *Formal Risk Analysis* particularly in the sub-domain of traffic monitoring and control, *UML* in the same sub-domain, and *Max Plus Algebra* as well as *Discrete Event Systems* particularly in the sub-domain of timetable scheduling; please see [11] for many further details.

As far as *future work* is concerned: Two of this paper's co-authors belong to an international planning committee, in which the table-of-contents of a forthcoming BoK book on the application of Formal Methods in the railway domain shall be prepared. The results published in this preparatory paper (on the basis of [11]) have clearly identified the predominant topics of 'settled' knowledge in the domain, i.e.: the knowledge, themes and topics which may soon await their further BoK-ification for the benefits of the engineers and professionals working in this domain. The future BoK book, with all its finer details, shall also be well-aligned with the higher-level *standards of quality* (such as CENELEC EN50128, EN50126-1, EN50129, EN ISO 9000, EN ISO 9001, ISO IEC 90003, ISO IEC

9126) which the international community of engineers has already accepted as normative and 'professionally binding' to a large extent. The ultimate purpose of the BoK book will be the provision of *'settled', problem-specific solution-templates*, which shall —when applied properly— *support the fulfillment* of the quality requirements stipulated by those normative standards at their coarser level of abstraction.

Epilogue

At the workshop in Paris on the 7th of November 2015, after the presentation of this paper, the question was asked *why* we have used *FCA instead of 'ontologies'*. The answer to this question is two-fold. First of all, FCA has already proven its practical value in various other application domains —see the annual *ICFCA* conferences published by Springer-Verlag in the LNAI— and is thus a trustworthy method in the field of formal epistemology. A second —and also more important— reason is the possibility of *numeric* assessment of 'stability', and subsequent elimination of 'noise', which is not possible in the framework of classical 'ontologies'. Last but not least we might perhaps conjecture —here without proof— that many practically relevant 'ontologies' could possibly be translated (more or less accurately) into (more or less equivalent) table representations of the typed needed and used in our work: in this case the suggested opposition —'ontologies' *versus* FCA— would disappear.

Acknowledgments. Many thanks to a number of experts, who have been helpful and supportive during the course of our project, especially: *Sergei Obiedkov, Markus Roggenbach, Anne Haxthausen, Hannes Gräbe, Jackie van der Westhuizen, René Hosse, Jan Welte, Francesco Flammini, Hans True, Jérôme Lalouette*, and *Stefan Östlund*. Many thanks also to the anonymous reviewers of FTSCS'15 for their constructive remarks. Last but not least many thanks to the workshop participants, particularly *José Meseguer*, for some interesting questions and comments during our meeting in Paris.

References

1. Arageorgis, A., Baltas, A.: Demarcating technology from science: problems and problem solving in technology. Zeitschrift für allgemeine Wissenschaftstheorie **20**(2), 212–229 (1989)
2. Bjørner, D.: Formal software techniques in railway systems. In: Proceedings 9th IFAC Symposium on Control in Transportation Systems, pp. 1–12. VDI/VDE (2000)
3. Bjørner, D.: TRain: the railway domain. http://euler.fd.cvut.cz/railwaydomain/
4. Bunge, M.: Philosophy of Science: From Explanation to Justification, vol. 2, Revised edn. Transaction Publ., Piscataway (1998)
5. Buzmakov, A., Kuznetsov, S., Napoli, A.: Is concept stability a measure for pattern selection? Procedia Comput. Sci. **31**, 918–927 (2014)
6. Fantechi, A.: Twenty-five years of formal methods and railways: what next? In: Counsell, S., Núñez, M. (eds.) SEFM 2013. LNCS, vol. 8368, pp. 167–183. Springer, Heidelberg (2014)

7. Ganter, B., Wille, R.: Formale Begriffsanalyse: Mathematische Grundlagen. Springer, Berlin (1996)
8. Gruner, S., Haxthausen, A., Maibaum, T., Roggenbach, M.: FM-RAIL-BOK organizers' message. In: Counsell, S., Núñez, M. (eds.) SEFM 2013. LNCS, vol. 8368. Springer, Heidelberg (2014)
9. Gruner, S., Haxthausen, A., Maibaum, T., Roggenbach, M.: Homepage of the workshop on a formal methods body of knowledge for railway control and safety systems (2013). https://ssfmgroup.wordpress.com/rel/
10. Jackson, M.: Formal methods and traditional engineering. J. Syst. Softw. **40**, 191–194 (1998)
11. Kumar, A.: A preparatory study towards a body of knowledge in the field of formal methods for the railway domain. Master-of-Applied Science Dissertation, McMaster University, Canada (2015). http://hdl.handle.net/11375/18416
12. Kuznetsov, S.: On stability of a formal concept. Ann. Math. Artif. Intell. **49**(1–4), 101–115 (2007)
13. Kuznetsov, S., Ignatov, D.: Concept stability for constructing taxonomies of website users. Computing Research Repository (CoRR) abs/0905.1424 (2009)
14. Maibaum, T.: What is a BoK? large: extended abstract. In: Counsell, S., Núñez, M. (eds.) SEFM 2013. LNCS, vol. 8368, pp. 184–188. Springer, Heidelberg (2014)
15. Poser, H.: On structural differences between science and engineering. Digital Library and Archives of the Virginia Tech University Libraries (1998)
16. Priss, U.: Formal concept analysis homepage. http://www.fcahome.org.uk/
17. Roth, C., Obiedkov, S., Kourie, D.G.: Towards concise representation for taxonomies of epistemic communities. In: Yahia, S.B., Nguifo, E.M., Belohlavek, R. (eds.) CLA 2006. LNCS (LNAI), vol. 4923, pp. 240–255. Springer, Heidelberg (2008)
18. Shaw, M.: The Coming-of-age of software architecture research. In: Proceedings 23rd ICSE, pp. 656–663. IEEE Computer Society (2001)
19. Vincenti, W.: What Engineers Know and How They Know It: Analytical Studies From Aeronautical History. John Hopkins University Press, Baltimore (1990)
20. Yevtushenko, S., ConExp,: Concept Explorer. http://conexp.sourceforge.net/

Towards Safety Analysis of ERTMS/ETCS Level 2 in Real-Time Maude

Phillip James[1], Andrew Lawrence[2], Markus Roggenbach[1], and Monika Seisenberger[1] ([✉])

[1] Swansea University, Swansea, UK
m.seisenberger@swansea.ac.uk
[2] Hitachi Data Systems, Poole, UK

Abstract. ERTMS/ETCS is a European signalling, control and train protection system. In this paper, we model and analyse this complex system of systems, including its hybrid elements, on the design level in Real-Time Maude. Our modelling allows us to formulate safety properties in physical rather than in logical terms. We systematically validate our model by simulation and error injection. Using the Real-Time Maude model-checker, we effectively verify a number of small rail systems.

1 Introduction

The European Rail Traffic Management System (ERTMS)/European Train Control System (ETCS) is a European signalling, control and train protection system designed to allow for high speed travel, to increase capacity, and to facilitate cross-border traffic movements [7]. ERTMS/ETCS is a complex system of systems, made up by distributed components. It is specified at four different levels, where each level defines a different use as a train control system. In our paper we consider ERTMS/ETCS Level 2, which is characterised by continuous communications between trains and a radio block centre.

The switch from classical railway signalling systems to ERTMS/ETCS train control poses a number of research questions for the formal methods community. Can safety be guaranteed? Can formal methods be used to confirm that such a switch improves capacity? Is it possible to predict capacity using formal methods? To address such questions it is necessary to develop and analyse timed or hybrid models. ERTMS/ETCS Level 2 takes speed and braking curves of each individual train into account. These determine the train's braking point well in advance of the end of authority that the signalling system had granted to this train. Such an approach is in contrast to classical signalling systems, which treat all trains in the same way. Therefore, they need to be designed for worst case braking. Consequently, in formal safety analysis, such traditional systems can be treated on a purely logical level, ignoring the aspect of time – see, e.g., [9,10].

An ERTMS/ETCS system consists of a controller, an interlocking (a specialised computer that determines if a request from the controller is "safe"), a radio block centre, track equipment, and a number of trains. While the ERTMS/ETCS standard details the interactions between trains and track equipment

C. Artho and P.C. Ölveczky (Eds.): FTSCS 2015, CCIS 596, pp. 103–120, 2016.
DOI: 10.1007/978-3-319-29510-7_6

(e.g., in order to obtain concise train position information) and radio block centre and trains (e.g., to hand out movement authorities), the details of how controller, interlocking and radio block centre interact with each other are left to the suppliers of signalling solutions such as our industrial partner Siemens Rail Automation UK. In this paper we work with the implementation as realised by Siemens. In the following we refer to this system simply as ERTMS.

One development step when building an ERTMS system consists of developing a so-called detailed design. Given geographical data such as a specific track layout and what routes through this track layout shall be used, the detailed design adds a number of tables that determine the location specific behaviour of interlocking and radio block centre. The objective of our modelling is to provide a formal argument that a given detailed design is safe. Here we focus on collision freedom, though our model is extensible for dealing with further safety properties, and possibly also with performance analysis.

We base our modelling approach on Real-Time Maude, which is a language and tool supporting the formal object-oriented specification and analysis of real-time and hybrid systems. In order to obtain a faithful model of ERTMS/ETCS level 2 on the design level, we follow a systematic approach, established by the Swansea Railway Verification Group.

This paper extends our location-specific modelling presented in past work [12] to a generic and far more detailed modelling. It is organised as follows. First, we introduce the ERTMS Level 2 standard, and briefly discuss high level safety properties for ERTMS. Then, we give a short presentation of Real-Time Maude with a focus on standard specification techniques for hybrid systems. In Sect. 4, we present our modelling of ERTMS in Real-Time Maude, discussing each component in detail. In Sect. 5, we validate our model by simulation and error injection. Finally, we present model checking results and put our approach in the context of related work.

2 ERTMS Level 2

ERTMS Level 2 extends classical railway signalling. To this end its location specific design[1] extends the classical notion of a scheme plan by information used for the radio block centre (RBC). ERTMS safety analysis also requires train characteristics such as maximum speed, acceleration and braking curves.

2.1 Scheme Plans

A scheme plan is a well-established concept within the railway domain. Figure 1 depicts such a *scheme plan* for a pass-through station. It comprises of a track plan, a control table, release tables and RBC tables. The *track plan* provides the topological information for the station. It consists of 8 tracks (e.g., BC) each with a length, 3 marker boards (e.g., MB1), and two points (e.g., P2). A topological

---

[1] We focus here on one ERTMS/ETCS system controlling a single, geographic region.

route is a piece of railway on which a train can travel, (typically) between two marker boards (e.g., from MB1 to MB2). The *control table* describes under which conditions a *route* can be set.[2] For example, a train can only proceed on route 1 A when point P1 is in normal (straight) position and tracks AA, AB and AC are clear, i.e., currently not occupied by any train. The *release table* is used to implement sequential release, a technique to improve capacity. The release table describes when a point is again free to move after being locked for a particular route. For example, when sending a train on route 1A, point P1 is free to move already, when this train has reached track AC. This allows to send another train on route 1B before the first train has reached track AD and thus completely left route 1A. Finally, the *RBC tables* are used for calculations within the RBC.

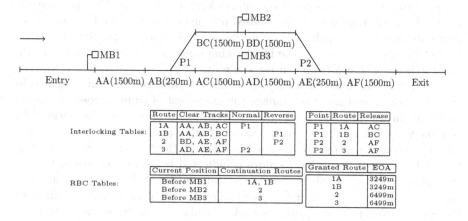

Fig. 1. Scheme plan for a pass-through station.

We consider open scheme plans with entry and exit tracks only. Furthermore, we assume that marker boards are placed at the end of tracks, and that the speed limit is the same for all tracks.

2.2 ERTMS System Architecture

Once a scheme plan has been designed, a number of control systems are implemented based around it. In the following we identify the entities of ERTMS, describe their abstract behaviour and determine the abstract information flow between them in line with the design by Siemens Rail UK, see Fig. 2.

The *controller* (manual or computerised) is responsible for controlling the flow of trains through the railway network. The controller completes this task by sending "route request" messages to the interlocking. These route requests are dependent upon elements such as the current timetable to be adhered to

---

[2] It is a design decision whether a topological route appears in the control table. The routes in the table are those available for use by trains.

and details on congestion within the network. For simplicity, we abstract from "route cancel" and "acknowledgement" messages.

The *interlocking* is responsible for setting and granting requested routes. Once the controller has requested a route, the interlocking will use information on current track occupation and point settings (from the track equipment) to determine if it is safe for the requested route to be set. Whether a route can be set or not is computed in a process based upon the conditions stipulated by the control table, see Fig. 1. Once the interlocking has checked that all points on the route are free to move or already in the right position, it will send a "route available" message to the RBC (Radio Block Centre). This informs the RBC that the route is free for use, however it is not yet reserved for a train. The RBC initiates the process of locking a route for a particular train by sending a "request to proceed" message to the interlocking. On receiving this message, the interlocking will then ensure that, based on the control table, all tracks for the route are free and that the points are indeed locked in the required positions. Once this step is completed, the interlocking sends a "proceed" message to the RBC indicating that a train can use the route.

The *RBC*'s main responsibility is to take the route information presented by the interlocking and use it to manage the movement of trains across geographic positions on the railway. To do this, the RBC and trains use the notion of a *movement authority*. A movement authority is an area of geographical railway that a train is permitted to move within. The furthest point along the railway to which a train is permitted to move is indicated by a point known as the *end of authority* (EoA) which is given to a train by the RBC. As a train moves across the railway network, it uses beacons on the track to continually calculate its position. When it is nearing its EoA, it makes a new "movement authority request" to the RBC indicating that it would like its movement authority to be extended. After receiving this request, the RBC will map the physical location of the train to an available continuation route that has been presented to it by the interlocking.[3] This calculation is performed based on a look-up table designed as part of the RBC for a scheme plan, an example of such a table is provided in Fig. 1. It will then issue a "request to proceed" message to the interlocking for this route. Once the RBC has received a "proceed" message from the interlocking, it will compute, based on the route that has been granted, a new EoA for the train. Again, this information is provided by a look-up table, see Fig. 1. This new EoA is then finally sent as a "movement authority" message to the train.

With regards to *trains*, their behaviour is parameterised by maximum speed, acceleration and braking curves. We make a maximum progress assumption for trains, i.e., trains are running as fast and as far as possible. Namely, if a train has a movement authority beyond its current position it will accelerate towards its maximum speed. When the maximum speed is reached, the train will continue to

---

[3] At this point, there should be maximally one route available that matches a particular train. This is ensured by the requests from the controller and also the ability of the interlocking to deny requests for conflicting routes.

travel at this speed. Whilst accelerating or travelling at maximum speed the train will start braking at the last possible time in order not to overrun its EoA. Trains are guided by the track layout, respecting the positions to which the interlocking has set points. As trains move along the track, track equipment senses track occupation and reports it to the interlocking. We assume that *track equipment* (points, track circuits, beacons etc.) functions correctly and that points move instantaneously. This is justified as our verification aim is to establish correctness of the location and train specific design parameters for a ERTMS system for a single geographic region. Therefore, we refrain from modelling track equipment.

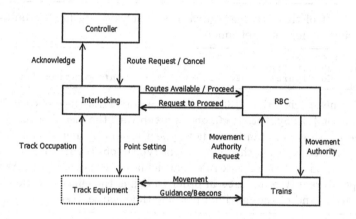

Fig. 2. ERTMS control architecture.

2.3 Safety Conditions

In the context of ERTMS, several high level safety conditions have been discussed such as collision freedom or derailment on a point. In this paper, we focus on collision freedom, i.e., excluding the possibility that two trains collide. In the context of classical signalling systems, this property usually is formulated logically, e.g., we verify that there are never two trains on the same track [9]. In contrast, for ERTMS we rather consider the physical invariant: the distance between trains never falls below a minimum threshold.

3   Maude/Real-Time Maude

The Maude system [5] is a multi-purpose tool with support for executable specification, simulation and verification. Its wide range of capabilities made us to favour Maude. Particularly, we are interested in the Maude LTL Model Checker [6]. Real Time Maude [13] is an extension of Maude containing specific support enabling the modelling and verification of real-time systems.

Object-based systems can be modelled as multisets of objects and messages where the messages define the communication between the objects and typically trigger actions of the objects. A class *C* with attributes of a_1 to a_n of sort Sort_1 to Sort_n, and an object O with attribute values v_1 to v_n of class C are written as, respectively

```
class C | a_1 : Sort_1, ... , a_n : Sort_n .
< O : C | a_1 : v_1, ... , a_n : v_n > .
```

Objects declared together with messages

```
msgs M_1 ... M_k : Sort_1 ... Sort_n -> Msg .
```

form a multiset of the sort Configuration, a subsort of Maude's built-in sort System, using __ for multiset union.

```
sorts Object Msg Configuration .
subsort Object Msg < Configuration .
op __ : Configuration Configuration -> Configuration [ctor] .
```

A real-time specification [13] consists of a sort Time (in our case PosRat), the constructor {_} : System− > Globalsystem with the meaning that {t} represents the whole system (and does not appear as an argument to another function - as is marked by using the independent type Globalsystem), instantaneous rewrite rules, and a so-called tick rule that defines how time elapses. As [17], we use the operators delta and mte in order to define the effect of time elapse on a configuration, and of the maximal possible time elapse, resp.

```
op delta : Configuration Time -> Configuration [frozen (1)] .
op mte : Configuration -> TimeInf [frozen (1)] .
```

Here, TimeInf is the sort Time enriched with an infinity element Inf. These two functions are distributed over objects and messages, i.e., each object has the same time available, and as the maximal time elapse for a message has value 0, time can only progress once all messages are consumed.

```
vars CON1 CON2 : NeConfiguration . var R : Time .
eq delta(none, R) = none .
eq delta(CON1 CON2, R) = delta(CON1,R) delta(CON2,R) .
eq mte(none) = INF .
eq mte(CON1 CON2) = min(mte(CON1),mte(CON2)) .
```

The argument R of type Time is determined by the tick rule

```
crl [tick] : {CURRENT} => {delta(CURRENT,R)} in time R
                if R <= mte(CURRENT) [nonexec] .
```

The default tick time is defined by

```
(set tick def 1 .)
```

This means we look at the configuration either at each time step, or more often in the case that some event occurs, for a justification see e.g. [15].

4   Modelling ERTMS in Maude

To the best of our knowledge, our modelling of ERTMS is the first one comprising all ERTMS subsystems required for the control cycle in ERTMS/ETCS Application Level 2, c.f. Fig. 6 in the ERTMS/ETCS System Requirements Specification [2]. For simplicity, we consider only uni-directional rail yards, as these exhibit many of the components of bi-directional rail yards, but are of a lower complexity with regards to the number of routes required within the model. Also, we make the standard assumption that trains have no length. This is the typical abstraction when one deals with trains whose length is shorter than any track length in the given scheme plan. For a detailed discussion of the topic see, e.g., our publication discussing train length [10].

In the following, we provide an overview of our model:[4] first we discuss the static data types; then we look at the instantaneously reacting sub-systems, i.e., controller, interlocking, and RBC; next, we describe how we capture train behaviour, which requires differential equations describing motion; finally, we address how to express collision-freedom. We note that our model is generic, with only location specific data as a parameter. This location specific data has been encoded manually, however this process could be automated within OnTrack [11].

4.1   Datatypes: Location Specific Data and Messages

We model the rail topology as a connected collection of tracks, points, and routes and provide a systematic translation into Maude. For the example given in Fig. 1, the location specific data Maude is encoded as follows:

```
sort RouteName .  ops RouteName1A ... : -> RouteName .
sort Track .      ops AA AB AC ... : -> Track         .
sort Point .      ops P1 P2 : -> Point                .
```

The connection between tracks is given by a next function. If the track under discussion is a point, as, e.g., track AB, it has two potential successors, namely AC and BC, depending on the current setting of the point.

```
op next : Track PointPos -> Track . var PPos : PointPos .
eq next(AA,PPos) = AB                                     .
eq next(AB,normal) = AC . eq next(AB,reverse) = BC        .
```

The various tables (clear and release tables for the scheme plan, the tables of the RBC) are encoded by defining a function for each column. A typical example is the "Clear Tracks" column[5] of the control table in Fig. 1:

```
op clearTracks : RouteName -> SetOfTracks    .
eq clearTracks(RouteName1A) = (AA, AB, AC) .
...
eq clearTracks(RouteName4)  = empty          .
```

---

[4] The models are available at: http://www.cs.swan.ac.uk/%7Ecsmarkus/Processes AndData/Models.

[5] Compared to the given control table, we add RouteName4 to cover the exit track.

The ERTMS components exchange a number of messages, see Fig. 2. As we are dealing with a single geographic region, controller, interlocking, and RBC are unique. Thus, for most messages no object identifier is needed:

```
msgs routerequest, proceedrequest, ... : RouteName -> Msg .
```

This is in contrast to messages involving trains. For instance, the message

```
msg magrant : Oid Nat -> Msg .
```

grants a movement authority (encoded as a natural number, determining the position to which the train is allowed to travel) to a specific train with an object identifier of type `Oid`. Messages are urgent, i.e., their processing time is 0:

```
eq mte(M:Msg) = 0 .
```

4.2   Instantaneously Reacting Sub-Systems

The processing time of controller, interlocking, and RBC is negligible compared to the time that it takes a train to pass a track. Thus, in our modelling we assume that these three components react instantaneously. In Maude this is expressed by saying that these components do not pose any time constrains. Here, written for the controller:

```
eq mte(< O1 : Controller | >) = INF .
```

Controller. An ERTMS controller issues route requests. For a general safety analysis, a *random controller* that can make any order of route requests should be considered:

```
op randomRoute : -> RouteName .
rl randomRoute => RouteName1A .
...
rl randomRoute => RouteName4 .
```

However, it is also possible to perform safety analysis relatively to a specific strategy, e.g., a *round-robin controller* that requests routes as follows – 1A first, followed by 1B, until route 4, starting over with 1A again:

```
eq routeOrder = (RouteName1A : RouteName1B : ... : RouteName4) .
```

Yet another parameter are the times at which the controller makes route requests. For both controllers we work with a constant frequency.

Interlocking. In rail control systems, the interlocking provides a safety layer between controller and track. To this end, it monitors the physical rail yard (`occ` says which tracks are currently occupied, `pointPositions` says for each point if it is in normal or in reverse position), manages locks (`pointslocked` says if a point is currently locked by a route), and stores which routes are currently set (`routeset`):

```
class Inter |  routeset : MapRouteName2Bool,
               pointslocked : MapPoint2Bool,
               occ : MapTrack2Bool,
               pointPositions : MapPoint2PointPos  .
```

The interlocking is a passive component, i.e., only upon receiving a message it possibly changes its state and/or sends a message. A typical rule for preserving safety is the following:

```
crl  routerequest(RN1)
       < 0 : Inter |  routeset : MAPRNB1,
                      occ : MAPTB1, pointslocked : MAPPB3 >
    => < 0 : Inter | > if (not checkClear(RN1, MAPTB1)) or
                      pointsLocked(RN1, MAPPB3) .
```

A route request by the controller is ignored in case that the tracks specified in the clear table for route RN1 are occupied or the points of route RN1 are locked in different positions.

RBC. The RBC mediates between requests from the trains to extend their movement authorities and the successful route requests by the controller. To this end it reconciles two different views on the rail yard: trains use continuous data to represent their position (in our model the distance from the leftmost point of the rail yard); the interlocking uses discrete data (track occupation, set routes, point positions) in its logic. In our model, we take a rather simplified and also abstract view on the challenges involved. We make the assumption that trains request a new movement authority only on the track on which their current authority ends. Furthermore, we abstract the mapping between continuous and discrete data to the two tables presented in Fig. 1.

In our model, the RBC only holds information on successful route requests (in availableRoutes) and for which trains (characterised by their Oid) it currently has an open "request to proceed" (in designatedRoutes):

```
class RBC |  availableRoutes  : SetOfRouteNames,
             designatedRoutes : MapOid2RouteName  .
```

Also, the RBC is a passive system component. A typical reaction is the following: When the interlocking sends a "proceed message" for a route RN, the RBC sends a new "end of authority" to the train and removes the corresponding request from its internal state.

```
rl proceedgrant(RN) < O2 : RBC | designatedRoutes : TRN >
   => magrant(getTrain(RN, TRN), endOfAuthority(RN))
      < O2 : RBC | designatedRoutes : removeRoute(_,_) >  .
```

4.3 Trains

The Train class is the only time dependent entity in our model. It is designed as an automaton with four states stop, acc for accelerating, cons for constant speed, and brake. There are transitions stop → acc → cons → brake, and acc → brake and vice versa. In addition, it has fields representing the current distance (relative to a given reference point 0), speed, acceleration, movement authority (relative to 0), maximum speed, and the current track segment.

```
class Train | state : TrainState , dist : NNegRat ,
              speed : NNegRat , ac : NNegRat , ma : NNegRat ,
              tseg : Track , maxspeed : NNegRat .
```

We assume that acceleration is linear, and – apart from Scenario 3 in Sect. 5.2 – use a value of 1 for both acceleration and deceleration. Trains move according to Newton's laws, i.e., if at time 0 a train is at DT with speed S and acceleration A, then the speed at time R is S + A*R and the location is DT + S*R + A*R*R/2. Its braking distance bd(S,A) is S*S/2*A. We show the rule for a train in the accelerating state.

```
crl [acc] :
  < 01 : Inter | pointPositions : PointSettings >
  delta(< 0 : Train | state : acc, dist : DT, speed : S,
         ac : A, ma : MA, tseg : AN, maxspeed : MAX >, R)
       =>
       < 01 : Inter | pointPositions : PointSettings >
       trackseg(PointSettings, < 0 : Train |
       state : if (S + A * R == MAX)
                  then cons
                  else (if R == mteMA(DT,S,A,MA)
                           then brake
                           else acc fi) fi,
       dist : DT + S * R + R * R * A * (1/2),
       speed : S + A * R > ) if not AN == Exit .
```

The rule computes the new configuration of a train after time R from its old configuration and the interlocking. It is sufficient to list those attributes that are updated, here speed, location, and, possibly, the state. The operator trackseg takes the new location of the train and the PointSettings from the interlocking and returns a new train object. In the case that the train has entered a new track it will update the train object accordingly. Here, we combine the delta rule together with a state transition, allowing us to exactly determine when a state transition occurs. An alternative approach would be to decouple these orthogonal concepts by expressing the rule as equation + rules. This, in turn, may lead to improvements when model checking.

The time R is determined by the maximal time elapse which is, in the acceleration state, the minimum of the following three cases. (1) maximum speed is reached, (2) the end of a track segment is reached, (3) the distance to the movement authority is not greater than the required braking distance.

```
ceq mte (< 0 : Train | state : acc,  dist : DT, speed : S,
          ac : A, ma : MA , tseg : AN, maxspeed : MAX >)
        = min((MAX monus S) / A,
              ((endof(AN) + 1) monus DT) / S,
              mteMA(DT,S,A,MA))   if S > 0 .
eq mteMA(DT, S, A, MA) = (((MA monus 1) monus DT) monus
                          (S * S / (2 * A))) / ( 2 * S) .
```

In case (1) we used monos for the maximum of the difference between two numbers and 0. For cases (2) and (3) the calculation of mte involves quadratic equations. From DT + S*R + A*R*R/2 < endof(AN)+1 we could determine R using an approximation via Newton's method. However, since, thanks to our default tick, we have 0 < R <= 1, and therefore 0 < A*R*R/2 <= A*R/2, we approximate the quadratic term either from below or from above depending on the context: in the case of entering a new track we ignore the quadratic term, and put the sampling point slightly late, as we want to be on the new track already; in the case of calculating where to start braking, we bring the event slightly forward, i.e., we start braking slightly too early. Both approximations are justified by the default tick.

4.4   Safety Condition

For classical railway signalling, we established the following finitisation theorem: if a signalling system is collision free for two trains, then it is collision free for any number of trains [9]. We conjecture that this result carries over to ERTMS and consider our ERTMS system to be safe if – within the scheme plan under consideration – two trains are always more than, say, 40 m apart. Thus, we check for the invariant "no collisions":

```
eq { REST   < train1 : Train |  tseg : T1 , dist : N1 >
             < train2 : Train |  tseg : T2 , dist : N2 > }
    |= nocrashDistance(train1, train2)
  =
    ( ( not (T1 == Entry) and not (T2 == Entry) and
        not (T1 == Exit ) and not (T2 == Exit ) )
    and ( T1 == T2 or
          T1 == next(T2, normal) or T1 == next(T2, reverse) or
          T2 == next(T1, normal) or T2 == next(T1, reverse) ) )
    implies ((N2 monus N1 > 100) or (N1 monus N2 > 100)) .
```

This formula reads: a configuration with two objects train1 and train2 of type train models the parameterised formula nocrashDistance iff the state of the two trains objects under consideration are in the relation specified after the equal sign. Here, T1 and T2 are the tracks and N1 and N2 are the positions on which the two trains are respectively. In the formula we check that the trains are more than 100 m apart, provided they are not on the Entry or Exit track, and provided they are on the same (T1 == T2) or on adjacent tracks.

The second condition is necessary as we model positions from a single reference point on the Entry track. For instance, on the track plan shown in Fig. 1, we can have one train on track BC and another train on track AC, both with the same distance, though by no means colliding with each other. We note that we use the value of 100 m for our invariant. This is different from the desired 40 m, but necessary due to our time sampling strategy: we sample the system only once every second. Within this time, the distance between two trains can reduce by maximally 60 m as we consider trains that travel at a maximum of 60 m/s.

4.5   Completeness

An important question is whether our modelling is complete, that is all errors can be detected by our modelling. Ölveczky and Meseguer give criteria for completeness in object oriented Real-Time Maude [15]. Essentially, one needs to prove that the maximal time elapse function is time robust. This is clearly the case if we consider movement without acceleration. It is almost all the time the case for our modelling with acceleration, however the small shifts of the sampling points require further analysis. We expect that a weakening of Theorem 4 [15], which takes approximation into account, holds. A necessary premise for this theorem is non-zenoness for which we give the following argument.

Our modelling is non-zeno in the sense of Henzinger [8] as there are no cycles in the behaviour of the automaton which allow time to converge. The argument is that any cycle will involve the accelerating state, which requires a new movement authority to be granted that will extend the current movement authority by at least one. This causes a minimal time elapse bounded away from zero by a fixed amount since the speed of a train is limited.

5   Validation Through Simulation and Error Injection

Here we give a number of scenarios to illustrate that our modelling is able to capture typical errors that are made when designing ERTMS subsystems. Concerning verification tools, we rely on the model checking capabilities of the Real-Time Maude Tool [16] to provide the relevant counter-examples. In carrying out the verification, our starting point is that the generic models of the interlocking, RBC and trains are correct. However, we make no assumptions about the correctness of the instantiation of our modelling with concrete *Control Tables*, *Release Tables* and *RBC tables*.

5.1   Simulation

We first demonstrate the behaviour of one train moving through the rail yard in Fig. 1 with a start position on track AA and a movement authority of 1498. For this we use the Real Time Maude `trew` command to execute our model upto a given time bound.

```
(trew {
  < inter1 : Inter | pointPositions : (P1 |-> normal,
                                        P2 |-> normal) , ... >
  < train1 : Train | state : acc, dist : 2, speed : 0, ac : 1,
                     ma : 1498, tseg : AA , maxspeed : 60 > }
in time <= 39 .)
```

The train accelerates until it begins to brake at the distance of 749.72m:

```
Result ClockedSystem : { < inter1 : Inter | ...>
  < train1 : Train | ac : 1, dist : 1499446241/2000000,
    ma : 1498, maxspeed : 60, speed : 38671/1000,
    state : brake, tseg : AA >} in time 38671/1000
```

A query one time step later shows that a movement authority request is made.

```
{marequest(train1,AA) < inter1 : ...>
  < train1 : Train | speed : 37671/1000, ... >} in time 39671/1000
```

Now, the system cannot progress, unless we add an RBC to our configuration.

```
(trew { < inter1 : Inter | ... > < train1 : Train | ... >
   < rbc1 : RBC | availableRoutes : empty ,
                  designatedRoutes : empty  >} in time <= 78 .)
```

As no follow-up route is available in the RBC, the train stops at 1497.46 m.

```
{< inter1 : Inter | ... > < rbc1 : RBC | ... >
   < train1 : Train | dist : 1497446241/1000000 , ma : 1498,
     speed : 0, state : stop, tseg : AA >} in time 38671/500
```

To continue, assume that we start in the configuration where the interlocking has set RouteName3 and the train has made a movement authority request.

```
(trew {marequest(train1,AA)
   < inter1 : Inter | routeset : RouteName3 |-> true,... >
   < train1 : Train | state : brake, dist : 760, speed : 37,
     ac : 1, ma : 1498, tseg : AA , maxspeed : 60 >
   < rbc1 : RBC | availableRoutes : (RouteName3), ...  >
   } in time <= 17 .)
```

Below we see that the authority is extended to 6499 m, and P2 gets locked. Time 17 is when the train crosses to track AB and can accelerate to maximum speed.

```
{ < inter1 : Inter | occ : (AA |-> false, AB |-> true),
    pointslocked : P2 |-> true, ... >
  < rbc1 : RBC | availableRoutes : empty, ... >
  < train1 : Train | dist : 3001/2, ma : 6499, speed : 52,
    state : acc,tseg : AB >} in time 17
```

5.2 Error Injection

We now show that our modelling is able to find errors in the design of various ERTMS components. The following scenarios use our random controller and check the safety condition presented in Sect. 4.4. Furthermore, we model one slow train (max speed 20 m/s) and one fast train (max speed 60 m/s).

```
eq initState = {...
   < train1 : Train | state : stop, dist : 0, speed : 0,
     ac : 1, ma : 1, tseg : Entry , maxspeed : 20 >
   < train2 : Train | state : stop, dist : 0, speed : 0,
     ac : 1, ma : 1, tseg : Entry , maxspeed : 60 > ...} .
```

Scenario 1 – Incorrect Control Tables. We consider a scheme plan where the designer forgets to put track section AC into the various interlocking tables in Fig. 1. Model checking highlights that two trains may be within 100 m of each other, with both trains on track AC.

```
{...< train1 : Train | ac : 1, dist : 3249, ma: 3249,
      maxspeed : 20, speed : 0, state : stop, tseg : AC >
    < train2 : Train | ac : 1, dist : 1939979/625, ma : 6499,
      maxspeed : 60, speed : 60, state : cons, tseg : AC > ...}
```

Scenario 2 – Incorrect RBC Tables. We consider a scheme plan where the designer incorrectly calculates an EoA of 3449m for route 1 A in the RBC tables given in Fig. 1. Model checking highlights that two trains may be within 100 meters with train1 overrunning onto track AD due to the incorrect EoA and train2 approaching on AC.

```
{...< train1 : Train | ac : 1,dist : 3449,ma : 3449,
      maxspeed : 20,speed : 0,state : stop,tseg : AD >
    < train2 : Train | ac : 1,dist : 12433788921/4000000,
      ma : 6499,maxspeed : 60, speed : 60,state : cons,
      tseg : AC > ...}
```

Scenario 3 – Incorrect Train Braking Parameters. The computation of the braking distance for a train is based on various parameters, some of which may be incorrectly entered by the driver. Hence the train's physical braking distance may differ from the computed one. Below we consider a starting scenario where a deceleration value of 1 (hard-coded, for illustration) has been incorrectly entered for `train2`, whilst the physical train has a deceleration value of 8/10. The other train has correct parameters.

```
{...< train1 : Train | state : stop, dist : 3249, speed : 0,
      ac : 1, ma : 6499, tseg : AD , maxspeed : 20 >
    < train2 : Train | state : stop, dist : 1, speed : 0,
      ac : 8/10, ma : 1, tseg : Entry , maxspeed : 60 > ...}
```

The incorrect parameter causes the two trains both to be on track `AF` within 100 m of each other. This is due to the incorrect behaviour of `train2` which overruns its movement authority thanks to its wrong braking parameter.

```
{...< train1 : Train | ac : 1,dist : 15662341/2500,ma : 6499,
      maxspeed : 20,speed : 20,state : cons,tseg : AF >
    < train2 : Train | ac : 4/5,dist : 968593576867/156250000,
      ma : 7999,maxspeed : 60,speed : 60,state : cons,
      tseg: AF > ...}
```

6   Model Checking Results

In this section we verify a number of rail yards with the Real-Time Maude Tool [16]. We check that the invariant "no collisions", c.f. Sect. 4.4, is globally true, either for all time

```
mc initState |=t [] nocrashDistance(train1,train2) .
```

or for 300 time steps:

```
mc initState|=t [] nocrashDistance(train1,train2) in time <= 300.
```

Here, `initState` is as given in Sect. 5.2. As track plans, we consider the pass-through station shown in Fig. 1 as well as some variations of it, see Fig. 3. This is in order to obtain an indication of how variations in the complexity of the rail yard influence the time required for model checking.

We check all three track plans with manually constructed tables that we consider to be correct. In all settings the model checking confirms that these rail yard designs are collision free (within the given time-bound, if applicable). The table shows verification times[6] and the number of rewrite steps for the three rail yards against the random controller and the round-robin controller (see Sect. 4.2). The following table presents our model checking results (Table 1).

---

[6] Using a PC running Xubuntu 14.04.2 with an i7 4790 @3.60 Ghz and 32 GB RAM.

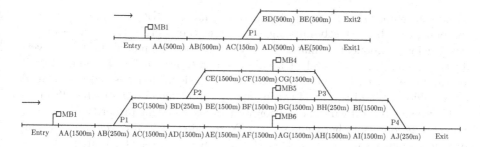

Fig. 3. Track plans for a junction and three platform station.

Table 1. Performance results of model checking three scheme plans.

Scheme Plan	Round Robin Controller Unbounded	Random Controller in Time 300
Junction	0.5 s/1,465,601 rewrites	361.1 s/151,564,627 rewrites
Pass-through Station	0.7 s/1,886,303 rewrites	589.0 s/500,397,040 rewrites
Three Platform Station	1.2 s/2,622,022 rewrites	1957.9 s/1,009,144,410 rewrites

The table shows that unbounded model checking is successful when control is restricted, e.g., to our round-robin controller. This is due to the restrictions that such a control strategy puts on train movements through the sheme plan. However, when using our random controller, the state space vastly increases. Thus, we provide results for up to a given time bound of 300s. Note that this time is enough to ensure that two trains can travel completely through the Junction and Station scheme plan. As expected, model checking times increase with the complexity of the scheme plans. It is future work, to consider further, more varied rail yards.

7   Related Work

ERTMS is a complex system of systems, made up of distributed components interconnected through standard (e.g. Euroradio) and proprietary (e.g. Siemens-specific) protocols and algorithms. Our approach reflects this by covering the full control cycle between controller, interlocking, radio-block centre and trains. Our objective is to verify the location specific data of railway designs in their early development stages, accompanying a standard design process performed by signalling companies such as our industrial partner Siemens.

Our approach to cover all components is different from several verification approaches with a focus on a single component only. Vu et al. [18] provide a generic and re-configurable model of ERTMS Level 2 on the design level sharing our objective. They present their model as a Kripke structure and verify high-level safety properties such as head-to-head collision or derailment on a point. Their approach abstracts from trains and the RBC and presumes these components to be correctly implemented. Thus, their verification focuses on the interlocking component. Cimatti et al. [4] apply software model checking to verify the implementation level of a subsystem responsible for the allocation of logical routes to trains. The software under consideration has been developed by Ansaldo-STS and is part of this company's implementation of ERTMS Level 2. They focus on software verification of a sub-component rather than on location specific data for the whole system. Nardone et al. [14] develop a new, rail specific specification language DSTM4Rail, an extension of hierarchical state machines. They employ DSTM4Rail to the modelling of specific functionalities of the ERTMS Radio Block Centre. Overall the objective is to obtain a formal model of ERTMS requirements for system testing purposes. This work is specialised to quality assurance for one ERTMS component.

The openETCS initiative [1] sets out to provide specifications that can be used for software generation for ETCS train control components, track elements, and functionality to be integrated in track side interlocking systems. This software development follows a model-driven approach, where the methods and tools shall comply with a SIL 4 development process.

Chiappini et al. [3] work towards the formalisation and validation of the overall ERTMS/ETCS specifications. To this end, they formalise a reference subset (including Movement Authority Management and RBC/RBC Handover) of the system requirements through a set of concepts and diagrams in UML, and through additional constraints in a defined controlled natural language. This formalisation then undergoes an automatic validation check covering questions concerning consistency, scenario compatibility, and if certain properties hold. Their work puts the ERTMS/ETCS specifications themselves under scrutiny.

8   Summary and Future Work

In this paper, we have modelled, validated, and verified a complex system of systems of hybrid nature. To this end, we presented an analysis of the ERTMS system, described its information flow, and provided a concise model in Real Time Maude. This model is astonishingly small: it consists of around only 1000 lines of code. We believe this is due to the advanced concepts, especially the object orientated features that Real Time Maude offers. Through simulation we have demonstrated that our model exhibits a number of expected behaviours. Furthermore, by systematic error injection, we have shown that safety in ERTMS depends on all its components. This simulation and error injection give us confidence that our model is valid. Finally, we have presented a number of model checking results that indicate that, for small rail yards, complexity of model checking of physical safety properties is under control.

It is future work to explore further, more complex rail yards, including bidirectional ones. On the practical side we intend to extend our modelling with further controller strategies and more complex train progression behaviour. On the more theoretical side, we plan to investigate completeness and abstraction techniques to reduce model-checking time, including finitisation.

Acknowledgement. The authors would like to thank Simon Chadwick, Siemens Rail Automation, UK, for his continued support and many helpful discussions. We also appreciate the helpful advice from Peter Ölveczky on Real-Time Maude and the constructive comments given by three anonymous referees. Finally, we thank Erwin R. Catesbeiana (Jr.) for timely hints on how to stay on track.

References

1. openETCS (2015). http://openetcs.org. Accessed 30 August 2015
2. Alcatel, Alstom, Ansaldo Signal, Bombardier, Invensys Rail and Siemens. System Requirements Specification, Chap. 2, Basic System Description (2006). SUBSET-026-2
3. Chiappini, A., Cimatti, A., Macchi, L., Rebollo, O., Roveri, M., Susi, A., Tonetta, S., Vittorini, B.: Formalization and validation of a subset of the european train control system. In: Proceedings of ICSE 2010. ACM Press (2010)
4. Rizzo, T., Sanseviero, A., Roveri, M., Narasamdya, I., Tchaltsev, A., Lazzaro, A., Corvino, R., Cimatti, A.: Formal verification and validation of ERTMS industrial railway train spacing system. In: Madhusudan, P., Seshia, S.A. (eds.) CAV 2012. LNCS, vol. 7358, pp. 378–393. Springer, Heidelberg (2012)
5. Clavel, M., Durán, F., Eker, S., Lincoln, P., Martí-Oliet, N., Meseguer, J., Talcott, C.L. (eds.): All About Maude. LNCS, vol. 4350. Springer, Heidelberg (2007)
6. Eker, S., Meseguer, J., Sridharanarayanan, A.: The Maude LTL model checker. In: WRLA 2002, vol. 71, ENTCS. Elsevier (2002)
7. European Railway Industry. ERTMS (2015). http://www.era.europa.eu/Core-Activities/ERTMS/Pages/home.aspx. Accessed 30 August 2015
8. Henzinger, T.A.: The theory of hybrid automata. In: Inan, M.K., Kurshan, R.P. (eds.) Verification of Digital and Hybrid Systems. NATO ASI Series, vol. 170, pp. 265–292. Springer, Heidelberg (2000)
9. James, P., Moller, F., Nga, N.H., Roggenbach, M., Schneider, S.A., Treharne, H.: Techniques for modelling and verifying railway interlockings. STTT **16**(6), 685–711 (2014)
10. James, P., Moller, F., Nguyen, H.N., Roggenbach, M., Schneider, S.A., Treharne, H.: On modelling and verifying railway interlockings: tracking train lengths. Sci. Comput. Program. **96**, 315–336 (2014)
11. James, P., Roggenbach, M.: Encapsulating formal methods within domainspecific languages: a solution for verifying railway scheme plans. Math. Comput. Sci. **8**(1), 11–38 (2014)
12. Lawrence, A., Berger, U., James, P., Roggenbach, M., Seisenberger, M.: Modelling and analysing the european rail traffic management system in Real-Time Maude. In: FTSCS 2014 - Preliminary Proceedings (2014)
13. Meseguer, J., Ölveczky, P.C.: Semantics and pragmatics of Real-Time Maude. Higher-Order Symbolic Comput. **20**(1–2), 161–196 (2007)
14. Nardone, R., Gentile, U., Peron, A., Benerecetti, M., Vittorini, V., Marrone, S., De Guglielmo, R., Mazzocca, N., Velardi, L.: Dynamic state machines for formalizing railway control system specifications. In: Artho, C., Ölveczky, P.C. (eds.) FTSCS 2014. CCIS, vol. 476, pp. 93–109. Springer, Heidelberg (2015)
15. Ölveczky, P.C., Meseguer, J.: Abstraction and completeness for Real-Time Maude. In: WRLA 2006, vol. 176, ENTCS (2007)

16. Meseguer, J., Ölveczky, P.C.: The Real-Time Maude tool. In: Ramakrishnan, C.R., Rehof, J. (eds.) TACAS 2008. LNCS, vol. 4963, pp. 332–336. Springer, Heidelberg (2008)
17. Thorvaldsen, S., Ölveczky, P.C.: Formal modeling and analysis of the OGDC wireless sensor network algorithm in Real-Time Maude. In: Bonsangue, M.M., Johnsen, E.B. (eds.) FMOODS 2007. LNCS, vol. 4468, pp. 122–140. Springer, Heidelberg (2007)
18. Vu, L.H., Haxthausen, A.E., Peleska, J.: Formal modeling and verification of interlocking systems featuring sequential release. In: Artho, C., Ölveczky, P.C. (eds.) FTSCS 2014. CCIS, vol. 476, pp. 223–238. Springer, Heidelberg (2015)

Modeling Railway Control Systems in Promela

Roberto Nardone[1]([⊠]), Ugo Gentile[1], Massimo Benerecetti[1], Adriano Peron[1],
Valeria Vittorini[1], Stefano Marrone[2], and Nicola Mazzocca[1]

[1] Università di Napoli Federico II, Naples, Italy
{roberto.nardone,ugo.gentile,massimo.benerecetti,adrperon,
valeria.vittorini,nicola.mazzocca}@unina.it
[2] Seconda Università di Napoli, Naples, Italy
stefano.marrone@unina2.it

Abstract. This paper presents an approach to systematically build
Promela models with the aim of generating test cases within the system level testing process of railway control systems. The paper focuses
on the encoding of the system model, of the aspects related to the representation of possible execution environments and their interaction with
the system. The input for building a Promela model of the system under
test is a state machine based specification. Indeed, state machines are
one of the most common notations used in industrial settings to model
critical systems and allow for easily obtaining the Promela model of the
system by applying a well structured transformational approach; furthermore, state-based formalism are also highly recommended by CENELEC
norms to model railway control systems.

In our approach Dynamic State Machines (DSTMs) are used, a newly
developed extension of hierarchical state machines which allow for modeling dynamic instantiation of processes. The approach is applied to a
functionality of the Radio Block Centre, the vital core of the ERTM-
S/ETCS Control System, in order to show the feasibility and effectiveness of the generation of the Promela model on a real system.

Keywords: Model checking · Promela · SPIN · Dynamic state
machine · CRYSTAL · Railway control systems · Test case generation

1 Introduction and Related Work

The extensive usage of model checking in the Verification&Validation (V&V)
activities in the context of control systems development is not a common practice in industry. One of the reasons is the difficulty of building a non trivial model
of the system under test (and expressing the properties to be verified) from the
artifacts produced during the verification and testing process, without requiring
radical changes in the process itself. Other reasons may be the lack of efficiency
of the available approaches or the lack of expressive power of the languages used
to build the system models. This paper addresses these problems with specific
reference to the railway domain. The European norm CENELEC EN50128 [3]

© Springer International Publishing Switzerland 2016
C. Artho and P.C. Ölveczky (Eds.): FTSCS 2015, CCIS 596, pp. 121–136, 2016.
DOI: 10.1007/978-3-319-29510-7_7

emphasizes the usage of model checking as one of the highly recommended techniques to be exploited for formal verification purposes. We propose an automatable approach to build a Promela model, which can be easily integrated into V&V activities. The resulting Promela model can be conceptually divided into two main parts: the first one consists of a set of Promela processes obtained by translating a state-based specification of the system under test (SUT), the second one is a dedicated Promela process modeling possible environment executions. In this work we adopt DSTM (Dynamic State Machine) [9] as the formal language used to model the SUT. DSTM extends Hierarchical State Machine (HSM, [1,8]) and allows for dynamic instantiation of machines (processes), procedure calls, parallelism, parameter passing, interrupts, communication through global variables and channels. The basic ideas underlying the proposed approach are not new. In past work [5] a model-based approach is proposed for the formal verification of the executable code of a railway control system. Several translations from state-based formalisms to model checkers have been proposed in the literature. For example, the work [13] describes an approach to automatically generate test cases for code coverage, by exploiting the capability of the NuSMV model checker. A similar approach is presented in the work [4], which focuses on a methodology to encode Abstract State Machine into Promela, in order to automatically generate test cases. In the past work [12] timing constraints, specified with MARTE Profile, are modeled as automata and then translated into Promela models for the verification of constraints fulfillment.

With respect to the literature, the major strength of our work resides in the definition of a structured approach to build non trivial Promela models taking into account both the issues to be faced in modeling the SUT and the (possibly non-deterministic) behaviors of the environment. The proposed approach is fully automatable starting from a DSTM specification and can be easily integrated in existing industrial settings. The ability of constraining the possible inputs to the SUT provided by the non-deterministic environment, allows, on the one hand, to achieve efficiency in terms of state space generation and analysis effort and, on the other, to prevent the generation of unfeasible test cases.

This paper provides a bird-eye view on the overall modeling approach, in particular a description of how some of the features of DSTM are translated into Promela and the definition of the environment model are presented by using a running example. A complete case study is also proposed, based on a functionality of the Radio Block Centre, a real railway control system. The paper is organized as follows: Sect. 2 summarizes the essential features of DSTM and introduces the running example. Section 3 presents the approach to construct the Promela model. Section 4 contains the railway case study and, finally, Sect. 5 provides some closing remarks and hints about future work.

2   Background and Running Example

DSTM [9] is a newly defined formalism developed within the context of the ongoing ARTEMIS Joint Undertaking project CRitical sYSTem engineering

AcceLeration[1] (CRYSTAL, [10]). It has been designed according to the needs expressed by a railway industry in order to be easily integrated in the testing process of signaling control systems. The ultimate goal is to develop an interoperable testing environment providing a high level of automation [2].

As the aim of the paper is to introduce an approach to build non trivial Promela models starting from a DSTM specification of the SUT, in the following we provide an informal introduction to DSTM by means of the toy running example depicted in Fig. 1. The example contains two machines: a machine modeling a Set-Reset (SR) flip-flop (Fig. 1(a)), and machine that models a 4-bit register (Fig. 1(b)) by activating four parallel instances of the flip-flop machine.

A DSTM is a collection of parametric machines, channels, variables and data-types. The evolution of a DSTM is a sequence of instantaneous reactions (*steps*). A step is a maximal set of transition firings which are triggered by the current set of available events avoiding sequential firings of transitions within the same step. DSTM allows for the definition of (*internal* or *external*) channels and global variables that allow for communication between machines. Additionally, DSTM gives the possibility to build complex types starting form basic ones. Specifically, basic types are integer, enumerations and channel names. Basic types can be composed to constitute compound types and multi-types. Compound types are structured types similar to records of basic types; multi-types, instead, are collections of basic and compound types. Channels may convey messages of any available type.

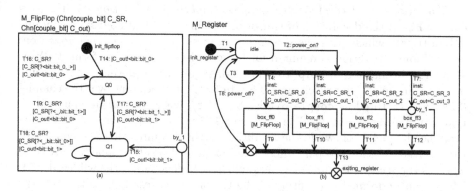

Fig. 1. (a) SR flip-flop model. (b) 4-bit register model

A single machine is composed of vertices, transitions and parameters. Different kinds of vertices may be included in a machine. *Nodes* represent the possible control states (e.g., node idle of M_Register in Fig. 1). An *initial node* is also present in each machine, corresponding to the default entry (e.g., node init_register of M_Register). Moreover, a machine may contain additional entering nodes (e.g., node by_1 of M_FlipFlop) and exiting nodes (e.g., node

---

[1] http://www.crystal-artemis.eu/.

exiting_register of M_Register). *Boxes* represent single or multiple machine invocations (parallel procedure calls). A transition entering a box models the invocation of the machine(s) associated with the box, while a transition leaving a box corresponds to a return from that machine(s). For instance, transitions T4-T7 perform invocations of the parametric machine M_FlipFlop, with suitable instantiation of its parameters, by entering boxes box_ff0, box_ff1, box_ff2 and box_ff3, respectively. Parallel behavior can be modeled either by associating multiple machines with a single box, or by explicitly splitting and merging the control flow using fork and join constructs. To this end, *Fork* and *Join* pseudonodes are provided in DSTM. A transition exiting a fork can execute either synchronously or asynchronously with the currently executing process. In the latter case, a transition from the fork node leads to a node of the caller machine. For instance, transition T2 triggers an asynchronous fork, instantiating four boxes whose associated machines execute asynchronously with the caller machine M_Register. *Join* nodes allow for merging of multiple control flows from concurrently executing processes. It either synchronizes the termination of the involved processes or forces their termination if a *preemptive* transition, marked by the symbol ⊗, enters the join node. Note that asynchronous forks, occurring within loops, allow for the dynamic instantiation of processes. This feature may lead to an unbounded number of processes and, as a consequence, to an unbounded state space. To allow Spin to analyze of the resulting designs, the generation of the corresponding Promela models bounds the number of instantiation of each machine.

Transitions are decorated with *triggers*, *conditions* and *actions*. With reference to Fig. 1, the decoration of transitions T2 in machine M_Register contains only a trigger which tests the presence of a message on the channel power_on, no additional condition is required for firing and no action is performed. Transition T16 in machine M_FlipFlop, instead, requires the presence of a specific message on the parametric channel C_SR. In fact, messages sent over the channel C_SR are structured as couple_bit = ⟨bit, bit⟩, where bit is an enumerative type bit = {bit_0, bit_1}. The trigger of T16 tests the presence of a message over the channel C_SR, while the condition further requires that the content of the received message is a pair whose first component has the value bit::bit_0, whereas the second component is simply ignored (denoted by the wildcard "_"). The action performed upon firing of the transition corresponds to the delivery of the value bit::bit_0 on the parametric channel C_out. Parameters associated to a machine (e.g., parameters C_SR and C_out of machine M_FlipFlop) are instantiated at invocation time.

3   Definition of the Promela Model

Starting from a DSTM specification of the SUT, we build a Promela model with the goal of generating test sequences, exploiting the capability of model checkers to build counterexamples of violated properties. By following a structured approach, a set of Promela processes is systematically built from the DSTM model of the SUT, together with a Promela process modeling a (non-deterministic) environment. We exemplify the generation of test sequences by assuming that the coverage of transitions is required. A more general discussion about requirements and how they are expressed is out of the scope of this work. Before describing how the Promela model can be automatically built, we provide a high level overview of the steps implementing the translation of DTSMs into Promela.

3.1   Generation Steps

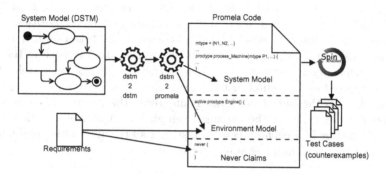

Fig. 2. Overview of the general approach.

Figure 2 depicts the steps which enable the automatic generation of the Promela model. Since Promela does not support hierarchical specifications, the encoding of a hierarchical DSTM model is performed in two phases. The first one is a *dstm2dstm*, where the hierarchical source model is flattened, to get rid of the hierarchical structure of a DSTM (the vertical modularity) and suitably encoding the horizontal modularity (i.e., parallelism). In this phase, all boxes, forks and joins are removed from the model and additional nodes are inserted when necessary. The dynamic instantiation of machines is translated into specific *run* commands, added to the action list of those transitions replacing the ones entering the boxes. During the second step, named *dstm2promela*, the flat DSTM model resulting from the previous phase is translated directly into Promela and a dedicated Promela process, called `Engine`, is generated to model the execution environment of the SUT.

The test goal and the assumptions about the execution environment of the SUT (if any) provide requirements that the model of the environment must satisfy. These requirements drive: (1) the refinement of the *Engine* process, by inserting constraints on the communication channels, and (2) the generation of *never claims*. Never claims are used to focus the analysis of the system to behaviors of special interest. In our case, never claims are used to describe those behaviors of the system that exhibit the occurrence of some desired transition. When a never claim is fulfilled, the model checker Spin provides a counterexample, which, in the present setting, corresponds to a possible test sequence that covers the specified transition.

3.2 Building the System Model

The step semantics of DSTM prevents sequential firings of transitions within the same execution step. Hence, we need to guarantee that at most one enabled transition can fire for each active process. To this aim, each DSTM machine M is translated into a Promela process, called process_M, which is instantiated by its caller process using the Promela command *run*, which allows for dynamic activation of processes. Each process encoding machine M is then executed until a termination message, sent by its caller, is received over a special channel ch_term_M (defined as a local channel to the caller). Each Promela process, modeling a DSTM machine, must own a token in order to fire an enabled transition. When a process owns a token it is scheduled, it consumes its token and: if none of its transitions is enabled, the process propagates the token to each of the child processes it has previously activated, if any; otherwise, one of the enabled transitions is selected and executed. At the beginning of each step only the process corresponding to the initial machine (main) owns the token. This machine is M_Register in the case of the running example. A set of global variables and channels is declared for each process. In Listing 1 all the automatically generated declarations for the running example are reported.

Listing 1. Global variables for the running example.

```
1.  #define MAX_PROC 6
2.  mtype last_transition;
3.  bit has_token [MAX_PROC];
4.  mtype = {init_register, idle, exiting_register};
5.  mtype = {T1, T2_T3_T4_T5_T6_T7, T8_T9_T10_T11_T12_T13};
6.  mtype = {init_flipflop, by_1, Q0, Q1};
7.  mtype = {T14, T15, T16, T17, T18, T19};
8.  mtype state_M_Register [MAX_PROC];
9.  mtype transition_M_Register [MAX_PROC];
10. mtype state_M_FlipFlop [MAX_PROC];
11. mtype transition_M_FlipFlop [MAX_PROC];
12. mtype = {bit_0, bit_1};
13. chan power_on = [2] of {bit};
14. chan power_off = [2] of {bit};
15. chan C_SR_0 = [2] of {mtype, mtype};
16. chan C_out_0 = [2] of {mtype};
17. chan C_SR_1 = [2] of {mtype, mtype};
18. chan C_out_1 = [2] of {mtype};
19. chan C_SR_2 = [2] of {mtype, mtype};
20. chan C_out_2 = [2] of {mtype};
21. chan C_SR_3 = [2] of {mtype, mtype};
22. chan C_out_3 = [2] of {mtype};
```

A global variable has_token, typed as a bit array, is used to store the assignment of the tokens described before (line 3). Specifically, this array contains 1 in the i-th location if the machine with *pid* equal to i currently has the token. Note that this array is global and visible to the entire Promela model. Two enumeration types (*mtype*) introduce symbolic names for nodes and transitions (e.g., lines 6 and 7 correspond to process_M_FlipFlop). The *mtype* vector variable state_M is used to maintain the current states of all the instances of machine M (e.g., line 10). Its elements are all initialized to the initial node of the corresponding machine. A *mtype* vector variable transition_M is used to keep track, for each instance of machine M, of the transition that fires in the current step (e.g., line 11). From lines 12 to 22 types and channels are declared. Both channels C_SR and C_out can store two messages, in order to correctly implement the step semantics, as it will be explained in Sect. 3.3. Finally, the variable last_transition (line 2) is used to store the name of the last transition covered in an execution. This information is used for instrumentation purposes, specifically it allows for the definition of the never claim requiring to find a the covering of a transition.

Promela Model of Machine _M_FlipFlop._ Each node of a machine is mapped into a *guarded statement* of the form *guard ->statement*. In Listing 2 an excerpt of the Promela translation of machine M_FlipFlop is reported. Notice that the channel names C_SR and C_out are parameters. The actual names are provided by the caller process, which can distinguish the different instances of M_FlipFlop. Furthermore, the ch_term channel is added as parameter: over this channel, defined locally to the caller, this latter sends the termination message to the one executing.

Listing 2. Promela code of machine M_FlipFlop (excerpt).

```
24.  proctype process_M_FlipFlop(chan C_SR; chan C_out, chan ch_term) {
25.    do
46.    :: (state_M_FlipFlop[_pid]==Q0 && has_token[_pid]==1) ->
47.       atomic {
48.         printf("<current node[\%d] = Q0>\n",_pid);
49.         has_token[_pid]=0;
50.         if
51.         :: (C_SR?[bit_0,_]) ->
52.            C_out!bit_0;
53.            printf("<firing transition[\%d] = T16>\n",_pid);
54.            transition_M_FlipFlop[_pid]=T16;
55.            state_M_FlipFlop[_pid]=Q0;
56.            last_transition=T16;
57.         :: (C_SR?[bit_1,_]) ->
58.            C_out!bit_1;
59.            printf("<firing transition[\%d] = T17>\n",_pid);
60.            transition_M_FlipFlop[_pid]=T17;
61.            state_M_FlipFlop[_pid]=Q1;
62.            last_transition=T17;
63.         :: else
64.         fi;
65.       }
86.    od unless {
87.       ch_term?1;
88.       printf("<Machine M_FlipFlop[\%d] terminated>\n",_pid);
89.    }
92.  }
```

The *guard* of the statement checks whether some enabled transition is allowed to fire from a node: the current node must be the source node of the transition (e.g., state_M_FlipFlop[_pid]==Q0 in Listing 2, line 45) and the process owns the token (has_token[_pid]==1, line 45). The statement is *atomic* and contains a sequence of statements executed indivisibly. The first statement in the sequence consumes the token. Then, a conditional statement contains one guarded statements for each transition exiting from that node (e.g., lines 51, 57). Their guards correspond to the enabling condition of the DSTM transitions and the associated statements translate the actions of the transitions. The actions (if any) associated with a DSTM transition are translated into basic Promela statements and operators, and they are executed when the associated guarded statement is selected. If more than one guarded statement is executable, one of them is non-deterministically selected. The *else* branch in the conditional statement (e.g., line 63) is taken when no transition can fire. The process is executed until a termination message, sent by its caller, is received by the caller over the channel ch_term (lines 86–89).

Promela Model of Machine M_Register. As opposed to the previous component, machine M_Register has a hierarchical structure, which requires to be flattened before translating it to Promela. The flattening phase removes all the boxes, fork and join constructs. In doing that, some transitions may be modified, eliminated or added. Moreover, additional variables and channels are introduced and proper conditions and actions are modified or added to the decorations of existing transitions. These elements are used to provide additional information and directives for the generation of the Promela code. The resulting flattened model of the DSTM in Fig. 1(b) is reported in Fig. 3.

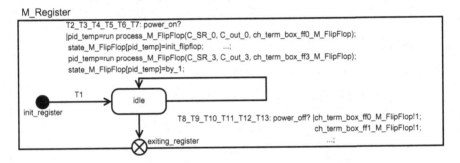

Fig. 3. Promela representation of the hierarchical machine M_Register.

The flattening of machine M_Register proceeds as follows. Since transition T2 (see Fig. 1(b)) enters a fork, the process continues its execution after the fork is performed. The DSTM model of M_Register is changed as follows:

- the fork and join nodes and the boxes are removed together with their entering and exiting transitions;
- a loop transition from the node idle is created which replaces transition T2, T3, T4, T5, T6 and T7. The decoration of this transition specifies the trigger of T2 (i.e., power_on?) and actions which contain all the information needed to instantiate the machines called inside the boxes; in particular, the actions specify the Promela statements to execute the four instances of the processes called by the fork operation (e.g., run process_M_flipflop) and set their initial state (e.g., state_M_flipflop[pid_temp]=initial).
- a transition from node idle to the exit node is created which replaces transitions T8, T9, T10, T11, T12 and T13. The decoration of this transition specifies the trigger of the preemptive transition T8 (power_off?) and actions encoding the preemptive join by requesting the termination of the four flip-flop processes through message on the termination channels (e.g., ch_term_box_ff0_M_FlipFlop!1) which are added to the model.

Listing 3 shows an excerpt of the Promela process encoding the flat machine depicted in Fig. 3 obtained by applying the technique explained above.

Listing 3. Promela code of machine M_Register (excerpt).

```
94.  proctype process_M_Register() {
95.     byte i;
96.     pid pid_temp;
97.     bit my_children[MAX_PROC];
98.     chan ch_term_box_ff0_M_FlipFlop , ch_term_box_ff1_M_FlipFlop ,
      ch_term_box_ff2_M_FlipFlop , ch_term_box_ff3_M_FlipFlop ;
99.     do
109.    :: (state_M_Register[_pid]==idle && has_token[_pid]==1) ->
110.       atomic {
111.          printf("<current node[\%d] = idle>\n",_pid);
112.          has_token[_pid]=0;
113.          if
114.          :: (power_on?[1]) ->
115.             pid_temp = run process_M_FlipFlop(C_SR_0, C_out_0,
      ch_term_box_ff0_M_FlipFlop);
116.             state_M_FlipFlop[pid_temp]=init_flipflop ;
117.             my_children[pid_temp] = 1;
118.             has_token[pid_temp]=1;

135.          :: (power_off?[1]) ->
136.             ch_term_box_ff0_M_FlipFlop!1;
137.             ch_term_box_ff1_M_FlipFlop!1;
138.             ch_term_box_ff2_M_FlipFlop!1;
139.             ch_term_box_ff3_M_FlipFlop!1;
140.             printf("<firing transition[\%d] = T8_T9_T10_T11_T12_T13}>\n",_pid);
141.             transition_M_Register[_pid]=T8_T9_T10_T11_T12_T13;
142.             state_M_Register[_pid]=exiting_register ;
143.             last_transition=T8_T9_T10_T11_T12_T13;
144.          :: else ->
145.             for (i : 0 .. MAX_PROC-1) {
146.                has_token[i]=my_children[i];
147.             }
148.          fi;
149.       }

155.    od unless {
156.       ch_term_M_Register?[1];
157.       printf("<Machine process_M_Register[\%d] terminated>\n",_pid);
158.    }
159. }
```

3.3   Modeling the Environment

As anticipated in the previous section, the possible environments of the SUT are modeled by a Promela process named **Engine**. This is the first process to be activated in the and it is the only process required to be running in the initial state by using the prefix **active** in its **proctype** declaration. The process **Engine** is in charge of: (1) instantiating the main machine of the system model; (2) non-deterministically generating messages, delivered by the environment on the external channels at the beginning of each execution step; (3) assigning the token to the main machine, starting the execution of a new execution step.

The **Engine** process is activated whenever no statement is executable in any process belonging to the system model. This situation is captured by the **timeout** Promela variable being true. This happens when each process belonging to the system model has *consumed* its own token, meaning that the execution current step is completed. Furthermore, **Engine** uses local variables to non-deterministically generate new messages in the external channels. These local variables are in correspondence to the fields of the compound types exchanged over those channels. Hence, in the running example, we have two variables, **temp1** and **temp2**, as declared at line 162 of the snippet of code reported in Listing 4.

Listing 4. Promela code of machine Engine - initialization

```
161.  active proctype Engine() {
162.     mtype temp1, temp2;
163.     pid pid_main;
164.     pid_main = run process_M_Register
         ();
165.     state_M_Register[pid_main]=
         init_register;
166.     printf(   <ENGINE: main machine
         has pid = %d\n>", pid_main);
167.     //Generation of first message
168.     power_on!0;
169.     power_off!0;
170.     C_SR_0!bit_0, bit_0;
171.     C_out_0!bit_0;
```

Listing 5. Promela code of machine Engine - generation of new messages

```
178.  generation:
179.     atomic {
180.        printf("<ENGINE: message
        generation>\n");
181.        //MESSAGES ON power_on
182.        if
183.        :: (len(power_on)==1) ->
184.           if
185.           :: (1) -> temp1=0;
186.           :: (1) -> temp1=1;
187.           fi;
188.           printf("<ENGINE: power_on -
        generated <%d>>\n", temp1);
189.           power_on!temp1;
190.        :: (full(power_on)) -> skip;
191.        fi;
192.        power_on?temp1;
      ...
343.        //GIVE TOKEN TO THE MAIN
        PROCESS
344.        has_token[pid_main] = 1;
345.        printf("<ENGINE: end execution
        >\n");
346.     }
347.  do
348.     :: timeout ->
349.        goto generation;
350.  od
351.  abort:
352.     skip;
353.  }
```

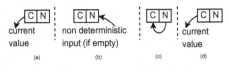

current value (a)   non deterministic input (if empty) (b)   (c)   current value (d)

Fig. 4. Message generation for the power_on channel.

First, the Engine process runs the main machine (i.e., process_M_Register()) and stores its *pid* in the local variable pid_main (Listing 4, line 164). Then, Engine initializes the channels (Listing 4, lines 167–171).

After those initialization steps, process Engine starts an *atomic* block in which it non-deterministically generates the messages to be sent over the channels (e.g., Listing 5, lines 182–187 initialize the power_on channel). The starting statement of this block is identified by the label generation at line 178 in Listing 5.

The subsequent evolution of the processes is driven by a suitable message handling mechanism, implemented as explained in the following. Each external channel has a buffer that stores two messages (Fig. 4). The first position C is used to store the message available in the current step, whereas the position N is used to store the message to be delivered in the next step (if any). During the execution of the current step, the processes modeling the SUT can read messages contained in positions C of any channels, without removing them. If a new message is produced by the SUT, it is stored in positions N of the corresponding channel (Fig. 4(a)). At the beginning of the next step, the Engine checks for the

Listing 6. Promela code of machine Engine - constraints.

```
212.  //MESSAGES ON C_SR_0
213.  if
214.  :: (len(C_SR_0)==1) ->
215.     if
216.     :: (1) -> temp1=0;
217.     :: (1) -> temp1=1;
218.     fi;
219.     if
220.     :: (1) -> temp2=0;
221.     :: (1) -> temp2=1;
222.     fi;
223.     if
224.     :: (temp1==1 && temp2==1)-> goto abort;
225.     :: else -> skip;
226.     fi;
```

presence of messages in positions N, (Listing 5, line 183). If a position N does not contain a message generated by the SUT processes during the previous step, the Engine generates a new message by using temp variables and if statements (Fig. 4(b), Listing 5, lines 184–189). Finally, the Engine consumes all the messages contained in positions C (line 192), by moving the content of position N in each channel to position C, thus making the messages previously generated for the next steps available (Fig. 4(c)).

Note that the *receive* statement at line 192 is always executable. This is ensured by the fact that the SUT never removes messages from the external channels. Therefore, that statement is never blocked, as two messages are always stored in each channel when it is executed.

The generation block ends by assigning the token to the main process (Listing 5, line 344). Then, the Engine process enters the do construct, where it waits until the Promela global variable timeout evaluates to true. This happens when no statement is executable in the active processes, hence when all the SUT processes have consumed their token. In this case, Engine executes a jump to the generation label, starting a new step.

3.4 Constraining Behaviors

The non-deterministic generation of messages to be sent over the channels can be constrained to a set of requirements that the desired environment must fulfill. Such constraints can be used to prevent the environment to prompt the system with unfeasible combinations of inputs.

The simplest constraint a designer may require is to avoid the generation of conflicting messages over the channels. As an example, the SR flip-flop cannot be prompted with both $R = 1$ and $S = 1$. This constraint can be expressed in Promela as shown in Listing 6. The constraint is included in the already described generation block for channel C_SR_0. After the generation of the values for the signals S and R in the variables temp_1 and temp_2 respectively, the statements reported at lines 223–225 check that these values are not both equal to 1. If the constraint is not satisfied, the Engine process jumps to the abort label (reported in Listing 5), which immediately ends this process, interrupting the related behavior. Note that the alternative handling of constraint violations that generates a new set of values for the messages is not an efficient solution, since it increases the number of possible execution paths in the state space, without adding meaningful behaviors. Similarly, we can express constraints involving different fields of the same compound message and constraining the generation of messages subject to the occurrence of specific events. These kinds of constraints are not described here for sake of space.

4   A Case Study in the Railway Domain

ERTMS/ETCS (European Rail Traffic Management System/European Train Control System, [11]) is a standard for the interoperability of the European railway signalling systems ensuring both technological compatibility among trans-European railway networks and integration of the new signalling system with the existing national interlocking systems. The ERTMS/ETCS specification identifies three functional levels featuring growing complexity. They can be implemented singularly or in conjunction and mainly differ in the communication mechanisms adopted to control the trains. Level 2 and Level 3 represent two more cutting-edge solutions than Level 1, at this moment Level 2 is the most widespread choice between Level 2 and Level 3. A reference architecture for ERTMS/ETCS systems consists of three main subsystems: the on-board system is the core of the control activities located on the train; the line side subsystem is responsible for providing geographical position information to the on-board subsystem; the trackside sub-system is in charge of monitoring the movement of the trains. The Radio Block Centre (RBC) is the most important component of the track side subsystem of the ERTMS/ETCS architecture. RBC is a computing system whose aim is to guarantee a safe inter-train distance on the track area under its supervision. It interacts with the on-board system by managing a communication session, by using the EURORADIO protocol and the GSM-R network. In the following, part of a realistic realization of an RBC procedure is described, together with the test generation procedure that demonstrates how the proposed approach can be effectively applied to obtain test sequences.

4.1 The Communication Procedure of the Radio Block Centre

The Communication procedure is modeled by the DSTM specification shown in Fig. 5. The main machine **M_CommunicationEstablishment** (Fig. 5(a)) is in charge of modeling the management of the connection requests issued by the trains. It accepts a limited number of requests (collected in variable V_cont) and for each accepted request it instantiates a new machine M_ManageTrain by entering the box MCE_manageTrain. Three transitions exit from node MCE_idle: MCE_T03, MCE_T06 and MCE_T02. MCE_T03 enters the fork, it is triggered by the availability of a message on channel C_request and it is guarded by the condition V_cont<=3. The action of this transition delivers acceptance message over channel C_answer, increments counter V_cont and stores in variables V_chSystemVersion, V_chAck and V_chSessionEstablished the names of the channels to be used to communicate with the train. The asynchronous control flow exiting from this fork returns back to node MCE_idle. When an instance of machine M_ManageTrain terminates its execution, transitions MCE_T06 and MCE_T07 merge the control flow by entering the join node; transition MCE_T08 exiting the join decrements the counter V_cont. Transition MCE_T02 from node MCE_idle, instead, is activated on receiving a connection request, when the maximal number of service requests has been reached. The action of this transition delivers of a suitable refusal message over channel C_answer. Machine M_ManageTrain (Fig. 5(b)) models the management of the communication procedure with a specific train. It takes the names of the channels, on which the train and RBC will communicate, as parameters. This machine enters node MMT_idle and then instantiates machine M_SessionEstablishment, which models the session establishment protocol, by entering the corresponding box. Machine M_SessionEstablishment (Fig. 5(c)) can terminate its execution with different exiting conditions (i.e., different exiting

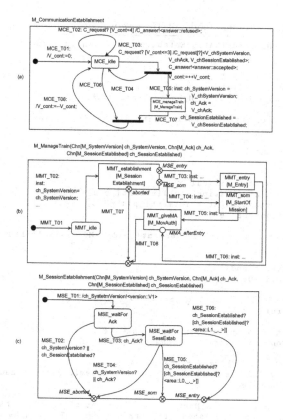

Fig. 5. DSTM model of the Communication Procedure.

nodes). If the communication session with the train has been successfully established, then the machine exits via either via node MSE_som or node MSE_entry, according to the specific communication mode established. Depending on the exit node of this machine, machine M_ManageTrain then instantiates either M_StartOfMission or machine M_Entry. If, on the other hand, the session establishment protocol aborts, then it terminates its execution in node MSE_aborted. Finally, machine M_MovAuth is instantiated after the termination of either one of mechines M_StartOfMission and M_Entry, which provides the train with the Movement Authority.

4.2   Results

The construction of the Promela model is automatically generated as explained in Sect. 3. The model contains as many processes as DSTM machines depicted in Fig. 5 plus the *Engine* process. As the structure of the Promela model is exactly the same of the code discussed in Sects. 3.2 and 3.3, only a portion of the code for **process_M_CommunicationEstablishment** is shown in Listing 7. The entire model of the case study contains around 1250 lines of code, where the first 75 of them are types and variable declarations.

Listing 7. Promela model of $M_C ommunicationEstablishment()$

```
proctype process_M_CommunicationEstablishment(chan ch_term) {
  byte i;
  pid pid_temp;
  bit my_children[MAX_PROC];
  chan ch_term_MCE_manageTrain_M_ManageTrain,
       ch_term_MCE_manageTrain_M_ManageTrain_exiting;
  do
  :: (state_M_CommunicationEstablishment[_pid]==MCE_initial && has_token[
     _pid]==1) ->
  atomic {
    printf("<current node[
    has_token[_pid]=0;
    V_cont=0;
    printf("<firing transition[
    transition_M_CommunicationEstablishment[_pid]=MCE_T01;
    state_M_CommunicationEstablishment[_pid]=MCE_idle;
    last_transition=MCE_T01;
  }
  :: (state_M_CommunicationEstablishment[_pid]==MCE_idle && has_token[_pid
     ]==1) ->
  atomic {
    printf("<current node[
    has_token[_pid]=0;
    if
    :: (C_request?[_,_,_] && V_cont==4) ->
      C_answer!refused;
      printf("<firing transition[
      transition_M_CommunicationEstablishment[_pid]=MCE_T02;
      state_M_CommunicationEstablishment[_pid]=MCE_idle;
      last_transition=MCE_T02;
    :: (C_request?[_,_,_] && V_cont<=3) ->
      C_request?V_chSystemVersion,V_chAck,V_chSessionEstablished;
      C_answer!accepted;
      V_cont++;
      pid_temp=run process_M_ManageTrain(V_chSystemVersion,V_chAck,
           V_chSessionEstablished, ch_term_MCE_manageTrain_M_ManageTrain,
           ch_term_MCE_manageTrain_M_ManageTrain_exiting);
      state_M_ManageTrain[pid_temp]=MMT_initial;
      my_children[pid_temp]=1;
      has_token[pid_temp]=1;
      printf("<firing transition[
      transition_M_CommunicationEstablishment[_pid]=MCE_T03_MCE_T04_MCE_T05;
      state_M_CommunicationEstablishment[_pid]=MCE_idle;
      last_transition=MCE_T03_MCE_T04_MCE_T05;
    :: (ch_term_MCE_manageTrain_M_ManageTrain_exiting?[1]) ->
      ch_term_MCE_manageTrain_M_ManageTrain_exiting?_;
      ch_term_MCE_manageTrain_M_ManageTrain!1;
      V_cont--;
      printf("<firing transition[
      transition_M_CommunicationEstablishment[_pid]=MCE_T06_MCE_T07_MCE_T08;
      state_M_CommunicationEstablishment[_pid]=MCE_idle;
      last_transition=MCE_T06_MCE_T07_MCE_T08;
    :: else ->
      for (i : 0 .. MAX_PROC-1) {
        has_token[i]=my_children[i];
      }
    fi;
  }
od unless {
    ch_term?1;
    printf("<Machine M_CommunicationEstablishment[
}
}
```

In order to show the effectiveness of the approach, we report the resulting performance of the Promela model for generating a test sequence that covers transition MSE_T06 of machine M_SessionEstablishment. The test sequence is obtained by generating a Promela never claim that checks for the existence of behaviors in which transition MSE_T06 is taken (i.e., such that the condition last_transition==MSE_T06 holds). The corresponding never claim is shown in Listing 8. This Promela model has been executed by SPIN [6] on a personal computer equipped with an Intel Core-i7, 8GB of RAM. The generation of the test sequence requires the exploration of **5211 states** analyzed in **0.234 s**.

Listing 8. Never claim

```
never {
step1:
  if
    :: (last_transition==MSE_T06) -> goto endStep
    :: else -> goto step1
  fi;
endStep: skip
}
```

5   Conclusions and Future Work

In this paper we presented a fully automatable approach to build a non trivial Promela model from a DSTM specification of a system under test. The approach has been defined to be integrated into existing testing environments in railway industrial settings and provide practical means to support the automatic generation of test sequences for gray-box testing of control systems. We are currently completing the process for the automatic translation of DSTM models into Promela and the construction of the Promela model modeling the environment of the SUT. This involves the implementation of a chain of model transformations partially written in ATL [7]. More work along several directions is needed to provide a complete test case generation environment. In particular, we are currently working on automating the construction of test specifications to obtain transition coverage, on optimizing the generation of the test cases, and on providing the end-user with a proper presentation of the generated sequences.

Acknowledgments. This paper is partially supported by research project CRYSTAL (Critical System Engineering Acceleration), funded from the ARTEMIS Joint Undertaking under grant agreement no. 332830 and from ARTEMIS member states Austria, Belgium, Czech Republic, France, Germany, Italy, Netherlands, Spain, Sweden, United Kingdom.

References

1. Alur, R., Kannan, S., Yannakakis, M.: Communicating hierarchical state machines. In: Wiedermann, J., Van Emde Boas, P., Nielsen, M. (eds.) ICALP 1999. LNCS, vol. 1644, pp. 169–178. Springer, Heidelberg (1999)

2. Di Martino, B., et al.: An interoperable testing environment for ERTMS/ETCS control systems. In: Bondavalli, A., Ceccarelli, A., Ortmeier, F. (eds.) SAFECOMP 2014. LNCS, vol. 8696, pp. 147–156. Springer, Heidelberg (2014)

3. CENELEC EN50128: communication, signalling and processing systems - software for railway control and protection systems (2011)

4. Riccobene, E., Rinzivillo, S., Gargantini, A.: Using spin to generate testsfrom ASM specifications. In: Börger, E., Gargantini, A., Riccobene, E. (eds.) ASM 2003. LNCS, vol. 2589, pp. 263–277. Springer, Heidelberg (2003)

5. Haxthausen, A.E., Peleska, J., Kinder, S.: A formal approach for the construction and verification of railway control systems. Formal Aspects Comput. **23**(2), 191–219 (2011)

6. Holzmann, G.J.: The SPIN Model Checker: Primer and Reference Manual, vol. 1003. Addison-Wesley, Reading (2004)

7. Jouault, F., Allilaire, F., Bézivin, J., Kurtev, I.: Atl: a model transformation tool. Sci. Comput. Program. **72**(1), 31–39 (2008)

8. Lanotte, R., Maggiolo-Schettini, A., Peron, A., Tini, S.: Dynamic hierarchical machines. Fundam. Inf. **54**(2–3), 237–252 (2002)

9. Nardone, R., et al.: Dynamic state machines for formalizing railway control system specifications. In: Artho, C., Ölveczky, P.C. (eds.) FTSCS 2014. CCIS, vol. 476, pp. 93–109. Springer, Heidelberg (2015)

10. Pflügl, H., El-Salloum, C., Kundner, I.: Crystal, critical system engineering acceleration, a truly european dimension. ARTEMIS Mag. **14**, 12–15 (2013)

11. UIC. ERTMS/ETCS class1 system requirements specification, ref. SUBSET-026, issue 2.2.2 (2002)

12. Yin, L., Mallet, F., Liu, J.: Verification of marte/ccsl time requirements in promela/spin. In: 16th IEEE International Conference on Engineering of Complex Computer Systems (ICECCS), pp. 65–74 (2011)

13. Zheng, Y., Zhou, J., Krause, P.: A model checking based test case generation framework for web services. In: Fourth International Conference on Information Technology, ITNG 2007, pp. 715–722. IEEE (2007)

Fault Tolerance

A Formal Model and Analysis of Feature Degradation in Fault-Tolerant Systems

Klaus Becker[✉] and Sebastian Voss

fortiss GmbH, An-Institut Technische Universität München,
Guerickestr. 25,80805 Munich, Germany
{becker,voss}@fortiss.org

Abstract. Fault-tolerant systems have to react on errors resulting from faults properly to avoid error propagation and finally a harmful failure of the entire system. Beside the detection of failing system elements, also the actions to handle failures are essential to cover the safety requirements. Actions reach from enabling fail-silent, fail-safe or fail-operational behavior of system elements, or also hybrids of this in a mixed-critical system design. Graceful degradation may be applied when system resources become insufficient, reducing the set of provided functional features. In this paper we address mixed critical systems, which partially comprise fail-operational functional features. We consider degradations of functional features in failure scenarios. We describe a formal model that contains i.a. the features of a system, possible feature degradations, the software components that realize these features, as well as the deployment of these components to execution units. We calculate valid deployments of software components to execution units and analyze them according to the level of graceful degradation on feature level and system level, as a consequence of failures of execution units or software components. We show an example from the automotive domain to illustrate our approach.

Keywords: Graceful-degradation · Fault-tolerance · Redundancy · Fail-operational · Mixed-critical · Diversity · Deployment · Dependability

1 Introduction and Motivation

Many embedded systems operate in safety-critical environments, in which faults could cause errors and failures of system elements, and finally a harmful failure of the entire system. This requires that these systems can detect failing elements, such as hardware or software components, and react properly. However, going into a fail-safe state may cause the loss of some provided functional features. This is not acceptable for features that require fail-operational behavior.

If system resources get lost due to hardware failures, the remaining resources should be used efficiently to keep those features alive that comprise the highest demand with respect to safety, reliability and availability (we use these terms as defined in [1]). For instance, if an execution unit has to be isolated from the remaining system due to a hardware failure, another execution unit has to be

© Springer International Publishing Switzerland 2016
C. Artho and P.C. Ölveczky (Eds.): FTSCS 2015, CCIS 596, pp. 139–154, 2016.
DOI: 10.1007/978-3-319-29510-7_8

able to provide some of those features that were provided by the failing unit. However, as the remaining system-resources may become insufficient to provide the full set of features, it may be needed to explicitly deactivate or degrade some features to handle this resource limitation. This results in graceful degradation of the system.

This paper relates to two previous publications. We introduced a formal model and formal constraints to calculate valid redundant deployments of software components (SWCs) to the execution units of a particular fault-tolerant system platform in [2]. We also treated the relationship of functional features and the SWCs that realize these features. We analyzed required degradations of the provided set of features in case of hardware failures of execution units. In another publication, we extended the model and the analysis by communication channels between the SWCs, again considering failing execution units [3].

In this paper, we consider additional faults, namely systematic faults of software components, which may be introduced by bugs in the software. In case a SWC fails to provide its intended function due to such a fault, it has to be isolated from the residual system to avoid failure propagation and harm. We assume an underlying platform runtime environment (RTE) which is able to detect such failures, to isolate failing components, and to trigger recovery mechanisms. Without activation of a backup, the functional features that are realized by a failing SWC cannot be provided anymore. Redundant backups of the same SWC would not be very helpful in this scenario, as the same systematic fault (e. g., a bug) would be contained in all backups. Hence, there is no use to deploy the same buggy SWC multiple times redundantly. Instead, diversity by alternative implementations is needed.

We consider a safety concept that incorporates degradations of failing features. We assume that diversity is introduced by implementing two similar features, which however are not providing exactly the same specification, but the second feature is a degraded version of the first full-fledged feature. This means, a failing full-fledged feature can be substituted by another degraded feature that fulfills a subset of the original requirements, with potentially less quality of service. An example is a full-fledged functional feature that provides a steer-by-wire application of a vehicle including active assistance functions, like lane-keeping or collision-avoidance. The degraded corresponding feature may support only rudimentary manual steering, without any assistance functions. Therefore, this paper introduces an approach to consider not only degradations on system level, like in the previous publications, but we also model degradations at feature level in order to be able to analyze the deployment of the resulting software component architectures onto the execution units. Also in scenarios of failing execution units, the existence of a degraded feature is helpful, if the system resources become insufficient to provide the initial full-fledged feature. In this case, the degraded feature can be activated, assuming that this requires less resources than the corresponding full-fledged feature.

Our approach is based on a formal system model and a set of formal constraints describing the validity of deployments with respect to the safety-concept.

The model and the constraints characterize an arithmetic problem that can be solved for instance by SMT-solvers, like Z3 [4,5].

In section 2, we present the basic concepts of an assumed underlying system platform. Section 3 shows the main contribution of this paper, which is an approach to analyze which feature degradations are required after isolations of execution units or software components. Section 4 contains an example, showing the applicability of our approach. The conclusion is given in section 5.

2   Assumed System Design

Fault-tolerance is the ability of a system to maintain control objectives despite the occurrence of a fault, while degradation of control performance may be accepted [6]. If a system has to support fail-operational features, it has to be capable to compensate for loss of failing execution units and of failing software components. We assume in this paper that the execution units of the system are homogeneous, allowing flexibility in the deployment, and are connected and communicating to each other by a reliable bus system.

As scheduling policy, we assume a system using the concept of logical execution times (LET), meaning that the software components are executed within fixed *cycles*. Each execution unit provides a budget of time per cycle that can be used to execute application software components (ASWCs).

We assume a system platform technology that is able to detect runtime failures of certain system elements, like sensors, actuators, execution units, communication links, and also software components. Furthermore, this system platform is able to isolate failing system elements from the residual system to avoid failure propagation and harm. The principles and more details about a platform that conforms to these assumptions have been presented in [7-9].

3   Deployment Calculation and Degradation Analysis

To handle systematic faults, diversity is needed. This can be achieved by providing two different realizations of the same functional feature. However, instead of realizing exactly the same functional feature by two different implementations, in this paper we address the substitution of a faulty realization of a full-fledged functional feature by a realization of a degraded functional feature, fulfilling less functional requirements and providing a less quality of service. The degradation of the feature may be required either because an ASWC of the full-fledged feature has to be isolated, or because an execution unit has to be isolated, resulting in reduced available computation resources. As we assume that a degraded feature requires less resources than the original full-fledged feature, such a degradation can be an adequate reaction in such hardware failure scenarios to deal with the decreasingly available resources.

For the case of failing hardware units, we also apply redundancy techniques to be able to keep alive fail-operational features without any degradation. For this, we deploy multiple instances of the realizing software components redundantly to the execution units. This enables the system to absorb loss of execution units and results in features being fully fail-operational without feature degradation. Due to this, these features can be kept alive in the presence of a limited number of hardware failures, while ensuring the absence of harm to the users or the environment.

Hence, there is a difference between full fail-operational behavior (the same functional feature is kept alive after a failure), and degraded fail-operational behavior (a degraded version of the functional feature is provided after a failure).

3.1 Formal System and Deployment Model

We define the system properties and the deployment problem as shown below. In the definitions, we write $\mathcal{P}^+(X)$ for the power set without empty set $\mathcal{P}(X) \setminus \emptyset$.

Definition 1. *A System* $\mathbb{V} = \langle F, S^A, H^A, \Phi \rangle$ *comprises a set of* Functional Features F, *an* Application Software Architecture S^A, *an* Execution Hardware Architecture H^A *and a* Configuration Φ.

Definition 2. *An Application Software Architecture* $S^A = \langle S, SC \rangle$ *is composed of a set* $S = \{s_1, ..., s_n\}$ *of Application Software Components (ASWCs) and a set* $SC = \{sc_1, ..., sc_q\}$ *of ASWC-Clusters (with* $n, q \in \mathbb{N}$*). The ASWCs are grouped by mapping them into the ASWC-Clusters. To describe the mapping of the* $s \in S$ *to a cluster* $sc \in SC$*, we define* $\alpha_s : S \to SC$*. To describe which* $s \in S$ *are contained in which* $sc \in SC$*, we define* $\alpha_{sc} : SC \to \mathcal{P}(S)$ *with* $\alpha_{sc}(sc) = \{s \in S \mid \alpha_s(s) = sc\}$*. Note that* α_s *is a total function, but neither injective nor surjective, as clusters might be empty in the formal model. For* $sc_i \neq sc_j$*, it holds that* $(\alpha_{sc}(sc_i) \cap \alpha_{sc}(sc_j) = \emptyset)$ *and* $\bigcup_{sc \in SC} \alpha_{sc}(sc) = S$.

For simplicity, we do not model communication channels between ASWCs in this paper. We introduced how we model the channels in [3].

Definition 3. *The set of functional features* $F = \{f_1, ..., f_m\}$ *contains the features of the system that can be recognized by the user. Each feature is realized by one or more ASWCs, while each ASWC contributes to realize one or more features. We define the relationship between ASWCs* $s \in S$ *and features* $f \in F$ *as* $\chi_s : S \to \mathcal{P}^+(F)$ *with* $\chi_s(s) = \{f \in F \mid s$ *contributes to realize* $f\}$*. Accordingly, we define* $\chi_f : F \to \mathcal{P}^+(S)$ *with* $\chi_f(f) = \{s \in S \mid f$ *is partially or totally realized by* $s\}$.

Definition 4. *An Execution Hardware Architecture* $H^A = \langle E, L \rangle$ *comprises execution units* E *and communication links* $L \subseteq E \times E$ *between these units.*

Definition 5. *The System Configuration* $\Phi = \langle \delta_P(S), \delta_A(S), \delta(S) \rangle$ *defines the solution of the deployment problem, namely how ASWCs* $s \in S$ *are deployed to execution units* $e \in E$*, either passively (*δ_P*) or actively (*δ_A*). For* $s \in S$*, we define* $\delta_P : S \to \mathcal{P}(E)$ *with* $\delta_P(s) = \{e \in E \mid s$ *is in memory of* e*, but not executed on* $e\}$*, as well as* $\delta_A : S \to \mathcal{P}(E)$ *with* $\delta_A(s) = \{e \in E \mid s$ *is in memory of* e *and executed on* $e\}$*. Furthermore,* $\delta(s) = \delta_A(s) \cup \delta_P(s)$.

We describe the system configuration as the deployment of single ASWCs onto execution units, not as the deployment of ASWC-Clusters onto execution units like done in [2], because the activity of the ASWCs within a cluster may become different in degradation scenarios. This means, some ASWCs within a cluster may become isolated due to detected failures of that ASWCs or passivated due to insufficient resources, while other ASWCs within the same cluster are still active. Due to this, the deployment has to be described on ASWC level.

We ensure by a constraint that ASWCs which are mapped to the same cluster, get deployed to the same execution units:

$$\forall s_i, s_j \in S, \forall sc \in SC : s_i \in \alpha_{sc}(sc) \wedge s_j \in \alpha_{sc}(sc) \implies \delta(s_i) = \delta(s_j)$$

The ASWC-Clusters are structure building elements. They group ASWCs with the same safety and reliability requirements, providing a basis for separating mixed critical ASWCs from each other, as different clusters can be separated using spatial and temporal partitioning mechanisms [10]. Furthermore, clusters can be used to group ASWCs with high communication dependencies, ensuring a high amount of local communication, instead of distributed communication.

3.2 Degradation of Functional Features

Definition 6. *For some of the functional features $f \in F$, there may exist a degraded version $f' \in F$ of that feature. A degraded functional feature is a feature fulfilling a subset of the functional requirements of the original full-fledged feature, potentially with a worse quality of service. We define $D_f : F \rightarrow F \cup \{\perp\}$ as the relationship between the original full-fledged feature $f \in F$ and the degraded version $f' \in F$ of that feature, with $\perp$ being no element.*

$$D_f(f) = \begin{cases} f' \in F \text{ if } f' \text{ is the degraded version of the feature } f \in F \text{ with } f \neq f' \\ \perp \quad \text{if the feature } f \in F \text{ has no degraded version} \end{cases}$$

Hence, $D_f(F)$ is not a total function, but it is a partial injective and surjective function (see Fig. 1).

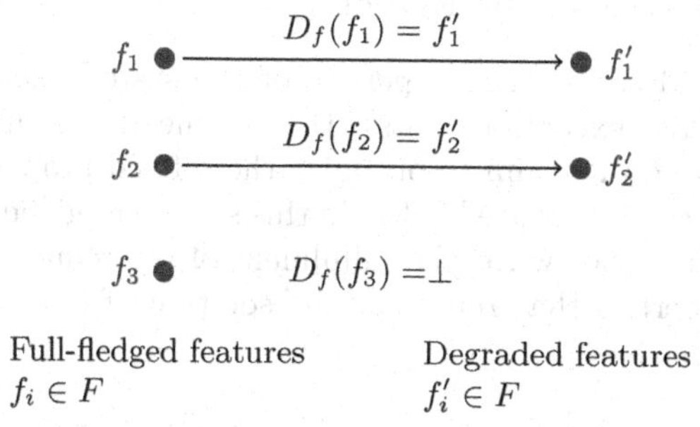

$$f_1 \bullet \xrightarrow{\quad D_f(f_1) = f_1' \quad} \bullet f_1'$$

$$f_2 \bullet \xrightarrow{\quad D_f(f_2) = f_2' \quad} \bullet f_2'$$

$$f_3 \bullet \qquad D_f(f_3) = \perp$$

Full-fledged features   Degraded features
$f_i \in F$ $f_i' \in F$

Fig. 1. Example partial injective and surjective function between full-fledged and degraded functional features

Definition 7. *For some ASWCs $s \in S$, there may exist a degraded version $s' \in S$ of that ASWC. We define $D_s : S \rightarrow S \cup \{\bot\}$ as the relationship between a normal ASWC $s \in S$ and its degraded version $s' \in S$, with $\bot$ being no element.*

$$D_s(s) = \begin{cases} s' \in S & \text{if } s' \text{ is the degraded version of the ASWC } s \in S \\ \bot & \text{otherwise, if the ASWC } s \in S \text{ has no degraded version} \end{cases}$$

$D_s(S)$ is a partial injective and surjective function (see Fig. 2).

Figure 2 shows how a degraded feature can be realized. For the realization of the degraded feature f_1', the ASWC s_1 is reused from the full-fledged feature f_1, a degraded version s_2' of ASWC s_2 is used, and ASWC s_3 is not used anymore. The motivation to introduce degraded ASWCs is providing diversity in the realization of features, as well as an efficient usage of decreasing system resources in case of failing system elements, assuming that s_2' requires less resources than s_2.

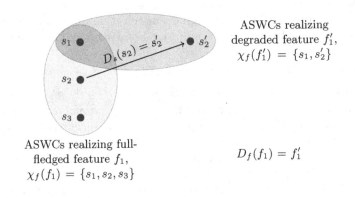

ASWCs realizing
degraded feature f_1',
$\chi_f(f_1') = \{s_1, s_2'\}$

ASWCs realizing full-
fledged feature f_1,
$\chi_f(f_1) = \{s_1, s_2, s_3\}$

$D_f(f_1) = f_1'$

Fig. 2. Example relation between normal and degraded ASWCs, realizing a full-fledged feature f_1 (green ellipse) and the corresponding degraded feature f_1' (orange ellipse) (Color figure online)

3.3   Fixed Properties of the Model

In this section, we describe the properties of the system elements (e. g., software components and execution units), that define the input problem model for our analysis. We do not aim to optimize these fixed properties. Instead, we consider the properties introduced below in this section as given and analyze possible degradation scenarios w.r.t. the fulfillment of the required fail-operational behavior. The properties that represent the solution of our analysis are introduced later in section 3.4.

Functional Features: Each functional feature $f \in F$ has properties defining in which sense it is required to behave fail-operational. We distinguish between full fail-operational and degraded fail-operational behavior. We express this distinction by assigning a property $failOp : F \rightarrow \mathbb{N}_0$ to $f \in F$ and $f' \in F$ with

$D_f(f) = f'$. If $failOp(f) > 0$, then feature $f \in F$ must be kept active with full-fledged functionality during the first $failOp(f)$ hardware or software failures, and is not allowed to be degraded meanwhile. More generally, it is allowed that feature f becomes degraded after $failOp(f) + 1$ hardware or software failures, and it is allowed that it becomes deactivated completely after $failOp(f') + 1$ failures. For instance, this means that if $failOp(f) = 1$ and $failOp(f') = 3$, then the full-fledged feature f has to survive the first failure and can be degraded to f' after a second failure. The degraded feature f' itself has to survive the third failure and can be deactivated after a fourth failure (see Fig. 3).

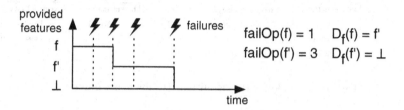

Fig. 3. Example of a feature degradation over time

In this paper, we consider at most one degradation step, meaning that degraded features do not have further degraded versions. However, our approach can be extended to allow such chains of multiple degradations.

Application Software Components: Each ASWC $s_i \in S$ is defined by several properties. Property $wcet : S \rightarrow \mathbb{N}^+$ defines the *Worst-Case Execution Time* of its cyclic executable function. Property $flash : S \rightarrow \mathbb{N}^+$ defines the required amount of flash memory to store the binary of the ASWC. Property $asil : S \rightarrow \{0..4\}$ defines the *Automotive Safety Integrity Level* (ASIL) of an ASWC [0: Quality-Management (QM), 1: ASIL-A, 2: ASIL-B, 3: ASIL-C, 4: ASIL-D]. Property $redncy : S \rightarrow \mathbb{N}_0$ defines the level of redundancy, with which an ASWC has to be deployed to the execution units [n: s_i has to be deployed $n + 1$ times (either passively or actively)].

Execution Units: For execution units $e \in E$, the following properties are defined. The property $providedTimeBudget : E \rightarrow \mathbb{N}^+$ defines the budget of time that is provided in each cycle to execute the ASWCs. We assume here that all ASWCs have the same execution rate and hence are executed in every cycle. The property $providedFlash : E \rightarrow \mathbb{N}^+$ defines the amount of flash memory that is provided to store binary images of ASWCs. For simplicity, we do not model other memory types, like RAM or NVRAM. These can be handled in a similar manner as the time budget and flash. Finally, the property $isolated : E \rightarrow \{0, 1\}$ defines if an execution unit $e \in E$ is isolated, after a failure of that unit has been detected.

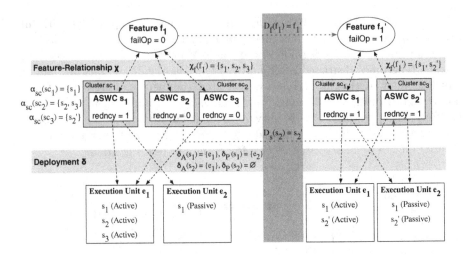

Fig. 4. Example for the definitions (Color figure online)

Figure 4 shows Definitions 6 and 7 in context, based on the example that was shown in Fig. 2. Also the mapping of ASWCs to clusters and some fixed properties are shown. The full-fledged feature f_1 is realized by overall three ASWCs s_1, s_2 and s_3. The three ASWCs are mapped to two different ASWC-Clusters sc_1 and sc_2. The ASWCs get deployed to the execution units e_1 and e_2, partially in a redundant manner (see s_1). Feature f_1 has a degraded version f_1', which is realized by overall two ASWCs s_1 and s_2'. The ASWC s_1 is reused from the realization of feature f_1, and s_2' is a degraded version of s_2, which was realizing parts of f_1. The degradations are indicated by the horizontal dashed red arrows.

3.4   Solution Properties of the Model

In this section we describe the model-properties that represent the solution of the deployment and degradation analysis.

ASWCs: To cover degradation scenarios that might be required after isolations of execution units, each ASWC $s \in S$ has the following properties:

- *hotStandbySlaveReq* $: S \to \{0, 1\}$ indicates if a redundant hot-standby *slave* is required. A hot-standby slave is active in the schedule, but it's output data is ignored by the system. Contrary to this, a cold-standby slave is only passively deployed and not in the schedule. The decision if a hot- or a cold-standby slave is required is based on a further *fault-tolerance time* property of the input model, which is not introduced in this paper.
- *hotStandbySlaveActive* $: S \to \{0, 1\}$ indicates if a required hot-standby *slave* can be kept active. In degradation scenarios, it can be valid that a hot-standby slave is deactivated due to insufficient resources, depending on the *failOp(f)* properties of the features $f \in \chi_s(s)$ for $f \in F$ and $s \in S$.

– *masterActive* : $S \rightarrow \{0,1\}$ indicates if one *master* instance can be kept active. In degradation scenarios, it is only allowed that no active master instance exists, if the requirements with respect to fail-operational behavior of the realized functional features $f_j \in \chi_s(s)$ are not violated.

ASWC Clusters: Certain properties of ASWC-Clusters $sc \in SC$ depend on the mapped ASWCs. Properties $asil : SC \rightarrow \{0..4\}$ and $redncy : SC \rightarrow \mathbb{N}_0$ define the ASIL and the redundancy level of a cluster. It is ensured by constraints that $\forall s \in \alpha_{sc}(sc) : asil(sc) = asil(s)$ and $redncy(sc) = redncy(s)$.

Execution Units: For execution units $e \in E$, property $usedTimeBudget : E \rightarrow \mathbb{N}_0$ is defined to be equal to $\sum_{s \in S \,|\, e \in \delta_A(s)} wcet(s)$, which is the sum of the $wcet(s)$ of those ASWCs that are active on execution unit e. A constraint ensures that $\forall e \in E : usedTimeBudget(e) \leq providedTimeBudget(e)$. Property $usedFlash :$ $E \rightarrow \mathbb{N}_0$ is the amount of flash memory which is occupied by the binaries of the ASWCs that are deployed to an execution unit actively or passively. Hence, $usedFlash(e) = \sum_{s \in S \,|\, e \in \delta(s)} flash(s)$, for $e \in E$.

System: The following two properties define the solution matrices that contain the mapping of ASWCs S to ASWC-Clusters SC and the deployment of the ASWCs S to the execution units E.

– *map* : $(S, SC) \rightarrow \{0,1\}$ is the mapping of ASWCs $s \in S$ to ASWC-Clusters $sc \in SC$. [0: $s \notin \alpha_{sc}(sc)$, 1: $s \in \alpha_{sc}(sc)$]
– *deploy* : $(S, E) \rightarrow \{0,1,2,3\}$ is the deployment of ASWCs $s \in S$ to execution units $e \in E$. [0: $e \notin \delta(s)$, 1: $e \in \delta_P(s)$,   2: $e \in \delta_A(s)$ while s is a *master* on e, 3: $e \in \delta_A(s)$ while s is a hot-standby *slave* on e]

3.5   Reconfigurations After Isolations

In this paper, we consider two different system elements which may fail:

1. a hardware execution unit $e \in E$
2. an application software component $s \in S$

We do not consider failures of physical communication links, because we assume a system platform with a reliable redundant communication backbone, like the platform introduced in [7]. Furthermore, we assume that the system platform is able to detect failing system elements with appropriate mechanisms (e. g., as sketched in [9]), and isolates these system elements to avoid further failure propagation and harm.

Reconfigurations in the deployment and in the schedules may be required after such isolations in order to ensure the fail-operational requirements of the functional features that are realized by the software components. ASWCs that realize non-fail-operational features may be deactivated (taken out of schedule) to enable the activation of redundant backups of ASWCs that realize fail-operational features. In section 4, we illustrate this based on an example.

Our objective is to maximize the value of the active ASWCs in a sense that the ASWCs with the highest requirements according to safety $(asil(s))$ and fail-operationality $(redncy(s))$ will be kept active as long as possible. ASWCs with low requirements according to these properties are deactivated first if the system resources become insufficient, for instance after isolations of execution units.

Priority Points: To fulfill the mentioned objective, we introduce so called *priority-points* that define the importance of a deployed ASWC instance. Each ASWC has the properties *prioPointsMaster* : $S \rightarrow \mathbb{N}^+$ and *prioPointsHotSlave* : $S \rightarrow \mathbb{N}^+$, storing the priority-points of instances of the ASWCs, deployed actively as master or as hot-standby slave. The priority-points are used to construct an order in which the active instances of ASWCs should be deactivated in case of insufficient resources in degradation scenarios. We derive the priority-points depending on the properties $asil(s)$ and $redncy(s)$.

On system level, the solution property *prioSumActiveASWCs* : $\mathbb{V} \rightarrow \mathbb{N}_0$ defines the sum of the priority-points of all (partially redundant) ASWC instances that are actively deployed in the current degradation scenario.

To implement the objective, we use an objective function of the Z3 SMT solver with optimization capabilities [5] over its Python API. Listing 1 shows a sketch of the implementation of the objective function. Line 1 creates an optimization solver. Lines 3–6 add a constraint that specifies the calculation of the sum of the priority-points of the active ASWC instances. An *If* statement is embedded into the calculation of the sum, defining that if an ASWC $s \in S$ is deployed as master to an execution unit $e \in E$, then *prioPointsMaster(s)* is added to the sum. Else, if s is deployed as hot-standby slave to e, then *prioPointsHotSlave(s)* is added to the sum. Finally, line 8 specifies that the objective is to maximize this sum. This objective function ensures that ASWC instances with low priority-points are deactivated first when resources become insufficient in degradation scenarios.

```
1 s = Optimize()
2
3 s.add(prioSumActiveASWCs == ∑_{s∈S,e∈E} (
4         If(deploy(s,e) == 2,
5             prioPointsMaster(s),
6             If(deploy(s,e) == 3, prioPointsHotSlave(s), 0) )))
7
8 s.maximize(prioSumActiveASWCs)
```

Listing 1. Objective to maximize the value of priority-points of active ASWCs

An ASWC with low priority-points has a low ASIL and low or no fail-operational requirements mirrored in their redundancy property. The redundancy property has a higher weight than the ASIL in the calculation of the priority-points. This is required to ensure that ASWCs with low ASIL but high fail-operational requirement are kept active with higher priority than ASWCs with high ASIL but low or no fail-operational requirement.

4   Example

In this section, we show an example of a feature set containing a feature degradation, as well as the corresponding ASWCs that realize these features. We show how this example can be degraded when execution units or ASWCs have to be isolated.

Table 1. Example set of functional features and realizing software components

Feature f_i	$failOp(f_i)$	ASWCs $s_i \in \chi_f(f_i)$	$asil(s_i)$	$redncy(s_i)$	$wcet(s_i)$ in ms	$flash(s_i)$ in kb
Full-fledged Features:						
f_1 : Steer-By-Wire (with assistance)	0	s_1	D	1 (hot-slave)	1.5	10
		s_2	C	0	1	10
		s_3	C	0	1	10
f_2 : Parking Assistance (active)	0	s_3	—	—	—	—
		s_4	C	1 (cold-slave)	0.5	10
f_3 : Drive-By-Wire	1	s_5	D	1 (cold-slave)	1.3	10
f_4 : Infotainment	0	s_6	QM	0	0.5	17
Degraded Features:						
f_1' : Steer-By-Wire (without assistance)	1	s_1	—	—	—	—
		s_2'	C	1 (cold-slave)	0.5	5
f_2' : Parking Assistance (passive)	1	s_4	—	—	—	—

Table 1 shows the properties of the example. The first two columns show four full-fledged features $\{f_1, f_2, f_3, f_4\}$ and two degraded features (f_1', f_2') with $D_f(f_1) = f_1'$ and $D_f(f_2) = f_2'$. The right five columns show the ASWCs that realize the features. The property values, like the ASIL levels, are fictional and not related to a real case-study. Some of the ASWCs contribute to realize multiple features, like s_3 which contributes to realize features f_1 and f_2, meaning that $\chi_s(s_3) = \{f_1, f_2\}$. Due to this, s_3 is shown in two rows. We write '—' in the property cells of the repetition rows, as the properties are the same.

Figure 5 shows the feature degradations of the example from a different perspective. As mentioned, ASWC s_3 contributes to realize both full-fledged functional features f_1 and f_2. Furthermore, ASWC s_1 is used to realize both the full-fledged feature f_1 (upper green ellipse) and the related degraded feature f_1' (upper orange ellipse). Hence, $\chi_s(s_1) = \{f_1, f_1'\}$. The same holds for s_4 and features f_2 and f_2'. It can be seen in the figure that the example contains also one

ASWC degradation, namely $D_s(s_2) = s_2'$, which is applied during the feature degradation $D_f(f_1) = f_1'$. Features f_3 and f_4 from the example are not shown in Fig. 5, as these have no degraded versions.

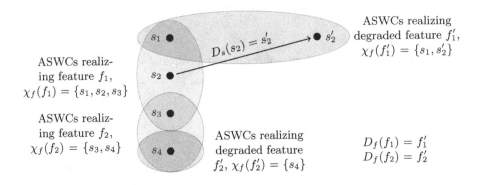

ASWCs realizing feature f_1, $\chi_f(f_1) = \{s_1, s_2, s_3\}$

ASWCs realizing feature f_2, $\chi_f(f_2) = \{s_3, s_4\}$

$D_s(s_2) = s_2'$

ASWCs realizing degraded feature f_2', $\chi_f(f_2') = \{s_4\}$

ASWCs realizing degraded feature f_1', $\chi_f(f_1') = \{s_1, s_2'\}$

$D_f(f_1) = f_1'$
$D_f(f_2) = f_2'$

Fig. 5. Realization of full-fledged features f_1 and f_2, as well as corresponding degraded features f_1' and f_2' by (partially shared) ASWCs (Color figure online)

4.1   Initial Deployment Solution for the Example

The shown example set of ASWCs should now be deployed on two execution units $e_1, e_2 \in E$, each having a provided time budget of 4ms to execute ASWCs in each execution cycle, *providedTimeBudget*(e_i) = *4ms*. Furthermore, both execution units have *providedFlash*(e_i) = *64kb* in this example.

We now consider four different failure scenarios. In scenario 1 the first execution unit e_1 has a failure and has to be isolated, with the result that no ASWCs can be executed anymore on e_1. In scenario 2 the second execution unit e_2 has to be isolated. In scenario 3 the ASWC s_2 has to be isolated, and in scenario 4 the ASWC s_3 has to be isolated.

We use the introduced formal model to calculate deployment solutions for these scenarios, using the Z3 SMT solver to calculate the results. Several formal constraints ensure the validity of follow-up deployments after isolations of execution units or ASWCs. For instance, one constraint defines that the master instance of an ASWC is not allowed to migrate to another execution unit in a follow-up deployment, if the execution unit to which the master was initially deployed is still alive.

Figure 6 shows the initial valid deployment solution for the example. Also exemplary schedules of the execution units are shown. In the schedule, it can be seen that for instance s_2' is not executed in the initial solution, as it is a passive cold-standby slave which only becomes active if s_2 gets lost. Also the redundant cold-standby slave of s_5 on e_1 is not executed initially, as it only is a backup for the case that the master of s_5 on e_2 gets lost. However, the components which are not executed in the schedule need flash memory space. On execution unit e_1, 55 kb of flash memory are used in this example (10+10+10+10+5+10).

Also the ASWC-Clusters are shown. Five clusters are created for the given set of ASWCs. Those ASWCs are mapped to the same cluster, which have the same properties of $asil(s_i)$ and $redncy(s_i)$.

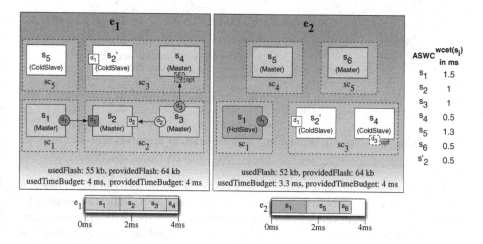

Fig. 6. An initial deployment solution for the example

In Fig. 6, there are also shown some communication channels between the ASWCs for illustration purpose. ASWC s_2 receives data from both s_1 and s_3. ASWC s_4 receives data from s_3 optionally, meaning that s_4 can also work without the input from s_3. The formalization of these communication dependencies in our model is described in [3].

4.2 Analysis of Degradations for the Example

Figures 7, 8, 9 and 10 show the follow-up deployments for the four mentioned considered failure scenarios. The solution property $usedTimeBudget(e_i)$ changes in the follow-up deployments, as the schedules change. However, the solution property $usedFlash(e_i)$ keeps unchanged, assuming that the binaries of isolated or deactivated ASWCs are kept stored in the flash memory. Notice that the solution property $deploy(s, e)$ equals to 1 for all ASWC instances that we call cold-standby slave, deactivated/inactive or isolated.

When the execution unit e_1 has to be isolated (Fig. 7), the cold standby-slaves of s'_2 and s_4 on e_2 have to be activated to be able to provide the degraded features f'_1 and f'_2 and by this fulfilling the required level of degraded fail-operationality. However, in order to be able to activate s'_2 and s_4 on e_2, the ASWC s_6 has to be deactivated, as otherwise the $providedTimeBudget(e_2)$ would be exceeded. This means, feature f_4 is lost in this scenario, what is okay.

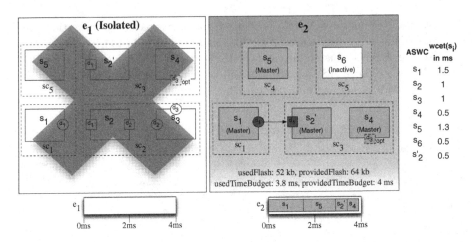

Fig. 7. Follow-Up deployment after isolation of execution unit e_1

When the execution unit e_2 has to be isolated (Fig. 8), the cold standby-slave of s_5 on e_1 has to be activated, because s_5 realizes feature f_3 which is required to behave fully fail-operational. In order to be able to activate s_5 on e_1, some other ASWCs have to be deactivated on e_1. However, deactivating s_1 would cause the loss of f_1 and f_1'. Deactivating s_4 would cause the loss of f_2 and f_2'. Hence, this is not allowed. Thus, s_2 and s_3 have to be deactivated to free enough space in the schedule to be able to activate s_5. Hence, s_2' has also to be activated on e_1 in order to be able to provide feature f_1'. Feature f_1 cannot be provided anymore in this scenario. Also f_2 cannot be provided anymore as s_3 is inactive, but f_2' can be provided because s_4 can operate standalone without the optional input.

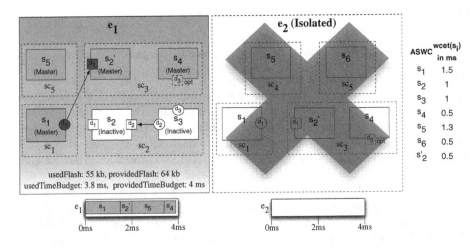

Fig. 8. Follow-Up deployment after isolation of execution unit e_2

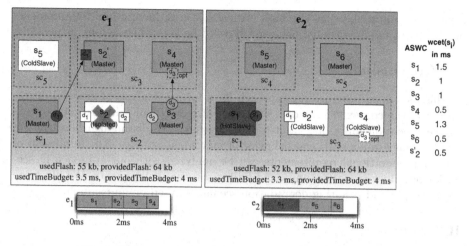

Fig. 9. Follow-Up deployment after isolation of ASWC s_2

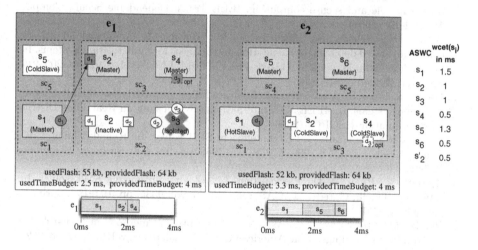

Fig. 10. Follow-Up deployment after isolation of ASWC s_3

When s_2 has to be isolated (Fig. 9), then feature f_1 cannot be provided anymore. ASWC s'_2 has to be activated to provide the degraded f'_1. ASWC s_3 is kept active to continue providing feature f_2.

When s_3 has to be isolated (Fig. 10), also s_2 has to be deactivated as s_2 needs mandatory data from s_3. Hence, features f_1 and f_2 cannot be provided anymore. But the degraded features f'_1 and f'_2 can be provided, as s_1, s'_2 and s_4 are active.

Hence, all requirements w.r.t. to full and degraded fail-operational behavior can be fulfilled in all considered scenarios. Our approach can be used to automatically analyze these and the other scenarios and obtain results about the subsets of functional features that can be kept alive in each case. We use an optimizing SMT solver [5] to calculate results for the problem model and use objective functions to describe that the high critical features, having high requirements according to fail-operational behavior, have to be kept alive as long as possible.

5 Conclusion

In this paper, we provided an approach for a formal analysis of graceful degradation in the context of the deployment of mixed-critical software components to the execution units of a fault-tolerant system. We distinguish between full and degraded fail-operational behavior of functional features. The fulfillment of these fail-operational requirements can be analyzed with our approach in scenarios of failing execution units and failing software components. We illustrate the concepts and resulting degradation scenarios based on an example.

References

1. Avizienis, A., Laprie, J., Randell, B., Landwehr, C.: Basic concepts and taxonomy of dependable and secure computing. IEEE Trans. Dependable Secure Comput. 1(1), 11–33 (2004)
2. Becker, K., Schätz, B., Armbruster, M., Buckl, C.: A formal model for constraint-based deployment calculation and analysis for fault-tolerant systems. In: Giannakopoulou, D., Salaün, G. (eds.) SEFM 2014. LNCS, vol. 8702, pp. 205–219. Springer, Heidelberg (2014)
3. Becker, K., Voss, S.: Analyzing graceful degradation for mixed critical fault-tolerant real-time systems. In: IEEE 18th International Symposium on Real-Time Distributed Computing (ISORC) (2015)
4. Bjørner, N.S., de Moura, L.: Z3: an efficient SMT solver. In: Ramakrishnan, C.R., Rehof, J. (eds.) TACAS 2008. LNCS, vol. 4963, pp. 337–340. Springer, Heidelberg (2008)
5. Bjørner, N., Phan, A.-D., Fleckenstein, L.: νZ - an optimizing SMT solver. In: Baier, C., Tinelli, C. (eds.) TACAS 2015. LNCS, vol. 9035, pp. 194–199. Springer, Heidelberg (2015)
6. Blanke, M., Staroswiecki, M., Wu, N.E.: Concepts and methods in fault-tolerant control. In: Proceedings of the American Control Conference, vol. 4, pp. 2606–2620. IEEE (2001)
7. Armbruster, M., Fiege, L., Freitag, G., Schmid, T., Spiegelberg, G., Zirkler, A.: Ethernet-based and function-independent vehicle control-platform: motivation, idea and technical concept fulfilling quantitative safety-requirements from ISO 26262. In: Meyer, G. (ed.) Advanced Microsystems for Automotive Applications 2012 (AMAA), pp. 91–107. Springer, Heidelberg (2012)
8. Sommer, S., Camek, A., Becker, K., Buckl, C., Knoll, A., Zirkler, A., Fiege, L., Armbruster, M., Spiegelberg, G.: RACE: a centralized platform computer based architecture for automotive applications. In: IEEE Vehicular Electronics Conference / International Electric Vehicle Conference (VEC-IEVC) (2013)
9. Becker, K., Frtunikj, J., Felser, M., Fiege, L., Buckl, C., Rothbauer, S., Zhang, L., Klein, C.: RACE RTE: a runtime environment for robust fault-tolerant vehicle functions. In: 3rd Workshop on Critical Automotive Applications : Robustness & Safety (CARS) (2015)
10. Rushby, J.: Partitioning in avionics architectures: Requirements, mechanisms, and assurance. Technical report, DTIC Document (2000)

Probabilistic Analysis of a Calculus for Wireless Sensor Networks

Xi Wu[✉] and Huibiao Zhu

Shanghai Key Laboratory of Trustworthy Computing,
East China Normal University, Shanghai, China
{xiwu,hbzhu}@sei.ecnu.edu.cn

Abstract. The CWQ Calculus (a Calculus for Wireless sensor networks from Quality perspective) was recently proposed for modeling and reasoning about Wireless Sensor Networks (WSNs). It has the flexibility that not all input data in a binder need to be received in order for the process to continue. Meanwhile, it has the unique and important characteristic that, in order for the decision of a system of a WSN to be of high trustworthiness, the decision is expected to be made by considering all data from all network nodes in the WSN. Consequently, decisions of a system may have different trustworthiness depending on which input data have actually been received. In this paper, we propose a data-driven probabilistic trust analysis of the CWQ Calculus for WSNs. We assume that data received from a channel have trust values that follow a probability distribution; that is, the trust value of a data represents the trust of the decision of a system made solely based on that data. Thus, we decouple the probability of receiving input data from the probability of data trustworthiness. The overall trustworthiness of the decision of a system is determined by performing a relational analysis to combine these probability distributions.

1 Introduction

As one of the key components of Cyber Physical Systems [7], Wireless Sensor Networks (WSNs) [1,2] have drawn a great deal of attentions recently. Due to significant applications of WSNs (e.g., distributed computing, medical systems, traffic security management systems, and disaster recovery), many calculi have been proposed in the literature for modeling and reasoning about WSNs; for example, [3,4,6,8–10,14,15]. One important feature of wireless systems is broadcast, and *wireless local broadcast* is the commonly adopted broadcast model in modeling and reasoning about WSNs, for example, in past works [4,6,8–10]. In wireless local broadcast, not all nodes but only the nodes within the transmission area of the sender can receive the message broadcasted by the sender. On the other hand, one critical problem of wireless systems is *unreliable communication* in WSNs. This problem may be mainly caused by deployment constraints and/or communication modalities; this may result in abnormalities and thus decrease the quality of the service provided by a wireless system. Therefore, it is of great importance to ensure the service quality offered by a wireless system.

© Springer International Publishing Switzerland 2016
C. Artho and P.C. Ölveczky (Eds.): FTSCS 2015, CCIS 596, pp. 155–171, 2016.
DOI: 10.1007/978-3-319-29510-7_9

The CWQ Calculus. To ensure wireless sensor nodes to behave in a reasonable manner even if they are in an unreliable communication network, CWQ Calculus (a Calculus for Wireless sensor networks from Quality perspective) [17] was recently proposed for modeling and reasoning about WSNs and applications based on WSNs. It *combines wireless local broadcast with quality predicate*; the topological structure is considered at the network level, and different node behaviours are represented by processes. In CWQ Calculus, default values are given to deal with the situations that the ideal behavior fails due to unreliable communications. The CWQ Calculus was modified and simplified to be a parametric framework by extracting the network topology as a configuration [16]; this makes it more flexible for modeling and reasoning about networks of different topological structures.

Probabilistic Trust Analysis. CWQ Calculus includes an input guard, *binder*, to specify the inputs to be performed before continuing. A simple binder is of the form $c^l?x$ describing that some value should be received over channel c and bound to variable x, and it has a trustworthiness l chosen from some finite lattice of trust values. By incorporating a *quality predicate* q, a general binder is of the form $\&_q(c_1^{l_1}?x_1, \cdots, c_n^{l_n}?x_n)$[1] indicating that several inputs are simultaneously active while the quality predicate q determines when sufficient inputs have been received to continue (e.g., $q \in \{\forall, \exists, \exists!, m/n\}$ [13,16,17]). That is, the CWQ Calculus has the flexibility that not all input data in a binder need to be received in order for the process to continue. Then, there comes the problem that one cannot be sure what data has actually been received. Nevertheless, the subsequent process can determine this by testing whether a particular data has actually been received (e.g., by using the case construct case x of some (y)), and decisions can be made accordingly. Consequently, decisions of a system may have different trustworthiness depending on which input data have actually been received. This calls the need to analyze the trust of the robustness of a system.

In the literature, Nielson and Nielson [12] developed a novel probabilistic *trust* analysis for supporting the Quality Calculus [13] to indicate the trust that a user can have in the overall robustness of a system. However, it is not applicable to the CWQ Calculus for WSNs, because the CWQ Calculus has a unique and important characteristic that is not part of the Quality Calculus. Specifically, the decision of a system of a WSN is expected to be made based on the data from all network nodes in the WSN, and the decision has the highest trustworthiness if data from all its constituent network nodes are received and considered. In other words, from the perspective of a single network node, its locally stored data may not be sufficient for making the best decision of a system. In Sect. 4, we illustrate this characteristic of WSNs in more detail, through a case study of refueling a car by using the information of gas stations stored in base stations.

---

[1] Details of binder $\&_q(c_1^{l_1}?x_1, \cdots, c_n^{l_n}?x_n)$ shall be introduced in Sect. 2.

Contributions. In this paper, we propose a data-driven probabilistic trust analysis of the CWQ Calculus for WSNs. Instead of the channel having a trust value, we assume that the data received from a channel have a trust value, where the trust value of a data represents the trust of the decision of a system made solely based on that data. Intuitively, data received from a channel of a network node is of high trustworthiness if it is essential for making a high-quality decision of the system, and it is not otherwise; for simplicity, we assume the data received from a channel has a probability distribution of trust values. To facilitate our probabilistic analysis, we change the syntax of binders in CWQ Calculus for WSNs to $\&_q^\pi(c_1^{l_1}?x_1, \cdots, c_n^{l_n}?x_n)$ at the beginning of our probabilistic analysis, where $\pi \in \mathcal{D}(\{x_1, \cdots, x_n\} \to \{\text{t}, \perp\})$ denotes whether an input data x_i is received (i.e., t) or not received (i.e., $\perp$) over channel c_i for $1 \leq i \leq n$, and $l_i \in \mathcal{D}(\mathcal{L})$ is a probability distribution of the trust of the input data received over channel c_i. Consequently, we consider data trustworthiness instead of channel trustworthiness, and decouple the probability of receiving input data from the probability of data trustworthiness. In such a way, it is possible to conduct more flexible probabilistic analysis, e.g., for analyzing systems based on WSNs. Finally, the overall trustworthiness of the decision of a system is determined by performing relational analysis to combine the probability distributions of π and $l_i(\forall 1 \leq i \leq n)$.

Organization. The rest of the paper is organized as follows. Firstly, we briefly review the CWQ Calculus in Sect. 2. In Sect. 3, we give a motivating example to illustrate the need for a data-driven probabilistic trust analysis to support the CWQ Calculus, while the formal detailed analysis is given in Sect. 4. Finally, Sect. 5 concludes the paper and points out some future directions.

2 Review of the CWQ Calculus

The CWQ Calculus [16,17] was recently proposed for modeling and reasoning about WSNs and applications based on WSNs. It ensures that sensor nodes, even if in an unreliable communication network, can behave in a reasonable manner. In the following, we briefly review the syntax and semantics of the CWQ Calculus.

Syntax of the CWQ Calculus. The processes and networks are interpreted by a two-level syntax in the CWQ Calculus.

Syntax of Process. For presentation simplicity, name restrictions are omitted in this paper. We employ P to range over the set of all processes, and N the set of all network nodes. We use the set $\mathcal{I}_n$ to denote the node identities, where $n_1, n_2,$ ... range over $\mathcal{I}_n$. The syntax of the CWQ Calculus is illustrated by the Backus-Naur form in Table 1. nil stands for the skip process. $c!v$ denotes an output of a value v, while the corresponding reception is represented by $c^l?x$ which receives a value via channel c and binds it to a variable x. Here, l indicates the trust

Table 1. The syntax of CWQ

Processes:

$P ::= \text{nil} \mid Act.P \mid \text{case } e \text{ of some}(y) : P_1 \text{ else } P_2 \mid A(\tilde{x})$

$Act ::= b \mid c!v \qquad b ::= c^l?x \mid \&_q(b_1, ..., b_n)$

$d ::= c \mid v \mid y \qquad e ::= x \mid \text{some}(d) \mid \text{none}$

Networks:

Network N has the form: $n_1[P_1] \parallel n_2[P_2] \parallel ... \parallel n_k[P_k]$

---

level of data received over channel c, and it is chosen from a finite trust lattice $\mathcal{L}$ with $\leq$ for the ordering on $\mathcal{L}$; for example, $\mathcal{L} = (\{\mathsf{L}, \mathsf{M}, \mathsf{H}\}, \leq)$. $A(\tilde{x})$ denotes a process with the (possibly recursive) definition of $A(\tilde{x}) =_{df} P$, where A is a process constant and $\tilde{x}$ contains all free variables in P.

The CWQ Calculus also has the *binder b*, an input guard inherited from the Quality Calculus, which is used to specify the inputs to be performed before continuing. It is of the form $\&_q(b_1, ..., b_n)$, where n is the total number of inputs and q is a quality predicate to be satisfied. Here, $q \in \{\forall, \exists, \exists!, m/n\}$ and the corresponding meanings are as follows: *all inputs are required* ($\forall$), *at least one of the inputs is required* ($\exists$), *only one input is required* ($\exists!$) and m *sufficient inputs among all n inputs are required* (m/n), respectively. Moreover, nested binders are also allowed; for example $\&_\exists(\&_\forall(c_1^{l_1}?x_1, c_2^{l_2}?x_2), c_3^{l_3}?x_3)$. Thus, it is possible that some variables in the binder do not get proper values when the process continues. Consequently, *data* are distinguished from *optional data*, and denoted by term d and expression e, respectively. In particular, $\text{some}(d)$ represents the presence of some data d and none for the absence of data. The construct case e of some$(y) : P_1$ else P_2 is used to check whether e evaluates to some data. If it does, then the data is bound to y and P_1 continues; otherwise, P_2 continues.

Syntax of Network. Networks are collections of nodes running in parallel. Each node, written as $n[P]$, is assigned a unique identity n and runs a process P. The topology T of a network is specified by an undirected graph G and a radius constraint Rad, where G consists of a finite set of nodes $Node$ and a set of edges $Edge$ between these nodes; $T = (G, Rad)$, and $G = (Node, Edge)$. Rad describes the transmission radius of a node in G, and is defined as a partial function of $Rad : Chan * Node \hookrightarrow R_0^+$, where $Chan$ is a finite set of channels and R_0^+ stands for non-negative real numbers. This partial function is used to distinguish between different kinds of channels; for example, $Rad(c_1, n_1) = 0$ for internal unicast communication while $Rad(c_2, n_2) = 3$ for broadcast communication. $Edge$ is also a partial function, $Edge : Node * Node \hookrightarrow R_0^+$, which assigns distances to node-pairs (n_i, n_j) in G, and it satisfies symmetry and the triangle inequality.

Labeled Transition Semantics of the CWQ Calculus. The labeled transition system is also divided into two levels: transitions for processes and for networks. The rule for process is of the form $P \xrightarrow{\lambda} P'$, where the syntax of the signal λ is, $\lambda ::= c!v \mid c^l?x$, where $c!v$ stands for sending data v via channel c, while $c^l?x$ represents the corresponding receiving and then assigning the value to variable x. Some auxiliary relations are also used; $c!v \vdash b \rightarrow b'$ and $b ::_\sigma \theta$ where $\sigma \in \{\mathsf{tt}, \mathsf{ff}\}$. The former one specifies that the binder b is changed to b' after receiving an output $c!v$. The latter one is used to check whether the required inputs in binder b have already been satisfied ($::_{\mathsf{tt}}$) or not ($::_{\mathsf{ff}}$). If all the required inputs are satisfied, a substitution θ is constructed to replace all the variables with the receiving values, i.e., $c^l?x::_{\mathsf{tt}}[\mathsf{some}(v)/x]$ and $c^l?x::_{\mathsf{ff}}[\mathsf{none}/x]$. Usually, a substitution has an id; thus, the composition $(\theta_1\theta_2)(x)$ is equivalent to $\theta_2(\theta_1(x))$ for all x.

Semantics of Processes. The operational semantics of processes are illustrated in Table 2. Rules *Send* and *Recv* refer to the primitive output and input of values respectively. After receiving a value via channel c, a substitution θ is constructed as $[\mathsf{some}(v)/x]$. Rules *Mat1* and *Mat2* stand for the case construct. $e \rhd \mathsf{some}(c)$ and $e \rhd \mathsf{none}$ are two relations for evaluating an expression e to a constant with the form $\mathsf{some}(c)$ and none, respectively. The next three rules denote the synchronization with quality binder. Rule *Qsd1* defines that after the binder b receiving an output, the required inputs in b still cannot be satisfied, thus more inputs are required; Rule *Qsd2* denotes that no more inputs are needed. The general idea of *Qrec* is to record the binding of the value received in the appropriate position. As mentioned before, the auxiliary relation $b ::_\sigma \theta$ is defined to evaluate the binder b for checking whether a sufficient number of inputs have been performed (i.e., recorded in σ) and for computing the associated substitution θ, which is shown by rules *Jdg1*, *jdg2* and *Sat*. The semantics of the example quality predicates are listed below:

Table 2. Semantics of processes

$[Send]$ $c!v.P \xrightarrow{c!v} P$ $\qquad$ $[Recv]$ $c!v \vdash c^l?x \rightarrow [\mathsf{some}(v)/x]$

$[Mat1]$ $\dfrac{e \rhd \mathsf{some}(v)}{\text{case } e \text{ of some}(y): P_1 \text{ else } P_2 \rightarrow P_1[v/y]}$ $\qquad$ $[Qsd1]$ $\dfrac{c!v \vdash b \rightarrow b' \quad b' ::_{\mathsf{ff}} \theta}{b.P \xrightarrow{c^l?x} b'.P}$

$[Mat2]$ $\dfrac{e \rhd \mathsf{none}}{\text{case } e \text{ of some}(y): P_1 \text{ else } P_2 \rightarrow P_2}$ $\qquad$ $[Qsd2]$ $\dfrac{c!v \vdash b \rightarrow b' \quad b' ::_{\mathsf{tt}} \theta}{b.P \xrightarrow{c^l?x} P\theta}$

$[Qrec]$ $\dfrac{c!v \vdash b_i \rightarrow b_i'}{c!v \vdash \&_q(b_1, \ldots, b_i, \ldots, b_n) \rightarrow \&_q(b_1, \ldots, b_i', \ldots, b_n)}$ $\qquad$ $[Rec]$ $\dfrac{A(\tilde{x}) =_{df} P}{A(\tilde{y}) \rightarrow P\{\tilde{y}/\tilde{x}\}}$

$[Jdg1]$ $[\mathsf{some}(v)/x] ::_{\mathsf{tt}} [\mathsf{some}(v)/x]$ $\qquad$ $[Jdg2]$ $c^l?x ::_{\mathsf{ff}} [\mathsf{none}/x]$

$[Sat]$ $\dfrac{b_1 ::_{\sigma_1} \theta_1 \ldots b_i ::_{\sigma_i} \theta_i \ldots b_n ::_{\sigma_n} \theta_n}{\&_q(b_1, \ldots, b_i, \ldots, b_n) ::_\sigma \theta_1 \ldots \theta_i \ldots \theta_n}$ $\qquad$ where $\sigma = [\{q\}](\sigma_1, \ldots, \sigma_i, \ldots, \sigma_n)$

- $[\{\forall\}](\sigma_1, ..., \sigma_n) = (|\{i|\sigma_i = \text{tt}\}| = n) = \sigma_1 \wedge ... \wedge \sigma_n$
- $[\{\exists\}](\sigma_1, ..., \sigma_n) = (|\{i|\sigma_i = \text{tt}\}| \geq 1) = \sigma_1 \vee ... \vee \sigma_n$
- $[\{\exists!\}](\sigma_1, ..., \sigma_n) = (|\{i|\sigma_i = \text{tt}\}| = 1)$
- $[\{m/n\}](\sigma_1, ..., \sigma_n) = (|\{i|\sigma_i = \text{tt}\}| \geq m)$

$|X|$ denotes the cardinality of a set X. Formally, $\exists(x_1, ..., x_n) \Leftrightarrow x_1 \vee \cdots \vee x_n$ and $\forall(x_1, ..., x_n) \Leftrightarrow x_1 \wedge \cdots \wedge x_n$. Here, we also allow to write the quality predicate as $[0 \wedge (1 \vee 2)](x_1, x_2, x_3)$ which is equivalent to $x_1 \wedge (x_2 \vee x_3)$. Rule *Rec* is a standard one for recursion. Finally, transitions can take place in contexts C by rule *Con* and the replacement in C is also allowed which is shown as follows:

$$[Con] \quad \frac{P \xrightarrow{\lambda} P'}{C[P] \xrightarrow{\lambda} C[P']} \quad \text{where } C ::= [\,] \mid C|P \mid P|C$$

Semantics of Networks. The formal transitional rules for the networks are defined by a parameterized operational semantics. Transitions are of the form $T \vdash N \xrightarrow{\alpha} N'$, where the action α is defined as, $\alpha ::= c!v@n \mid c^l?x@n \mid \tau$. The parameter T refers to the topology of the entire network and N refers to the network. For the actions, $c!v@n$ denotes that a node identified n sends a message v to its neighbors using channel c, $c^l?x@n$ refers to the corresponding receiving from a node identified n, and τ is an internal action inside a network.

The labeled transition system for networks is defined in Table 3. One node can either do an internal action in rule *Int1* or keep unchanged in rule *Int2*, where rule *Int2* is a preliminary of rules *BSyn* and *τSyn* which shall be explained shortly. Rule *Bro* denotes that a node, identified n, can send a message v via channel c and the executing process P evolves into P'. Three corresponding receivings are listed in rule *BRcv1*, *BRcv2* and *BRcv3*. Taking local broadcast into account, only the nodes that are located inside the transmission area of the sending node can receive the message according to rule *BRcv1*. The other nodes that are outside the transmission area of the sender or cannot execute receiving

Table 3. Semantics of networks

$$[Int1] \quad \frac{P \xrightarrow{\tau} P'}{n[P] \xrightarrow{\tau} n[P']} \qquad [Int2] \quad n[P] \xrightarrow{\tau} n[P] \qquad [Bro] \quad \frac{P \xrightarrow{c!v} P'}{T \vdash n[P] \xrightarrow{c!v@n} n[P']}$$

$$[BRcv1] \quad \frac{P \xrightarrow{c^l?x} P' \wedge (n,m) \in G(T) \wedge Rad(c,n) \geq Edge(n,m)}{T \vdash m[P] \xrightarrow{c^l?x@n} m[P']}$$

$$[BRcv2] \quad \frac{(n,m) \in G(T) \wedge Rad(c,n) < Edge(n,m)}{T \vdash m[P] \xrightarrow{c^l?x@n} m[P]} \qquad [BRcv3] \quad \frac{P \xrightarrow{c^l?-}}{T \vdash m[P] \xrightarrow{c^l?x@n} m[P]}$$

$$[BSyn] \quad \frac{T \vdash n_i[P_i] \xrightarrow{c!v@n_i} n_i[P_i'] \qquad \forall j \neq i \quad T \vdash n_j[P_j] \xrightarrow{c^l?x@n_i} n_j[P_j']}{T \vdash n_1[P_1]||...||n_i[P_i]||...||n_k[P_k] \xrightarrow{c!v@n_i} n_1[P_1']||...||n_i[P_i']||...||n_k[P_k']}$$

$$[\tau Syn] \quad \frac{\forall i \quad T \vdash n_i[P_i] \xrightarrow{\tau} n_i[P_i']}{T \vdash n_1[P_1]||...||n_i[P_i]||...||n_k[P_k] \xrightarrow{\tau} n_1[P_1']||...||n_i[P_i']||...||n_k[P_k']}$$

actions will remain unchanged, based on rules *BRcv2* and *BRcv3*, respectively. Rule *BSyn* specifies the parallel of the entire network when the nodes execute the sending action, as well as the rule *τSyn*, for the internal action.

3   Motivating Example

As presented in Sect. 2, the CWQ Calculus has the flexibility that not all input data in a binder need to be received in order for the process to continue (e.g., see P_{user} in Fig. 3). Thus, decisions of a system may have different trustworthiness depending on which input data have actually been received.

In the literature, Nielson and Nielson [12] developed a novel probabilistic *trust* analysis for supporting the Quality Calculus to indicate the trust that a user can have in the overall robustness of a system. They assume each channel has a trust and change the syntax of binders from $\&_q(c_1^{l_1}?x_1, \cdots, c_n^{l_n}?x_n)$ to $\&_q^{\pi}(c_1^{l_1}?x_1, \cdots, c_n^{l_n}?x_n)$. Here, $\pi \in \mathcal{D}(\{x_1, \cdots, x_n\} \to \mathcal{L}_{\perp})$ is a probability distribution indicating the probability of the various inputs having been received where $\perp$ denotes the absence of input and $\mathcal{L}_{\perp}$ is the lifted trust lattice obtained from $\mathcal{L}$ by adding $\perp$ as the new least element. Then, they use information about the probabilities that expected input will be absent to associate probability distributions with all program points of interest, where the probabilities indicate the trust level of the data.

The trust analysis performed for Quality Calculus in past work [12] however is not applicable to the CWQ Calculus for WSNs, because the CWQ Calculus has a unique and important characteristic which is not part of the Quality Calculus. Specifically, the decision of a system of a WSN is expected to be made based on data from all network nodes in the WSN, and the decision has the highest trustworthiness if data from all its constituent network nodes are received and considered. In other words, from the perspective of a single network node, its locally stored data may not be sufficient for making the best decision of a system; this characteristic of WSNs is elaborated more through a case study. Thus, in this paper, we propose a new data-driven probabilistic trust analysis of the CWQ calculus for WSNs. Firstly, we give a case study in the following.

Case Study. We give a case study of refueling a car by using the information of gas stations stored in base stations. Specifically, we consider the scenario that a car on the road is running out of gas and thus the car driver (i.e., the user) wants to find the nearest gas station for refueling the car.

The request of finding the closest gas station (GS) is accomplished by broadcasting the request in a wireless network and then receiving replying messages that contain locations of GSs. The wireless network consists of a set of base stations (BSs), where the user can also be regarded as a BS. Each BS has a transmission area constraint (e.g., illustrated as dotted circles in Fig. 1). That is, when a BS broadcasts a message, only other BSs that are within its transmission area (i.e., within a certain distance) can receive the message. We assume that each BS stores some information of GSs (i.e., locations of a subset of GSs)

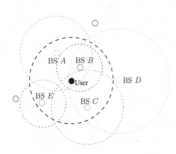

$$\text{Network} \overset{df}{=} \text{User} \parallel (\prod_{i \in \mathbb{Z}} \text{BS}_i \parallel \prod_{k \in \mathbb{Z}} \text{GS}_k)$$

$$\text{User} \overset{df}{=} n_{11}[\text{P}_{user}] \parallel n_{12}[\text{Local}_{user}]$$
$$\parallel n_{13}[\text{Timer}_{user}]$$

$$\text{BS}_i \overset{df}{=} n_{2i}[\text{P}_{bs}]$$

$$\text{GS}_k \overset{df}{=} n_{3k}[\text{P}_{gs}]$$

$$\text{Using } us^{H \vee M}, local^L, timer^H.$$

Fig. 1. Communication in a WSN   **Fig. 2.** The system

so that the location of a GS is stored in the local cache of the closest BS (or several closest BSs).

To find the closest GS to the location of the user, the user broadcasts a request to BSs in a wireless network and then waits for replies. Ideally, if every BSs in the wireless network replies its locally stored GSs to the user, then the user can obtain the closest GS by iterating through all the replied GSs. However, in real wireless networks, a BS cannot (or may not) send its stored GSs to the user due to several reasons. For example, (1) the BS does not receive the request since it is not in the transmission area of the user (e.g., BS D in Fig. 1); (2) the user is not in the transmission area of the BS even if the BS receives the request (e.g., BS E in Fig. 1); (3) although the BS sends its replying message to the user and the user is in its transmission area, the message may be lost in the transmission process due to unreliable wireless communications. Consequently, the user has to make a decision based on the locations of a subset of GSs it received, and the GSs stored at each BS have a probability to contain the closest GS to the user. In the worst case, the user may not even receive any replies. Therefore, we assume the user has a local computer (or other electronic devices) which caches previously searched closest GSs, and the user will choose the closest one among these locally cached GSs as a candidate if it receives no replies.

Since the GSs replied by BSs are preferred to the locally cached ones, the user uses a clock to set a waiting time which will wait for at least t_1 time units but at most t_2 time units. When t_1 time units are reached, the user will check the received replies. If at least one reply is received, then the user will choose the closest replied GS for refueling the car and the process continues. Otherwise, it waits for another $t_2 - t_1$ time units. Once t_2 time units are reached, the user will choose the closest replied GS. Note that, if there is still no reply received, then the locally cached GS will be chosen. The overall scenario is illustrated in Fig. 2, which is similar to that in [16]. We give details of the P_{user} process in Fig. 3, which is the main subject of our probabilistic *trust* analysis, and omit details of other processes.

$\mathsf{P}_{user} \overset{df}{=} us^{H\vee M}!req.local^L!req.timer^H!(t_1, t_2).$

    $\&_\forall(timer^H?x_{t_1}, \&_\exists(us^{H\vee M}?x_{rep_A}, us^{H\vee M}?x_{rep_B}, us^{H\vee M}?x_{rep_C}, local^L?x_{rep'})).$

    case x_{rep_A} of some(y_{rep_A}) :

      case x_{rep_B} of some(y_{rep_B}) :

        case x_{rep_C} of some(y_{rep_C}) :[1] use$(\widehat{min}(y_{rep_A}, y_{rep_B}, y_{rep_C})).\mathsf{P}_{user}$

        else[2] use$(\widehat{min}(y_{rep_A}, y_{rep_B})).\mathsf{P}_{user}$

      else case x_{rep_C} of some(y_{rep_C}) :[3] use$(\widehat{min}(y_{rep_A}, y_{rep_C})).\mathsf{P}_{user}$

        else[4] use$(y_{rep_A}).\mathsf{P}_{user}$

    else case x_{rep_B} of some(y_{rep_B}) :

      case x_{rep_C} of some(y_{rep_C}) :[5] use$(\widehat{min}(y_{rep_B}, y_{rep_C})).\mathsf{P}_{user}$

      else[6] use$(y_{rep_B}).\mathsf{P}_{user}$

    else case x_{rep_C} of some(y_{rep_C}) :[7] use$(y_{rep_C}).\mathsf{P}_{user}$

    else $\&_\forall(timer^H?x_{t_2}, \&_\exists(us^{H\vee M}?x_{rep_A}, us^{H\vee M}?x_{rep_B}, us^{H\vee M}?x_{rep_C}, local^L?x_{rep'})).$

      case x_{rep_A} of some(y_{rep_A}) :

        case x_{rep_B} of some(y_{rep_B}) :

          case x_{rep_C} of some(y_{rep_C}) :[8] use$(\widehat{min}(y_{rep_A}, y_{rep_B}, y_{rep_C})).\mathsf{P}_{user}$

          else[9] use$(\widehat{min}(y_{rep_A}, y_{rep_B})).\mathsf{P}_{user}$

        else case x_{rep_C} of some(y_{rep_C}) :[10] use$(\widehat{min}(y_{rep_A}, y_{rep_C})).\mathsf{P}_{user}$

          else[11] use$(y_{rep_A}).\mathsf{P}_{user}$

        else case x_{rep_B} of some(y_{rep_B}) :

          case x_{rep_C} of some(y_{rep_C}) :[12] use$(\widehat{min}(y_{rep_B}, y_{rep_C})).\mathsf{P}_{user}$

          else[13] use$(y_{rep_B}).\mathsf{P}_{user}$

        else case x_{rep_C} of some(y_{rep_C}) :[14] use$(y_{rep_C}).\mathsf{P}_{user}$

          else case $x_{rep'}$ of some$(y_{rep'})$:[15] use$(y_{rep'}).\mathsf{P}_{user}$

          else[16] 0

Fig. 3. Model of the process P_{user}

Discussion. In P_{user} in Fig. 3, for ease of exposition we assume that there are three BSs (i.e., BSs A, B, and C in Fig. 1) that can communicate with the user. The binder of the second line in Fig. 3, denoted binder1, is equivalent to

$$\&_{[1\wedge(2\vee3\vee4\vee5)]}(timer^H?x_{t_1}, us^{H\vee M}?x_{rep_A}, us^{H\vee M}?x_{rep_B},$$
$$us^{H\vee M}?x_{rep_C}, local^L?x_{rep'}).$$

That is, when t_1 time units are reached, the process continues when the input from either BSs A, or B, or C, or the local computer is performed. Alternatively, we might use the binder, denoted binder2,

$$\&_{[1\wedge((2\wedge3)\vee(2\wedge4)\vee(3\wedge4)\vee5)]}(timer^H?x_{t_1}, us^{H\vee M}?x_{rep_A},$$
$$us^{H\vee M}?x_{rep_B}, us^{H\vee M}?x_{rep_C}, local^L?x_{rep'}),$$

This binder requires that at least two BSs from $\{A, B, C\}$ must reply messages before the process can proceed. We will show through probabilistic trust analysis in Sect. 4.3 that binder2 is better than binder1 as far as the quality of the GS (i.e., how close is it to the user), obtained by the system, is concerned.

4   Data-Driven Probabilistic Trust Analysis

For the case study, ideally, if every BSs in the wireless network replies its locally stored GSs to the user, then the user can obtain the closest GS by iterating through all the replied GSs. However, from the perspective of a single BS, the locally stored GSs may not include the closest GS to the user. In other words, the set of locally stored GSs in a BS may be of high trustworthiness if it includes the closest GS to the user, and it may not otherwise.

To incorporate the above intuitions, instead of the channel having trust values we assume that data received from a channel have trust values, where the trust value of a data represents the trust of the decision of a system made solely based on that data. Intuitively, data received from a channel of a network node is of high trustworthiness if it is essential for making a high-quality decision of the system, and it is not otherwise. Since it is hard to judge whether a data is essential for making the decision of a system without actually evaluating the system, we assume that the data received from a channel has a probability distribution of trust values. To facilitate our probabilistic analysis, we change the syntax of binders in CWQ Calculus for WSNs to $\&_q^\pi(c_1^{l_1}?x_1, \cdots, c_n^{l_n}?x_n)$, where $\pi \in \mathcal{D}(\{x_1, \cdots, x_n\} \to \{\mathsf{t}, \perp\})$ denotes whether an input data x_i is received (i.e., t) or not received (i.e., $\perp$) over channel c_i for $1 \le i \le n$, and $l_i \in \mathcal{D}(\mathcal{L})$ is a probability distribution of the trust of the input data received over channel c_i (i.e., l_i is a probability distribution of the trust of x_i). Consequently, we consider data trustworthiness instead of channel trustworthiness, and decouple the probability of receiving input data from the probability of data trustworthiness which makes more flexible probabilistic analysis possible (e.g., for analyzing systems based on WSNs). The overall trustworthiness of the decision of a system is determined by performing relational analysis to combine the probability distributions of π and $l_i(\forall 1 \le i \le n)$.

4.1   Trust Propagation

The judgement of our analysis is of the form $\vdash p, \pi, \mathbb{L}@P$. Here, p is the probability that we will reach the process P, π is a distribution from $\mathcal{D}(V \to \{\mathsf{t}, \perp\})$ where $V = \{x_1, \cdots, x_{n'}\}$ is a set of optional data variables, and $\mathbb{L} = \{l_1, \ldots, l_{m'}\}$ is a set of distributions of the trust level of data variables y_i for $1 \le i \le m'$ (i.e., distributions from $\mathcal{D}(\mathcal{L})$). The mappings of $V \to \{\mathsf{t}, \perp\}$ indicate whether optional data are received or not and π specifies the distribution of these mappings when P is reached. Similarly, $\mathbb{L}$ specifies the distributions of the trust levels of data variables y, and we assume l_i and l_j ($i \ne j$) are independent. Note that, this judgement is different from that in [12] which is of the form $\vdash p, \pi@P$.

The main judgement is of the form $\vdash 1, \pi_o, \mathbb{L}_o@N$ as shown in Table 4, where N stands for the entire program (or network) in the CWQ Calculus, and the choice of $p = 1$ reflects that the main process must be called in order to reach other program points. Here, we let $\pi_o = \emptyset$ and $\mathbb{L}_o = \emptyset$, since there are no optional data variables or data variables when reaching the main process. Note that, it is also possible to incorporate constants into π (and π_o) and $\mathbb{L}$ (and $\mathbb{L}_o$); however,

Table 4. Trust propagation

$$\vdash 1, \pi_o, \mathbb{L}_o@(n_1[P_1]\|...\|n_k[P_k]) \qquad \vdash 1, \pi_o, \mathbb{L}_o@n_1[P_1] \qquad \cdots \qquad \vdash 1, \pi_o, \mathbb{L}_o@n_k[P_k]$$

$$\frac{\vdash p, \pi, \mathbb{L}@(n_1[P_1]\|...\|n_k[P_k])}{\vdash p, \pi, \mathbb{L}@P_1} \qquad \cdots \qquad \frac{\vdash p, \pi, \mathbb{L}@(n_1[P_1]\|...\|n_k[P_k])}{\vdash p, \pi, \mathbb{L}@P_k}$$

$$\frac{\vdash p, \pi, \mathbb{L}@(\mathsf{case}\ x\ \mathsf{of}\ \mathsf{some}(y) : P_1\ \mathsf{else}\ P_2)}{\vdash p \cdot \pi_{[x\neq\perp]}, (\pi_{\downarrow[x\neq\perp]})|_x^\mathsf{C}, \mathbb{L} \oplus l_x[y := x]@P_1} \quad \text{if}\ \pi_{[x\neq\perp]} \neq 0$$

$$\frac{\vdash p, \pi, \mathbb{L}@(\mathsf{case}\ x\ \mathsf{of}\ \mathsf{some}(y) : P_1\ \mathsf{else}\ P_2)}{\vdash p \cdot \pi_{[x=\perp]}, (\pi_{\downarrow[x=\perp]})|_x^\mathsf{C}, \mathbb{L}@P_2} \quad \text{if}\ \pi_{[x=\perp]} \neq 0$$

$$\frac{\vdash p, \pi, \mathbb{L}@(c!v.P)}{\vdash p, \pi, \mathbb{L}@P} \qquad \frac{\vdash p, \pi, \mathbb{L}@(b.P) \quad \vdash b \blacktriangleright \pi_b}{\vdash p, (\pi|_{\mathsf{bv}(b)}^\mathsf{C}) \otimes \pi_b, \mathbb{L}@P}$$

---

we omit the constants in these distributions for ease of presentation, and all constants are assumed to exist and be of the highest trustworthiness.

Operations on π and $\mathbb{L}$. To do the trust propagation, we need to define several operations on π and $\mathbb{L}$. First is *lookup* on a name for π. That is, given a distribution $\pi : \mathcal{D}(V \to \{\mathsf{t}, \perp\})$ and a name u, we want to know the probabilities $\pi_{[u\neq\perp]}$ and $\pi_{[u=\perp]}$, corresponding to the probabilities that u is received or not, respectively.

$$\pi_{[u=\perp]} = \sum_{(\sigma \in \pi\ \text{s.t.}\ \sigma(u)=\perp)} \pi(\sigma)$$

Here, σ is a mapping $\sigma : V \to \{\mathsf{t}, \perp\}$. $\pi_{[u\neq\perp]}$ is similarly defined, and moreover $\pi_{[u\neq\perp]} = \pi_{[u=\mathsf{t}]} = 1 - \pi_{[u=\perp]}$. These operations are used in the analysis of the construct $\mathsf{case}\ x\ \mathsf{of}\ \mathsf{some}(y) : P_1\ \mathsf{else}\ P_2$; $\pi_{[x\neq\perp]}$ is the probability that the first branch is taken and $\pi_{[x=\perp]}$ is that the second branch is taken.

The next operation for π is *selection* on a name. That is, given a distribution $\pi : \mathcal{D}(V \to \{\mathsf{t}, \perp\})$ and a name u, we want to construct a new distribution $\pi_{\downarrow[u\neq\perp]}$ that gives 0 probability to all mappings σ with $\sigma(u) \neq \perp$ and rescales the remaining probabilities, and this is defined only if $\pi_{[u\neq\perp]} \neq 0$.

$$(\pi_{\downarrow[u\neq\perp]})(\sigma) = \begin{cases} \frac{\pi(\sigma)}{\pi_{[u\neq\perp]}} & \text{if}\ \sigma(u) \neq \perp, \\ 0 & \text{otherwise.} \end{cases}$$

Similarly, we define $\pi_{\downarrow[u=\perp]}$. These two operations are used in the analysis of the construct $\mathsf{case}\ x\ \mathsf{of}\ \mathsf{some}(y) : P_1\ \mathsf{else}\ P_2$; $\pi_{[x\neq\perp]}$ is the distribution of the first branch if it is taken and $\pi_{[x=\perp]}$ is the distribution of the second branch if taken.

The next operation for π is *projection* on a subset of names. That is, given a distribution $\pi : \mathcal{D}(V \to \{\mathsf{t}, \perp\})$ and a subset of names $U \subseteq V$, we want to obtain the distribution $\pi|_U$ in $\mathcal{D}(U \to \{\mathsf{t}, \perp\})$. It is defined as,

$$(\pi|_U)(\sigma) = \sum_{(\sigma' \in \pi\ \text{s.t.}\ \sigma=\sigma'|_U)} \pi(\sigma').$$

Here, $\sigma'|_U$ is the restriction of the mapping $\sigma' : V \rightarrow \{\mathsf{t}, \bot\}$ to the domain of U; that is $(\sigma'|_U)(u) = \sigma(u)$ if $u \in U$, and $(\sigma'|_U)(u)$ is undefined otherwise. Similarly, we define the projection on the complement of U, $\pi|_U^C$, which is the same as $\pi|_{V \setminus U}$. These operations are used to reduce the size of a distribution.

The last operation of π is *product* of two distributions. That is, given two distributions $\pi_1 : \mathcal{D}(V_1 \rightarrow \{\mathsf{t}, \bot\})$ and $\pi_2 : \mathcal{D}(V_2 \rightarrow \{\mathsf{t}, \bot\})$ over two disjoint sets of names (i.e., $V_1 \cap V_2 = \emptyset$), we construct a new distribution $\pi_1 \otimes \pi_2$ in $\mathcal{D}(V_1 \cup V_2 \rightarrow \{\mathsf{t}, \bot\})$. It is defined as,

$$(\pi_1 \otimes \pi_2)(\sigma) = \pi_1(\sigma|_{V_1}) \cdot \pi_2(\sigma|_{V_2}).$$

They are used when combining two stochastically independent distributions.

For $\mathbb{L}$, we define two operations, *replace* and *addition*. Given a distribution l_x in $\mathcal{D}(\mathcal{L})$ and a name y, the replace operation $l_x[y := x]$ is to construct another distribution l_y in $\mathcal{D}(\mathcal{L})$ with the same probabilities as l_x; that is, $l_y(t) = l_x(t), \forall t \in \mathcal{L}$. That is, the replace operation is to replace the name of a distribution while all other information remains unchanged. Given a set of distributions $\mathbb{L}$ and a distribution l_y, the addition operation $\mathbb{L} \oplus l_y$ is to add l_y into $\mathbb{L}$ (i.e., $\mathbb{L} \cup \{l_y\}$). Both operations are used in the analysis of the construct case x of $\mathsf{some}(y) : P_1$ else P_2. That is, when the optional data x is actually received, then the process will continue on the first branch P_1; since y instead of x will be visible and used in P_1, the distribution of the trust level of x is copied and stored into data y to be prepared for being used in P_1.

Propagation. Armed with the above operations on π and $\mathbb{L}$, the detailed trust propagation is shown in Table 4. The logic-flow of our analysis is similar to that in the program analysis [11] and in the Quality Calculus [13]. That is, the propagation operates in a top-down manner instead of a more conventional bottom-up manner. As shown in Table 4, our propagation starts from an axiom $\vdash 1, \pi_\circ, \mathbb{L}_\circ @ (n_1[P_1] \| ... \| n_k[P_k])$ saying that the program (or network) is reachable. Two inference rules for parallel composition are presented at the second row; it means that if $p, \pi, \mathbb{L}$ describe the program point just before the entire network $n_1[P_1] \| ... \| n_k[P_k]$, then they also describe the program point just before each of the k constitute processes.

For the case construct case x of $\mathsf{some}(y) : P_1$ else P_2, there are two inference rules as shown at the third and fourth rows. If $\pi_{[x \neq \bot]} \neq 0$, then there is a non-zero probability that the optional data x can be received. Thus, we will continue with process P_1 with probability $p \cdot \pi_{[x \neq \bot]}$. Now since we are sure that $x \neq \bot$ (since we reach P_1), we need to do a selection on π conditioned on the fact that $x \neq \bot$; we can also do a project on the set of names excluding x to simplify the distribution. Moreover, the data y is assigned and may be used in P_1; since the trust level of y is the same as the optional data x, we construct a new distribution by replacing the x in l_x with y, and add the new distribution to $\mathbb{L}$. Note that, the set of distributions $\mathbb{L}$ is used for conducting trust analysis at program points. If $\pi_{x=\bot} \neq 0$, then there is a similar inference rule for continuing with process P_2.

The last row illustrates inference rules for output and input, respectively. The rule for output is straightforward, as $p, \pi, \mathbb{L}$ directly pass forward to the following process. The rule for input binding makes use of another auxiliary judgement $\vdash b \blacktriangleright \pi_b$, which obtains the distribution π_b; note that, π_b is computed by using standard statistical inference, based on the probability distributions of all the optional data and channels in b. When reaching P (i.e., successfully passing b), the distribution π will be augmented by π_b while p and $\mathbb{L}$ remain the same.

Remarks. Note that the probabilistic analysis of CWQ Calculus proposed above is different from that conducted by Nielson et al. for probabilistic trust analysis of the Quality Calculus. Firstly, the CWQ Calculus has a unique characteristic that is not part of the Quality Calculus, as discussed in Sect. 3. Secondly, we decouple the probability of receiving input data from the probability of data trustworthiness. That is, the judgement of our analysis is of the form $\vdash p, \pi, \mathbb{L}@P$ where π and $\mathbb{L}$ are distributions with $\pi : \mathcal{D}(V \rightarrow \{t, \bot\})$, while the judgement of the analysis in past work [12] is of the form $\vdash p, \pi'@P$ with $\pi' : \mathcal{D}(V' \rightarrow \mathcal{L}_\bot)$.

Note that, the set of distributions, $\mathbb{L}$, in our analysis can be also regarded as a distribution as follows. Given $\mathbb{L} = \{l_1, \ldots, l_{m'}\}$ with each l_i being a distribution $l_i : \mathcal{L}$, we can construct a new distribution $\mathbb{L}' = L_1 \otimes \cdots \otimes L_{m'}$ where $L_i : \mathcal{D}(x_i \rightarrow \mathcal{L})$ and $\otimes$ is the product operation. It is easy to show that $\mathbb{L}'$ is equivalent to $\mathbb{L}$. In this paper, we consider the set of distributions, $\mathbb{L}$, due to its compact form and the independence of l_i and l_j ($i \neq j$); note that, the size of $\mathbb{L}'$ is much (i.e., exponentially) larger than that of $\mathbb{L}$.

The analysis can be implemented using Standard ML. Each distribution can be represented as a list of pairs (σ, p); for example, the distribution π can be represented in the form as shown in Tables 5 and 6. Other improvements towards the representation and the probability inference are also possible, we omit the discussions in this paper since it is orthogonal to the content of this paper.

4.2   Trust Analysis

Now, we show how to extract information about outputs from the analysis. Firstly, we consider an output of the form $c!v$; that is, we want to compute the trust level of the value v sent over channel c. Assume the analysis gives the form $\vdash p, \pi, \mathbb{L}@c!v.P$ when reaching P; this means that P is reached with probability p, and the distributions of trust levels of data y, which may be used in v or P, are given in $\mathbb{L}$. The trust level of v over channel c can be represented as a distribution ϕ in $\mathcal{D}(\mathcal{L})$ and is defined as follows,

$$\phi(t) = \sum_{\sigma \in \mathbb{L} \text{ s.t. } \sigma(v) = t} \mathbb{L}(\sigma).$$

Note that, for ease of presentation, we assume $\mathbb{L}$ is in the form of a distribution as discussed in above. Thus, if v is a single data y, then $\phi(y)$ is the same as $l_y \in \mathbb{L}$. Otherwise, v is of the form $f(y_1, \ldots, y_n)$ where $f(\cdot)$ is a function (e.g., min in Fig. 3). Given a set of data $\{y_1, \ldots, y_n\}$ with trust levels $\{t_1, \ldots, t_n\}$, respectively, the trust of the function $f(y_1, \ldots, y_n)$ is assume to be the greatest lower bound of $\{t_1, \ldots, t_n\}$ in the trust lattice $\mathcal{L}$. For example, given y_1, y_2, y_3 of trust $\mathsf{H}, \mathsf{M}, \mathsf{L}$, respectively, the trust of $\widehat{min}(y_1, y_2, y_3)$ is H; that is, y_1 is the most important and sufficient data for the function.

Secondly, we consider all outputs of the form $c!\cdot$; that is, we want to compute the trust level of the decision of the system in the form $c!\cdot$ across all branches of the case constructs. For simplicity, we assume that no occurrence of $c!\cdot$ prefixes another. Then, the distribution Φ_c in $\mathcal{D}(\mathcal{L}_\perp)$ is defined as follows,

$$\Phi_c(t) = \sum\nolimits_{\vdash p, \pi, \mathbb{L}@c!v.P} \sum\nolimits_{\sigma \in \mathbb{L} \text{ s.t. } \sigma(v) = t} \mathbb{L}(\sigma).$$

The probability of the trust level of $\perp$ is $\Phi_c(\perp) = 1 - \sum_{t \in \mathcal{L}} \Phi_c(t)$.

4.3   Probabilistic Trust Analysis of the Case Study

We illustrate how to compute such a trust of the decision of a system through two examples in the following.

Example 1. We consider the binder, binder1, which is described in Fig. 3,

$$\&^{\pi}_{[1 \wedge (2 \vee 3 \vee 4 \vee 5)]}(timer^{\mathsf{H}}?x_{t_1}, us^{\mathsf{H} \vee \mathsf{M}}?x_{rep_A}, us^{\mathsf{H} \vee \mathsf{M}}?x_{rep_B},$$
$$us^{\mathsf{H} \vee \mathsf{M}}?x_{rep_C}, local^{\mathsf{L}}?x_{rep'}).$$

Here, the trust l_{rep_A} of x_{rep_A} received over channel us may be either H or M (i.e., $\mathsf{H} \vee \mathsf{M}$). Let us assume that $l_{rep_A}(\mathsf{H}) = l_{rep_A}(\mathsf{M}) = 0.5$. Note that, l_{rep_A} is a probability distribution in $\mathcal{D}(\mathcal{L})$. l_{rep_B} and l_{rep_C} are similarly defined, while l_{t_1} and $l_{rep'}$ have deterministic trust H and L, respectively. For presentation simplicity, Let us assume that $l_i, l_j (i \neq j)$ are independent.

Let us assume that the process of receiving input data through channels us and $local$ are exponentially distributed with rates λ_{us} and λ_{local}, respectively. For ease of presentation, assume the probability of receiving replying messages through channels us and $local$ are $p_{us} = 0.6$ and $p_{local} = 0.8$, respectively; that is, the probability of not receiving replying messages through channels us and $local$ are $1 - p_{us} = 0.4$ and $1 - p_{local} = 0.2$, respectively. One can show that the distribution π, indicating whether input data are received or not, is computed as that in Table 5, with $\pi(\delta) = 0$ for all other cases.

For presentation simplicity, we assume that there is only one time out (i.e., t_1) in P_{user} in Fig. 3; that is, only labels, $1, \ldots, 6, 16$, are reachable, while those branches corresponding to labels $7, \ldots, 15$ are ignored. Now, we illustrate how to obtain the trust of the decision of the system. First, let us consider $\pi_1(x_{t_1} \mapsto \mathsf{t}, x_{rep_A} \mapsto \mathsf{t}, x_{rep_B} \mapsto \mathsf{t}, x_{rep_C} \mapsto \mathsf{t}, x_{rep'} \mapsto \mathsf{t}) = 0.1750$ in Table 5. Since all optional data, x_{rep_A}, x_{rep_B} and x_{rep_C}, have actually been received, the decision of the system is made based on the combination of these three data; note that, π_1 and π_2 in Table 5 together correspond to label 1 in Fig. 3. Thus, when reaching label 1, the trust of the decision is M with probability $l_{rep_A}(\mathsf{M}) \times l_{rep_B}(\mathsf{M}) \times$

Table 5. π for binder1

id	x_{t_1}	x_{rep_A}	x_{rep_B}	x_{rep_C}	$x_{rep'}$	p
π_1	t	t	t	t	t	0.1750
π_2	t	t	t	t	$\perp$	0.0438
π_3	t	t	t	$\perp$	t	0.1167
π_4	t	t	t	$\perp$	$\perp$	0.0292
π_5	t	t	$\perp$	t	t	0.1167
π_6	t	t	$\perp$	t	$\perp$	0.0292
π_7	t	$\perp$	t	t	t	0.1167
π_8	t	$\perp$	t	t	$\perp$	0.0292
π_9	t	t	$\perp$	$\perp$	t	0.0778
π_{10}	t	t	$\perp$	$\perp$	$\perp$	0.0196
π_{11}	t	$\perp$	t	$\perp$	t	0.0778
π_{12}	t	$\perp$	t	$\perp$	$\perp$	0.0196
π_{13}	t	$\perp$	$\perp$	t	t	0.0778
π_{14}	t	$\perp$	$\perp$	t	$\perp$	0.0196
π_{15}	t	$\perp$	$\perp$	$\perp$	t	0.0513

Table 6. π for binder2

id	x_{t_1}	x_{rep_A}	x_{rep_B}	x_{rep_C}	$x_{rep'}$	p
π_1	t	t	t	t	t	0.1860
π_2	t	t	t	t	$\perp$	0.0465
π_3	t	t	t	$\perp$	t	0.1245
π_4	t	t	t	$\perp$	$\perp$	0.0315
π_5	t	t	$\perp$	t	t	0.1245
π_6	t	t	$\perp$	t	$\perp$	0.0315
π_7	t	$\perp$	t	t	t	0.1245
π_8	t	$\perp$	t	t	$\perp$	0.0315
π_9	t	t	$\perp$	$\perp$	t	0.0827
π_{10}	t	t	$\perp$	$\perp$	$\perp$	0
π_{11}	t	$\perp$	t	$\perp$	t	0.0827
π_{12}	t	$\perp$	t	$\perp$	$\perp$	0
π_{13}	t	$\perp$	$\perp$	t	t	0.0827
π_{14}	t	$\perp$	$\perp$	t	$\perp$	0
π_{15}	t	$\perp$	$\perp$	$\perp$	t	0.0514

$l_{rep_C}(M) = 0.125$, and it is H with probability $1 - 0.125 = 0.875$; recall that each $l_x \in \mathcal{D}(\mathcal{L})$ is a probability distribution. Based on the above, we can see that the probability that the trust of the decision is H includes 0.1750×0.875, and the probability to be M includes 0.1750×0.125. Similarly, π_3 and π_4 in Table 5 together correspond to label 2 in Fig. 3, and $\pi_3 = 0.1167$. When reaching label 2, the trust of the decision is M with probability $l_{rep_A}(M) \times l_{rep_B}(M) = 0.25$, and it is H with probability $1 - 0.25 = 0.75$. Thus, the probability that the trust of the decision is H also includes another 0.1167×0.75, and the probability to be M also includes another 0.1167×0.25.

Overall, the probability that the trust of the decision is H is $(\pi_1 + \pi_2) \times 0.875 + (\pi_3 + \cdots + \pi_8) \times 0.75 + (\pi_9 + \cdots + \pi_{14}) \times 0.5 = 0.2188 \times 0.875 + 0.4377 \times 0.75 + 0.2922 \times 0.5 = 0.6658$, and the probability that the trust of the decision is M is $(\pi_1 + \pi_2) \times 0.125 + (\pi_3 + \cdots + \pi_8) \times 0.25 + (\pi_9 + \cdots + \pi_{14}) \times 0.5 = 0.2188 \times 0.125 + 0.4377 \times 0.25 + 0.2922 \times 0.5 = 0.2829$

Example 2. Now, we consider binder2 which is discussed in the case study, as follows,

$$\&_{[1\wedge((2\wedge3)\vee(2\wedge4)\vee(3\wedge4)\vee5)]}(timer^H?x_{t_1}, us^{H\vee M}?x_{rep_A},$$
$$us^{H\vee M}?x_{rep_B}, us^{H\vee M}?x_{rep_C}, local^L?x_{rep'}).$$

Here, l_{rep_A}, l_{rep_B}, l_{rep_C}, and $l_{rep'}$ are the same as in Example 1 in above. Note that, the process P_{user} needs to be modified accordingly, and we also assume there is only one time out (i.e., t_1); we omit the details here. Similar to Example 1, one can show that the distribution π, indicating whether input data are received or not, is computed as that in Table 6.

We illustrate how to obtain the trust of the decision of the system. First, let us consider $\pi_1(x_{t_1} \mapsto t, x_{rep_A} \mapsto t, x_{rep_B} \mapsto t, x_{rep_C} \mapsto t, x_{rep'} \mapsto t) = 0.1860$ in Table 6. Since all optional data, x_{rep_A}, x_{rep_B} and x_{rep_C}, have actually been received, the decision of the system is made based on the combination of these three data. Thus, similar to that in Example 1, the probability that the trust of the decision is H includes 0.1860×0.875, and the probability to be M includes 0.1860×0.125. Similarly, when considering $\pi_3 = 0.1245$, the probability that the trust of the decision is H also includes another 0.1245×0.75, and the probability to be M also includes another 0.1245×0.25. Overall, the probability that the trust of the decision is H is 0.6785, and the probability that it is M is 0.2701.

Remark. By comparing the above two examples, we can see that the probability of the trust of the decision based on binder2 to be H is 0.6785 and it is larger than the probability of the trust of the decision based on binder1 to be H which is 0.6658. Thus, by using probabilistic analysis we can quantify the trustworthiness of decisions based on different binders, based on which we choose the better one.

5   Conclusion and Future Work

In this paper, we proposed a data-driven probabilistic trust analysis of the CWQ Calculus for WSNs. The CWQ Calculus has the flexibility that not all input data in a binder need to be received in order for the process to continue; thus, decisions of a system may have different trustworthiness depending on which input data have actually been received. We assumed that data received from a channel have trustworthiness values which follow probability distributions, and the trust value of a data represents the trust of the decision of a system made solely based on that data. Then, we proposed to decouple the probability of receiving data from the probability of data trustworthiness which makes more flexible probabilistic analysis possible (e.g., for analyzing systems based on WSNs). The overall trustworthiness of the decision of a system is then determined by performing a relational analysis to combine these probability distributions.

Future directions for our research may include considering the topological structure changing in the analysis and also incorporating the mobility of sensor network nodes. It is also possible to use PRISM [5] for automatic probabilistic analysis. Moreover, we are continuing to explore the denotational semantics and algebraic semantics of the CWQ Calculus. Giving a deduction system of the calculus may also be another interesting topic.

Acknowledgement. This work was partly supported by the Danish National Research Foundation and the National Natural Science Foundation of China (Grant No. 61361136002) for the Danish-Chinese Center for Cyber Physical Systems. It was also supported by National Natural Science Foundation of China (Grant No. 61321064) and Shanghai Collaborative Innovation Center of Trustworthy Software for Internet of Things (No. ZF1213).

References

1. Akyildiz, I.F., Su, W., Sankarasubramaniam, Y., Cayirci, E.: Wireless sensor networks: a survey. Comput. Netw. **38**, 393–422 (2002)
2. Bulusu, N., Jha, S.: Wireless Sensor Networks: A Systems Perspective. Artech House, Norwood (2005)
3. Ene, C., Muntean, T.: A broadcast-based calculus for communicating systems. In: Proceedings of 15th International Parallel and Distributed Processing Symposium (IPDPS 2001), pp. 149–149, San Francisco, CA, April 2001
4. Fehnker, A., van Glabbeek, R., Höfner, P., McIver, A., Portmann, M., Tan, W.L.: A process algebra for wireless mesh networks. In: Seidl, H. (ed.) Programming Languages and Systems. LNCS, vol. 7211, pp. 295–315. Springer, Heidelberg (2012)
5. Kwiatkowska, M., Norman, G., Parker, D.: PRISM 4.0: verification of probabilistic real-time systems. In: Gopalakrishnan, G., Qadeer, S. (eds.) CAV 2011. LNCS, vol. 6806, pp. 585–591. Springer, Heidelberg (2011)
6. Lanese, I., Sangiorgi, D.: An operational semantics for a calculus for wireless systems. Theor. Comput. Sci. **411**(19), 1928–1948 (2010)
7. Lee, E.A.: Architectural support for cyber-physical systems. In: Proceedings of 12th International Conference on Architectural Support for Programming Languages and Operating Systems (ASPLOS 2015), pp. 14–18, Istanbul, Turkey, March 2015
8. Liu, S., Zhao, Y., Zhu, H., Li, Q.: A calculus for mobile ad hoc networks from a group probabilistic perspective. In: Proceedings of 13th IEEE International Symposium on High-Assurance Systems Engineering (HASE 2011), pp. 157–162. IEEE Computer Society (2011)
9. Merro, M., Sibilio, E.: A timed calculus for wireless systems. In: Arbab, F., Sirjani, M. (eds.) FSEN 2009. LNCS, vol. 5961, pp. 228–243. Springer, Heidelberg (2010)
10. Mezzetti, N., Sangiorgi, D.: Towards a calculus for wireless systems. Electr. Notes Theor. Comput. Sci. **158**, 331–353 (2006)
11. Nielson, F., Nielson, H.R., Hankin, C.: Principles of Program Analysis. Springer, Heidelberg (1999)
12. Nielson, H.R., Nielson, F.: Probabilistic analysis of the quality calculus. In: Proceedings of 8th International Federated Conference on Distributed Computing Techniques (DisCoTec 2013), pp. 258–272, Florence, Italy (2013)
13. Nielson, H.R., Nielson, F., Vigo, R.: A calculus for quality. In: Păsăreanu, C.S., Salaün, G. (eds.) FACS 2012. LNCS, vol. 7684, pp. 188–204. Springer, Heidelberg (2013)
14. Prasad, K.: A calculus of broadcasting systems. Sci. Comput. Program. **25**(2–3), 285–327 (1995)
15. Prasad, K.: A prospectus for mobile broadcasting systems. Electr. Notes Theor. Comput. Sci. **162**, 295–300 (2006)
16. Wu, X., Nielson, H.R., Zhu, H.: A SAT-based analysis of a calculus for wireless sensor networks. In: Proceedings of 9th IEEE International Symposium on Theoretical Aspects of Software Engineering (TASE 2015), pp. 23–30. IEEE Computer Society (2015)
17. Wu, X., Zhu, H.: A calculus for wireless sensor networks from quality perspective. In: Proceedings of IEEE 16th International Symposium on High Assurance Systems Engineering (HASE 2015), pp. 223–231, Daytona Beach, FL, USA, January 2015

Leveraging Abstraction to Establish Out-of-Nominal Safety Properties

Jackson R. Mayo[✉], Robert C. Armstrong, and Geoffrey C. Hulette

Sandia National Laboratories, P.O. Box 969, Livermore, CA 94551-0969, USA
{jmayo,rob,ghulett}@sandia.gov

Abstract. Digital systems in an out-of-nominal environment (e.g., one causing hardware bit flips) may not be expected to function correctly in all respects but may be required to fail safely. We present an approach for understanding and verifying a system's out-of-nominal behavior as an abstraction of nominal behavior that preserves designated critical safety requirements. Because abstraction and refinement are already widely used for improved tractability in formal design and proof techniques, this additional way of viewing an abstraction can potentially verify a system's out-of-nominal safety with little additional work. We illustrate the approach with a simple model of a turnstile controller with possible logic faults (formalized in the temporal logic of actions and NuSMV), noting how design choices can be guided by the desired out-of-nominal abstraction. Principles of robustness in complex systems (specifically, Boolean networks) are found to be compatible with the formal abstraction approach. This work indicates a direction for broader use of formal methods in safety-critical systems.

Keywords: Abstraction · Refinement · Model checking · Fault tolerance · Soft errors · Temporal logic of actions · NuSMV

1 Introduction

Due to the combinatorial complexity of digital systems, not only is exhaustive testing infeasible as a means to ensure safety, but even the reasoning techniques used by formal methods face scalability challenges in verifying large designs and complex safety requirements. A widely used technique to improve the tractability of formal verification is to work with abstractions (or overapproximations), which can be simpler to analyze and are conservative in the sense that their verified safety properties are guaranteed to hold also in the actual implementation. This guarantee applies because a valid abstraction permits all behaviors that occur in the implementation and possibly additional behaviors. In current formal methods, abstractions are used in two main contexts:

1. *Proof techniques* that search for a post-hoc abstraction suitable for verifying desired properties of a given implementation, as in counterexample-guided abstraction refinement (CEGAR) [3].

© Springer International Publishing Switzerland 2016
C. Artho and P.C. Ölveczky (Eds.): FTSCS 2015, CCIS 596, pp. 172–186, 2016.
DOI: 10.1007/978-3-319-29510-7_10

2. *Design techniques* that start from an abstraction in which desired properties can be proven and then create an implementation by refinement, as in the Event-B method [1].

In both cases, the abstraction is a means to an end: either generating a proof of an existing design, or generating a provable design. The abstraction is of value because it can be tractably verified for safety and because it has an overapproximation relationship to the implementation, but serves little purpose beyond these points. If the implementation could be verified directly, the need for the abstraction would be obviated.

Here we present a different perspective on abstraction – useful when, under some conditions, a system is physically capable of additional behaviors beyond its "nominal" operation. In this approach, we note that a typical formal model of the implementation makes certain assumptions about the environment that are not universally valid. Thus, the requirements that are verified on this implementation model, which may include not only safety but also reliability, etc., are proven to hold in this nominal environment. This is practically sufficient for some requirements, given that the nominal environment can be maintained often enough for the system to be useful. But critical safety properties may need to be guaranteed under a less restrictive model that permits particular "out-of-nominal" behaviors, if such behaviors may physically occur often enough to be of concern for the risk of catastrophic failure. Our observation is that the abstraction concept, already commonly used in formal methods as a mathematical technique, can be reinterpreted as defining a space of possible "real-world" out-of-nominal behaviors for which the abstraction-verified safety properties are still guaranteed to hold. Thus, by leveraging suitable abstractions, we can gain out-of-nominal safety verification for free.

A primary example of out-of-nominal behavior is the response of digital hardware to electrical or other physical stimuli that produce states not accounted for in the logic design – with the abnormal physical dynamics generating a nominally disallowed digital state transition such as a bit flip. A variety of formal techniques have been investigated for modeling and verifying such behavior [4,7,8]; recognizing that out-of-nominal behavior may overlap with other formal abstractions can increase the applicability of these techniques, particularly in earlier stages of the design process. More generally, other types of unexpected but not totally unforeseeable inputs from the environment can be treated as out-of-nominal behavior. For example, in modular verification of a system where each component is verified subject to assumptions on the behavior of other components with which it interacts, a conservative approach that verifies safety for a suitable overapproximation can create a "firebreak" around each component that mitigates the possibility of catastrophic cascading failure in the event of isolated malfunctions. A complex systems theory of such firebreaks has been developed previously [15].

In the remainder of this paper we present the formal abstraction framework for understanding out-of-nominal behavior (Sect. 2), the definition of a simple example model of a turnstile (Sect. 3), an illustration of the framework using the example (Sect. 4), a conclusion (Sect. 5), and the formalization of aspects of the example in the temporal logic of actions or TLA (Appendix A) and in NuSMV (Appendix B).

2 Modeling Out-of-Nominal Safety Properties

The safety properties of a given model are required to hold at all times over all possible behavioral paths. Such properties, when imposed on an abstraction, require that every path in the abstraction conforms to the properties, and thus every refinement will as well. The use of abstraction in verifying safety requirements is well established.

Here we distinguish "critical" safety requirements that must hold even in out-of-nominal environments (Fig. 1). These out-of-nominal fail-safe requirements are less strict (allow more behaviors) than the requirements for nominal operation and thus constitute an abstraction of the nominal requirements. Safety-critical devices where failure modes can be anticipated are likely candidates for this technique. Nominal requirements can be relaxed to admit acceptable modes of failure. The resulting out-of-nominal safety requirements reflect an engineering decision that certain properties must be preserved even in exceptional circumstances that may be considered unlikely to occur.

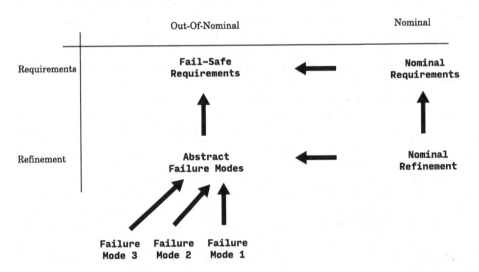

Fig. 1. Refinement/abstraction conceptual diagram for treating out-of-nominal and nominal models in a unified way. The arrows point in the direction of abstraction.

The safety requirements must ultimately be verified on formal models that reflect the actual nominal and out-of-nominal behavior of the system being designed. Such models are typically tied to the requirements via one or more abstraction/refinement steps ultimately leading to a model of a practical implementation. In our approach, upon refinement, the out-of-nominal model remains an abstraction of the nominal one (Fig. 1). By stipulating that the out-of-nominal refinement has a superset of the behaviors of the nominal refinement, we ensure that the safety properties verified for out-of-nominal operation also hold for nominal operation. These critical safety properties take the form of a fail-safe mode where nominal function is no longer guaranteed but essential safety invariants still hold. Of course, the approach is limited to those out-of-nominal failure modes that can be foreseen and modeled.

Not all foreseeable failure modes may manifest an abstraction or overapproximation of the system's nominal behavior. A particular failure mode may render the system incapable of performing some nominal behaviors. The removal of possible behavioral paths, by itself, does not invalidate any of the nominal safety properties, but can affect functional requirements that are outside the scope of the formal refinement methodology applied in this work. Out-of-nominal scenarios of concern for safety would involve adding at least some new behaviors. In typical cases, failures can occur to varying degrees or not at all depending on practically unpredictable events. Thus, it is often natural for out-of-nominal behavior to be represented in a way that includes nominal behavior as a possibility. Regardless, an out-of-nominal model can be *made* an overapproximation by simply adding the nominal behavior to it as an allowed nondeterministic branch.

If we are to apply critical safety requirements globally across all failure modes, then the high-level out-of-nominal refinement will represent the union of all failure modes together with the nominal behavior. In this way, all models of particular failure modes are refinements of the global failure refinement and inherit any safety property proven for this global refinement. The nominal model is *also* a refinement and inherits the same safety properties (Fig. 1). Not admitted in this work is a case where a safety property is required to hold *only* for out-of-nominal operation and is not present in the nominal model. Though such cases exist, it is considered rare for a nominal implementation to lack a safety requirement present in a failure mode for that system.

Viewing behaviors of anticipated malfunctions as an abstraction of the nominal behavior has some advantages. For complex safety-critical systems that are prone to failure, it is important to "design-in" anticipated failures with their own fail-safe requirements. Recasting such requirements into the familiar abstraction/refinement design practice means that the same tools can be brought to bear on these designed-in benign failure requirements as part of the normal design process. Another advantage is that anticipated failure modes are incorporated into the design process up-front rather than as an afterthought.

3 Example Turnstile Model

For an illustration, we use the familiar turnstile model [6] in simplified form. A turnstile requires a coin to permit the patron admission by pushing on the bar. In a simplified description, we can identify three Boolean state variables for the device: C, P, and L, indicating whether a coin is present, whether the bar is being pushed, and whether the bar is locked. We idealize the operation of the turnstile as a sequence of discrete instants at which C and P can be set arbitrarily from the outside and L updates at the next instant in response. If the coin is present and the bar is locked, the bar should become unlocked and remain so until the patron pushes through, after which it should become locked again. If the coin is absent, the bar should remain locked. We can synthesize the desired nominal properties into a TLA+ [11] formula:

$$
\begin{aligned}
S1 \quad &\triangleq (\neg C \wedge L \Rightarrow L') \ldots\ldots \qquad \textbf{critical safety property} \\
S2 \quad &\triangleq (C \wedge L \Rightarrow \neg L') \\
S3 \quad &\triangleq (\neg P \wedge \neg L \Rightarrow \neg L') \qquad\qquad\qquad\qquad\qquad (1) \\
S4 \quad &\triangleq (P \wedge \neg L \Rightarrow L') \\
Safety \quad &\triangleq \Box[S1 \wedge S2 \wedge S3 \wedge S4]_{\langle C,P,L \rangle}.
\end{aligned}
$$

Here, each Sn defines a safety property in terms of a TLA action, which relates the variables C, P, and L in the "current" instant to L', representing the value of L in the "next" instant. TLA formulas describe *behaviors*, infinite sequences of states over a set of named variables, and so we have to lift the description of individual steps into a predicate on behaviors. To combine the safety properties into the requirement *Safety*, we require that each step must satisfy the conjunction of the safety properties, or else be a "skip" step where the next state is identical to the current one. In TLA+ this is expressed as $\Box[S1 \wedge S2 \wedge S3 \wedge S4]_{\langle C,P,L \rangle}$.

While all of the implications in (1) can be thought of as safety properties, the "critical safety property" $S1$ is one that we wish to preserve in a design for anticipated out-of-nominal conditions. We could have designated another one (or more) of the safety conditions as "critical" – there is nothing special about the property $S1$ other than our choice of it for this example. We can interpret $S1$ as "the turnstile will remain locked unless a coin is present" $(\neg C \wedge L \Rightarrow L')$. Out-of-nominal designs will be discussed further in Sect. 4.

The nominal requirements in (1) can be used as an abstraction suitable for refinement. If the refinement is valid, all of $S1$ through $S4$ will be true of the implementation. One initial refinement of the requirements is described by the action

$$
L' = (\neg C \wedge L) \vee (P \wedge \neg L), \qquad\qquad (2)
$$

and this can be elaborated into a full TLA+ model, shown in Fig. 4 in Appendix A. The TLC model checker can prove that the behaviors of this model, encoded in a TLA formula *Spec*, refine *Safety*, i.e., satisfy the safety conditions $S1$ through $S4$. Since the model is finite, TLC readily verifies that $Spec \Rightarrow Safety$.

The refinement (2) would need to be "compiled" (i.e., further refined) into a program running on a processor, or in the ensuing example for this paper, synthesized into logic gates. It is the specifics of the implementation that determine whether this circuit is robust to the anticipated failure modes.

4   Design and Out-of-Nominal Verification via Abstraction

4.1   Refinement (High Level)

We now consider a method by which abstraction and refinement can be used in a formal design process in order to account for out-of-nominal conditions. The process starts, as any design process should, with the requirements. These are gathered in the usual ways and must be formalized. These are the nominal requirements.

Next, certain of these requirements are designated as "critical" – these are the out-of-nominal requirements, i.e., those that must hold even under some (predicted) mode of system failure or inconsistency. Our methodology dictates that now the designer must prove that the nominal requirements refine the out-of-nominal requirements. If the out-of-nominal requirements are a subset of the nominal requirements then this proof is trivial, since any system behavior satisfying a set of requirements will also satisfy any subset of those requirements.

Next, we refine the nominal requirements. The refined model is closer to an implementation, although it may still be quite abstract. Refinement of the nominal model is done in the usual way [1,11], ensuring that the level above simulates the level below.

Finally, we must construct the out-of-nominal refinement such that it both *refines* the out-of-nominal requirements *and abstracts* the nominal refinement, completing the commuting square diagram (shown for the turnstile example in Fig. 2). This step might be quite difficult, and we know of no general approach to construct this model. However the turnstile example may be typical of certain cases. In this case, our out-of-nominal requirement is only that $\neg C \wedge L \Rightarrow L'$. In the nominal refinement, L evolves based on the action

$$L' = (\neg C \wedge L) \vee (P \wedge \neg L).$$

Since the first disjunct alone already satisfies the out-of-nominal requirement that $\neg C \wedge L \Rightarrow L'$, we can consider the second disjunct to behave "randomly" and, at any step, draw its value from either the nominal behavior $P \wedge \neg L$ or its negation $\neg(P \wedge \neg L)$. In the model, we denote by X a value from this set, and the out-of-nominal refinement is derived by replacing the action above with

$$L' = (\neg C \wedge L) \vee X.$$

This model is shown in Fig. 5 in Appendix A. We have verified with TLC that it both refines the out-of-nominal requirements and abstracts the nominal refinement, thus completing the commuting diagram.

By contrast, if we had used the logically equivalent nominal refinement

$$L' = (\neg C \vee \neg L) \wedge (P \vee L),$$

it would not have been straightforward to obtain an out-of-nominal abstraction preserving the critical safety requirement $S1$. That is, while the disjunctive and

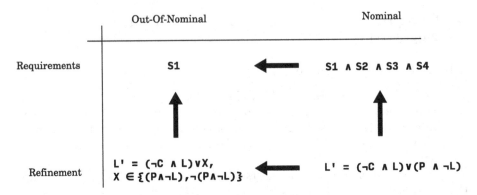

Fig. 2. Refinement/abstraction diagram for the turnstile example. The arrows point in the direction of abstraction. Existing formal abstractions can be reinterpreted in this framework; a technique like CEGAR might already prove that the nominal design (lower right) satisfies a safety property (upper left) by finding an abstraction (lower left) that satisfies the safety property.

conjunctive normal forms are of course equivalent in their nominal behavior, in this example one particular choice of design offers the ability to tolerate a faulty out-of-nominal operation. This interpretation gives abstraction an even more central role in driving the design process.

It is useful to ask: How generalizable and automatable is the use of abstraction techniques to understand out-of-nominal behavior? While we present only a preliminary exploration of this type of approach, we suggest that there are likely insights to be gained on many specific digital system models by viewing already-used abstraction techniques through the out-of-nominal lens. In traditional nominal verification, discovering a useful abstraction in which given safety properties can be proven is typically an iterative process, either automated or manual. The goal of capturing some realistic out-of-nominal behavior in the abstraction can be an additional criterion guiding this process.

For example, in design by refinement, a high-level model satisfying critical safety properties could be constrained to be assembled from abstracted component models that are known to represent the behavior of implementable devices including both nominal and out-of-nominal environments of interest. This would ensure that subsequent refinement can match a physically realizable implementation while preserving the out-of-nominal requirements. Moreover, the choice of physical implementation itself could be directly informed by abstractions that are found in other ways. If CEGAR is applied to a critical safety property and discovers a suitable abstraction of the nominal model automatically, the system design could be adjusted to ensure that its out-of-nominal behavior falls within this abstraction. In the turnstile model, CEGAR might produce the abstraction $L' = (\neg C \wedge L) \vee X$ in the course of proving $\neg C \wedge L \Rightarrow L'$. More realistic applications of CEGAR [10] result in other abstractions that may correspond to out-of-nominal behavior, such as allowing the values of variables to be corrupted as long as certain predicates are not altered. This could define the strength of error correction needed in an implementation.

4.2 Implementation (Low Level)

We now discuss how the refined logic design for the turnstile (on both the out-of-nominal and nominal sides) can be related to a notional implementation in hardware gates. This corresponds to adding another level of detail to the model that could be reified in raw gates, moving from the second to the third row in Fig. 3. We could initially interpret the nominal logic $L' = (\neg C \wedge L) \vee (P \wedge \neg L)$ directly in terms of AND and OR gates. Then the out-of-nominal logic $L' = (\neg C \wedge L) \vee X$ implies that the $P \wedge \neg L$ term can be computed by an unreliable gate, but the remaining gates must remain reliable even under out-of-nominal conditions. Often this is achieved using some physically more robust but more expensive type of gate, and is ineluctably tied to the physical failure mode(s) that the designer has in mind. To illustrate an alternative technique, we discuss an intrinsically robust implementation using Boolean networks (BNs) informed by principles of digital error damping. Such BNs have several advantages:

1. The analysis draws on the rich body of science developed for BNs [9] as previously applied to discrete system robustness, including digital and biological applications; error creation, propagation, and extinction in BNs are well characterized.
2. The statistics of error damping in BNs have been previously evaluated [12] for a digital half-adder. Because of this, the example implementations used here are known to be representative of the class of BNs from which they are chosen.
3. The dynamical systems principles illustrated by BNs are applicable to much more complex designs than the turnstile example and to broader types of faults, offering a means of assessment even for systems beyond the reach of exhaustive formal verification.

We draw on previous work [12] in which example BNs were constructed to compute a half-adder function and their robustness was analyzed with the NuSMV [2] model checker. For present purposes, we ignore the "sum" output and use only the "carry" output, which corresponds directly to an AND operation. Conventionally, a BN is interpreted as a sequential logic circuit. To implement combinational logic, we replicate the gates in "tiers", with each tier providing its results as input to the next, and with the final output being read at the end of a specified number of tiers (here, 20). This corresponds to "unrolling" the conventional BN steps and can analyzed identically using model checkers, etc. The BNs are used here as a notional means of implementing the turnstile's combinational logic in a way that is systematic (rather than idiosyncratic) and representative of more complex designs.

Two BNs were constructed, differing in the design parameter k, the average number of inputs per node [12]. In accordance with complex systems analysis [9],

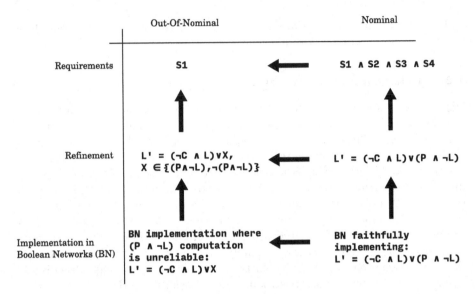

Fig. 3. Continuation of Fig. 2 where we add an implementation in gate-level Boolean networks. It is at this lowest implementation level that the failure mode will evidence itself and must be anticipated and accounted for in the out-of-nominal design.

the BN with $k = 1.5$ shows "quiescent" behavior (perturbations are damped) and the BN with $k = 2.5$ shows "chaotic" behavior (perturbations are amplified). Typical real-world digital implementations are found empirically to be chaotic [13]; such implementations are cheaper to create because they impose fewer restrictions on programmability. Quiescent implementations that damp bit-flip errors are more constrained and generally more difficult to create. Our strategy here is to use the cheaper chaotic implementation for parts of the design that do not impact the critical safety property, and to use the more expensive quiescent implementation for parts that need robustness to preserve the critical safety property.

In using the BNs for the turnstile, we take advantage of the higher-level abstraction properties already established. Specifically, we implement each of the two AND operations in $L' = (\neg C \land L) \lor (P \land \neg L)$ with a BN. This means that the two values $\neg C$ and L are wired to the inputs of a BN and the carry output is used for the result $\neg C \land L$, and similarly for $P \land \neg L$. We assume that the other operations, such as the NOT initially applied to some inputs and the OR performed at the end, are fully reliable for this example.

Each of the two AND operations in $L' = (\neg C \land L) \lor (P \land \neg L)$ can be implemented with either of the BNs as far as *nominal* behavior is concerned. This is verified by exhaustive testing as well as model checking with NuSMV [12], and is as expected because the BNs were chosen to compute their function correctly when operating with their nominal logic. Thus, the abstraction arrow leading upward from the bottom right of Fig. 3 is valid.

For out-of-nominal behavior, as before [12], we consider the possibility of any single bit flip (incorrect gate output) within some range of tiers in the BN, again using a nondeterministic formal model of the kind used in other work on soft errors [14]. We have adapted the NuSMV analysis in this case to check the correctness of the carry bit specifically. A portion of our NuSMV model is shown in Fig. 6 in Appendix B. In these BNs, because bit flips occurring at or shortly before the output stage may not have a chance to self-correct, the bit flip is restricted to the first $n_{\max}$ tiers, where we consider $1 \leq n_{\max} \leq 20$. The NuSMV analysis finds that for no such value of $n_{\max}$ does the chaotic BN reliably implement the AND operation, while the quiescent BN does so for any $n_{\max} \leq 15$. That is, most of the computations performed by the quiescent BN can be susceptible to a bit flip, and relatively few of them (the last 5 tiers) need to be protected. Thus, if we can arrange that the effect of the out-of-nominal environment is not felt in the last 5 tiers, then the quiescent BN can be used to implement the "critical" term $\neg C \wedge L$ and correctly refines it on the out-of-nominal side – the abstraction arrow leading upward from the lower left in Fig. 3. Meanwhile, either BN (or for that matter, any nominally correct implementation) can be used for $P \wedge \neg L$ because the out-of-nominal side imposes no constraint on this term.

Hence, we have shown that for a suitable out-of-nominal environment, a BN-based implementation of the turnstile logic with quiescent $\neg C \wedge L$ and arbitrary $P \wedge \neg L$ can complete the bottom row in Fig. 3, conforming to the previous abstractions on both the out-of-nominal and nominal sides. As mentioned, quiescent implementations are harder to design, and so limiting the need for them (here to one half of the turnstile logic) is useful.

In accordance with the remarks at the end of Sect. 4.1, the relation between the higher-level models and the BN implementations illustrates the potential for two-way interaction in the design process. The robustness that is designed-in at the gate level can be targeted at the goal of making the out-of-nominal behavior conform to a chosen abstraction; resources need not be spent on correcting errors that are allowed by the abstraction. Conversely, the availability and efficiency of robust implementations can motivate the use of particular abstractions in a formal design methodology.

5 Conclusion

We have presented an approach for modeling out-of-nominal behavior in digital systems so that critical safety properties can be established, in a way that leverages existing formal design and verification techniques. Our approach takes advantage of a key observation: The relation between nominal and out-of-nominal behavior can be viewed as an instance of the same kind of formal abstraction that is used for other purposes, and so analysis techniques and specific abstractions can be shared. Nominal and out-of-nominal requirements and implementations are connected by an interlocking set of abstraction relationships.

This work can contribute to new digital design and verification techniques that ensure safety in out-of-nominal environments as an inherent property rather than addressing it after the fact. This will likely benefit from an iterative design process in which the nominal and out-of-nominal requirements and implementations can be adjusted until the network of abstractions is complete and consistent. For a design already created with only nominal analysis, abstractions can reveal what properties are preserved in what out-of-nominal environments, and thus may enlarge the usefulness of the design or suggest ways of improving it.

Possible extensions of this work include:

1. Generalizing the dichotomy of nominal and out-of-nominal to a larger family of different environments, each of which may have its own set of safety requirements based on likelihood of occurrence and consequences of failure.
2. Enabling statistical reasoning with probabilistic (rather than merely nondeterministic) models of out-of-nominal behavior, probabilistic safety requirements, and probabilistic model checkers [5], using suitable notions of abstraction and refinement.
3. Further integrating robust-design principles from formal methods and complex systems theory to enable out-of-nominal verification with as much confidence as possible for systems beyond the reach of exhaustive analysis.

Acknowledgments. Sandia National Laboratories is a multi-program laboratory managed and operated by Sandia Corporation, a wholly owned subsidiary of Lockheed Martin Corporation, for the U.S. Department of Energy's National Nuclear Security Administration (NNSA) under contract DE-AC04-94AL85000. This work was funded by NNSA's Advanced Simulation and Computing (ASC) Program.

A   High-Level Model for Turnstile in TLA

As discussed in Sect. 3 and Sect. 4.1, TLA+ is used to specify and verify both nominal and out-of-nominal models for the turnstile example. The nominal model is shown in Fig. 4 and the out-of-nominal model in Fig. 5. Both models have three variables *lock*, *coin*, and *push*, corresponding to the variables L, C, and P described in Sect. 3. The specifications are given in the idiomatic TLA+ style: *Init* constrains the initial conditions, *Next* describes the "next step" relation, and *Spec* expresses the complete temporal logic specification [11].

The relation *Next* is defined by existential quantification over parameters c and p, representing new values of *coin* and *push* in the relation *Step*. This somewhat contorted idiom is used because a step must completely describe the evolution of each variable. The existential expresses that *coin* and *push* may each evolve nondeterministically at each step.

The property *TypeInvariant* states that each variable is limited to Boolean values, while *Safety* expresses the set of safety properties drawn from $S1$ through $S4$ that apply to each model. In the nominal model, *OutOfNominalSpec* imports the out-of-nominal specification for use in proving refinement (see Sect. 4.1). The type invariant, safety, and refinement properties were checked for correctness using the TLC model checker.

```
┌──────────────────── MODULE Turnstile ────────────────────┐

VARIABLES lock, coin, push

Init ≜
    ∧ lock  = TRUE
    ∧ coin ∈ BOOLEAN
    ∧ push ∈ BOOLEAN

Step(c, p) ≜
    ∧ lock' = ((¬coin ∧ lock) ∨ (push ∧ ¬lock))
    ∧ coin' = c
    ∧ push' = p

Next ≜ ∃ c, p ∈ BOOLEAN : Step(c, p)

vars ≜ ⟨lock, coin, push⟩

Spec ≜ Init ∧ □[Next]vars
├──────────────────────────────────────────────────────────┤

TypeInvariant ≜
    ∧ lock ∈ BOOLEAN
    ∧ coin ∈ BOOLEAN
    ∧ push ∈ BOOLEAN

THEOREM Spec ⇒ □ TypeInvariant
├──────────────────────────────────────────────────────────┤

S1 ≜ ¬coin ∧ lock ⇒ lock'
S2 ≜ coin ∧ lock ⇒ ¬lock'
S3 ≜ push ∧ ¬lock ⇒ lock'
S4 ≜ ¬push ∧ ¬lock ⇒ ¬lock'

Safety ≜ □[S1 ∧ S2 ∧ S3 ∧ S4]vars

THEOREM Spec ⇒ Safety
├──────────────────────────────────────────────────────────┤

OutOfNominal ≜ INSTANCE OutOfNominal
OutOfNominalSpec ≜ OutOfNominal! Spec

THEOREM Spec ⇒ OutOfNominalSpec
└──────────────────────────────────────────────────────────┘
```

Fig. 4. TLA+ specification for the nominal turnstile.

―――――――――――― MODULE *OutOfNominal* ――――――――――――

VARIABLES *lock, coin, push*

Init $\triangleq$
    $\wedge$ *lock* = TRUE
    $\wedge$ *coin* $\in$ BOOLEAN
    $\wedge$ *push* $\in$ BOOLEAN

Step(*c, p, x*) $\triangleq$
    $\wedge$ *lock'* = $((\neg coin \wedge lock) \vee x)$
    $\wedge$ *coin'* = *c*
    $\wedge$ *push'* = *p*

Next $\triangleq$
    $\exists\, c, p \in$ BOOLEAN :
    $\exists\, x \in \{(push \wedge \neg lock), \neg(push \wedge \neg lock)\}$:
    Step(*c, p, x*)

vars $\triangleq$ $\langle lock,\ coin,\ push \rangle$

Spec $\triangleq$ *Init* $\wedge\ \square[Next]_{vars}$

―――

TypeInvariant $\triangleq$
    $\wedge$ *lock* $\in$ BOOLEAN
    $\wedge$ *coin* $\in$ BOOLEAN
    $\wedge$ *push* $\in$ BOOLEAN

THEOREM *Spec* $\Rightarrow$ $\square$ *TypeInvariant*

―――

S1 $\triangleq$ $\neg coin \wedge lock \Rightarrow lock'$

Safety $\triangleq$ $\square[S1]_{vars}$

THEOREM *Spec* $\Rightarrow$ *Safety*

――

Fig. 5. TLA+ specification for the out-of-nominal turnstile.

B   Boolean Network Model for Turnstile in NuSMV

As described in Sect. 4.2, the NuSMV model checker is used to verify the robustness of the tiered combinational logic implementing the safety-critical term $\neg C \wedge L$, along the lines of previous work [12]. The inputs are taken as node 0 ($\neg C$) and node 1 (L), and the output is taken as node 18. The Boolean network (BN) is checked for conformance to the abstraction in the presence of any single internal bit flip in one of the first n_{max} tiers, where $n_{max} \in \{1, \ldots, 20\}$. Figure 6 shows an extract from the model in the case where node 2 can be flipped

```
-- ...
   init(n02) := 0ub1_0;

   init(xfer02) := 0ub4_0011;

   init(nfn02) := 0ub1_0;
   init(latchn02) := FALSE;
   init(flipn02) := {FALSE, TRUE};

   next(flipn02) := {FALSE, TRUE};
   next(latchn02) := flipn02 | latchn02;
-- (flipn02 & (! latchn02)) happens at most once

-- xfern02 is the static transfer function for node 02
   next(n02) := ((0 <= tier) & (tier < 14) &
      (flipn02 & (! latchn02))) ? (! xfern02) : xfern02;

-- nfn02 is here to keep track of what the non-flipped bit would be
   next(nfn02) := xfern02;
-- ...
-- Property to be verified:
LTLSPEC F ((tier = 20) & (n18 = (n00 & n01)));
```

Fig. 6. Extract from a NuSMV model that is programmatically generated so that all tiers and all nodes can be checked for susceptibility to bit flips. The linear temporal logic (LTL) property at the end expresses conformance of the out-of-nominal output to the abstraction $\neg C \wedge L$.

and $n_{max} = 14$. It is found that the quiescent BN is immune to any single bit flip up to $n_{max} = 15$, whereas the chaotic BN can be corrupted by a single bit flip for any value of n_{max}.

References

1. Abrial, J.R.: Modeling in Event-B: System and Software Engineering, 1st edn. Cambridge University Press, Cambridge (2010)
2. Cimatti, A., Clarke, E., Giunchiglia, E., Giunchiglia, F., Pistore, M., Roveri, M., Sebastiani, R., Tacchella, A.: NuSMV 2: an opensource tool for symbolic model checking. In: Brinksma, E., Larsen, K.G. (eds.) CAV 2002. LNCS, vol. 2404, pp. 359–364. Springer, Heidelberg (2002)
3. Clarke, E., Grumberg, O., Jha, S., Lu, Y., Veith, H.: Counterexample-guided abstraction refinement for symbolic model checking. J. ACM **50**, 752–794 (2003)
4. Fey, G.: Assessing system vulnerability using formal verification techniques. In: Kotásek, Z., Bouda, J., Černá, I., Sekanina, L., Vojnar, T., Antoš, D. (eds.) MEMICS 2011. LNCS, vol. 7119, pp. 47–56. Springer, Heidelberg (2012)
5. Güdemann, M., Ortmeier, F.: Probabilistic model-based safety analysis. In: Proceedings of the 8th Workshop on Quantitative Aspects of Programming Languages, pp. 114–128, March 2010

6. Jackson, M., Zave, P.: Deriving specifications from requirements: an example. In: Proceedings of the 17th International Conference on Software Engineering, pp. 15–24 (1995)
7. Joshi, A., Heimdahl, M.P.E., Miller, S.P., Whalen, M.W.: Model-based safety analysis. NASA Contractor Report CR-2006-213953, February 2006
8. Joshi, A., Miller, S.P., Whalen, M., Heimdahl, M.P.: A proposal for model-based safety analysis. In: Proceedings of the 24th Digital Avionics Systems Conference, October 2005
9. Kauffman, S.A.: The Origins of Order: Self-Organization and Selection in Evolution. Oxford University Press, Oxford (1993)
10. Kobayashi, N., Sato, R., Unno, H.: Predicate abstraction and CEGAR for higher-order model checking. In: Proceedings of the 32nd ACM SIGPLAN Conference on Programming Language Design and Implementation, pp. 222–233, June 2011
11. Lamport, L.: Specifying Systems: The TLA+ Language and Tools for Hardware and Software Engineers. Addison-Wesley, Boston (2002)
12. Mayo, J.R., Armstrong, R.C., Hulette, G.C.: Digital system robustness via design constraints: the lesson of formal methods. In: Proceedings of the 9th Annual IEEE International Systems Conference, pp. 109–114, April 2015
13. Mytkowicz, T., Diwan, A., Bradley, E.: Computer systems are dynamical systems. Chaos 19, 033124 (2009)
14. Seshia, S.A., Li, W., Mitra, S.: Verification-guided soft error resilience. In: Proceedings of the Conference on Design, Automation and Test in Europe, pp. 1442–1447, April 2007
15. Vorobeychik, Y., Mayo, J.R., Armstrong, R.C., Ruthruff, J.R.: Noncooperatively optimized tolerance: decentralized strategic optimization in complex systems. Phys. Rev. Lett. 107, 108702 (2011)

Automotive Systems

A Controller Safety Concept Based on Software-Implemented Fault Tolerance for Fail-Operational Automotive Applications

Majdi Ghadhab[1](✉), Matthias Kuntz[1], Dmitrii Kuvaiskii[2],
and Christof Fetzer[2]

[1] BMW AG, Munich, Germany
{majdi.el.ghadhab,matthias.kuntz}@bmw.de
[2] Technische Universität Dresden, Dresden, Germany
{dmitrii.kuvaiskii,christof.fetzer}@tu-dresden.de

Abstract. We propose to build a fail-operational computing system from a primary self-checking controller and a secondary limp-home controller to guarantee an emergency operation in the case of hardware failure of the primary controller. A self-checking controller commonly builds on hardware-implemented fault detection, e.g. lock-stepping to reach a high diagnostic coverage of hardware faults. Such techniques come into contradiction with new features of modern CPUs such as inherent nondeterminism of execution. Thus an interesting alternative to hardware-based self-checking in the primary controller is to implement software-based fault detection and recovery on the primary controller to detect and mask its hardware failures. We prove by means of stochastic model checking and prototype fault detection technique that the proposed approach not only reduces costs, but also guarantees higher availability of the computing system at the same safety level as common replicated execution on redundant hardware.

Keywords: Automotive controller · Functional safety · Availability · Fail-operational · Stochastic model checking · Markov model · Coded processing

1 Introduction

It is commonplace that modern automobiles are abundantly equipped with electronic systems that provide the driver with additional driving comfort, assistance, and safety. Regardless of the purpose of the electronic systems, often they impose high requirements for performance, availability, and functional safety. In the near future enhanced functionality like automated or autonomous driving will increase the aforementioned demands and in particular impose a shift in the automotive safety philosophy from fail-safe to fail-operational. In this context, fail-operational means, that on the occurrence of failures of the primary highly comfortable automated driving function, a comfort- but not safety-reduced emergency function can be maintained for a certain time. The challenge will not only

C. Artho and P.C. Ölveczky (Eds.): FTSCS 2015, CCIS 596, pp. 189–205, 2016.
DOI: 10.1007/978-3-319-29510-7_11

be to satisfy these technical properties given the constraints of automotive electronics such as limited computing resources, but also to comply with high cost pressure, short development cycles, and customer expectations on functionality.

In this paper, we show for a simple fail-operational system how to meet these demands by means of software-implemented fault tolerance. Typically the embedded system architecture is provided with mechanisms such as diverse or homogenous redundancy and monitoring devices to detect safety-critical hardware failures with high probability and initiate transition into a safe behavior. These techniques, however, generally raise negative side effects on costs, complexity, and availability of the embedded system. Therefore we propose to make use of software-implemented fault detection which reliably shifts the diagnosis of execution errors into the application software. We prove per stochastic model checking that such techniques yield to appreciable customer advantages. Moreover we recommend implementing a combination of coded processing and instruction-level duplication (Δ-encoding), as it allows an optimized trade-off between diagnostic coverage and computing overhead.

The paper is organized as follows: We introduce the transition from fail-safe to fail-operational in Sect. 2. In Sect. 3 we propose a fail-operational computing platform based on a self-checked primary controller and a limp-home controller. Two variants of this platform are also presented in Sect. 3: a self-checked primary controller by hardware redundancy in platform 1 and by software fault detection in platform 2. In Sect. 4 we model the computing platform using the stochastic model checker PRISM and compare platform 1 and 2 with regards to customer-relevant criteria including availability. Furthermore we extend platform 2 by a recovery mechanism (platform 3) and prove further improvements. In Sect. 5 we introduce Δ-encoding as a novel software-implemented fault detection technique which fulfills the diagnostic coverage assumed for platforms 2 and 3 and present experimental results in terms of fault detection capabilities and performance overhead. Finally we give in Sect. 6 a brief overview and discuss a selected current research in dependable automotive computing.

2 From a Fail-Safe to a Fail-Operational System Architecture

Current safety-critical automotive systems are fail-safe, which means they generally go into a safe state in the case of failure by stopping operation. Systems where a shutdown in case of failure might lead to a dangerous or non-controllable driving situation are referred to as fail-operational. In this case fault tolerance measures must be provided to allow at least an emergency operation. This means that the E/E[1]- system is designed with regard to its fault tolerance so that necessary functionality can be maintained in the case of failures within a critical operating phase. Figure 1 shows a typical fail-safe architecture. The basic principle consists of a monitoring of safety-critical elements, e.g. sensor or processing.

---

[1] Electric/Electronic.

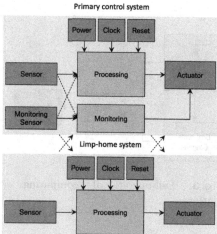

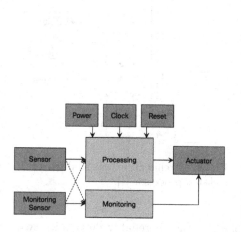

Fig. 1. Example of a fail-safe architecture [2].

Fig. 2. Example of a hybrid redundancy approach [2].

Alternatively, structural redundancy is used in applications where the complexity or the physical conditions do not permit a simpler monitoring. Examples of structural redundancy include lockstep-CPUs [1], where two CPU cores execute the same sequence of instructions in a tightly-coupled manner.

In contrast to a fail-safe system, a fail-operational system should continue operation after a failure of one of its components (e.g. sensor, processor or actuator). Therefore, the transition from fail-safe to fail-operational requires a significant extension of the system architecture. Typical architectures for a fail-operational behavior include 2-out-of-3 and duo-duplex systems [3,4]. In practice, especially for vehicles, a fully symmetric redundancy is often not necessary since only a short emergency operation - so-called "Limp-home" phase - is required to continue operation when the primary control system fails. Figure 2 shows a so-called hybrid redundancy approach. This approach consists of a primary control system designed with appropriate self-checking and a limp-home system for an emergency operation. If the primary control system fails, the limp-home system takes over the control for a short time.

3   Fail-Operational Computing Platform

This paper focuses on the fail-operability of the processing. For this purpose, we design a computing platform according to the hybrid redundancy approach with a self-monitored primary controller and a limp-home controller (Fig. 3). A switch is integrated into the architecture to control the outputs to the actuators depending on the health state of each controller. In case the primary controller fails, the command of the actuators is switched to the limp-home controller.

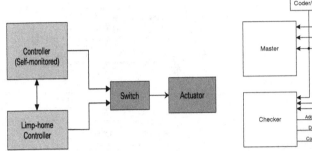

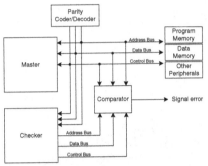

Fig. 3. Fail-operational computing Platform.

Fig. 4. Architecture of a dual-core lockstep processor [1].

The primary controller is self-monitored, so that it reliably detects its own failures in order to give over the control to the limp-home controller. To ensure a high diagnostic coverage through self-monitoring, the primary controller typically uses a redundant processor (structural redundancy). The most straightforward way to duplicate and compare a microprocessor is the technique of lockstepping (Fig. 4). Each processor is expected to generate the same outputs given the same inputs. The main disadvantage of this approach is that lock-step microprocessors double the computing resources while providing just the same performance as single processing and requiring high synchronization and comparison overhead. Lock-step processors are also susceptible to non-determinism; a number of mechanisms in current CPUs (e.g. pipelining) increase non-determinism, potentially resulting in false positives that might disconnect such lock-step CPUs from the latest developments in processor technology [5].

Furthermore, the expected relying on general-purpose processing units [6], due to their high performance per price [7], requires safety techniques without changes on the hardware architecture of these processors. To cope with the dilemma of high performance, high safety integrity, and high cost-efficiency, software-implemented fault detection achieves reliability using unreliable commodity hardware and redundancy on the application level [7].

Apart from that, we expect a better availability of the system by reducing the redundancy level within the dependable computing platform. To prove and quantify these benefits, we perform a stochastic model checking of the fail-operational computing platform and compare the results, when designing the primary controller as a duplex controller (Platform 1, Fig. 5) or as a single controller (Platform 2, Fig. 6). The duplex primary controller provides redundant processing channels for the purpose of self-checking, whereas the single controller performs self-checking by extending the single processing channel with software-implemented fault detection mechanisms. Our stochastic model checking indicates that fail-operational systems with a single-processor approach in the primary controller perform better in terms of availability and repair costs than with a dual-processor approach.

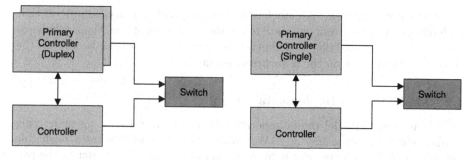

Fig. 5. Duplex primary controller (Platform 1).

Fig. 6. Single primary controller (Platform 2).

4   Stochastic Model Checking of the Fail-Operational Computing Platform

To prove the benefits of a fail-operational computing system with a single-processor primary controller, we use stochastic model checking. We choose the model-checker PRISM [10] to build and verify our model. First we give a short introduction to stochastic model checking and to the tool PRISM. Then we show the results of a simple comparison between platform 1 and platform 2 from the previous section with regards to availability. Based on experiments (see Sect. 5) platform 2 can exhibit a very high diagnostic coverage similar to platform 1 by implementing an adequate fault detection mechanism. Enhancing platform 2 with recovery, which is difficult to install on platform 1, leads to further significant improvement of the computing platform (the extension of platform 2 with a recovery mechanism is called platform 3). Finally we interpret the results to illustrate the reached improvement.

4.1   Technical Background

In **stochastic model checking** [8] the property to be verified is specified using a stochastic variant of a temporal logic, such as CTL. The temporal logic used in this paper is CSL (continuous stochastic logic) [9]. It is tailored to reason about stochastic quantitative system behavior, including the performance, safety, and reliability of a system. Given an appropriate system model and a CSL specified property, a stochastic model checking tool such as PRISM can verify automatically whether the model satisfies that property or not. The verification process essentially consists of the numerical analysis of a huge continuous-time Markov chain (CTMC), i.e., the efficient solution of a large system of linear equations.

PRISM [10] is a free, open source stochastic model checker developed at the University of Birmingham. It accepts stochastic models described in its modeling language, a simple, high-level state-based language. Three types of stochastic models are supported directly; these include discrete-time Markov chains (DTMCs) and continuous-time Markov chains (CTMCs).

A **Markov chain** [11] is a stochastic (random) and memoryless process that undergoes transitions from one state to another on a state space. Memorylessness means that the probability distribution of the next state depends only on the current state and not on the sequence of events that preceded it.

4.2   Modeling and Implementation

PRISM is used to model the fail-operational system from Fig. 3. Its underlying Markov chain is shown in Fig. 7. We assume that the Switch has a negligible failure rate and therefore omit it from the model. PC and LHC refer to the primary controller and the limp-home controller respectively. States of the system (primary controller, limp-home controller) are defined as follows:

2: Operational; 1: Failed detected; 0: Failed undetected

The initial state of (2,2) means that both primary and limp-home controller are operational and fault-free. The state of (1,2), for example, means a failed detected primary and an operational limp-home controller that takes over. Further we assume that:

- The control system is **intact**, only if both controllers are processing correctly (green).
- The control system is **degraded**, if only one of the controllers is processing correctly (yellow).
- The control system is **failed**, if the primary fails silently or the limp-home controller is not correct with failed primary controller (red).

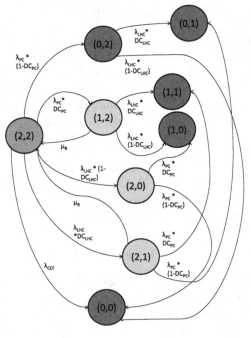

Fig. 7. Markov model of platforms 1 and 2

Table 1 specifies the parameters of platform 1 and 2. The data used are intended as examples only in order to investigate the behavior of the platforms qualitatively and quantitatively. These data do not reflect the parameters of an existing platform and have of course to be adapted for each specific design.

Commonly backup systems are designed according to significantly lower integrity requirements than corresponding primary systems. Therefore we assume a higher failure rate and a lower diagnostic coverage for the limp-home controller compared to the primary controller. Additionally to the failure rate and the diagnostic coverage of each controller, we consider a common-cause failure rate that is one order of magnitude lower than the failure rate of the primary controller and a repair rate of once per day for each computing platform (we show in the appendix that lower repair rates lead to higher relative improvement of the considered platform properties).

Table 1. Parameters of the platforms 1 and 2.

Parameters	λ_{PC}	λ_{LHC}	DC_{PC}	DC_{LHC}	λ_{CCF}	μ_R
Platform 1	2000	10000	99	60	200	0,04
Platform 2	1000	10000	99	60	100	0,04

λ_{PC} Failure rate of the primary controller (FIT[2])
λ_{LHC} Failure rate of the limp-home controller (FIT)
DC_{PC} Diagnostic coverage of the primary controller (%)
DC_{LHC} Diagnostic coverage of the limp-home controller (%)
λ_{CCF} Common-cause failure rate (FIT)
μ_R Repair rate (1/h)

Due to the processor redundancy in the primary controller of platform 1, we assume a higher failure rate λ_{PC} for platform 1 than for platform 2. It might be counterintuitive that the failure rate of the hardware-redundant controller (primary controller of platform 1) is two times the failure rate of the self-checked single controller (primary controller of platform 2). However, note that the failure rates of the redundant hardware modules in platform 1 are independent, and that the failure of one module leads to the failure of the whole controller. Therefore, such redundancy increases fault coverage but at the same time decreases MTTF.

Moreover, the diversity between the primary and the limp-home controller is higher in platform 2 than in platform 1. Additionally to the software diversity due to software-implemented fault tolerance, the hardware independence of the fault detection mechanism in platform 2 allows to use different commodtiy processors with high hardware diversity (e.g. from different manufacturers). "The diversity provides effective coverage for common cause failures and systematic failures" [12]. Hence we consider a lower common-cause failure rate for platform 2 than for platform 1.

4.3 Properties

To compare both platforms we evaluate 3 properties:

- **Availability**: "readiness for correct service" [13]. In our case, it is the probability that the computing platform is working correctly at an operation time T. The computing platform is considered available if at least one of the controllers, the primary or the limp-home, is working correctly: State "available" = State "intact" OR State "degraded".

---

[2] FIT: Failure in Time (1/10^{-9}h).

- **Duration of Limp-Home Mode**: expected time where the limp-home controller is taking control after an operation time T. We expect that only a reduced functionality is provided within the limp-home mode; therefore this property is significant for customer satisfaction.
- **Number of Repairs**: Expected repairs after an operation time T.

4.4   Results of the Stochastic Model Checking with PRISM

Figure 8 shows the same "intact"-probability for both platforms (the graphs of `Platform1_Intact` and `Platform2_Intact` are overlapping). This behavior is due to the low failure rate and the high repair rate considered in the model (see the sensitivity analysis in Appendix). Instead, the "degraded"-probability is higher for platform 2 and the "fail"-probability is lower. In sum the availability of platform 2 is significantly higher than the availability of platform 1, especially at high operation times (Fig. 9).

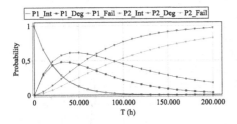

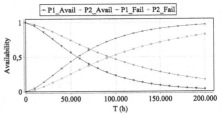

Fig. 8. Probability of each state at an operation time T.

Fig. 9. Availability of platforms 1 and 2 at an operation time T.

Regarding the duration of the limp-home mode (Fig. 10) and the number of repairs (Fig. 11) after an operation time T, clear improvements can be observed when moving from platform 1 to platform 2. These improvements result mainly from the lower failure rate of the primary controller of platform 1.

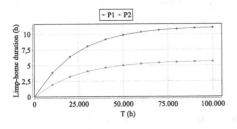

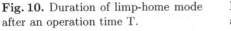

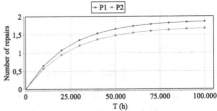

Fig. 10. Duration of limp-home mode after an operation time T.

Fig. 11. Expected number of repairs after an operation time T.

4.5   Recovery from Transient Faults

Up until now our model considers all hardware failures of the same type irrevocably leading to a failure of the primary controller.

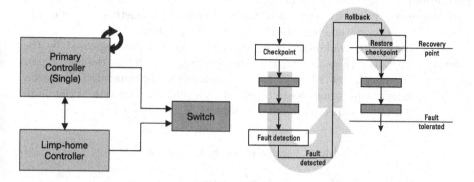

Fig. 12. Single primary controller with recovery (Platform 3).

Fig. 13. Backward recovery [14].

Next we introduce a refined model that distinguishes between two types of execution errors: transient (soft) and permanent (hard) ones. In the case of transient faults, to re-start the incorrectly executed software generally allows to recover with a high probability. A backward recovery (Fig. 13) is easier, faster, and more efficient when the underlying fault detection is performed in the application software rather than on the hardware level. A recovery mechanism building on a lockstep architecture (platform 1) for example requires a much higher development effort. In the following we propose to

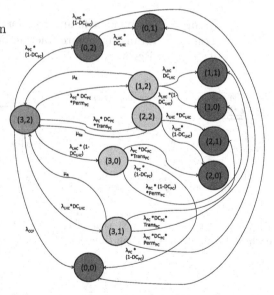

Fig. 14. Markov model of computing platform 3.

implement the recovery mechanism on the primary controller of platform 2 and call the new computing platform "platform 3" (Fig. 12).

To model and evaluate the platform 3, we expand the states of the primary controller as follows (Fig. 14):

3: Operational
2: Failed detected transient
1: Failed detected permanent
0: Failed undetected

Furthermore, a distribution of permanent and transient faults is introduced as well as a recovery rate from transient faults. The new parameters are defined in Table 2. The other parameters are the same as for platform 2.

Surprisingly, the availability of the control system is not improved by the recovery mechanism (Figs. 15 and 16). The reason for this lies in the high repair rate considered in the model (see sensitivity analysis in the appendix). However, again significant improvements are observed regarding the duration of the limp-home mode and the expected number of repairs (Figs. 17 and 18).

Table 2. Parameters of the platform 3.

Parameters	$Perm_{PC}$	$Trans_{LHC}$	μ_{Re}
Platform 3	10	90	1

$Perm_{PC}$ Permanent failure fraction of primary controller (%)
$Trans_{PC}$ Transient failure fraction of primary controller (%)
μ_{Re} Recovery rate (1/h)

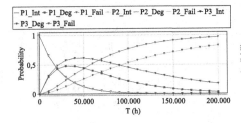

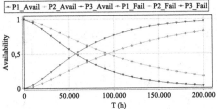

Fig. 15. Probability of each state of each platform at an operation time T.

Fig. 16. Availability of each platform at an operation time T.

4.6   Interpretation of the Results

To better illustrate the results of the stochastic model checking, we consider a fleet of 100,000 vehicles with an average operation time of 1 hour per vehicle per day. This leads to an operation time of 100,000 hours per day for the complete fleet. Considering Fig. 18 we expect a number of repairs of 2, 1.75 or 1.5 per day when respectively platform 1, 2 or 3 is used. This means a saving of repair costs

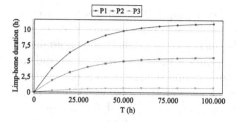

Fig. 17. Duration of limp-home mode after an operation time T.

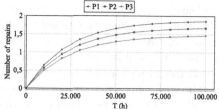

Fig. 18. Expected number of repairs after an operation time T.

up to 25 % for platform 3 compared to platform 1. This improvement becomes more significant when future vehicles are equipped with a plurality of such systems. A similar improvement can be pointed on the availability. Considering an unavailability probability of 0.75 after 100,000 hours of operation (Fig. 17), 0.75 vehicles will not be available every day due to a failure of one of the computing platforms. This number can be reduced to 0.5 by a single-processor safety concept instead of processor redundancy.

In the following we introduce Software Coded Processing (SCP) as an adequate single-processor safety technique that enables a high detection of hardware faults at an acceptable computing overhead.

5   Software Coded Processing

5.1   Theory About Software Coded Processing

Software coded processing is a pure software-based fault-tolerant approach to detect and possibly recover from hardware errors such as bit-flips and stuck-at faults. At the heart of it lies the idea of information redundancy: all data is augmented with additional, redundant bits and an error can be detected by checking against these bits.

The most well-known encodings are parity bits and Error Correcting Codes (ECC). However, they were introduced for data transmission, e.g., TCP/IP packet transmission in the Internet, but not for data processing. If, say, an addition is to be performed on two ECC-encoded integers, then both integers have to be decoded first, an addition is done, and the result is again ECC-encoded.

As such, a handful of arithmetic encodings - also referred to as Software Coded Processing (SCP) techniques were developed. Among them are residue codes, AN-encodings, and Δ-encoding. The first two were introduced in the 1960 s [15,16] and are successfully implemented in hardware and software nowadays [17–19]. These techniques share a common feature of producing encoded results from encoded inputs without any interim decoding; this enables fault tolerance, since at any point in time a hardware error can affect only an encoded value, which is easily detected by a following check.

Consider a straight-forward idea of AN-encoding [20]: each integer variable is multiplied by some predefined constant A. This multiplication increases the number of bits to represent the variable and also "stretches" the domain of possible values. Assume an original 2-bit domain of values 0, 1, 2, 3 and an A = 7. Encoding a variable x transforms an original domain to a 5-bit encoded domain with only possibly correct values in the set 0, 7, 14, 21. Values from this set are called code words (note that they are multiples of A), whereas all other 5-bit values 1-6, 8-13, 15-20, 22-31 are considered invalid words. Now if we observe a value of say 23 in the encoded variable x_e, this can only happen due to a hardware error.

In short, AN-encoding provides the following 3 basic operations:

(a) encoding: $x_e = x * A$; (b) decoding: $x = x_e / A$; (c) checking: $x_e \bmod A = 0$

Moreover, it is easy to see that other arithmetic operations such as addition, subtraction, multiplication can be mapped to work on encoded values. For example, an addition of two encoded values results in an encoded value:

$$z_e = x_e + y_e = A * (x + y) = A * z$$

Not all operations can be easily performed on AN-encoded values. For example, bitwise XOR, AND, OR, shifts and division are notoriously difficult to reproduce in AN-encoding. Another important disadvantage of AN-encoding is its expensive decoding operation division, which requires many cycles even on modern CPUs. To overcome these problems, Δ-encoding has been introduced [21].

5.2 Δ-encoding

Δ-encoding is a combination of AN-codes and instruction-level duplication [22,23]. The general idea is to have not one, but two constants A1 and A2 and duplicate all program flow including all program variables and all program operations. In comparison to AN-encoding, Δ-encoding has the following advantages. Firstly, a clever choice of A1 and A2 enables fast and operation-diverse checking and decoding operations. Secondly, bitwise operations can now be performed on decoded values, and fault tolerance is still provided by the fact that a hardware error cannot corrupt both copies. In comparison to instruction-duplication approaches [22,23], Δ-encoding detects not only transient (soft) hardware errors, but also intermittent and permanent (hard) ones. To this end, Δ-encoding provides very high fault detection guarantees at moderate performance costs. More details can be found in [21].

In the following, we concentrate on Δ-encoding, its costs, and gains.

5.3   Evaluation of Δ-encoding

Previous work on Δ-encoding [21] indicates fault coverage of 99.997 % and performance overheads of 2–4×. These results were produced on a diverse set of benchmarks imitating programs typical for embedded domain. To evaluate Δ-encoding in a real-world environment, we applied it to a clutch-by-wire program. The evaluation was held on an Intel Xeon CPU E5-2683 v3 @ 2.00 GHz with Intel Haswell micro-architecture.

The results are as follows: Δ-encoded clutch-by-wire showed normalized run-times of 2.45× in comparison to unmodified native version. In terms of fault coverage, Δ-encoding detected 100 % of transient faults, 99.9 % of intermittent faults (10 faults went undetected) and 99.98 % of permanent faults (2 faults went undetected). Notice that we injected 10000 faults for each experiment, and the native version exhibited 5828, 1873, and 2507 data corruptions respectively.

We conclude that Δ-encoding drastically reduced the number of data corruptions - up to 3 orders of magnitude in case of permanents - and increased fault coverage - from ~50 % to 100 % in case of transients - at the moderate cost of ~2.5× performance slowdown. We find these results encouraging and proving the applicability of software coded processing techniques in the field of embedded automotive systems.

6   Related Work

RACE: A centralized fail-operational platform computer for automotive applications

The increasing amount of automotive complex functionalities up to highly and fully automated driving results in dependability and expandability requirements on the E/E-architecture. Such architecture is proposed in the RACE[3] project [24,25]. The fail-operational centralized platform consists of a redundant communication infrastructure based on a switched Ethernet topology, redundant power supply, and redundant high performance multi-core controllers. The centralized platform computer is composed from two or more homogeneous duplex control computers (DCC). In order to guarantee fail-safe behavior, a DCC has two execution lanes that monitor input and output data mutually. In case an error occurs their results are discarded. Fail-operational behavior is guaranteed by a second DCC, which takes over the control in case the first DCC has failed.

Figure 19 shows a snapshot of the communication from DCC1 to DCC2 and DCC3. The redundant data exchange is used to detect failures of a sending lane immediately. Therefore each lane of DCC1 sends out its data (control data, application status, and platform status) cyclically to DCCs 2 and 3. As long as DCC1 is fault-free, the output data of DCC lane A and lane B are identical. In case of disparity, the receiver can immediately detect the failure and discard the received data. After a well-defined confirmation time, a fault is indicated and a system reconfiguration is initiated. Moreover, each line of a DCC sends its output data to its neighboring lane within the same DCC. Each lane monitors its opposite lane and may passivate itself, and thus the DCC, in case of inequality.

---

[3] Robust and Reliant Automotive Computing Environment for Future eCars, www.projekt-race.de/

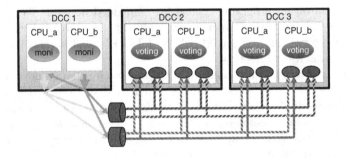

Fig. 19. The logical topology of the RACE centralized computing platform [25].

DCCs are recognized as passive if at most one lane keeps sending data; proper operation of the remaining platform is not endangered because only consistent DCC output is processed and all nodes unanimously identify the failed DCC.

In summary, the proposed platform ensures integrity and availability of the computing and communication hardware by using duo-duplex redundancy to detect and isolate faulty DCCs and to provide a second DCC (slave) to guarantee availability. If an application is configured to run redundantly, it is executed on two lanes of a DCC to ensure integrity. A slave DCC can be configured as hot-standby to ensure fail-operational behavior.

Due to redundancy of computing and communication, the costs of the proposed architecture are high. Moreover, the centralized platform requires a significant communication and monitoring overhead. In order to avoid false positives, the parallel software execution must be deterministic. This leads to a high synchronization overhead and to a slowing of the execution. In contrast, an important benefit of the proposed fail-operational architecture with software-implemented fault tolerance is that it supports non-determinism in distributed multi-core executions, by virtue of single processing and subsequent fault detection without comparison. Furthermore, the hardware homogeneity of the lanes in the RACE approach does not allow the detection of systematic hardware faults which restricts the choice of processors to those complying with ISO26262 [12] or requires costly additional measures like software diversity.

7   Conclusion

In this paper we proposed a fail-operational computing architecture based on a self-monitored primary controller and a limp-home controller ensuring a reliable take-over when the primary controller fails. For a cost-efficient, future-proof and hardware-independent self-monitoring of the primary processing, we recommended software-implemented fault tolerance, as it enables the use of low-priced and high-performance commodity processors for automotive applications. Apart from that, we showed per stochastic model checking significant benefits on availability and repair costs of the computing system when fault detection and recovery are implemented in software on the primary controller instead of common replicated execution on redundant cores. The key technique for the proposed safety architecture is a combination of software coded processing and instruction-level replication (Δ-encoding) allowing to reach a very high diagnostic coverage of hardware faults at a moderate performance overhead.

Appendix: Sensitivity analysis

To understand the sensitivity of the measured properties to the failure rate and the repair rate of the computing platform, we vary one of these parameters (see Tables 3 and 4) by keeping the rest of the specification unchanged.

Table 3. Variation of failure rate λ.

$\lambda 1$	$\lambda 2$	$\lambda 3$	$\lambda 4$
1000	50000	100000	1000000

Table 4. Variation of repair rate μ.

$\mu 1$	$\mu 2$	$\mu 3$	$\mu 4$	$\mu 5$
1/24	1/(24*7)	1/(24*30)	1/(24*365)	1/(24*365*10)

Part 1 - Sensitivity of the "intact"-probability to the parameters failure rate and repair rate (platform 1 vs. 2)

The improvement reached by platform 2 compared to platform 1 regarding the probability of the state "intact" is more significant at high failure rates (Fig. 20) and low repair rates (Fig. 21). At low failure rates or high repair rates, the probability of the state "intact" is almost identical between platform 1 and platform 2.

Part 2 - Sensitivity of the availability to the parameters failure rate and repair rate (platform 2 vs. 3)

The improvement reached by platform 3 compared to platform 2 regarding the availability of the computing platform is almost independent from the failure rate of the primary controller. The improvement is actually negligible at high as well as at low failure rates (Fig. 22). However, Fig. 23 shows a clear availability improvement at low repair rates.

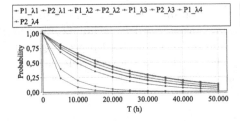

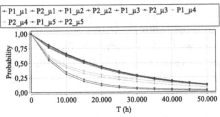

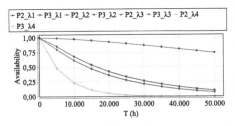

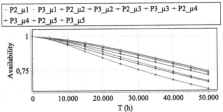

Fig. 20. Impact of the failure rate of the primary controller on the probability of the state "intact".

Fig. 21. Impact of the repair rate on the probability of the state "intact".

Fig. 22. Impact of the failure rate of the primary controller on the availability of the computing platform.

Fig. 23. Impact of the repair rate on the availability of the computing platform.

References

1. Beckschulze, E., et al.: Fault handling approaches on dual-core microcontrollers in safety-critical automotive applications. RWTH Aachen University, Germany, Embedded Software Laboratory (2008)
2. Temple, C., Vilela, A.: Fehlertolerante Systeme im Fahrzeug: von "fail-safe" zu "fail-operational". Infineon Technologies. www.elektroniknet.de
3. Wanner, D., et al.: Survey on fault-tolerant vehicle design. In: EVS26 International Battery, Hybrid and Fuel Cell Electric Vehicle Symposium, Los Angeles (2012)
4. Powel Douglass, B.: Real-Time Design Patterns: Robust Scalable Architecture for Real-Time Systems. Addison-Wesley, Boston (2002)
5. Bernick, D., et al.: Nonstop advanced architecture. Hewlett Packard Company. In: Proceedings of the International Conference on Dependable Systems and Networks (DSN), Yokohama, Japan (2005)
6. German Electrical and Electronic Manufacturers Assosciation (ZVEI): Consumer-Components in Safe Automotive Applications. Position paper (2014)
7. Ghadhab, M., Kaienburg, J., Süßkraut, M., Fetzer, C.: Is software coded processing an answer to the execution integrity challenge of current and future software-intensive applications? In: Schulze, T., Müller, B., Meyer, G. (eds.) Advanced Microsystems for Automotive Applications 2015 Smart Systems for Green and Automated Driving. LNIM, pp. 263–275. Springer, Heidelberg (2015)
8. Kwiatkowska, M., Norman, G., Parker, D.: Stochastic Model Checking. School of Computer Science, University of Birmingham Edgbaston, Birmingham B15 2TT (2007)

9. Baier, C., et al.: Model-checking algorithms for continuous-time Markov chains. IEEE Trans. Softw. Eng. **29**(7), 524–541 (2003)
10. PRISM - Probabilistic Symbolic Model Checker. www.prismmodelchecker.org
11. Häggström, H.: Finite Markov Chains and Algorithmic Applications. Cambridge University Press, Cambridge (2002)
12. International Organization for Standardization: ISO 26262: Road vehicles - Functional safety. International standard, 1st edn. (2011)
13. Avizienis, A., Laprie, J.-C., Randell, B.: Fundamental concepts of dependability. Research report, no. 1145, LAAS-CNRS (2001)
14. Pullum, L.L.: Software Fault Tolerance Techniques and Implementation. Artech House Computing Library, Boston, London (2001)
15. Brown, D.T.: Error detecting and correcting binary codes for arithmetic operations. IRE Trans. Electron. Comput. **3**, 333–337 (1960)
16. Massey, J.L.: Survey of residue coding for arithmetic errors. Int. Comput. Cent. Bull. **3**, 3–17 (1964)
17. Nathan, R., Sorin, D.J.: Nostradamus: Low-cost hardware-only error detection for processor cores. In: Design, Automation and Test in Europe Conference and Exhibition (DATE), pp. 1–6 (2014)
18. Reick, K., et al.: Fault-tolerant design of the IBM Power6 microprocessor. IEEE Micro **28**(2), 30–38 (2008)
19. Forin, P.: Vital coded microprocessor principles and application for various transit systems. In: IFAC-GCCT, pp. 79–84, Paris, France (1989)
20. Schiffel, U.: Hardware error detection using AN-codes. Ph.D thesis, Technische Universität Dresden (2011)
21. Kuvaiskii, D., Fetzer, C.: Δ-encoding: practical encoded processing. In: Proceedings of the 45th Annual IEEE/IFIP International Conference on Dependable Systems and Networks, Rio de Janeiro, Brazil (2015)
22. Oh, N., et al.: Error detection by duplicated instructions in superscalar processors. IEEE Trans. Reliab. **51**(1), 63–75 (2002)
23. Reis, G.A., et al.: SWIFT: Software Implemented Fault Tolerance. In: Proceedings of the International Symposium on Code Generation and Optimization (2005)
24. Sommer, S., et al.: RACE: a centralized platform computer based architecture for automotive applications. In: Vehicular Electronics Conference (VEC) and the International Electric Vehicle Conference (IEVC) (2013)
25. Armbruster, M., Freitag, G., Schmid, T., Spiegelberg, G., Fiege, L., Zirkler, A.: Ethernet-based and function-independent vehicle control-platform: motivation, idea and technical concept fulfilling quantitative safety-requirements from ISO 26262. In: Meyer, G. (ed.) Advanced Microsystems for Automotive Applications 2012 Smart Systems for Safe, Sustainable and Networked Vehicles, pp. 91–107. Springer, Heidelberg (2012)

Modeling Safety Requirements of ISO26262 Using Goal Trees and Patterns

Toshiaki Aoki[1]([✉]), Kriangkrai Traichaiyaporn[1], Yuki Chiba[1],
Masahiro Matsubara[2], Masataka Nishi[2], and Fumio Narisawa[2]

[1] JAIST, 1-1, Asahidai, Nomi, Ishikawa 923-1292, Japan
toshiaki@jaist.ac.jp
[2] Research and Development Group,
Center for Technology Innovation - Controls, Hitachi, Ltd., Tokyo, Japan

Abstract. In ISO 26262, safety requirements are constructed step by step. The construction is started to set safety goals to be achieved in a system up, then they are refined into hardware and software requirements which the system consists of. Such stepwise construction of the safety requirements provides traceability among them and allows us to confirm that the system surely realizes the goals. The traceability also helps us to exhaustively extract requirements which are necessary to achieve safety. On the other hand, the quality of a document describing them is important to obtain those merits. If the document contains ambiguities, contradictions and many of requirements are missed, those lead to the unsafety of the system. In fact, we found many of missing implicit assumptions and ambiguous requirements by analyzing a document which describes safety requirements. To solve this problem, we proposed a method to describe the safety requirements based on the goal tree of KAOS and its patterns. We confirmed the effectiveness of the method by applying it to an electronic power steering system as a case study. In this paper, we show the case study which is not trivial but a real system in addition to the proposed method.

Keywords: Functional safety · Safety requirements · ISO 26262 · Automotive systems

1 Introduction

Recently, the safety of automotive systems is becoming a big concern of our society. Although vehicles have been controlled by mechanical machines in the past, many of electronic parts are embedded to them at present according to the progress of electronic control technology and its performance. Those electronic parts can realize the complex control of the vehicles, and make it possible to provide high functionality to them such as electronic power steering systems and emergency braking systems. On the other hand, it makes hard to analyze and design the safety of the vehicles because there are a number of systematic failures and hardware failures which have to be taken into account. To achieve

© Springer International Publishing Switzerland 2016
C. Artho and P.C. Ölveczky (Eds.): FTSCS 2015, CCIS 596, pp. 206–221, 2016.
DOI: 10.1007/978-3-319-29510-7_12

the safety of the vehicles, international standards of functional safety such as IEC 61508 [2] and ISO 26262 [1] have been proposed.

ISO 26262 is an adaptation of IEC 61508 for automotive electric and electronic systems. ISO 26262 defines functional safety for automotive equipment applicable throughout the lifecycle of all automotive electronic and electrical safety-related systems. One of the most important implication obtained from such functional safety standards is to make documents which explain reasons why a developed system is safe. In ISO 26262, safety requirements are constructed step by step. The construction is started to set safety goals to be achieved in a system up, then they are refined into hardware and software requirements which the system consists of. That allows us to confirm that the system satisfies the goals because the reasons are traceable from the goals to the software and hardware requirements. Such traceability also helps us to exhaustively extract requirements which are necessary to achieve safety. On the other hand, the quality of a document describing them is important to obtain those merits. If the document contains ambiguities, contradictions and many of requirements are missed, those lead to the unsafety of the system. Thus, it is very important to rigorously describe the requirements so that they are traceable.

We are working on the formalization and verification of safety requirements for ISO26262 as a joint work of JAIST and Hitachi. We conducted a case study to make safety requirements document in which traceability of the requirements is realized. The target of the case study is an electronic power steering system. We call the system EPS below. We first analyzed a safety document. It was being constructed and still in a draft version at that time. The document was described in the form of spreadsheets with English. The spreadsheets are used to correspond safety requirements with each other. We analyzed the document using a goal tree which is proposed in the field of requirement engineering. We realized the traceability by relations between a parent and children of the goal tree. By this analysis, we found that the original document has problems such as containing inappropriate descriptions and missing requirements. To solve those problems, we proposed a method to describe the safety requirements based on the goal tree and its patterns. We confirmed the effectiveness of the method by applying it to an electronic power steering system as a case study. In this paper, we show the case study which is not trivial but a real system in addition to the proposed method.

The rest of the paper is organized as follows. Section 2 discusses related works. Section 3 introduces safety requirements of ISO 26262 and the goal tree. Section 4 reveals problems of the safety document which was developed by engineers. Section 5 explains our approach for describing the safety requirements so that the traceability can be achieved. Section 6 shows a case study of a real system and its results. Section 7 discusses the approach and results. Finally, Sect. 8 concludes this paper.

2   Related Works

We adopted the goal tree of KAOS [3] which is an approach for requirement engineering in order to describe safety requirements. There is another model named GSN (Goal Structuring Notation) [5] which is for describing safety cases. A safety case is a structured argument which has evidences to justify that a target system is acceptably safe. Patterns to reuse safety cases are proposed as well [8]. The reason why we adopted the goal tree of KAOS instead of GSN is that the goal tree has clear and simple semantics. Such semantics is important since we also aim at formally verifying the safety requirements. There are works on the formalization of GSN and its patterns [6,7]. These works mainly formalize the syntactical aspect of GSN. Unlike them, in our approach, we focus on semantical aspect of safety requirements. We represent the safety requirements using propositional logic and relations among them which rely on the semantics of the goal tree.

There are works on patterns of the goal tree as well. Darimont and Lamsweerde proposed a set of generic goal refinement patterns based on KAOS [11]. These generic patterns are proved to be complete and correct based on temporal logic. They are designed to be domain-independent, that is, the patterns can be reused in the construction of any goal tree for requirements elaboration. One successful example applying these patterns can be found in [9], which uses the patterns for policy refinement. The patterns proposed in this paper are domain-dependent, that is, specific to series of EPS.

3   Safety Requirements and Goal Tree

3.1   Safety Requirements

ISO 26262 is an international standard which is specialized for automotive systems. It provides an automotive safety lifecycles and supports tailoring necessary activities during these lifecycle phases. ISO 26262 is applied from preliminary vehicle development phases through the whole of the development. It adopted a top-down approach which refines a safety goal into more detailed safety requirements step by step. The objective of the safety requirements is called a safety goal, shortly SG. Phases to obtain the safety requirements starts at defining SG which is obtained from hazard analysis and risk assessment activities. Then, the initial requirement called functional safety requirements, shortly FSR, are defined based on SG. FSR is refined into technical safety requirements and hardware/software safety requirements stepwise. Those requirements are abbreviated as TSR, HSR and SSR respectively. TSRs are the technical requirements which are necessary to implement FSRs. In this refinement, item-level functional safety requirements are transformed into system-level technical safety requirements. TSRs are allocated to hardware and software. The requirements that are allocated to both are further partitioned to yield hardware/software only safety requirements, that is, HSRs/SSRs.

We refer to a preliminary architecture assumption, shortly PAA, throughout the refinement from SG to HSR/SSR. PAA is an abstract architecture of the system, which is defined in the early stage of the development. In our approach, the structure defined in PAA is refined according to the progress of the refinement. We also call such refined structure PAA for the simplicity of technical words. In this case, components appearing in FSR, TSR, HSR and SSR are defined in PAA.

3.2 Goal Tree

It is hard to analyze the safety requirements described in the form of the spreadsheet with English because they do not have explicit semantics. In order to analyze the safety requirements, we adopted a goal tree as a model which they follow. The goal tree is the central model of KAOS which is an approach for requirement engineering. A goal is a prescriptive statement of intent that the system should satisfy through the cooperation of its agents such as human, devices or software. The goal tree is for expressing relationships among goals by showing how higher-level goals are refined into lower-level ones and, conversely, how lower-level goals contribute to higher-level goals. The higher-level goals and lower-level goals are called parent-goals and sub-goals respectively. A property named *completeness of the goal tree* is defined to represent such relationships. Let sub-goals $G_1, G_2, \ldots, G_n$ and a parent-goal G. The completeness is formally defined as $\{G_1, G_2, \ldots, G_n\} \models G$ which means that the sub-goals $G_1, G_2, \ldots, G_n$ are sufficient for deriving the parent goal G. The goal tree is an appropriate for the reference model of the safety requirements since its completeness is fitted to the notion of the traceability of ISO 26262.

4 Safety Requirements of EPS

4.1 PAA of EPS

In the case study, we focus on safety requirements of EPS. EPS is a system which assists the movement of steering by a motor which is electronically controlled. Figure 1 shows PAA of EPS. Boxes and arrows represent components and flows respectively. The power supply unit provides electric power to operate motor. The flows of electric power is represented by solid lines in Fig. 1. The dotted lines represent the other data such as signals and values. The electric power has to be changed so that it can fit to the motor. Pre-Driver and Inverter changes the voltage and waveform of the electric power with PWM respectively.

This system realizes fail safe mechanisms to safely stop the system if the electric power is failed. It is monitored by Pre-Driver Voltage Monitor and Inverter Voltage Monitor. They provide the values of voltages supplied to Pre-Driver and Inverter to Diagnostic Function module. Diagnostic Function module decides whether the electric power is failed or not based on those values provided by Pre-Driver Voltage Monitor and Inverter Voltage Monitor. If the electric power failure is detected by Diagnostic Function module, that fact is notified to Fail-safe

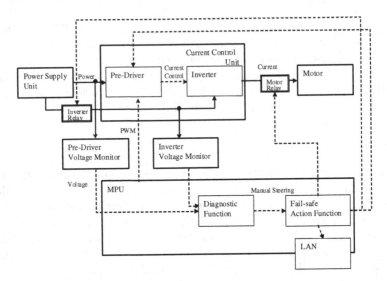

Fig. 1. Overview of PAA

Action Function module by sending a demand to transit to 'Manual Steering'. Then, Fail-safe Action Function module cuts the power supply to the motor. To make sure to cut the power supply, it is stopped by Pre-Driver, Inverter Relay and Motor Relay. We use short names CCU, PD, Inv, DF and FSF which stand for Current Control Unit, Pre-Driver, Inverter, Diagnostic Function and Fail-safe Action Function respectively. MPU is generic reference to DF and FSF.

4.2   Analysis of Safety Requirements

We analyzed a document which specifies safety requirements of EPS. The document is described in the form of spreadsheets with English. In this analysis, we constructed a goal tree consisting of safety requirements appeared in the document. As as result, we found that the following problems.

- There exist implicit assumptions.
  Many of implicit assumptions are put and do not appear in the document. This is because there are many assumptions as well as they appear in the documents many times. Such implicit assumptions are harmful. If a system is developed by multiple engineers, such assumptions may not be shared by them. This might lead to making the system unsafe.
- Safety requirements are described ununiformly.
  The safety requirements are expressed as different sentences even though they represent the same or similar requirement. In addition, the abstraction of the descriptions is not appropriate for ensuring the traceability as big gaps often exist among FSR, TSR, HSR and SSR.

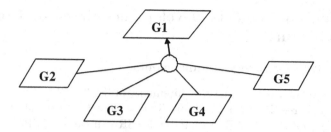

Fig. 2. Safety Requirements in terms of Goal Tree

– Some of safety requirements are missing.
We found that some of safety requirements were missing in the document. Missing the requirements directly leads to the unsafety of the system.

Figure 2 shows a part of the goal tree which corresponds to the document. The descriptions of its nodes are shown in the following.

G1 System shall make transition to 'Manual Steering' If failure of voltage supplied to Current Control Unit has been detected.
G2 Demand for transition to 'Manual Steering' shall be sent to ECU Processing Unit if failure of voltage supplied to inverter has been detected.
G3 Demand for transition to 'Manual Steering' shall be sent to ECU Processing Unit if failure of voltage supplied to Pre-Driver has been detected.
G4 ECU Processing Unit shall send 'Stop Demand' to Pre-Driver if ECU Processing Unit has received demand for transition to Manual Steering.
G5 Pre-Driver shall stop according to 'Stop Demand'.

Firstly, there is implicit assumptions in the safety requirements. The expected behavior of the system is that the failure of voltage supplied to Inv and the failure of voltage supplied to PD will lead to the failure of voltage supplied to CCU. 'Stop Demand' will be sent to PD after the detection of the failure. However, such behavior is not described in the safety requirements. This are implicit assumptions put in the document. Secondly, there is a big gap between the parent goal and its sub-goal of the goal tree. Although we have to derive the parent goal from the sub-goals for the traceability, it is impossible in this case because a relation among CCU, Inv and PD is not described. Furthermore, names used in the document are not uniform. Despite that ECU Processing Unit does not appear in PAA, it is used in this document. ECU Processing Unit represents DF and FSF, and sometimes it is referred to as MPU in the other parts of the document. Finally, the safety requirements for message transmissions among CCU, Inv and PD are missing. The other part of the document contains the safety requirement that demands have to be sent and received without failure, however; it does not appear such one here.

5   Safety Requirements Development Based on Goal Tree and Patterns

5.1   Goal Tree for Safety Requirements

The stepwise refinement of safety requirements of ISO26262 is fitted to the concept of the goal tree. FSR is refined into TSR so that FSR can satisfy TSR, and TSR is refined into HSR/SSR so that HSR/SSR can satisfy TSR. The correctness of this refinement can be regarded as the completeness of the goal tree, and that provides the traceability among FSR, TSR, HSR and SSR. On the other hand, the completeness is defined formally based on temporal logic in KAOS. It is well-known that correctly representing what we want to describe in temporal logic is difficult [10]. In addition, as far as we analyze the document of EPS, temporal properties are not essential in it. Thus, we decided to describe the safety requirements not in temporal logic but in propositional logic with some syntax sugars. Although the descriptive power of propositional logic is limited, we think that it is sufficient to describe the safety requirements. In fact, we could describe safety requirements in propositional logic within the scope of our case study. In addition, reasoning with a rich logic tends to be hard to convince us that it is valid as well as what we describe is correctly represented. We think that simpler logic is better for the safety requirements.

Our concern on the safety requirements is that there is no missing requirement or contradiction of them. In fact, there are many safety requirements having the form of implications. In this case, what we worry about them is whether a upper safety requirement such as FSR can be logically derived from lower safety requirements such as TSR with Modus Ponens. Modus Ponens is an inference rule to derive a fact B from facts A and $A \Rightarrow B$. There are many safety requirements in the document. Reasonings on the safety requirements might become unsound due to implicit assumptions and their ambiguity. Propositional logic is useful to ensure that upper safety requirements are surely derived from lower ones with sound reasonings. For example, G1 and G2 shown in figures are described as follows.

G1 $CCU.VoltFailureDetected \Rightarrow S.State = `Manual\ Steering'$
G2 $Inv.VoltFailureDetected \Rightarrow DF.Send(`Manual\ Steering', DF, MPU)$

$CCU.VoltFailureDetected$, `$S.State=Manual\ Steering$', $Inv.VoltFailure\ Detected$ and $DF.Send$ (`$Manual\ Steering$', DF, MPU) are propositional variables. One may think that $=$ is an equality operator, however; it is a part of the name of the propositional variable $S.State=`Manual\ Steering'$. $DF.Send(`Manual\ Steering', DF, MPU)$ is not an application of a function but a propositional variable. $CCU.VoltFailureDetected$ and $Inv.VoltFailureDetected$ represent the the failure detection of voltage supplied to CCU has been detected and that of voltage supplied to Inv respectively. $S.State=`Manual\ Steering'$ represents the fact that the mode of the system moves to manual steering. $DF.Send$ (`$Manual\ Steering$', DF, MPU) represents the fact that a demand message `Manual Steering' is sent to MPU from DF. Note that MPU is the abstract representation of FSF here.

Although ECU Processing Unit is used to represent a source or destination of message transmissions in the document of EPS, it usually refers to the whole of the system. This is an ambiguity of the safety requirements, that is, the sources and destinations are ambiguous. DF and FSF are used to describe message transmissions in the goal tree since the messages are transmitted between them. On the other hand, there are the ones in which the sources and destinations are not designated to abstractly describe safety requirements. In this case, we use MPU which appears in PAA shown in Fig. 1. The abstraction is different from the ambiguity. Using those symbols allow us to remove such ambiguity. In addition, there exists an implicit assumption about relations among CCU, Inv and PD. It can be described formally as $CCU.VoltFailureDetected ==$ $(Inv.VoltFailureDetected || PD.VoltFailureDetected)$.

5.2 Safety Requirement Patterns

In safety requirements, there are usually small variations of mechanisms to achieve the safety of a system. It implies that we can prepare mechanisms to achieve the safety before making safety requirements. In addition, those mechanisms can be common in an application domain. For example, systems that we focus on deal with detections of components' failure and notifying the failure to components which are in charge to deal with the failure. Despite that there are many components to detect the failure and those to deal with it, there are a small number of safety mechanisms for the detection and communication. Thus, in our approach, we define patterns for the mechanisms. We call such patterns safety requirement patterns or shortly patterns below if there is no confusion in a context.

We show an example of safety requirement patterns in Fig. 3. It is a partial goal tree which has parameters to be replaced with logical expressions and strings. This pattern represents a mechanism that a message M is safely transmitted from S to D. M, S and D are parameters which represent a message to be transmitted, a source of the transmission and a destination of the transmission respectively. Those parameters are replaced with strings which constitute propositional variables when the pattern is instantiated. C and TC are parameters to be replaced with logical expressions which represent a condition to transmit the message and a condition which holds after receiving it respectively.

The pattern ensures that sub-goals derive a parent goal for any replacement of the parameters. In Fig. 3, $C \Rightarrow D.Received(M,D)$ is derived from the facts $C \Rightarrow D.Send(M,S,D)$, $D.SendWithoutFailure$ (M,S,D) and $D.Send(M,S,D) \wedge D.SendWithoutFailure(M,S,D) \Rightarrow D.Received(M,D)$ for any M, S, D, C and TC. In addition, the upper goal $C \Rightarrow TC$ is derived from the facts $C \Rightarrow D.Received(M, D)$ and $D.Received(M, D) \Rightarrow TC$. Hence, the parent goal is derived from the sub-goals even if the parameters are replaced.

The patterns are documented like design patterns [15]. The description of each of the patterns consists of a partial goal tree with parameters as shown in Fig. 3, its explanation, applicability, example and formal proof as mentioned in the above.

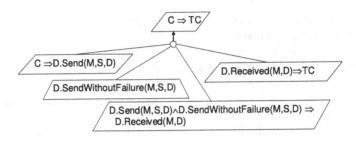

Fig. 3. Safety requirements pattern

We found that safety requirement patterns are effective to solve the problems pointed in Sect. 4.2. Firstly, the patterns allows us to explicitly describe necessary assumptions for a specific mechanism. The primary reason why many assumptions are omitted is that it is very tedious and costly to describe all of them. Assumptions appearing many times in the documents tend to be omitted. However, as we pointed out, omitting them might lead to making the system unsafe. We should describe all of the assumptions even though they are obvious for engineers who describe the document. To solve this problem, the patterns are useful. Assumptions appearing many times in the document are defined once in the pattern, and then we instantiate descriptions of the safety requirements from the patterns. It allows us to avoid tedious and costly tasks in making safety requirements. Secondly, the patterns are useful to uniformly describe the safety requirements because they provide appropriate abstraction of the safety requirements. What facts are essential for ensuring the safety is described in the patterns. Thus, we do not need describe too concrete details because what described in the patterns are sufficient to ensure the completeness of the safety requirements. Finally, the patterns help us not to miss the safety requirements. Mechanisms to achieve the safety are given by the patterns, that is, what is needed is described in them. When we instantiate the patterns, we have to find elements and conditions fitted to them. That makes it possible to notice missing safety requirements.

5.3   Application of Safety Requirement Pattern

The safety requirement pattern describes requirements of a specific safety mechanism. The pattern shown in Fig. 3 represents a mechanism of the safe message transmission which is used to communications among components to be made when the electric power failure is detected. We prepared the other two patterns, that is, there are totally three patterns, for mechanisms of the transmission. There are three variations for the transmission in this system. Firstly, communication is completed within a chip. A communication means is not needed in this case. Secondly, the communication means is needed and it is reliable enough. Thirdly, the communication means is needed and it is unreliable. Error correction mechanisms such as CRC are used in this case. Which mechanism is adopted is determined according to the degree of reliability of the transmission. The degree of the reliability is determined by communication types and signal types. The communication types mean where the transmission takes place. The signal types mean contents of the communication. There are three communication types, communications inside of a chip, between chips and between controllers. We refer those communication types to In-chip, Inter-chip and Inter-controller respectively. The reliability of the transmission is higher in the order of In-chip, Inter-chip and Inter-controller. There are three signal types, digital data, analog data and series of digital data. We refer those signal types to Digital, Analog and DigitalCom. The reliability of the transmission is higher in this order.

The degree of the reliability of the transmission is determined by combination of a communication type and signal type. It is shown in Table 1. There are three degrees of the reliability, high, mid and low. For example, the degree of the reliability in transmitting digital data within a chip is high and that in transmitting series of digital data between controllers is low. We prepared three mechanisms as well as safety requirement patterns for each of the degrees. The pattern shown in Fig. 3 is the one for the transmission with high reliability.

Table 1. Reliability of transmission

Com./sig.	Digital	Analog	DigitalCom
In-chip	High	High	—
Inter-chip	High	Mid	Low
Inter-controller	Mid	—	Low

In developing safety requirements of EPS, we identify a communication type and signal type based on PAA, then select a safety requirement pattern to be used. Table 2 shows the patterns used for the transmissions in the safety requirements of EPS. HS, MS and HS represent the patterns for high, middle and low reliability transmissions respectively. For example, in the third row of Table 2, since voltage data is transmitted from PD to MPU, the pattern MS is used for that transmission. In this way, the patterns are systematically used to develop the safety requirements.

6   Case Study

6.1   Development of Goal Tree

Figure 4 shows a part of the goal tree obtained by our approach proposed in Sect. 5. Firstly, the safety requirement pattern shown in Fig. 3 is instantiated by replacing the parameters S, D, M, C and TC with DF, MPU, 'Manual Steering', $CCU.VoltFailureDetected$ and $S.State=$'Manual Steering' respectively. Then, G2 and G5 which appear in the document are manually formalized.

Table 2. Patterns applications

src	dst	Com.	Sig.	Data	Pattern
DF	FSF	In-chip	Digital	Signal	HS
PD	MPU	Inter-chip	Analog	Voltage	MS
MPU	PD	Inter-chip	Digital	Signal	HS
MPU	PD	Inter-chip	Digital	PWM	HS
⋮	⋮	⋮	⋮	⋮	⋮

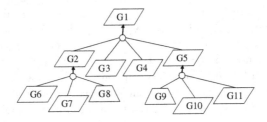

Fig. 4. Goal tree for EPS

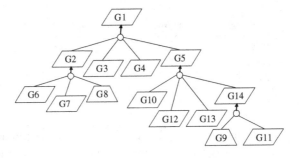

Fig. 5. Complete goal tree

The descriptions and their logical expressions of the goals of the goal tree are found in Fig. 6. We can see from them that the parent goal G1 is derived from sub-goals from G2 to G5 with Modus Ponens. Similarly, G2 is derived from those from G6 to G8.

In Fig. 4, there is a sub-tree consisting of G5, G9, G10 and G11 which describes that a stop demand is sent from MPU to PD and PD shall stop by receiving the demand. Since the sub-tree represents a safe message transmission mechanism, the pattern shown in Fig. 3 should be applied to it according to Tables 1 and 2. Although $D.SendWithoutFailure$ which represents the requirement that a message is sent without failure exists in the pattern, such requirement does not appear in Fig. 4. We can see from this fact that some requirements are missing in the sub-tree. Here, we apply the pattern to the sub-tree by replacing the parameters S, D, M, C and TC with MPU, PD, '$StopDemand$',

G1 System shall make transition to 'Manual Steering' If failure of voltage supplied to Current Control Unit has been detected.

CCU.VoltFailureDetected ⇒ *S.State = 'Manual Steering'*

G2 Demand for transition to 'Manual Steering' shall be sent to ECU Processing Unit if failure of voltage supplied to Current Control Unit has been detected.

CCU.VoltFailureDetected ⇒ *DF.Send('Manual Steering', DF, MPU)*

G3 Demand for transition to 'Manual Steering' shall be sent without failure.

DF.SendWithoutFailure('Manual Steering', DF, MPU)

G4 Demand for transition to 'Manual Steering' shall be received if it is sent without failure.

(DF.Send ('Manual Steering', DF, MPU) ∧ DF.SendWithoutFailure ('Manual Steering', DF, MPU)) ⇒ DF.Received ('Manual Steering', MPU)

G5 System shall make transition to 'Manual Steering' if Demand for transition to 'Manual Steering' shall be received.

DF.Received('Manual Steering', MPU) ⇒ S.State = 'Manual Steering'

G6 Demand for transition to 'Manual Steering' shall be sent to ECU Processing Unit if failure of voltage supplied to inverter has been detected.

Inv.VoltFailureDetected ⇒ *DF.Send('Manual Steering', DF, MPU)*

G7 Demand for transition to 'Manual Steering' shall be sent to ECU Processing Unit if failure of voltage supplied to Pre-driver has been detected.

PD.VoltFailureDetected ⇒ *DF.Send('Manual Steering', DF, MPU)*

G8 failure of voltage supplied to Current Control Unit has been detected if failure of voltage supplied to inverter or Pre-Driver has been detected.

CCU.VoltFailureDetected ⇔ *(Inv.VoltFailureDetected || PD.VoltFailureDetected)*

G9 System shall make transition to 'Manual Steering' if Pre-Driver stops.

PD.Status = 'Stop' ⇒ *S.State = 'Manual Steering'*

G10 ECU Processing Unit shall send 'Stop Demand' to Pre-Driver if ECU Processing Unit has received demand for transition to Manual Steering.

DF.Received ('Manual Steering', MPU) ⇒ PD.Send ('Stop Demand', MPU, PD)

G11 Pre-Driver shall stop according to 'Stop Demand'.

PD.Received('Stop Demand', PD) ⇒ PD.Status = 'Stop'

Fig. 6. Safety requirements

DF.Received('Manual Steering', MPU) and *S.State = 'Manual Steering'* respectively. As a result, the goal tree becomes the one shown in Fig. 5 and its goals are described as follows.

G5 *DF.Received ('Manual Steering', MPU) ⇒ S.State='Manual Steering'*

G10 *DF.Received ('Manual Steering', MPU) ⇒ PD.Send ('Stop Demand', MPU, PD)*

G12 *PD.SendWithoutFailure ('Stop Demand', MPU, PD)*

G13 *PD.Send ('Stop Demand',MPU ,PD)∧ PD.SendWithoutFailure ('Stop Demand',MPU,PD) ⇒ PD.Received ('Stop Demand',PD)*

G14 *PD.Received ('Stop Demand',PD) ⇒ S.State = 'Manual Steering'*

The completeness which means the fact that a parent goal is derived from sub-goals for each sub-tree holds in this goal tree. In this way, we can obtain formally traceable safety requirements based on the goal tree.

6.2   Result

We have applied our approach to the development of safety requirements. We focus on safety mechanisms to deal with electric power failure in EPS. There was a document which was described informally in the form of the spreadsheet as we already mentioned. Even though the document was in a draft version, all of safety requirements of the mechanisms were described. We developed a goal tree based on the document as shown in Sect. 6.1. There were 24 safety requirements in the document. As the completeness does not hold in a goal tree consisting of only safety requirements appearing the document, we added necessary ones so that it can hold.

As a result, there were 53 goals of the goal tree for which the completeness holds. In the goal tree, each of the goals represents a safety requirement. There were 17 goals which were brought from the document without any modification, 3 goals which appeared in the document but did not appear in the goal tree, that is, deleted, 4 goals which were modified from the document, and 32 goals which did not appear in the document, that is, added, out of 53 goals. It means that 67 % of the safety requirements were added or modified from the document. In addition, we analyzed the safety requirements related to the safety requirement patterns. 29 out of 53 goals were instantiated by means of the safety requirement patterns. Thus, the safety requirement patterns cover 55 % of the whole of the safety requirements. There were 12 goals which were brought from the document without any modification, 4 goals which were modified and 13 goals which were added out of 29. It means that 59 % of safety requirements were added or modified from the document by the safety requirement patterns out of the instantiated ones. The percentage of them in the whole of the safety requirements was 32 %.

6.3   Evaluation

We can say from this result that we have successfully complemented the safety requirements of EPS by our approach. Many safety requirements were missing in the original document so that it could be traceable. The most of missing safety requirements were implicit assumptions put in it, however; they might cause missing important safety requirements. In fact, an important safety requirement representing that a message is sent without failure was missing as pointed out in Sect. 6.1. We can see from the case study that our approach enables to find missing important safety requirements although many safety requirements have to be described. As the unsafety of automotive systems may cause fatal troubles such as the loss of human lives, they have to be developed very carefully even if it costs a lot.

We prepared three safety requirement patterns to develop the safety requirements. As a result, they cover more than half of the safety requirements. The purpose of the patterns is to identify essential and typical safety requirements. The patterns greatly contribute to efficiently describing the safety requirements despite that their purpose is not to cover everything. On the other hand, the percentage of safety requirements which were added or modified by the patterns was 67 % among the ones related to the patterns but 32 % on the whole. It means that many of the safety requirements related to the patterns were appeared in the original document. We can see from this fact that the safety requirement patterns captured the essential safety requirements of EPS. We observed from the development of the safety requirements that it was started to describe essential safety requirements, then the ones related to them were identified, finally we obtained traceable safety requirements. Thus, we can say that the safety requirement patterns play an important role to develop the safety requirements.

7 Discussion

The traceability of safety requirements which is introduced in ISO 26262 is not well-defined. Many engineers feel trouble about how it should be ensured. Thus, we adopted the completeness of the goal tree in order to ensure the traceability. It actually revealed many of missing safety requirements because we carefully described them so that the completeness can be maintained. Introducing such clear definition of the traceability is important to guide the development of the safety requirements as well as improve the quality of them.

We took a shallow approach to formalize safety requirements based on propositional logic. This approach is not so heavy like formal specifications [12–14] in which everything is described formally. Introducing the existing formal specification languages to practical developments is very hard because there are many problems such as education of engineers, change of development processes and so on. The reason why we took such a shallow approach is that we aim at easily expanding it to daily developments done by engineers. On the other hand, the shallow approach does not likely have sufficient effectiveness. Unlike this, in our approach, we confirmed that it achieved drastic improvement of the quality of the safety requirements. We found an appropriate way to describe the safety requirements so that it can be sufficiently effective as well as easy to be expanded to the developments.

On the other hand, one may think that propositional logic is insufficient because computation and timing are important for automotive systems [4]. They are definitely important in some development phases, for example, design of control logics. What we focus on here is not design but descriptions of safety requirements. Some safety requirements may contain complicated statements like arithmetics or differential equations. Reasonings based on their underlying theories should not be taken into account in describing the safety requirements. Such reasonings should be resolved before describing them. For example, if $f(x)$ implies $g(x)$ based on a particular theory, the fact $f(x) \Rightarrow g(x)$ should be described as a safety requirement. The timing can be dealt with similarly. For example, we show safety requirements that the timing of transmissions between DF and MPU is taken into account. The safety requirements G5 and G7 of Fig. 6 are changed as follows.

G5' *DF.EventuallyReceived('Manual Steering', MPU)* $\Rightarrow$ *S.State= Manual Steering'*

G7' *PD.VoltFailureDetected* $\Rightarrow$ *DF.AlwaysSend('Manual Steering', DF, MPU)*

DF.AlwaysSend ('Manual Steering', DF, MPU) and *DF.ReceivedEventually ('Manual Steering', MPU)* mean that a demand *'Manual Steering'* always sends and it is received eventually respectively. In order to establish the communication, we need the following safety requirement.

G15 *DF.AlwaysSend ('Manual Steering', DF, MPU)* $\Rightarrow$ *DF.EventuallyReceived ('Manual Steering', MPU)*

In temporal logic, this fact is not needed because it is derived by its inference rules. On the other hand, in our approach, we do not rely on the inference rules but explicitly describe what holds about the timing in propositional logic like G15. In this approach, although inconsistencies in the timing might be introduced, it makes underlying logic simple.

We think that our approach is useful to explain the reason why the safety requirements are traceable. We adopted propositional logic to formally describe the safety requirements. Propositional logic is simple and easy to understand. In our approach, a parent goal is derived from sub-goals by inference rules of propositional logic, mainly, Modus Ponens. Such inference rules are also intuitively understandable. Explaining the traceability using such simple and intuitive logic makes it easier to convince others that the safety requirements are traceable. On the other hand, one may think that propositional logic is too simple to describe the safety requirements. In fact, it was possible to describe all of the safety requirements within propositional logic. We think that rich logic is not needed to reason the safety requirements in terms of the traceability because complex computation such as differential equations does not appear in reasoning them. Even if it appears, it should be abstracted as propositional facts for the safety requirements.

8   Conclusion

In this paper, we presented a case study to make safety requirements for ISO 26262. The target of the case study is to develop the safety requirements of EPS. We identified a few major problems of the original document of EPS in its preliminary analysis. To solve those problems, we adopted a goal tree proposed in KAOS and proposed patterns of the goal tree for the safety requirements. We confirmed that the quality of the safety requirements are drastically improved by applying the goal threes and the patterns. In fact, more than half of the safety requirements were modified or added. Such improvements were admitted by engineers developing EPS. What we learned in the case study is as follows. Firstly, propositional logic is sufficient and effective to ensure the traceability of the safety requirements. Ensuring the traceability mainly relies on Modus

Ponens inferences. Secondly, the notion of patterns is well-fitted to the development of safety requirements. There are small variations of essential and typical safety mechanisms. The safety requirements which correspond to them should be defined as the patterns.

Currently, we are developing a tool to manage and verify the safety requirements based on the approach proposed in this paper. The verification is fully automated using a SAT solver [16] because the traceability is verified based on propositional logic. We are going to expand the tool to daily developments of automotive systems after the tool is released.

References

1. ISO 26262 Road vehicles - functional safety (2011)
2. IEC 61508: Functional safety of electrical/electronic/programmable electronic safety-related systems (1998)
3. van Lamsweerde, A.: Requirements Engineering: From System Goals to UML Models to Software Specifications. Wiley, New York (2011)
4. Broy, M., Kruger, I.H., Stauner, T.: Software engineering for automotive systems: a roadmap. In: Future of Software Engineering, pp. 55–71 (2007)
5. Weaver, R.A., Kelly, T.P.: The goal structuring notation-a safety argument notation. Workshop on Assurance Cases, Dependable Systems and Networks (2004)
6. Denney, E., Pai, G., Whiteside, I.: Formal foundations for hierarchical safety cases. In: High Assurance Systems Engineering, pp. 52–59 (2015)
7. Denney, E., Pai, G.: A formal basis for safety case patterns. In: Bitsch, F., Guiochet, J., Kaâniche, M. (eds.) SAFECOMP. LNCS, vol. 8153, pp. 21–32. Springer, Heidelberg (2013)
8. Kelly, T.P., McDermid, J.A.: Safety case construction and reuse using patterns. In: Daniel, P. (ed.) SAFECOMP, pp. 55–69. Springer, London (1997)
9. Rubio-Loyola, J., Serrat, J., Charalambides, M., Flegkas, P., Pavlou, G.: A functional solution for goal-oriented policy refinement. In: Policies for Distributed Systems and Networks, pp. 133–144 (2006)
10. Dwyer, M.B., Avrunin, G.S., Corbett, J.C.: Patterns in property specifications for finite-state verification. In: International Conference on Software Engineering, pp. 411–420 (1999)
11. Darimont, R., van Lamsweerde, A.: Formal refinement patterns for goal-driven requirements elaboration. ACM SIGSOFT Softw. Eng. Notes 21(6), 179–190 (1996)
12. Abrial, J.R.: Modeling in Event-B: System and Software Engineering. Cambridge University Press, Cambridge (2010)
13. Jones, C.B.: Systematic Software Development using VDM, 2nd edn. Prentice Hall International, Upper Saddle River (1990)
14. Spivey, J.M.: The Z Notation: A Reference Manual. Prentice-Hall, New York (1992)
15. Gamma, E., Helm, R., Johnson, R., Vlissides, J.: Design Patterns - Elements of Reusable Object-Oriented Software. Pearson Education, London (1995)
16. Minisat: http://minisat.se/

Software and Systems Analysis

An Approach to Static-Dynamic Software Analysis

Pablo Gonzalez-de-Aledo[1]([⊠]), Pablo Sanchez[1], and Ralf Huuck[2]

[1] University of Cantabria, Santander, Spain
{pabloga,sanchez}@teisa.unican.es
[2] NICTA and UNSW, Sydney, Australia
ralf.huuck@nicta.com.au

Abstract. Safety-critical software in industry is typically subjected to both dynamic testing as well as static program analysis. However, while testing is expensive to scale, static analysis is prone to false positives and/or false negatives. In this work we propose a solution based on a combination of static analysis to zoom into potential bug candidates in large code bases and symbolic execution to confirm these bugs and create concrete witnesses. Our proposed approach is intended to maintain scalability while improving precision and as such remedy the shortcomings of each individual solution. Moreover, we developed the SEEKFAULT tool that creates local symbolic execution targets from static analysis bug candidates and evaluate its effectiveness on the SV-COMP loop benchmarks. We show that a conservative tuning can achieve a 98 % detecting rate in that benchmark while at the same time reducing false positive rates by around 50 % compared to a singular static analysis approach.

1 Introduction

Quality assurance for safety-critical systems is no longer only challenged by hardware reliability and the complexity of the environment these systems are operating in, but to a large degree these systems are suffering from the growth of their software bases. In the automotive space a state-of-the-art car contains over 50 million lines of source code. And although the industry has stringent quality assurance processes in place, complies to strict standards such as ISO 26262 and uses restrictive coding guidelines such as MISRA [1], safety is continuously challenged. As shown by Miller et al. [2,3] modern automobiles are open to numerous attack vectors, almost exclusively being exposed by software bugs such as buffer overruns, null pointer dereferences and command injections.

Pablo gratefully thanks the funding and support of DATA61 and the Australian Government as a Research intern and Fellow Student. Authors acknowledge the funding from projects TEC2011-28666-C04-02, TEC2014-58036-C4-3-R and grant BES-2012-055572, awarded by the Spanish Ministry of Economy and Competitivity.

Funded by the Australian Government through the Department of Communications and the Australian Research Council through the ICT Centre of Excellence Program.

© Springer International Publishing Switzerland 2016
C. Artho and P.C. Ölveczky (Eds.): FTSCS 2015, CCIS 596, pp. 225–240, 2016.
DOI: 10.1007/978-3-319-29510-7_13

Industry has extensive experience designing and testing safety-critical systems. However, the growing software sizes pose problems to many of the existing quality assurance methods and processes. This includes common practices such as dynamic software testing and static program analysis. Software testing does not scale well and is both expensive as well as time consuming. On the other hand, static analysis scales well but suffers from both *false positives* and/or *false negatives*. This means, there are spurious warnings not related to actual defects and instances of software bugs that are part of checked defect classes, but missed. Both false positives as well as false negatives are a serious concern in industry.

In this work we present a first approach that bridges some of the gaps between the existing techniques and their shortcomings. In particular, we present a combination of static program analysis and symbolic dynamic execution to minimize false positives and false negatives, while at the same time maintaining scalability. The core idea is to use static program analysis to broadly zoom in on a potential software defect and treat that as a bug candidate. Next, we make this bug candidate a precise target for symbolic execution. This has a number of advantages:

1. Scalability is maintained by a broad static analysis pass that zooms in on bug candidates.
2. Fine grained symbolic execution has a concrete target as opposed to an unguided crawl, which allows for additional symbolic execution heuristics.
3. Performance can be tuned by relaxing static analysis constraints and removing false negatives at the expense of potential false positives, which in turn can potentially be ruled out by symbolic execution. Conversely, only true positives can be reported where symbolic execution provides a concrete witness execution.

Moreover, we present the first steps of an integrated tool called *SEEKFAULT* using static analysis and symbolic execution, which borrows some of the underlying technology of the respective tools Goanna [4] and Forest [5]. As a first benchmark we apply SEEKFAULT to the loop category of the SV-COMP verification competition set. Relaxing static analysis to allow for over-approximations we are able to detect 98 % of the defect cases in SV-COMP while reducing the false positive rate by over 50 % compared to a single static analysis approach.

The remainder of this paper is structured as follows: In Sect. 2 we present the overall ideas and their relation with existing work. In Sect. 3 we give a brief introduction to the formal verification based static analysis we employ as well as our symbolic execution framework for C/C++ code. This is followed by an explanation of our new combined analysis framework and its architecture in Sect. 4. We present our initial results from the tight integration of static analysis and symbolic execution in Sect. 5 and conclude with a summary and future work in Sect. 6.

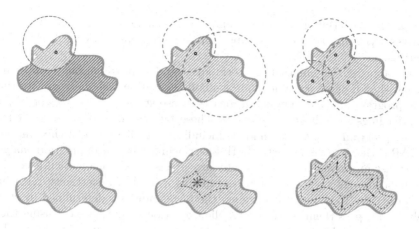

Fig. 1. Top row: static analysis coverage; bottom row: symbolic execution coverage.

2   Overview and Related Work

Software testing is extensively used to validate the safety-critical system (or a unit thereof) against requirements to ensure coverage of both the requirements and the actual code. However, it is well understood that only a fraction of the actual semantic behavior can be realistically tested and many of the known vulnerabilities result from corner cases of a particular input leading to vulnerabilities [2]. For instance, even when a path with a particular division is covered, the semantic case where that divisor happens to become zero might not. As a result even full traditional test coverage does not equate to full semantic coverage.

There are various approaches to remedy this shortcoming including symbolic execution [6] and concolic testing [7,8]. These techniques increase semantic coverage criteria by treating inputs and undetermined return values symbolically. As such, this enables the investigation of an execution not only for a single value, but for a symbolic range of values at once. However, as shown in industry case studies [9,10] symbolic techniques are prone to scalability limitations and current tools are not well suited yet for deep embedded applications. As such, their adoption in safety-critical industries has so far been limited.

One widely used technology in safety-critical industries is static program analysis. Static analysis approximates the behavior of source code and detects common coding violations such as the ones defined by MISRA, but also possible software bugs that lead to runtime errors such as null pointer dereferences, memory leaks and buffer overruns. Many commercial tools are based on earlier academic work and are routinely used in industry [4,11–13]. However, while static analysis is scalable to very large code bases, it approximates program behavior and as such is prone to false positives (false alarms) and/or false negatives (missed bugs).

Static analysis and dynamic testing can be seen as two different approximation methods to cover the program semantics as shown in Fig. 1. While (sound) static analysis over-approximates the program behavior and as such allows false positives, dynamic analysis under-approximates program behaviour leaving false negatives.

Our approach combines both techniques and approximations to obtain a solution that is more scalable than symbolic execution, yet more precise than static program analysis. The main idea is to use static analysis to 'zoom' into potential bugs we call *bug candidates*. These bug candidates are identified by modern program analysis techniques including data flow, model checking and CEGAR-style trace refinement [14]. However, while this type of program analysis can be fast and scalable, it is typically less precise than some actual execution or simulation. As such, there always remains a level of uncertainty regarding false positives. To counter this, we use the bug candidates determined by static analysis and pass them on to a symbolic execution execution pass, using those candidates as local reachability targets. This means, we attempt to confirm that a bug candidate is indeed a real bug. This allows us to boost the rate of true positives. The reachability targets assist additional heuristics that guide the search and are more efficient than classical *crawling* approaches [15].

Bug candidates that cannot be confirmed by symbolic execution remain potential bugs due to the under-approximating nature of symbolic execution unless, however, symbolic execution is able to explore all paths (symbolically) and as such can make a precise decision whether a bug candidate exists or not.

Most of the work in the symbolic execution and the static program analysis area has been focusing on improvements and heuristics in each individual field [15–18]. Combining the different domains gained less attention and is mostly related to improving symbolic execution search strategies by adding static analysis information [19,20]. In [21], Young and Taylor use static analysis to compute a concurrency graph and then to prune equivalent symbolic states by dynamic execution. Their ideas focus on concurrency errors for Ada programs and the goals are similar to symmetry and partial order reduction. Another combined approach is presented in [22]. However, the authors focus on obtaining maximal-coverage test cases for C programs. In contrast, our work focuses on the reach-ability of a set of error locations. Moreover, we use these locations to guide the symbolic execution search while [22] aims at heuristics for path coverage.

3   Our Approach to Static Analysis and Symbolic Execution

We deploy two complementary program analysis techniques: Static code analysis and symbolic execution. As the names suggest, the former is a static technique that takes the source code and builds an abstraction that is analyzed using a range of approaches including model checking and trace refinement. The latter is a dynamic technique that symbolically executes the program under test by building constraints over concrete execution paths and checking their validity using SMT solving.

```
void example() {
l0 :  int i, *q;
l1 :  int* p = malloc(sizeof(int));
      for (l2 :  i = 100000; l3 :  i >= 0; l7 :  i--) {
         l4 :  q = p;
         l5 :  if (i == 0)
            l6 :  free(p);
      }
}
```

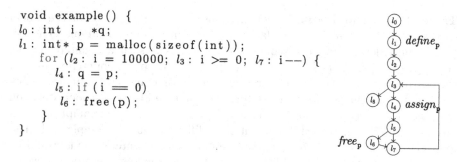

Fig. 2. Original program and automatically annotated CFG.

3.1   Static Analysis Using Model Checking and Trace Refinement

Static analysis comprises a number of techniques including data flow analysis, abstract interpretation and software model checking [18,23]. The approach we use in this work is based on model checking and trace refinement as originated in the Goanna tool [24]. The core ideas are based on the observation that data flow analysis problems can be expressed in modal μ-calculus [25]. This has been developed further by Fehnker et al. in [26] and later expanded in [14].

The main idea is to abstractly represent a program (or a single function) by its control flow graph (CFG) annotated with labels representing propositions of interest. Example propositions are whether memory is allocated or freed in a particular location, whether a pointer variable is assigned *null* or whether it is dereferenced. In this way the possibly infinite state space of a program is reduced to the finite set of locations and their propositions.

The annotated CFG consisting of the transition system and the (atomic) propositions can then be transformed into the input language of a model checker. Static analysis bug patterns can be expressed in temporal logic and evaluated automatically by a model checker. To illustrate the approach, we use a contrived function **example** shown in Fig. 2. It works as follows: First a pointer variable p is initialized and memory is allocated accordingly. Then, in a loop, a second pointer variable q is assigned the address saved in p. After hundred-thousand assignments p is freed and the loop is left.

To automatically check for a use-after-free, i.e., whether the memory allocated for p is still accessed after it is freed, we define atomic propositions for allocating memory $define_p$, freeing memory $free_p$ and accessing memory $assign_p$, and we label the CFG accordingly. The above check can now be expressed in CTL as:

$$\forall p : \mathbf{AG}(define_p \Rightarrow \mathbf{AG}(free_p \Rightarrow \mathbf{AG}\neg assign_p))$$

This means, whenever memory is allocated, after $free_p$ there is no occurrence of a $assign_p$. Note that once a check has been expressed in CTL, the proposition can be generically pre-defined as a template of syntactic tree patterns on the abstract syntax tree of the code and determined automatically. Hence, it is possible to automatically check a wide range of programs for the same requirement.

Trace Refinement Loop. Model checking the above property for the model depicted in Fig. 2 will find a violation and return a counterexample. The following path denoted by the sequence of locations is such a counterexample: $l_0, l_1, l_2, l_3, l_4, l_5, l_6, l_7, l_3, l_4, l_5$. However, if we match up the counterexample in the abstraction with the concrete program, we see that this path cannot possibly be executed, as the condition i == 0 cannot be true in the first loop iteration and, therefore, l_5 to l_6 cannot be taken. This means, the counterexample is spurious and should be discarded. We might get a different counterexample in the last loop iteration $\ldots, l_5, l_6, l_7, l_3, l_4, l_5$. But again, such a counterexample would be spurious, because once the condition i == 0 holds, the loop condition prevents any further iteration.

To detect the validity of a counterexample we subjected the path to a fine-grained simulation using an SMT solver. In essence, we perform a backward simulation of the path computing the *weakest precondition*. If the precondition for the initial state of the path is unsatisfiable, the path is infeasible and the counterexample spurious. We use an efficient SMT encoding and a refinement loop by creating *observer automata* to successively eliminate sets of infeasible traces. For the example in Fig. 2 the approach is able to create two observer automata from minimal unsatisfiable cores of a single path leading to the elimination of all paths of the same nature, i.e., avoiding an unrolling of the loop. This approach is similar to interpolation-based solutions and more details can be found in Junker et al. [14].

False Positives and Tuning. Even in this formal verification based framework of static program analysis there are possibilities for false positives (wrongly warned bugs) and false negatives (missed bugs). This is caused by the abstraction and encoding into the model checker, which is necessarily sound. For instance, certain semantic constructs such as function pointers are typically not modelled and their behaviour is optimistically assumed. And, finally, the false positive elimination itself might time out and a judgment call whether to report a potential bug or not is made.

Industrial static analysis tools regularly make the aforementioned trade-offs. In this work we scale back the potential false negatives and counter the increasing false positives with symbolic execution.

3.2   SMT Solving Based Symbolic Execution

Symbolic execution is a faithful technique to observe program behavior by evaluating it symbolically in an abstract or constraint-based domain [6]. This means, values, variables and expressions are encoded as constraints over program paths and solvers are used to determine the (symbolic) program state at each location. The most common use case is to determine test inputs and coverage criteria [27], which is generalized to the concept of concolic testing [7,8].

These approaches basically divide executions into equivalence classes exhibiting the same behavior under a given symbolic value or constraint of input parameters and path conditions. The advantage of these approaches is the ability to take into account a wide range of (equivalent) inputs within one interpreted execution. However, besides building a faithful symbolic interpreter, the challenges of semantic coverage and dealing with a potentially exponential set of execution paths with respect to the number of decision points remain.

A bug detected by symbolic execution or concolic testing is basically the same as if discovered by dynamic testing. Hence, it provides some concrete validation that the program under test exposes some vulnerability. This is a clear advantage over static program analysis, where false positives are possible and further investigation of the results is often required. The downside is that both from a practical and theoretical point of view, not all execution paths can typically be explored. As such symbolic execution helps for confirming bugs, but less so for ruling them out.

In the following we describe our approach to symbolic execution using multi-process execution and multi-theory SMT solving.

Our Approach to Symbolic Dynamic Execution. Symbolic execution evaluates the code under test using symbolic variables. The symbolic variables can take any value of the replaced concrete variable range they substitute. This is in particular true for free (input) variables. Moreover, all operations on symbolic variables are recorded as a mathematical constraint over a pre-defined logic of an SMT solver as detailed below. In our approach, whenever the evaluator hits a conditional branch, the SMT solver is evaluating the two possible branching outcomes (true and false) to see if any or all of the branches are feasible. As a result, on each path the evaluator keeps a record of the set of constraints that must hold to follow this path and it only keeps the feasible paths in memory. This approach has proven to be a good compromise between generality, i.e., each path is represented as a formula that is valid for different input values, and specificity, i.e., only possible paths are considered, and they are considered explicitly.

To exemplify the approach, we can use the example shown in Fig. 5 and the associated execution tree of Fig. 3. When this example is run in the symbolic execution engine, it is emulated in a virtual environment that logs every access to a variable and every operation performed on a variable. In the example we start at the beginning of $\mathtt{main}$. The first operation that takes place is the assignment of the constant 0 to the variable i. Then i is compared to 10. The framework keeps record of the fact that i comes from a constant, so there is no need to explore two branches in the condition, because only one can be executed. If i was not assigned to the constant 0 at the beginning, i would only have a symbolic assignment when reaching the condition. In that case, an SMT solver is called for the two possible outcomes of the branch, and the branch condition is added to a set of constraints that is independent for every path. If the solver gives a satisfying assignment for that branch output, we obtain two outcomes: Firstly, we know that the path starting at the beginning of $\mathtt{main}$ is feasible. Secondly, we get a concrete input vector for all free variables demonstrating the reachability.

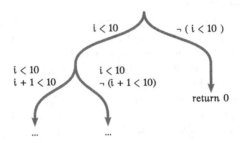

Fig. 3. Tree representation of the execution of program in Fig. 5

Multi-process Execution. As it can be intuitively seen in Fig. 3, the number of paths grows exponentially with the number of branches in the code. To find non-trivial bugs and to scale to larger programs we use parallelization as one of the architectural solutions. This means for every decision point, i.e., every branching, we spawn separate processes for the true and false branches. This enables us to parallelize the SMT solver computation as well as to independently follow different search strategies for different paths.

Multi-theory Solving. Another technique to speed up the process is to adjust the representation of the symbolic variables and their encoding in the SMT solver. For proving certain properties the sign of the variables might be enough or a representation as intervals is appropriate. If we want to account for overflows, or precisely capture sign-extension or bitwise operations, a bit-level representation for every variable is used. Some other representations we support are linear equations, where each variable is represented as a linear formula dependent of input variables, and polynomials, where sets of variables are represented as a polynomial equation. In our work we deploy heuristics to switch between different SMT solver theories dynamically based on the current context [5].

Execution Monitors. While the main goal of symbolic execution is to generate input test vectors, it is possible to instrument the code on top of the symbolic execution framework to introduce *monitors* on it. Those monitors are observer code that check for errors during run-time. For instance, we add a monitor that on every pointer dereference checks that the value of the index to an array is in the range of allocated memory. Monitors can be expressed as SMT-formulas and their generation can be automated avoiding manual code annotations.

Although the semantics of symbolic execution precisely capture the set of program behaviors, the program is still under-approximated, since not all paths can necessarily be explored, neither in theory nor in practice. This is caused by (non-regular) loops and recursion in programs leading to infinitely sized spaces. In order to maximize the set of explored states, different heuristics have been added to these frameworks [15,28]. These heuristics do not solve, however, the fundamental problem of a potentially exponentially growing number of execution paths. Hence, our goal is to use static analysis for defining more constrained bug

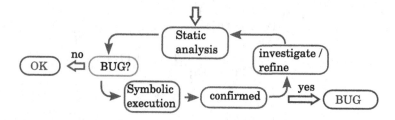

Fig. 4. SEEKFAULT architecture: static-dynamic integration.

candidates and provide a guidance of the symbolic execution framework in the search strategy.

4   An Integrated Static-Dynamic Approach

4.1   Architecture

We illustrate our approach in Fig. 4: We start off with a static security analysis phase. If there is no vulnerability found the process stops. Otherwise, we submit the bug candidate to the symbolic execution engine. If the symbolic execution engine is able to confirm the issue it generates a concrete trace and an input vector. Otherwise, the bug candidate is neither confirmed nor ruled out automatically and needs to be subjected to a manual investigation. Depending on that outcome either the issue will be manually confirmed or it proves to be a false positive that can be used to improve the static analysis checking algorithm or the exact CTL specification.

4.2   Implementation

We implement our approach in a new tool called SEEKFAULT. The SEEK-FAULT engine makes use of two approaches: Static analysis based on model checking and SMT-based trace refinement as used in Goanna [29], and symbolic execution based on multi-theory SMT solving as used in Forest [5]. Z3 is used as the underlying SMT solver. SEEKFAULT itself is developed in a mixture of C/C++ and OCaml.

At the current stage of development, the integrated SEEKFAULT tool first runs a static analysis pass to determine bug candidates and for each potential bug creates location information as well as a possible counter-example trace that is then passed on to the dynamic execution phase. Unlike traditional symbolic execution, the combined approach in SEEKFAULT enables new search heuristics by applying the trace information as well as by using the bug locations as *reachability targets*. For instance, as one heuristic, we calculate a distance measure from the last visited node in the program to the reachability target. This distance is computed statically over the control flow graph. The symbolic execution engine can then use that distance to sort the set of candidate paths during the guided search. To do so, we use the standard A* graph traversal algorithm.

```
int main (...) {
  int a[10];
  int i;
  for(i=0; i < 10; i++){
    a[i] = 10;
  }
  a[i] = 0;
  return 0;
}
```

Fig. 5. Overflow detection static analysis

Finally, we use time outs on each branch of the symbolic execution if we are unable to reach a particular target.

5   Experiments

In this section we outline some of the experiments we performed and some of the experiences we gained so far. While implementation for larger projects is still underway, it provides some valuable results.

5.1   Examples

We firstly demonstrate our idea by some examples from our internal test suite. The first example program is shown in Fig. 5. An array with 10 elements ranging form 0 to 9 is initialized in a loop. However, in the last loop iteration the counter is increased to one beyond the array size and the subsequent access to that array would result in an out of bounds violation.

This error can be detected by our SEEKFAULT static analysis engine alone as the following command shows:

```
$ seekfault --static-only overflow.c
 SEEKFAULT - analyzing file overflow.c
 line 5: warning: Array 'a' subscript 10 is out of bounds [0,9].
```

For that example the analyzer is able to determine the array bounds as well as the number of loop iterations that are executed and, therefore, can derive the buffer overrun. However, in certain scenarios when the complexity of reasoning is increased by for instance copying memory around or reasoning about strings, the analysis might lose precision. We do not warn in the latter cases. An example is shown in Fig. 6. In the example, the buffer overflow introduces a real vulnerability, as it can be used to write in the memory occupied by the variable access, and grant the access to the application with an incorrect password.

This occurs when the size of the string passed as first parameter to the program is larger than 10 characters. In that case, the strcpy function writes in a space that was not allocated to store the variable password_buffer, but for

```
void main (...) {
  char password_buffer [10];
  int access = 0;
  strcpy(password_buffer, argv[1]);
  if (!strcmp(password_buffer, "passwd"))
    access = 1;
  printf("Access %d", access);
}
```

Fig. 6. Overflow detection symbolic execution

access. Once access is overwritten with a different value than the initial 0, the access to the application is granted.

To be able to detect these kind of errors we tune the static analysis engine of SEEKFAULT to always emit an error when it is not certain that a bug is absent. This means it will generate a vulnerability candidate for the example in Fig. 6. Moreover, using our symbolic execution engine on the target location of the static analysis candidate we get a concrete confirmation of that bug. The SEEKFAULT engine produces:

```
$ seekfault pwd.c
SEEKFAULT - analyzing file pwd.c
line 5: Array 'password_buffer' subscript 10 is out of bounds:
Symbolic analysis:
Testcase  12 : aaaaaaaaac\0
Testcase  13 : aaaaaaaaba\0
Testcase  14 : aaaaaaaaaba\0 < BufferOverflow
```

This shows this two-tiered approach where static analysis defined the bug candidate and symbolic execution is able to provide a real exploitable scenario in case the input is the aaaaaaaaaba\0 string.

5.2   SV-COMP Benchmark Results

For the evaluation of our integrated solution we use the well known SV-COMP benchmark[1], in particular, the *loop* category. SV-COMP is a set of competition benchmarks used in the automated verification community to highlight complex verification problems and to test the strength of individual tools.

The loop category is comprised of 117 files. All of the test cases expose a potential error, but only a minority of 34 files exhibit a real bug. Hence, any brute force approach by warning at any uncertainty will overwhelmingly exhibit false positives.

We show the results of our integrated approach in Table 1. This table is broken down by the different analysis phases as well as the final verdict, where *SA* denotes static analysis, *SE* symbolic execution and *SF* SEEKFAULT. A tick

---

[1] http://sv-comp.sosy-lab.org/.

means proven to be correct, a cross that a bug has been confirmed and a warning triangle means for static analysis that it flags a potential issue and for symbolic execution that it times out. The file names shaded in gray are those containing a bug.

We have broken the table in five groups, which are separated by horizontal lines.

1. In the first set of examples, the static analysis engine is able to conclude that the program is correct. This is because our static analysis phase over-approximates the possible behavior and the program does not contain any approximation breaking constructs such as function pointers.
2. In the second group, SEEKFAULT's static analysis engine produces some potential bug candidates that are passed to the symbolic analysis pass. However, the symbolic analysis engine was able to faithfully cover all the possible branches in the program and conclude that all of them are bug-free.
3. In the third group, the full potential of the SEEKFAULT approach is shown. In these cases static analysis concludes that there is a potential bug in the code and provides a set of candidate locations that exhibit the undesired behavior. This set of locations is used as target locations for the symbolic execution heuristics. In each case SEEKFAULT was able to find the bug and provide a test case that demonstrates this behavior.
4. In the next two groups, the relaxation of the rules in the static analysis tool makes the analysis to produce error candidates in programs that however do not exhibit undesired behavior under the fully-accurate semantics of the operations of the program. The set of feasible paths, however, is too big to be fully exercised by symbolic execution, so under the requirements of a sound analysis, the algorithm has to output an inconclusive output. We observe, however that the fact of having a concrete goal to reach helps a lot in the symbolic execution framework so most of these cases (41 over 43) are actually correct. Considering the two remaining cases as correct would break the soundness of the approach but would leave us with an error rate of only 2/117.

In summary, the combined approach has a detection rate (number of detected errors over files with an error) of 98 %. The true negative rate of the combined approach (number of files "proven" as correct when they are correct) is 35 %, which is approximately 50 % above the rate obtained by only using a static analysis approach.

5.3   Observations and Limitations

It is worth noting some observations: Firstly, our SEEKFAULT solution is quite capable of detecting bugs. All bugs have been identified by SEEKFAULT and all apart from two have been confirmed with symbolic execution inputs and traces. Secondly, the SEEKFAULT approach gives a slightly better coverage to demonstrate the absence of bugs compared to single static analysis approach.

Table 1. Results of each engine and the integrated SEEKFAULT solution. SA = static analysis, SE = symbolic execution, SF = SEEKFAULT, gray = bug

Filename	SA	SE	SF	Filename	SA	SE	SF	Filename	SA	SE	SF
nested6_true-u...	✓	⚠	✓	simple_false-u...	⚠	✗	✗	functions_true...	⚠	⚠	⚠
nested9_true-u...	✓	⚠	✓	terminator_01_...	⚠	✗	✗	simple_true-un...	⚠	⚠	⚠
heapsort_true-...	✓	⚠	✓	underapprox_fa...	⚠	✗	✗	simple_true-un...	⚠	⚠	⚠
apache-escape-...	✓	⚠	✓	sum01_bug02_su...	⚠	✗	✗	simple_true-un...	⚠	⚠	⚠
apache-get-tag...	✓	⚠	✓	while_infinite...	⚠	✗	✗	SpamAssassin-1...	⚠	⚠	⚠
count_by_k_tru...	✓	⚠	✓	for_bounded_lo...	⚠	✗	✗	sum03_true-unr...	⚠	⚠	⚠
diamond_true-u...	✓	⚠	✓	count_up_down_...	⚠	✗	✗	trex03_true-un...	⚠	⚠	⚠
gj2007_true-un...	✓	⚠	✓	sum01_bug02_fa...	⚠	✗	✗	count_up_down_...	⚠	⚠	⚠
gr2006_true-un...	✓	⚠	✓	sum01_false-un...	⚠	✗	✗	ddlm2013_true-...	⚠	⚠	⚠
seq_true-unrea...	✓	⚠	✓	sum04_false-un...	⚠	✗	✗	jm2006_true-un...	⚠	⚠	⚠
down_true-unre...	✓	⚠	✓	terminator_02_...	⚠	✗	✗	jm2006_variant...	⚠	⚠	⚠
phases_true-un...	✓	⚠	✓	trex02_false-u...	⚠	✗	✗	overflow_true-...	⚠	⚠	⚠
up_true-unreac...	✓	⚠	✓	sum03_false-un...	⚠	✗	✗	half_true-unre...	⚠	⚠	⚠
bhmr2007_true-...	✓	⚠	✓	trex03_false-u...	⚠	✗	✗	nest-if3_true-...	⚠	⚠	⚠
hhk2008_true-u...	✓	⚠	✓	terminator_03_...	⚠	✗	✗	MADWiFi-encode...	⚠	⚠	⚠
half_2_true-un...	✓	⚠	✓	trex01_false-u...	⚠	✗	✗	trex04_true-un...	⚠	⚠	⚠
string_concat-...	✓	⚠	✓	simple_false-u...	⚠	✗	✗	trex01_true-un...	⚠	⚠	⚠
eureka_01_true...	✓	✓	✓	functions_fals...	⚠	✗	✗	sum01_true-unr...	⚠	⚠	⚠
n.c40_true-unr...	✓	✓	✓	simple_false-u...	⚠	✗	✗	string_true-un...	⚠	⚠	⚠
lu.cmp_true-un...	⚠	✓	✓	overflow_false...	⚠	✗	✗	vogal_true-unr...	⚠	⚠	⚠
veris.c_sendma...	⚠	✓	✓	phases_false-u...	⚠	✗	✗	afnp2014_true-...	⚠	⚠	⚠
eureka_05_true...	⚠	✓	✓	eureka_01_fals...	⚠	✗	✗	array_true-unr...	⚠	⚠	⚠
cggmp2005_true...	⚠	✓	✓	id_trans_false...	⚠	✗	✗	array_true-unr...	⚠	⚠	⚠
diamond_true-u...	⚠	✓	✓	string_false-u...	⚠	✗	✗	array_true-unr...	⚠	⚠	⚠
underapprox_tr...	⚠	✓	✓	vogal_false-un...	⚠	✗	✗	array_true-unr...	⚠	⚠	⚠
large_const_tr...	⚠	✓	✓	NetBSD_loop_tr...	⚠	⚠	⚠	cggmp2005b_tru...	⚠	⚠	⚠
nec40_true-unr...	⚠	✓	✓	sendmail-close...	⚠	⚠	⚠	const_true-unr...	⚠	⚠	⚠
sum04_true-unr...	⚠	✓	✓	simple_true-un...	⚠	⚠	⚠	count_by_1_tru...	⚠	⚠	⚠
terminator_02_...	⚠	✓	✓	terminator_03_...	⚠	⚠	⚠	count_by_1_var...	⚠	⚠	⚠
array_false-un...	⚠	✗	✗	trex02_true-un...	⚠	⚠	⚠	count_by_2_tru...	⚠	⚠	⚠
array_false-un...	⚠	✗	✗	css2003_true-u...	⚠	⚠	⚠	count_by_nonde...	⚠	⚠	⚠
const_false-un...	⚠	✗	✗	n.c11_true-unr...	⚠	⚠	⚠	gauss_sum_true...	⚠	⚠	⚠
diamond_false-...	⚠	✗	✗	while_infinite...	⚠	⚠	⚠	gj2007b_true-u...	⚠	⚠	⚠
diamond_false-...	⚠	✗	✗	while_infinite...	⚠	⚠	⚠	gsv2008_true-u...	⚠	⚠	⚠
ludcmp_false-u...	⚠	✗	✗	while_infinite...	⚠	⚠	⚠	id_build_true-...	⚠	⚠	⚠
multivar_false...	⚠	✗	✗	cggmp2005_vari...	⚠	⚠	⚠	multivar_true-...	⚠	⚠	⚠
nec11_false-un...	⚠	✗	✗	for_infinite_1...	⚠	⚠	⚠	nested_true-un...	⚠	⚠	⚠
phases_false-u...	⚠	✗	✗	for_infinite_1...	⚠	⚠	⚠	nec20_false-un...	⚠	⚠	⚠
simple_false-u...	⚠	✗	✗	fragtest_simpl...	⚠	⚠	⚠	verisec_NetBSD...	⚠	⚠	⚠

However, the SEEKFAULT solution is not yet very capable to prove the absence of bugs in general.

Having said that, the SV-COMP results need to be taken with a grain of salt: Many of the competition tools are variants of bounded model checking tools that declare a program bug free if no violation up to a certain bound can be found.

In our case, if we declared a program bug free when both SEEKFAULT phases cannot come to a combined negative conclusion, we would correctly identify all benchmark cases apart from two, keeping the overall error rate at around 1 %. This is better than the rate exhibited by more mature state-of-the-art tools in this set of programs.

Finally, we expect SEEKFAULT to shine outside the small but very complex SV-COMP cases. The main reason is that symbolic execution adds a lot of precision to static analysis, but is typically hampered by scalability. In the SEEKFAULT approach, however, static analysis takes care of scalability and provides local bug candidates that should be easier to identify. Implementation work for those additional experiments is underway.

6   Conclusions

In this work we presented an integrated approach of static program analysis and symbolic execution. In this new two-phased solution static analysis is tuned to not miss bugs at the expense of higher false positives, which are filtered in the second phase using symbolic execution. We implemented the solution in the tool SEEKFAULT.

Our experiments on the challenging SV-COMP benchmark shows a 98 % vulnerability detection rate with a 50 % reduced false positive rate compared to a singular static analysis solution. Moreover, the overall true negative rate remains at around 35 %, which is quite reasonable for this set of benchmarks. However, overall the false positive rate is still too high, unless we add the soundness breaking assumption that inconclusive symbolic execution results indicate the absence of a bug.

Future work is to experiment on larger open source projects. Our conjecture is that most detectable bugs are less complex than the SV-COMP ones and we should see lower false positive rates. However, this will largely depend on the scalability results for the symbolic execution phase. Earlier experiments with the use of reachability targets, however, showed that our symbolic analysis scales well to around several hundred to thousand lines of code.

Moreover, right now we still manually adjust the static analysis engine whenever possible to feedback the new information we gained from the symbolic execution phase. Another line of future work is to investigate a learning mechanism to at least partially automate that process.

References

1. MISRA Ltd: MISRA-C:2004 Guidelines for the use of the C language in Critical Systems. MISRA, October 2004
2. Miller, C., Valasek, C.: A survey of remote automotive attack surfaces. Black Hat USA (2014)

3. Checkoway, S., McCoy, D., Kantor, B., Anderson, D., Shacham, H., Savage, S., Koscher, K., Czeskis, A., Roesner, F., Kohno, T., et al.: Comprehensive experimental analyses of automotive attack surfaces. In: USENIX Security Symposium, San Francisco (2011)
4. Huuck, R.: Technology transfer: formal analysis, engineering, and business value. Sci. Comput. Program. **103**, 3–12 (2015)
5. Gonzalez-de-Aledo, P., Sanchez, P.: Framework for embedded system verification. In: Baier, C., Tinelli, C. (eds.) TACAS 2015. LNCS, vol. 9035, pp. 429–431. Springer, Heidelberg (2015)
6. Clarke, L.A.: A system to generate test data and symbolically execute programs. IEEE Trans. Softw. Eng. **2**(3), 215–222 (1976)
7. Sen, K., Marinov, D., Agha, G.: CUTE: a concolic unit testing engine for C. In: Proceedings of the 10th European Software Engineering Conference, ESEC/FSE-13, pp. 263–272. ACM, New York, NY, USA (2005)
8. Godefroid, P., Klarlund, N., Sen, K.: Dart: directed automated random testing. In: Programming Language Design and Implementation (PLDI) (2005)
9. Qu, X., Robinson, B.: A case study of concolic testing tools and their limitations. In: International Symposium on Empirical Software Engineering and Measurement (ESEM), pp. 117–126, September 2011
10. Cadar, C., Godefroid, P., Khurshid, S., Păsăreanu, C.S., Sen, K., Tillmann, N., Visser, W.: Symbolic execution for software testing in practice: preliminary assessment. In: Proceedings of the 33rd International Conference on Software Engineering, ICSE 2011, pp. 1066–1071. ACM, New York (2011)
11. Bessey, A., Block, K., Chelf, B., Chou, A., Fulton, B., Hallem, S., Henri-Gros, C., Kamsky, A., McPeak, S., Engler, D.: A few billion lines of code later: using static analysis to find bugs in the real world. Commun. ACM **53**(2), 66–75 (2010)
12. GrammaTech: CodeSurfer. http://www.grammatech.com/
13. O'Hearn, P.W., Calcagno, C., Distefano, D., Lee, O., Cook, B., Yang, H., Berdine, J.: Scalable shape analysis for systems code. In: Gupta, A., Malik, S. (eds.) CAV 2008. LNCS, vol. 5123, pp. 385–398. Springer, Heidelberg (2008)
14. Junker, M., Huuck, R., Fehnker, A., Knapp, A.: SMT-based false positive elimination in static program analysis. In: Aoki, T., Taguchi, K. (eds.) ICFEM 2012. LNCS, vol. 7635, pp. 316–331. Springer, Heidelberg (2012)
15. Marre, B., Mouy, P., Williams, N., Roger, M.: PathCrawler: automatic generation of path tests by combining static and dynamic analysis. In: Dal Cin, M., Kaâniche, M., Pataricza, A. (eds.) EDCC 2005. LNCS, vol. 3463, pp. 281–292. Springer, Heidelberg (2005)
16. Cadar, C., Sen, K.: Symbolic execution for software testing: three decades later. Commun. ACM **56**(2), 82–90 (2013)
17. Escalona, M.J., Gutierrez, J.J., Mejías, M., Aragón, G., Ramos, I., Torres, J., Domínguez, F.J.: An overview on test generation from functional requirements. J. Syst. Softw. **84**(8), 1379–1393 (2011)
18. D'Silva, V., Kroening, D., Weissenbacher, G.: A survey of automated techniques for formal software verification. IEEE Trans. Comput.-Aided Des. Integr. Circ. Syst. (TCAD) **27**(7), 1165–1178 (2008)
19. Pasareanu, C.S., Visser, W.: A survey of new trends in symbolic execution for software testing and analysis. Int. J. Softw. Tools Technol. Transf. **11**(4), 339–353 (2009)
20. Qu, X., Robinson, B.: A case study of concolic testing tools and their limitations. In: International Symposium on Empirical Software Engineering and Measurement (ESEM), pp. 117–126, September 2011

21. Young, M., Taylor, R.N.: Combining static concurrency analysis with symbolic execution. IEEE Trans. Softw. Eng. **14**(10), 1499–1511 (1988)
22. Williams, N., Mouy, P., Roger, M., Marre, B.: PathCrawler: automatic generation of path tests by combining static and dynamic analysis. In: Dal Cin, M., Kaâniche, M., Pataricza, A. (eds.) EDCC 2005. LNCS, vol. 3463, pp. 281–292. Springer, Heidelberg (2005)
23. Nielson, F., Nielson, H.R., Hankin, C.L.: Principles of Program Analysis. Springer, Berlin (1999)
24. Fehnker, A., Seefried, S., Huuck, R.: Counterexample guided path reduction for static program analysis. In: Dams, D., Hannemann, U., Steffen, M. (eds.) Concurrency, Compositionality, and Correctness. LNCS, vol. 5930, pp. 322–341. Springer, Heidelberg (2010)
25. Schmidt, D.A., Steffen, B.: Program analysis *as* model checking of abstract interpretations. In: Levi, G. (ed.) SAS 1998. LNCS, vol. 1503, pp. 351–380. Springer, Heidelberg (1998)
26. Fehnker, A., Huuck, R., Jayet, P., Lussenburg, M., Rauch, F.: Model checking software at compile time. In: Proceedings of the First Joint IEEE/IFIP Symposium on Theoretical Aspects of Software Engineering, TASE 2007, pp. 45–56. IEEE Computer Society, Washington, DC, USA (2007)
27. Cadar, C., Dunbar, D., Engler, D.: Klee: Unassisted and automatic generation of high-coverage tests for complex systems programs. In: Proceedings of the 8th USENIX Conference on Operating Systems Design and Implementation, OSDI 2008, pp. 209–224. USENIX Association, Berkeley, CA, USA (2008)
28. Burnim, J., Sen, K.: Heuristics for scalable dynamic test generation. In: Proceedings of the 2008 23rd IEEE/ACM International Conference on Automated Software Engineering. ASE 2008, pp. 443–446. IEEE Computer Society, Washington, DC, USA (2008)
29. Bradley, M., Cassez, F., Fehnker, A., Given-Wilson, T., Huuck, R.: High performance static analysis for industry. ENTCS, Third Workshop on Tools for Automatic Program Analysis (TAPAS 2012), vol. 289, pp. 3–14 (2012)

Towards Verifying VDM Using SPIN

Hsin-Hung Lin[(✉)], Yoichi Omori, Shigeru Kusakabe, and Keijiro Araki

School of Information Science and Electrical Engineering,
Kyushu University, Fukuoka, Japan
{h-lin,yomori,kusakabe}@ait.kyushu-u.ac.jp, araki@csce.kyushu-u.ac.jp

Abstract. The Vienna Development Method (VDM) is a formal method that supports modeling and analysis of software systems at various levels of abstraction. Case studies have shown that applying VDM, or formal specification, in general, in software development processes is the key to achieving high-quality software development. However, to derive full benefit from the use of VDM in software development, associative activities such as validating and verifying VDM models are crucial. Since the primary way of verifying a VDM model is specification animation, we aim to utilize the animation feature of VDM to apply model checking techniques. In this paper, we propose an approach to supporting model check VDM models by constructing a hybrid verification model combining VDMJ, a VDM interpreter, and SPIN, one of the most popular model checkers, especially in practical use. Two case studies are reported, and the usability, scalability, and efficiency of our approach are discussed.

Keywords: Vienna Development Method · SPIN · Model checking

1 Introduction

The Vienna Development Method (VDM) [5,6,13] is a formal method which supports modeling and analysis of software systems at various levels of abstraction. A VDM specification, i.e. software specifications described in a VDM model, uses a combination of implicit and/or explicit definitions of functionalities to describe software specifications acquired from software requirements.

VDM has a strong record of industrial application for design and specification of software systems [14,15,17]. The well-known basic benefits of using VDM to describe software specifications are from the accuracy and unambiguity of VDM, which is common for other formal methods like B or Z. However, to derive the full benefit from VDM to achieve high-quality software development, validation and verification of VDM models are crucial. For example, the FeliCa IC card development team [23] takes the testing (specification animation) approach to validating the specifications of FeliCa IC card written in VDM++ [6] models, a dialect of VDM specification language. The FeliCa IC card development team

This work was partly supported by KAKENHI, Grant-in-Aid for Scientific Research(S) 24220001.

ⓒ Springer International Publishing Switzerland 2016
C. Artho and P.C. Ölveczky (Eds.): FTSCS 2015, CCIS 596, pp. 241–256, 2016.
DOI: 10.1007/978-3-319-29510-7_14

put the most effort on the issues of how to construct the style of VDM++ models and the design of test cases for better confidence in software quality.

On the other hand, when considering concurrency and/or reactivity of software systems, it is not enough to specify each functionality with pre/post-conditions and invariants. This is because (1) the dynamic properties related to execution runs/traces of a concurrent/reactive system are more important and usually formalized using temporal logics, and (2) the correctness of temporal properties and constraints specified in a VDM model is hard to be validated by pure testing/animation. In this case, techniques like model checking [4] can help a lot.

Since testing is the primary means to validate/verify a VDM model, there is not yet any direct way of applying model checking on VDM models. Model translation, for example, to translate VDM to Alloy [20], is considered. However, data types and expressions in VDM are translated in a limited way since VDM has abstract but rich data types and expressions. Therefore, we take a different approach that utilizes the animation feature of VDM for applying model checking techniques.

In our approach, we construct a hybrid verification model combining a VDM interpreter VDMJ [1], and PROMELA, the modeling language of SPIN [9] model checker. More specifically, in a PROMELA model, the embedded C code feature of SPIN is applied to incorporate VDMJ's functionality of evaluating corresponding VDM expressions based on VDM models to be checked. By our approach, we model check VDM models by interpretation, not model translation. Instead, implementations for incorporating VDMJ are needed instead.

One of the advantages of our approach we want to address is the extensibility to other VDM dialects. Our approach can check every dialect of VDM as long as there is a supporting interpreter, and the VDM dialect's features are handled appropriately in embedded C code. In fact, VDMJ supports every dialect of VDM including VDM-SL, VDM++, and VDM-RT.

The structure of this paper is as follows: Sect. 2 gives a brief introduction to the basic knowledge of VDM and SPIN; Sect. 3 explains our approach, including the definitions of a hybrid model and the construction of a hybrid model by combining PROMELA and VDMJ; Sect. 4 demonstrates two case studies with discussions; Sect. 5 describes the related work and clarifies the position of our approach; Sect. 6 gives conclusions and the future plans.

2   Preliminaries

In this section, we give some introductions about the basic knowledge of the technologies used in this paper.

2.1   The Vienna Development Method

The Vienna Development Method (VDM) was originally developed in the 1970's at the IBM laboratories in Vienna [3]. The VDM Specification Language

```
1 module SIMPLE
2 exports all
3 definitions
4
5 types
6   myNat = nat
7   inv n == n in set {0,...,9};
8
9 state S of
10    pool : set of myNat
11    init s == s = mk_S({0,4,9})
12    inv s == s <> mk_S({2,8}) /* two danger numbers */
13 end
14
15 operations
16    putintoS : set of myNat ==> set of myNat
17    putintoS(a) == ( pool := pool union a; return pool )
18    pre card a <= 2 and card a > 0
19    post card pool >= card pool~;
20
21    takefromS : set of myNat ==> set of myNat
22    takefromS(a) == ( pool := pool \ a; return pool )
23    pre card a <= 2 and card a > 0
24    post card pool <= card pool~;
25 end SIMPLE
```

Fig. 1. A simple VDM-SL model: SIMPLE module

(VDM-SL) is a higher-order language with formally defined syntax and semantics [18,19]. VDM provides various abstract data types: basic types such as booleans, natural numbers, and tokens; advanced types such as record, product, set, and map. Typed variables (state) may be restricted by invariants and operations/functions may be specified with preconditions and postconditions. For example, Fig. 1 shows a VDM-SL model, module SIMPLE, with a state of a pool of digits represented by a set of numbers from 0 to 9. The module has operations that can put or take numbers in/from the pool. Invariants for type myNat and state S are specified as well as pre/postconditions of operations putintoS and takefromS. From this example, it is easy to understand that there are two essential parts of a VDM model: (1) constraints: pre/post-conditions and invariants, and (2) abstract data type and corresponding operators for specifying functionalities of a system.

Existing tools such as Overture Tool [16] and VDMTools [7] provide graphical user interfaces for easy editing/building of VDM models. These tools also provide functionalities such as type/syntax checking and testing/animation (execution by the interpreter [19]) for validation and verification of VDM models.

There are other dialects of VDM: VDM++ [6] and VDM Real-Time (VDM-RT) [26]. VDM++ is the extension of VDM-SL with object-orient concepts;

VDM-RT further extends VDM++ with scheduling controls of threads or processes. Our approach applies to both VDM-SL and VDM++ though the construction of verification models will be slightly different from each other. We use VDMJ [1] as the engine of executing VDM expressions based on specified VDM models. VDMJ is a Java implementation of VDM interpreter, which is used as the base interpreter of Overture Tool.

2.2 The SPIN Model Checker

Model checking [4] is a promising verification technology for both hardware and software systems. The basic idea of model checking is to explore the state space of a system systemically, and various techniques and tools are developed. Among these tools, the SPIN model checker [9] is one of the most popular model checkers especially in practical use such as mission critical software verification [10].

From the model specified in PROMELA with given properties to be checked, SPIN will generate a verifier pan.c that is the C program performs the model checking. Several configurable settings are provided to tune the verification process to match available computing resources such as CPU and memory usage.

SPIN has a special feature called *embedded C code* that incorporates external C codes in PROMELA model [12]. With this feature, verifying a hybrid model that consists of behavior fragments specified in PROMELA and specified by external code is possible. Usually, the external code is part of the target software itself, and PROMELA fragments capture the environment or user behavior against the software. In our approach, the external code plays the role of executing a VDM model through VDMJ interactively guided by the PROMELA fragments.

3   Model Checking VDM Using SPIN

In this section, we firstly show the basic idea of our approach, the hybrid verification model concept, then give definitions related to the construction of a hybrid verification model. Finally, we describe our implementation strategy.

3.1   Hybrid Model

Figure 2 shows the concept of hybrid verification model in our approach. The concept is inspired by SPIN's embedded C and take VDM models into consideration. A hybrid model is considered a statechart-like finite transition system where global variables and VDM models of a system are defined. In this system, current state location and values of global (state) variables together represent the overall state space. Although only one transition of the transition system is showed, it is easy to analogize from UML state diagrams: a transition is in the *[condition]/action* style where *condition* represents the guard of executing *action*, and a state may have entry/exit actions. An action on a transition may evaluate functions/operations of defined VDM models and update the values of corresponding global variables.

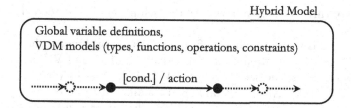

Fig. 2. A hybrid model

3.2 Hybrid Model as Extended Automata

Although we analogize UML state diagrams to our hybrid model, we do not restrict our hybrid model to a UML state diagram model. Here we define the hybrid model as an extended automaton system that consists of definitions of global variables and VDM models. Before defining the extended automaton, we define the notation of a VDM model at first in Definition 1.

Definition 1 (VDM Model). *A VDM model is represented as a 6-tuple:* $\mathcal{M} =$ (*Types, Var, Values, Inv, Fun, Ope), where*

- *Types is the finite set of types.*
- *Var is the finite set of variables (states);*
    - *type(v) $\in$ Types is the type of $v \in$ Var.*
- *Values is the finite set of values (constants);*
    - *type(v') $\in$ Types is the type of $v' \in$ Values.*
- *inv = {inv_t | t $\in$ Types} $\cup$ {inv_Var} is the finite set of invariants;*
- *Fun is the finite set of functions.*
    - *in_f and out_f represent the type signature of input and output of $f \in$ Fun respectively;*
    - *pre_f and post_f represent the precondition and postcondition of $f \in$ Fun respectively.*
- *Ope is the finite set of operations.*
    - *in_op and out_op represent the type signature of input and output of op $\in$ Ope respectively;*
    - *pre_op and post_op represent the precondition and postcondition of op $\in$ Ope respectively.*

Definition 1 shows that a VDM model consists of several definition blocks: types, values, variables, invariants, functions, and operations. The definition blocks are abstracted from a subset of VDM-SL and VDM++ syntax since it is not necessary to look into the detailed syntax of VDM when focusing on the construction of a hybrid verification model. For the purpose of verification, it is reasonable seeing a VDM model as one module (VDM-SL) or class (VDM++) containing these definition blocks. For convenience, we will focus on VDM-SL models and use the module shown in Fig. 1 as the explanatory example in the remainder of this section. We now give the definition of an extended automaton called EA^{VDM}.

Definition 2 is the automaton definition of the hybrid model shown in Fig. 2. An EA^{VDM} is a finite automaton with global variables and VDM models specified. In Definition 2, the set of variables V includes (state) variables defined in the VDM model $\mathcal{M}$. Also, a variable in V is allowed to be of the type defined in $\mathcal{M}$. For an event/action on a transition, the guard condition is a Boolean expression, and the update function is an expression composed of a sequence of arithmetic expressions. The expressions used in an EA^{VDM} may update the global variables including (state) variables defined in the VDM model.[1]

Definition 2 (EA^{VDM}). *Given a VDM model $\mathcal{M} = ($ Types$_{\mathcal{M}}$, Var$_{\mathcal{M}}$, Values$_{\mathcal{M}}$, Inv$_{\mathcal{M}}$, Fun$_{\mathcal{M}}$, Ope$_{\mathcal{M}}$), a hybrid model is an extended automaton EA^{VDM}: $\mathcal{P} = (\mathcal{S}, s_0, \mathcal{V}, \mathcal{E}, \mathcal{T}, \mathcal{A}, \mathcal{F})$, where*

- $\mathcal{S}$ *is the finite set of locations;*
- $s_0 \in \mathcal{S}$ *is the initial location;*
- $\mathcal{V}$ *is the finite set of variables. Var$_{\mathcal{M}} \in V$.*
- ρ *is the finite set of mappings from type signatures to subsets of variables;*
- $\mathcal{E} = \mathcal{G} \times \Theta$ *is the finite set of events/actions;*
    - $\mathcal{G}$ *is the finite set of guard conditions;*
    - Θ *is the finite set of variable update functions;*
- $\mathcal{A}$ *is the finite set of propositions;*
- $\mathcal{T} \subseteq \mathcal{S} \times \mathcal{E} \times \mathcal{S}$ *is the finite set of transitions.*
- $\mathcal{F} \subseteq \mathcal{S}$ *is the finite set of final states;*

In an expression, either boolean or arithmetic, if a function or operation defined in the VDM model is involved, the evaluation is not computed directly but instead the VDM interpreter is invoked for the evaluation. For this case, we define evaluation functions in Definition 3. In Definition 3, an evaluation requires specifying the related VDM expression for evaluating a function/operation along with corresponding variables as the inputs and outputs. The evaluation functions evaluate a VDM expression with specified input variables and assign the evaluation result to the specified output variables.

Definition 3 (VDM Evaluation Function). *For a VDM model $\mathcal{M} = ($ Types$_{\mathcal{M}}$, Var$_{\mathcal{M}}$, Fun$_{\mathcal{M}}$, Ope$_{\mathcal{M}}$), and a set of variables $\mathcal{V}$ where $\forall v \in \mathcal{V}, type(v) \in$ Types$_{\mathcal{M}}$.*

- $eval_{VDM} = 2^{\mathcal{V}} \times (Fun_{\mathcal{M}} \cup Ope_{\mathcal{M}}) \times 2^{\mathcal{V}} \rightarrow ()\ |\ Error$
- $booleval_{VDM} = 2^{\mathcal{V}} \times (Fun_{\mathcal{M}} \cup Ope_{\mathcal{M}}) \rightarrow Bool\ |\ Error$

In Definition 3, we defined two evaluation functions for boolean and arithmetic expressions. For boolean expressions mainly used as a guard condition of a transition, only a truth value is returned. For arithmetic expressions mainly used as actions of a transition, assigning the result to output variables is included.

---

[1] To avoid ambiguity, in Definition 2, S is called location to distinguish from state variables.

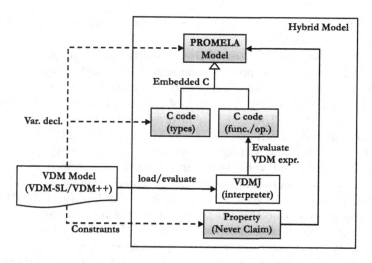

Fig. 3. Constructing hybrid model using PROMELA and VDMJ

Note that if an operation is being evaluated by an evaluation function, according to the semantics of VDM, variables of the VDM model might be updated during the evaluation. Therefore, not only the output variables but also state variables of the VDM model, i.e. $Var_{\mathcal{M}}$ in Definition 2, will be updated after evaluation.

The evaluation functions return *Error* if a runtime error, i.e. a violation of constraints defined in the VDM model $\mathcal{M}$, is encountered during the evaluation. For example, when evaluating an operation, variables defined in the VDM model will be updated during the evaluation. If the updated variables violate one of the variable invariants, the VDM interpreter captures the violation and makes the evaluation function to return *Error* as the result of the evaluation.

3.3 Constructing Hybrid Model Based on EA^{VDM}

This section describes how to construct a hybrid verification model defined in Definitions 2 and 3 using PROMELA and VDMJ. Figure 3 shows the structure of the hybrid model which consists of several parts. The main part is the PROMELA model that specifies behaviors of the environment or user against the specified system, the VDM model. For the module SIMPLE, specifying a general behavior which invokes operations putintoS and takefromS nondeterministically from its initial state would cover all possible scenarios.

C code that defines type definitions and implements the evaluation functions in Definition 3 should be prepared to invoke functions/operations defined in the VDM model. More specifically, the evaluation functions in Definition 3 are implemented as C code separately for each operation in the VDM model. For example, for module SIMPLE there would be four evaluation functions for evaluating the two operations and their preconditions, where the preconditions are used as guard conditions.

In our implementation strategy, VDMJ is started as an independent process, and the SPIN/PROMELA process communicates through pipes with VDMJ using the evaluation functions implemented as embedded C code. Note that PROMELA and VDMJ keep their state of variables individually but only the variables in the PROMELA model are involved in the checking process. Therefore, to keep the state of variables synchronized between PROMELA and VDMJ, operations for reading and writing state variables are added to the VDM model.

Type definitions and variable declarations can be specified in either the PROMELA model or in the embedded C code. Though there is no standard way of mapping abstract types such as *set*, *map*, and *seq* in VDM to PROMELA/C, according to our experiences, a structure comprised of an array and a length indicator shall cover most cases. For basic types of VDM except integers, usually `mtype` or `enum` can be used to define corresponding storages.

The inputs of a function/operation usually are not defined as state variables in the VDM model but has to be defined and assigned in the PROMELA model. Currently, our approach does not yet have intuitive or direct means to encode type invariants in VDM to type definitions in PROMELA/C. Therefore, when assigning values to variables in the PROMELA model that is related to a type or variable defined in the VDM model with invariants specified, the variables must be carefully assigned to not violate these invariants.

4   Case Study

4.1   Module SIMPLE

We have applied our approach on the simple VDM-SL module shown in Fig. 1. The verification of this module is to find the violation of the state invariant in line 12 which says that numbers 2 and 8 can not be put together alone in the pool. In other words, the verification is to check the reachability of a particular state of the pool in a state space of $2^{10} = 1,024$ states.

We took the intuitive behavior for module SIMPLE: a transition system that fires the two operations `putintoS` and `takefromS` nondeterministically and continuously after initialization:

```
1 c_decl{\#include "simple_types.c"}
2 c_code{\#include "simple_ops.c"}
3
4 // state of SIMPLE module
5 typedef SIMPLE_S {
6   byte length = 0;  // size
7   byte pool[10]; // pool : set of myNat  (0~9)
8 }
9
10 // set of nat (input of operations in SIMPLE module)
11 typedef set_myNat {
```

```
12   byte length = 0;
13   byte numbers[2]; // max length: 2
14 }
15
16 SIMPLE_S state_simple;
17 set_myNat param;
18 bool VDM_Error = 0;
19
20 active proctype simple() {
21   c_code{ initialization(); read_state_SIMPLE(); };
22   do
23   :: sel_set_mynat_param(param);
24      if
25      :: c_expr{ pre_SIMPLE_putintoS(); } ->
26         c_code{ write_state_SIMPLE(); }
27         c_code{ SIMPLE_putintoS(); }
28         c_code{ read_state_SIMPLE(); };
29      :: c_expr{ pre_SIMPLE_takefromS() } ->
30         c_code{ write_state_SIMPLE(); }
31         c_code{ SIMPLE_takefromS(); }
32         c_code{ read_state_SIMPLE(); };
33      fi;
34   :: break
35   od;
36 }
```

The above code shows the related part of PROMELA model.[2] Firstly, two C files are included using c_decl and c_code (lines 1–2). The former is to include type definitions, and the latter is to include functions implementing the evaluation functions of the VDM-SL operations and other support functions. Types of S and set of myNat are defined in the SIMPLE module using struct in PROMELA, with an array of byte and length indicator length (lines 4–14).

In the transition part (lines 21–35), synchronizations of state variables between PROMELA and VDMJ are required. Therefore, after initialization (line 21), read_state_SIMPLE() is called to retrieve the value of initialized S in VDMJ and assign it to state_simple in PROMELA. Firing a transition contains three steps: synchronization from PROMELA to VDMJ, operation execution, and synchronization from VDMJ to PROMELA (lines 26–28, 30–32).

To address the C code implementing evaluation functions for module SIMPLE, we show the operation for synchronizing state variables as follows:

```
get_state : () ==> S
get_state() == ( return S );

set_state : S ==> ()
set_state(a) == ( pool := a.pool );
```

---

[2] We skipped the detail of sel_mynat_param which is used to enumerate the input of operations: a set of myNat containing one or two digits (0–9).

To execute these operations through VDMJ, we implemented two operations: read_state_SIMPLE() and write_state_SIMPLE() in the embedded C code. read_state_SIMPLE() sends a string print get_state() to VDMJ process[3] and gets VDMJ's response = mk_S(0,4,9). Similarly, assuming the current value of state S is mk_S(0,4,9), write_state_SIMPLE() sends print write_state(mk_S(0,4,9)) and ignores the returned message if no runtime error is detected.

The property we checked was specified as !<> VDM_error == 1. We declared a special variable VDM_error (line 18) to monitor whether *Error* is returned by an evaluation function. In module SIMPLE, the evaluation functions need to be monitored are SIMPLE_putintoS() and SIMPLE_takefromS(). If any of the two functions returns *Error*, i.e., a violation of the invariants of module SIMPLE occurs, VDM_error will be set to 1 and an assertion violation will be detected by SPIN. The checking result is as follows:

```
pan:1: assertion violated !(VDM_Error==1) (at depth 406680)
pan: wrote simple.pml.trail
...
State-vector 32 byte, depth reached 406687, errors: 1
    545237 states, stored
     52645 states, matched
    597882 transitions (= stored+matched)
         0 atomic steps
hash factor: 246.164 (best if > 100.)
bits set per state: 3 (-k3)
Stats on memory usage (in Megabytes):
    18.719   equivalent memory usage for states
    16.000   memory used for hash array (-w27)
    16.000   memory used for bit stack
    38.147   memory used for DFS stack (-m1000000)
    70.733   total actual memory usage
pan: elapsed time 33.5 seconds
pan: rate   16266.02 states/second
```

The above report from SPIN shows that the verifier found a violation of the LTL property and output an error trace. The verification was performed on a machine with Intel Core i5 2.3 GHz CPU and 4 GB RAM. The search was set to use bit state-space search with search depth 1,000,000.

4.2   SAFER

We also applied our approach to a more realistic example SAFER [2]. SAFER stands for "Simplified Aid For EVA (Extravehicular Activity) Rescue" and is designed by NASA for space crewmembers in an EVA (Extravehicular Activity). In [2], a VDM-SL model[4] partly translated from a PVS model by NASA was

---

[3] VDMJ process is in interactive mode.

[4] The VDM-SL model can be downloaded at Overture tool example download page: http://overturetool.org/download/examples/VDMSL/.

validated using specification animation (testing). This VDM-SL model focused on the thruster selection logic and was specified as an operation with a postcondition:

```
ControlCycle: HCM'SwitchPositions * HCM'HandGripPosition * AUX'RotCommand
               ==> TS'ThrusterSet
ControlCycle(mk_HCM'SwitchPositions(mode,aah),raw_grip,aah_cmd) ==
  let grip_cmd  = HCM'GripCommand(raw_grip,mode),
      thrusters = TS'SelectedThrusters(grip_cmd,aah_cmd,AAH'ActiveAxes(),
                                       AAH'IgnoreHcm())
  in
      (AAH'Transition(aah,grip_cmd,clock);
      clock := clock + 1;
      return thrusters)
post card RESULT <= 4 and
     ThrusterConsistency(RESULT);
```

The above code shows the signature, body, and postcondition of the operation ControlCycle specified in module SAFER which has three inputs of types referring to other modules: HCM'SwitchPositions and HCM'HandGripPosition are of type "record of quote"; AUX'RotCommand is of type "map of quote to quote".

In [2], a huge test that executes the operation with all 8,748 combinations of inputs was conducted. However, the state variables are not considered in the huge test due to the difficulty of building test cases exhaustively to state variables. We conducted the same verification using our model checking approach with state variables considered. We built a PROMELA model for verifying the operation ControlCycle with an abstraction on clocks in the state variables.[5] Below shows part of the PROMELA code.

```
c_decl{\#include"safer_types.c"}
c_code{\#include "safer_ops.c"}

// quote types of SAFER specification
mtype = { m_Rot, m_Tran }; // HCM'ControlModeSwitch
mtype = { m_Up, m_Down };   // HCM'ControlButton
mtype = { m_Neg, m_Zero, m_Pos };   // AUX'AxisCommand
mtype = { m_Roll, m_Pitch, m_Yaw }; // AUX'RotAxis
mtype = { m_AAH_off, m_AAH_started, m_AAH_on, m_pressed_once,
          m_AAH_closing, m_pressed_twice }; // AAH'EngageState
// state of SAFER module
typedef SAFER_SAFER {
  byte clock = 0; // clock : nat
}
// state of AAH module
typedef AAH_AAH {
```

---

[5] There are two clocks of type nat in the state variables defined in module SAFER and AAH we found that only two cases were worth considering in the verification.

```
    mtype active_axes[3];     // active_axes : set of AUX'RotAxis
    mtype ignore_hcm[3];      // ignore_hcm  : set of AUX'RotAxis
    mtype toggle = m_AAH_off; // toggle      : AAH'EngageState
    byte mytimeout = 0;       // timeout     : nat
}

typedef HCM_SwitchPositions {
    mtype mode = m_Rot; // mode: HCM'ControlModeSwitch
    mtype aah = m_Up;   // aah : HCM'ControlButton
};

typedef HCM_HandGripPosition {
    mtype vert = m_Zero;   // vert  : AUX'AxisCommand
    mtype horiz = m_Zero;  // horiz : AUX'AxisCommand
    mtype trans = m_Zero;  // trans : AUX'AxisCommand
    mtype twist;           // twist : AUX'AxisCommand
};

// RotCommand = map RotAxis to AxisCommand
//   inv cmd == dom cmd = rot_axis_set;
typedef AUX_RotCommand {
    mtype key[3] = { m_Roll, m_Pitch, m_Yaw };
    mtype val[3];
};


... ... ...


SAFER_SAFER state_safer;
AAH_AAH     state_aah;

HCM_SwitchPositions param1;
HCM_HandGripPosition param2;
local AUX_RotCommand param3;
bool VDM_Error = 0;

active proctype safer() {
    c_code{ initialization(); };

    sel_SAFER_SAFER(state_safer);
    sel_AAH_AAH(state_aah);
    sel_HCM_SwitchPositions(param1);
    sel_HCM_HandGripPosition(param2);
    sel_AUX_RotCommand(param3);

    c_code{ write_state_SAFER(); write_state_AAH(); SAFER_ControlCycle(); }
}
```

As above code shows, firstly, the elements of quote types are defined as mtype in PROMELA. Then we define types of states of SAFER and AAH, and types of inputs of ControlCycle. In this case study, we intended to confirm that there is no violation of post-condition. Therefore the value of the output TS'ThrusterSet is not needed and is ignored in the PROMELA model. Also, to reduce the depth of search in SPIN, the process in PROMELA enumerates all combination of inputs and state variables, so loops are eliminated in the PROMELA model. The result is as follows where no violation of the postcondition was found:

```
State-vector 36 byte, depth reached 131, errors: 0
 33593277 states, stored
 20155223 states, matched
 53748500 transitions (= stored+matched)
        0 atomic steps
hash factor: 127.852 (best if > 100.)
bits set per state: 3 (-k3)
Stats on memory usage (in Megabytes):
 1281.482   equivalent memory usage for states
  512.000   memory used for hash array (-w32)
  512.000   memory used for bit stack
    0.382   memory used for DFS stack (-m10000)
 1024.577   total actual memory usage

pan: elapsed time 1.42e+04 seconds
pan: rate 2369.6754 states/second
```

The time consumed was about 4 h with the memory usage of about 1 GB. Other settings are similar to verifying module SIMPLE.

4.3   Discussion

From the case study on module SIMPLE, we showed how to apply our approach to verifying VDM models. From the case study on SAFER, we showed that our approach can be applied to real-world systems. In this section, we discuss some issues of our approach with the results of the two case studies.

Usability: The cost of constructing a hybrid model for model checking a VDM model is still high since we have to build PROMELA model manually including implementing the embedded C codes. Fortunately, from the two case studies, we have built some code blocks and functions that are reusable. For example, the code for establishing the connection between PROMELA and VDMJ is directly reusable, while the code implementing evaluation functions for operations in SIMPLE and SAFER can be taken as templates for construction of hybrid models for other VDM models. We have also implemented a built-in parser for reading VDM literals which is mainly used in synchronization of variables between PROMELA and VDMJ.

Scalability: From the SAFER case study, state explosion is easily encountered, and we have to tune the verifier with care. Besides abstraction on VDM models, we may also apply the swarm verification technique [11] to deal with large state space. To reduce the computation complexity on enumerating variables of types like set and map, we are considering to integrate constraint logic programming (CLP) [25] to SPIN. CLP is expected to make the encoding of VDM invariants much easier.

Efficiency: It should be noticed that the execution time is quite long compared to verifying pure PROMELA models because the verification has two processes, pan verifier and JVM (VDMJ is a Java software), which communicate with each other through pipes. As a result, the I/O usage inevitably and significantly increases the execution time. One choice to improve the efficiency is to implement the evaluation functions using C++ APIs of VDMTools to eliminate frequent I/O access in verification.

5   Related Work

There is little work on applying model checking techniques on VDM models. K. Lausdahl [20] proposed a semantics-preserving translation that constructs an Alloy model from a subset of VDM-SL model. This work aims to support the validation of implicitly specified VDM-SL model by applying Alloy to find instances of the scenarios described in requirements that meet the constraints specified in a VDM-SL model. K. Lausdahl et al. [21] aim to interpret implicitly specified VDM-SL/VDM++ models using the constraint solving functionality of ProB [22]. Specifically, their approach encodes the precondition and postcondition of functions/operations with invariants. By giving an input, the ProB produces a solution based on the encoding, and the solution is encoded back to VDM model as the body of the explicit specification.

The above two works are both based on model translation to Alloy or ProB and aim to support validation of implicitly specified VDM models. Since VDM has a rich syntax for specifying data types and expressions, it is difficult to translate a VDM model to another formal model. Therefore, it is reasonable to restrict the scope of translation to implicitly specified VDM models within a subset of VDM.

On the other hand, our approach requires explicitly specified VDM models, which is executable by VDM interpreter (VDMJ). Our approach does not use model translation but constructs a hybrid model combing PROMELA and VDMJ using embedded C code feature of SPIN. We argue that our approach is more practical because using SPIN is easier for software engineers to learn and think, and a state-diagram-like model is more adaptable to existing software development processes. Furthermore, as mentioned in Sect. 1, our approach is easier to extend to other VDM dialects.

The technique used in our approach can be recognized as an aspect of combining source codes with VDM specifications. B. Frohlich and P.G. Larsen [8] proposed an extension of VDM-SL Toolbox for integrating C++ codes into VDM-SL specifications. C.B. Nielsen et al. [24] illustrated the use of external call interface and remote control interface for linking VDM interpreter with Java codes.

These techniques are useful for GUI-based simulation/animation of VDM specifications. Though our approach is currently using an indirect way of combining source codes (PROMELA) with VDM models (VDMJ), it is one of the future directions for improving the efficiency of our approach as discussed in Sect. 4.3.

6 Conclusion and Future Work

In this paper, we have presented an approach of applying model checking on VDM models for validation and verification of VDM specifications to increase software reliability. Our approach constructs a hybrid model that combines SPIN model checker and VDMJ interpreter using the embedded C code feature of SPIN. Thus, we can apply traditional logic model checking on VDM without model translation. The greatest advantage of our approach is that it can be extended to VDM-RT, the real-time dialect of VDM, if the scheduling of threads and time are handled with care.

We also reported two case studies and discussed issues about usability, scalability, and efficiency to point out the future directions. For usability, though we have built reusable code blocks and templates, how to define types of VDM in PROMELA/C especially types with invariants still needs more work such as introducing constraint logic programming. For scalability, the SAFER case study shows that our approach is scalable for real-world systems. Besides applying data abstraction on VDM models, we may also utilize SPIN's ability to handle large state space. For efficiency issue, we plan to introduce C++ APIs of VDMTools to improve the execution time of checking.

References

1. VDMJ. http://sourceforge.net/projects/vdmj/
2. Agerholm, S., Larsen, P.G.: Modeling and validating SAFER in VDM-SL. In: Proceedings of the Fourth NASA Langley Formal Methods Workshop, NASA Conference, Publication 3356 (1997)
3. Bjorner, D., Jones, C.B. (eds.): The Vienna Development Method: The Meta-Language. LNCS, vol. 61. Springer, Heidelberg (1978)
4. Clarke Jr., E.M., Grumberg, O., Peled, D.A.: Model Checking. The MIT Press, Cambridge (1999)
5. Fitzgerald, J., Larsen, P.G.: Modelling Systems: Practical Tools and Techniques in Software Development, 2nd edn. Cambridge University Press, New York (2009)
6. Fitzgerald, J., Larsen, P.G., Mukherjee, P., Plat, N., Verhoef, M.: Validated Designs For Object-Oriented Systems. Springer, Santa Clara (2005)
7. Fitzgerald, J., Larsen, P.G., Sahara, S.: VDMTools: advances in support for formal modeling in VDM. SIGPLAN Not. 43(2), 3–11 (2008)
8. Fröhlich, B., Larsen, P.: Combining VDM-SL specifications with C++ code. In: Gaudel, M.C., Woodcock, J. (eds.) FME 1996. LNCS, vol. 1051, pp. 179–194. Springer, Heidelberg (1996)
9. Holzmann, G.: SPIN Model Checker: The Primer and Reference Manual. Addison-Wesley Professional, Reading (2003)

10. Holzmann, G.J.: Mars code. Commun. ACM **57**(2), 64–73 (2014)
11. Holzmann, G.J., Joshi, R., Groce, A.: Swarm verification techniques. IEEE Trans. Softw. Eng. **37**(6), 845–857 (2011)
12. Holzmann, G.J., Joshi, R.: Model-driven software verification. In: Graf, S., Mounier, L. (eds.) SPIN 2004. LNCS, vol. 2989, pp. 76–91. Springer, Heidelberg (2004)
13. Jones, C.B.: Systematic Software Development Using VDM, 2nd edn. Prentice-Hall Inc, Upper Saddle River (1990)
14. Kurita, T., Chiba, M., Nakatsugawa, Y.: Application of a formal specification language in the development of the "Mobile FeliCa" IC chip firmware for embedding in mobile phone. In: Cuellar, J., Sere, K. (eds.) FM 2008. LNCS, vol. 5014, pp. 425–429. Springer, Heidelberg (2008)
15. Kurita, T., Nakatsugawa, Y.: The application of VDM to the industrial development of firmware for a smart card IC chip. Int. J. Softw. Inf. **3**(2–3), 343–355 (2009)
16. Larsen, P.G., Battle, N., Ferreira, M., Fitzgerald, J., Lausdahl, K., Verhoef, M.: The overture initiative integrating tools for VDM. SIGSOFT Softw. Eng. Notes **35**(1), 1–6 (2010)
17. Larsen, P.G., Fitzgerald, J.: Recent industrial applications of VDM in Japan. In: Proceedings of the 2007th Internatioanal Conference on Formal Methods in Industry, FACS-FMI 2007, p. 8. British Computer Society, Swinton (2007)
18. Larsen, P.G., Pawlowski, W.: The formal semantics of ISO VDM-SL. Comput. Stand. Interfaces **17**(5–6), 585–601 (1995)
19. Larsen, P., Lassen, P.: An executable subset of meta-IV with loose specification. In: Prehn, S., Toetenel, W. (eds.) VDM 1991. LNCS, vol. 551, pp. 604–618. Springer, Berlin Heidelberg (1991)
20. Lausdahl, K.: Translating VDM to alloy. In: Johnsen, E.B., Petre, L. (eds.) IFM 2013. LNCS, vol. 7940, pp. 46–60. Springer, Heidelberg (2013)
21. Lausdahl, K., Ishikawa, H., Larsen, P.G.: Interpreting implicit VDM specifications using ProB. In: Battle, N., Fitzgerald, J. (eds.) Proceedings of the 12th Overture Workshop, Newcastle University, 21 June, 2014. School of Computing Science, Newcastle University, UK, Technical report CS-TR-1446, January 2015
22. Leuschel, M., Butler, M.: ProB: a model checker for B. In: Araki, K., Gnesi, S., Mandrioli, D. (eds.) FME 2003. LNCS, vol. 2805, pp. 855–874. Springer, Berlin Heidelberg (2003)
23. Nakatsugawa, Y., Kurita, T., Araki, K.: A framework for formal specification considering review and specification-based testing. In: TENCON 2010–2010 IEEE Region 10 Conference, pp. 2444–2448, November 2010
24. Lausdahl, K., Larsen, P.G., Nielsen, C.B.: Combining VDM with executable code. In: Derrick, J., Fitzgerald, J., Gnesi, S., Khurshid, S., Leuschel, M., Reeves, S., Riccobene, E. (eds.) ABZ 2012. LNCS, vol. 7316, pp. 266–279. Springer, Heidelberg (2012)
25. Triska, M.: The finite domain constraint solver of SWI-Prolog. In: Schrijvers, T., Thiemann, P. (eds.) FLOPS 2012. LNCS, vol. 7294, pp. 307–316. Springer, Heidelberg (2012)
26. Larsen, P.G., Hooman, J., Verhoef, M.: Modeling and Validating Distributed Embedded Real-Time Systems with VDM++. In: Misra, J., Nipkow, T., Sekerinski, E. (eds.) FM 2006. LNCS, vol. 4085, pp. 147–162. Springer, Heidelberg (2006)

Tools

Statistical Model Checking of Simulink Models with Plasma Lab

Axel Legay and Louis-Marie Traonouez[(✉)]

Inria Rennes – Bretagne Atlantique, Rennes, France
louis-marie.traonouez@inria.fr

Abstract. We present an extension of the statistical model-checker Plasma Lab capable of analyzing Simulink models.

1 Introduction

Formal methods comprise a wide range of techniques capable of proving or evaluating the safety of a system. Model based techniques, like model-checking, rely on a formal model of the system in order to perform an exhaustive exploration of its state-space. The technique reaches its limit when the state-space of the model is too large to be explored entirely, or when the model mixes heterogeneous data like time, quantities and probabilities. Statistical Model Checking (SMC) is an alternative technique that combines formal analysis with statistical methods. It relies on a finite number of simulations of a formal model in order to compute an evaluation of the system's safety as a probability measure. This lightweight approach can be applied on complex systems, even with infinite state-space.

SMC can be implemented easily for a wide range of formal models or even directly applied to a system simulator. It only depends on three basic components: 1. a simulator of the model or the system, capable of generating random traces, specified as a finite sequence of states; 2. a monitor, that determines if a trace satisfies a property expressed in a formal logic like the Bounded Linear Temporal Logic; 3. an SMC algorithm from the statistic area that evaluates the probability to satisfy the formal property. For instance, the Monte Carlo algorithm computes N executions ρ and it estimates the probability γ that the system satisfies a logical formula φ using the following equation:

$$\tilde{\gamma} = \frac{1}{N} \sum_{i=1}^{N} \mathbf{1}(\rho \models \varphi)$$

where $\mathbf{1}$ is an indicator function that returns 1 if φ is satisfied and 0 otherwise. It guarantees that the estimate $\tilde{\gamma}$ is close enough to the true probability γ with a probability of error that is controlled by the number N of simulations.

Several model-checking tools have added SMC as a complement to exhaustive model-checking. This includes the model-checker UPPAAL [5] for timed automata, the probabilistic model-checker PRISM [7], and the model-checker

© Springer International Publishing Switzerland 2016
C. Artho and P.C. Ölveczky (Eds.): FTSCS 2015, CCIS 596, pp. 259–264, 2016.
DOI: 10.1007/978-3-319-29510-7_15

Ymer [9] for continuous time Markov chains. Plasma Lab [3] is the first platform entirely dedicated to SMC. Contrary to other tools, that target a specific domain and offer several analysis techniques, including basic SMC algorithms, Plasma Lab is designed as a generic platform that offers several advanced SMC algorithms that can be applied to various models. Indeed to apply Plasma Lab algorithms to a new model or system it is only required to implement a simulator that extends public interfaces from Plasma Lab API. Currently, Plasma Lab can already be used with the PRISM language, biological models, the SystemC language, and Simulink models, the extension presented in this paper.

Simulink is a graphical programming language for multidomain dynamic systems. It is part of the MATLAB environment, a widely used tool in the industry. Simulink models can be formally translated to hybrid automata [1], that interleave discrete state automata with complex dynamic behaviors described by differential equations. Model-checking of these models is however undecidable. It is therefore interesting to use SMC to provide a formal analysis technique for these models. Rather than translating Simulink models to a specific formal language, we have been able to directly interface Plasma Lab and Simulink, and we apply SMC algorithms by using the simulation engine provided by Simulink. This approach facilitates the adoption of formal methods by non experts, who can launch SMC analyses directly from a small MATLAB App.

2   Plasma Lab Architecture

Plasma Lab is a compact, efficient and flexible platform for SMC. The tool offers a series of SMC algorithms, included advanced techniques for rare events simulation, distributed SMC, non-determinism, and optimization. The main difference between Plasma Lab and other SMC tools is that Plasma Lab proposes an API abstraction of the concepts of stochastic model simulator, property checker (monitoring) and SMC algorithm. In other words, the tool has been designed to be capable of using external simulators, input languages, or SMC algorithms. This not only reduces the effort of integrating new algorithms, but also allows us to create direct plug-in interfaces with industry used specification tools. The latter being done without using extra compilers.

Figure 1 presents Plasma Lab architecture. More specifically, the relations between model simulators, property checkers, and SMC algorithms components. The simulators features include starting a new trace and simulating a model step by step. The checkers decide a property on a trace by accessing to state values. They also control the simulations, with a *state on demand* approach that generates new states only if more states are needed to decide the property. A SMC algorithm component is a runnable object. It collect samples obtained from a checker component. Depending on the property language, their checker either returns Boolean or numerical values. The algorithm then notifies progress and sends its results through the Controller API.

In coordination with this architecture, we use a plugin system to load models and properties components. It is then possible to support new model or property

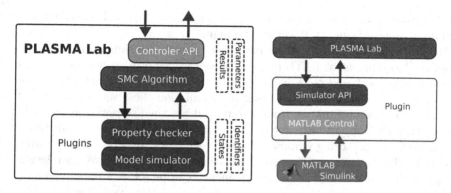

Fig. 1. Plasma Lab architecture

Fig. 2. Interface between Plasma Lab and Simulink

languages. Adding a simulator or a checker is pretty straightforward as they share a similar plugin architecture. Thus, it requires only a few classes and methods to get a new component running. Each plugin contains a factory class used by Plasma Lab to instantiate component objects. These components implement the corresponding interface defining their behavior. Some companion objects are also required (results, states, identifiers) to allow communication between components and the Controller API.

One of the goal of Plasma Lab is also to benefit from a massive distribution of the simulations, which is one of the advantage of the SMC approach. Therefore Plasma Lab API provides generic methods to define distributed algorithms.

3   Plasma Lab and Simulink Integration

We now show how we have integrated Plasma Lab within Simulink, hence lifting the power of our simulation approaches directly within the tool.

In order to obtain significant results with SMC the Simulink models should include randomly generated events. By default the Simulink library provides some random generators, but these are not compatible with SMC: they always generate the same random sequence of values at each execution. To overcome this limitation we use some custom C-code blocks that generate independent sequences of random draws.

Our objective was to reuse the simulation engine provided with Simulink and to integrate it in Plasma Lab. To do so, we developed a simulator plugin whose architecture is showed in Fig. 2. One of the key points of our integration has been to exploit MATLAB Control,[1] a library that allows to interact with MATLAB from Java. This library uses a proxy object connected to a MATLAB session. Function calls and variables access are transmitted and executed on the MATLAB session through the proxy. This allowed us to implement a MATLAB

---

[1] https://code.google.com/p/matlabcontrol/.

program that controls a Simulink simulation. Calls to this implementation are then done in Java from the Plasma Lab plugin.

Regarding the monitoring of properties, we exploit the simulation output of Simulink. More precisely, BLTL properties are checked over sequences of states and time stamps, based on a set of state variables defined by declaring some Simulink signals as log output. During the simulation these signals are logged in a data structure containing time stamps and are then retrieved as states in Plasma Lab. One important point is that Simulink discretizes the signals trace, its sample frequency being parameterized by each block. In terms of monitoring this means that the sample frequency must be configured to observe any relevant change in the model. In practice, the frequency can be set as a constant value, or, if the model mixes both continuous data flow and state flow, the frequency can be aligned on the transitions, i.e., when a state is newly visited.

Usage. We provide a Simulink plugin for the main interface of Plasma Lab. Simulink models can be loaded in the interface and a MATLAB instance is started to simulate the models. Alternatively we provide PLASMA2Simulink, a MATLAB App that can be installed in MATLAB. It contains all the necessary components to verify Simulink models: the simulator plugin, a BLTL monitor and SMC algorithms. Then, SMC experiments can be directly started in MATLAB from this App: it allows to select a model, a property and an algorithm, to specify the parameters of the experiment and it displays the results. Both Plasma Lab and PLASMA2Simulink can be downloaded from our website.[2]

Applications. We also describe in this webpage[3] two case-studies developed with Simulink and verified with Plasma Lab. The first is a fuel control system provided by MathWorks. The second described the temperature controller of a pig shed.

In the first one, we replace manual switches, used in the standard model to introduce failures in the system sensors, by random generators that implement a Poisson probability distribution using C-code blocks. We then analyze the probability of a long engine shutdown and compare our results obtained with Plasma Lab with the results from [10].

4 Related Works

A first experiment with SMC and Simulink was presented by Zuliani et al. [10]. Their approach consists in programming one SMC algorithm within the Simulink toolbox. On the contrary, the flexibility of our tool will allow us to incrementally add new algorithms to the toolbox without new programming efforts.

A few other works consider formal verification of Simulink models via model-checking. None consider adding stochastic behaviors to Simulink, but consider the hybrid automata semantics of these models. However, model-checking hybrid automata is undecidable, and therefore, the existing approaches restrict the type

---

[2] https://project.inria.fr/plasma-lab/download/.

[3] https://project.inria.fr/plasma-lab/examples/.

of blocks that can be used in Simulink models: in general by removing continuous behaviors in order to obtain a finite state machine. For instance Honeywell presents in [8] a tool that translates certain Simulink models to the input language of the model-checker NuSMV. Barnat et al. [2] also presents a tool chain that translates Simulink models to the input language of the LTL model-checker DiViNE. This tool chain uses the tool HiLiTe [6], also developed by Honeywell, that can perform semantic analyses of Simulink models. Contrary to these model-checking approaches, SMC techniques are not restricted by the model, and our Simulink plugin for Plasma Lab is able to handle any type of Simulink and Stateflow diagrams, with both continuous and discrete behaviors.

Finally, our approach is also different from [4] that consists in translating parts of Simulink models into the UPPAAL language. This makes it difficult to analyze counter examples as it implies remapping traces from UPPAAL to the Simulink model. Therefore Plasma Lab offers the first integrated verification tool for Simulink models with stochastic information.

Acknowledgement. This work was supported by the European Union Seventh Framework Programme under grant agreement number 318490 (SENSATION).

References

1. Agrawal, A., Simon, G., Karsai, G.: Semantic translation of simulink/stateflow models to hybrid automata using graph transformations. Electron. Notes Theor. Comput. Sci. **109**, 43–56 (2004)
2. Kratochvíla, T., Ročkai, P., Brim, L., Barnat, J., Beran, J.: Tool chain to support automated formal verification of avionics simulink designs. In: Stoelinga, M., Pinger, R. (eds.) FMICS 2012. LNCS, vol. 7437, pp. 78–92. Springer, Heidelberg (2012)
3. Corre, K., Boyer, B., Sedwards, S., Legay, A.: PLASMA-lab: a flexible, distributable statistical model checking library. In: Joshi, K., Siegle, M., Stoelinga, M., D'Argenio, P.R. (eds.) QEST 2013. LNCS, vol. 8054, pp. 160–164. Springer, Heidelberg (2013)
4. David, A., Du, D., Larsen, K.G., Legay, A., Mikucionis, M., Poulsen, D.B., Sedwards, S.: Statistical model checking for stochastic hybrid systems. In: Proceedings of HSB. EPTCS, vol. 92, pp. 122–136 (2012)
5. Legay, A., Wang, Z., Larsen, K.G., David, A., Mikučionis, M.: Time for statistical model checking of real-time systems. In: Gopalakrishnan, G., Qadeer, S. (eds.) CAV 2011. LNCS, vol. 6806, pp. 349–355. Springer, Heidelberg (2011)
6. Bhatt, D., Madl, G., Oglesby, D., Schloegel, K.: Towards scalable verification of commercial avionics software. In: Infotech@Aerospace. AIAA (2010)
7. Norman, G., Parker, D., Kwiatkowska, M.: PRISM 4.0: verification of probabilistic real-time systems. In: Gopalakrishnan, G., Qadeer, S. (eds.) CAV 2011. LNCS, vol. 6806, pp. 585–591. Springer, Heidelberg (2011)
8. Bhatnagar, A., Meenakshi, B., Roy, S.: Tool for translating simulink models into input language of a model checker. In: Liu, Z., Kleinberg, R.D. (eds.) ICFEM 2006. LNCS, vol. 4260, pp. 606–620. Springer, Heidelberg (2006)

9. Younes, H.L.S.: Verification and planning for stochastic processes with asynchronous events. Ph.D. thesis, Carnegie Mellon (2005)
10. Zuliani, P., Platzer, A., Clarke, E.M.: Bayesian statistical model checking with application to Stateflow/Simulink verification. Formal Methods Syst. Des. **43**(2), 338–367 (2013)

g-HOL: A Graphical User Interface for the HOL Proof Assistant

Fahd Arshad[✉], Hassan Mehmood, Fauzan Raza, and Osman Hasan

School of Electrical Engineering and Computer Sciences (SEECS),
National University of Sciences and Technology (NUST), Islamabad, Pakistan
{10besefarshad,11besehmehmood,10besefraza,
osman.hasan}@seecs.nust.edu.pk

Abstract. Given the high expressiveness of higher-order logic, their proof assistants are being widely advocated for formally verifying cyber-physical systems these days. However, the usage of higher-order-logic proof assistants is mostly restricted to academia. One of the main reasons for the hesitancy of their usage in industrial setting is the associated long learning curve. We believe that one of the foremost factors behind this slow learning process is the user-unfriendly text-based interfaces of the proof assistants. To facilitate the first experience of users with a proof assistant, this paper presents a user-friendly graphical user interface (GUI) g-HOL for the higher-order-logic (HOL) proof assistant. g-HOL is developed in Java swing and is supported by the Windows, Linux and MAC operating systems. It tends to minimize syntax errors and the need to memorize and type commands and facilitates the searching process, which is frequently required in interactive formal reasoning. The paper describes the architecture and main features of g-HOL using an illustrative example.

Keywords: Higher-order logic · Proof assistants · Theorem proving · HOL

1 Introduction

Theorem proving is one of the most widely used formal verification methods [4]. The system that needs to be analyzed is mathematically modeled in an appropriate logic and the properties of interest are verified using computer-based formal tools called theorem provers or proof assistants. The human interaction or the manual proof effort required for proving logical formulas in a theorem prover varies from trivial to complex depending on the underlying logic. For instance, propositional logic [4] is decidable, i.e., the logical correctness of a formula specified in propositional logic can be automatically verified using an algorithm. However, it provides very limited expressiveness. On the other hand, higher-order logic [4] allows quantification over functions and sets and is thus much more expressive than propositional logic. The added expressiveness of higher-order logic comes at the cost of explicit user guidance required to verify all formulas

© Springer International Publishing Switzerland 2016
C. Artho and P.C. Ölveczky (Eds.): FTSCS 2015, CCIS 596, pp. 265–269, 2016.
DOI: 10.1007/978-3-319-29510-7_16

expressed in higher-order-logic, due to its undecidable nature. The user interacts with a proof assistant by providing it with the necessary tactics to prove goals. This process could be very tedious and usually takes thousands of lines of script and hundreds of man-hours for verifying analysis described in a page.

Despite the great potential of higher-order-logic theorem proving in verifying the correctness of complex engineering systems, this technology is very rarely used in the industry [3]. We believe that besides the manual proof guidance requirement, the user-unfriendly command-line interfaces of proof assistants are also mainly responsible for this limited usage. The need for a user-friendly interface for proof assistants was majorly felt in the interactive theorem proving course that we teach at NUST, Islamabad. Most of the undergraduate students struggle with syntax errors and finding appropriate theorems from the libraries during their initial hands-on experiences with the proof assistants for at least a couple of weeks. These issues usually hinder the development of interest of the students in this field. In order to alleviate this problem, this paper presents a Graphical User Interface (GUI) called g-HOL [2], for the widely used HOL proof assistant [1], which has been successfully used as a verification framework for both software and hardware as well as a platform for the formalization of pure mathematics. It is important to note that g-HOL has been developed for the sole purpose of facilitating the learning process of proof assistants for novice users and thus should not be considered as an alternative to the far more powerful and efficient command-line based interface of HOL.

2   g-HOL's Architecture and Features

g-HOL [2] is developed using Java Swing [5], i.e., a framework specifically for designing and developing GUIs in Java. This choice was made due to the flexibility, platform independence and the large user community of the Java language. The g-HOL GUI follows a simple Model view controller (MVC) pattern. The architecture of g-HOL is composed of 5 main components:

1. HOL Theorem Prover (Back-end Software that does all the theorem proving)
2. Linker (Bridge between the HOL theorem Prover and g-HOL)
3. g-HOL (Front end Graphical Use Interface)
4. GraphicView Plugin (To create the layout using Java Swing)
5. View Controller (This consists of different types of listeners that handle interrupts, like button clicks etc.)

The g-HOL user-interface, depicted in Fig. 1, tends to facilitate the HOL learning process and enhance the productivity, usefulness and effectiveness of HOL users by providing them with the following key features:

– Archiving and loading proof scripts.
– A built-in text editor that dynamically maintains the proof script corresponding to mouse clicks on the g-HOL interface.

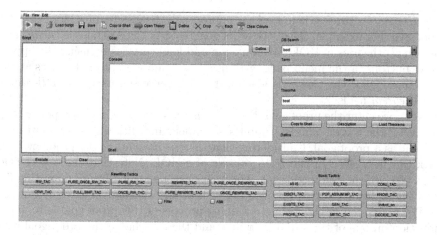

Fig. 1. g-HOL screen shot

- Ability to define and save definitions and theorems by just providing the logical formulas and names, as required, without worrying about following the HOL specific syntax.
- Availability of most of the commonly used HOL tactics (proof strategies) as clickable buttons. The user is allowed to define her own proof strategy buttons and replace the default ones with these.
- A simple to use search box, which accepts a logical formula and returns the matching theorems within the loaded theories by a simple mouse click.
- An auto-complete suggestions based string search feature that accepts theorem and definition names and returns the corresponding logical statements.

To the best of our knowledge, g-HOL is the first graphical user interface (GUI) for the HOL proof assistant. One of its foremost distinguishing features is the ability to conduct most of the commonly used formal reasoning steps using click-able buttons. The other user interfaces, such as Isabelle/jEdit and CoqIDE, are usually 'Emacs' style interfaces for other proof assistants (Isabelle and Coq) and do not allow using click-able buttons for proof strategies. This ability to conduct formal reasoning steps greatly minimizes the number of syntax errors and spelling mistakes and thus significantly reduces the proof time. Another useful feature of g-HOL is its flexibility to be used with any proof assistant in the HOL family, like HOL4 or HOL-Light, due to the independence of the GUI layer. The path for the target theorem prover can be selected from within the g-HOL interface and the tactics (proof strategies) can be defined corresponding to the target theorem prover.

3   Illustrative Example

In this section, we illustrate various features of g-HOL by working through a simple proof example: $(x^{(m+n)} = x^m x^n)$, using the HOL4 proof assistant. The first step in the proof process is to load the appropriate theories required for the given proof goal. For example, the above proof goal requires the Arithmetic (*arith*) and Real (*real*) theories in HOL. We can open and load theories by using the appropriate buttons in the menu pane. g-HOL allows loading multiple theories at the same time. Once the theory is loaded, it can be accessed using the *DB-Search* and *Theorem* fields.

Next, we enter the proof goal, i.e., !x m n. x pow (m + n) = x pow m * x pow n (! is the $\forall$ symbol in HOL) in the *Goal* field and click the *Define* button to define it as a proof goal. Considering that there is no syntax error, the new goal stack can be viewed in the *HOL console* of g-HOL. Note that the *Script* field keeps track of the running script. The script can be loaded from an existing file or by highlighting selected text from the editor and clicking the *Execute* button.

The main step in the formal reasoning process of this proof goal is to apply induction on one of the variables m or n and then discharge the proof goal generated by induction using real-theoretic reasoning. The induction can be done by applying the HOL tactic: *Induct_on*, which is available in the *Misc* button section of g-HOL. Upon clicking this button, we get the message of identifying the variable name where induction needs to be applied. We mentioned m, which breaks the goal into 2 sub-goals that are given in the console window.

The first step in the formal reasoning about the first sub-goal, i.e., $\forall$.x n. x pow (0 + n) = x pow 0 * x pow n, requires rewriting with the definition of the function pow. This can be done by clicking the REWRITE_TAC button and giving pow as an argument. This step simplifies the subgoal to $\forall$.x n. x pow (0 + n) = 1 * x pow n. This goal can be discharged by arithmetic rewriting using the facts that $0 + n = n$ and $1 * x = x$. We find the corresponding HOL theorems by using the strings 0+n and 1*x in the DB search field of g-HOL to find the theorems ADD_CLAUSES and REAL_MUL_LID from the arith and real theories, respectively. Rewriting with these two theorems can now be done by clicking the REWRITE_TAC button and giving ADD_CLAUSES and REAL_MUL_LID as arguments, which discharges the first subgoal.

We proceed with the verification of the subgoal corresponding to the step-case of induction, i.e., $\forall$.x n. x pow (SUC m + n) = x pow SUC m * x pow n given $\forall$.x n. x pow (m + n) = x pow m * x pow n, by rewriting it to bring it to the form where the definition of the function pow, i.e., $\forall$(x. x pow 0 = 1) $\wedge$ $\forall$ x n. x pow SUC n = x * x pow n, can be applied. This can be done by representing (SUC m + n) as SUC (m + n) and we use the DB search field on the arithmetic theory to find the corresponding theorem name, i.e., ADD_CLAUSES. Rewriting with ADD_CLAUSES using the REWRITE_TAC button simplifies the proof goal as mentioned above. This subgoal can now be simplified by rewriting it with the definition of the function pow along with the assumption by clicking the ASM_REWRITE_TAC button with an argument pow, which makes the proof goal to become $\forall$x n. x * (x pow m * x pow n) = x * x pow m * x pow n. This sub-goal can be discharged using the associative property of real numbers and we find the corresponding theorem from the real theory using the DB search field in the g-HOL interface and rewriting with it using the REWRITE_TAC. This completes the proof of our main proof goal. Once the goal is verified, a prompt appears asking the user to save the theorem by giving an appropriate name. Moreover, the complete script for the formal reasoning is also available in the `Script` window of g-HOL.

In the above interactive proof example, the user of g-HOL only required the working knowledge of induction (`induct_on`), rewriting (`REWRITE_TAC` and `ASM_REWRITE_TAC` and searching the HOL libraries (`DB search`) and she did not have to care about the syntax issues of these features. This freedom of not worrying about the syntax related issues makes the users more focussed on concentrating and learning the interactive theorem proving processes. We chose a simple example to illustrate the interaction with g-HOL here but it can be equally used to verify more complex theorems as well. The screen shots corresponding to a couple of more examples, involving transcendental functions and HOL probability theory, can be found in [2].

4   Conclusions

The paper describes a GUI for the HOL proof assistant. The main motivation of g-HOL is to facilitate learning the interactive theorem proving process and thus pave the path for their usage in the industry. In order to evaluate the effectiveness of g-HOL, we used it in a classroom, of 60 under-graduate students of software engineering, as an alternative to the command line interface of HOL. These students were taking their first course in Logic, which was 16 weeks long and the HOL proof assistant was used to illustrate the process of natural deduction and formal reasoning to them. Half of the class students were taught interactive theorem proving using the command-line interface of HOL while g-HOL was used for the other half. After the same amount of training time, the g-HOL users were found to be about 4-times more-effective in terms of the time spent to verify simple arithmetic proofs than their counterparts. The amount of syntax errors were also predictably much less for the g-HOL users. These statistics clearly indicate the effectiveness of the proposed ideas. We are currently working on enhancing the features of g-HOL and would appreciate suggestions and comments about our interface, which is available for download for all major operating systems at [2].

References

1. Hol Proof Assistant (2015). hol.sourceforge.net/
2. Arshad, F., Mehmood, H., Raza, F.: g-HOL - a graphical user interface for the HOL proof assistant (2015). save.seecs.nust.edu.pk/projects/g-HOL/g-HOL.html
3. Geuvers, H.: Proof assistants: history, ideas and future. Acad. Proc. Eng. Sci. **34**, 3–25 (2009). Springer-Verlag
4. Hasan, O., Tahar, S.: Formal verification methods. In: Encyclopedia of Information Science and Technology. IGI Global Pub. (2014)
5. Oracle: Java documentation (2015). docs.oracle.com/javase/tutorial/uiswing/

Author Index

Printed in the United States
By Bookmasters